FAMILIES AS RELATIONSHIPS

47. Individuation , 47 desire (attachment) Jones

5a Family socialising

Series Information

This book forms one of a series of paperbacks that are dedicated to the study and application of processes by which individuals relate to each other in social and family settings. Each book provides an *expanded* and *up-to-date* version of a section in the original *Handbook of Personal Relationships* (second edition) edited by Steve Duck and his colleagues.

The series is aimed at students taking courses studying personal relationships and related subjects, researchers and scholars in the relationships field, community/health psychologists, counsellors, therapists and social workers.

The Social Psychology of Personal Relationships
Edited by William Ickes and Steve Duck
ISBN: 0-471-99881-8

The Developmental Psychology of Personal Relationships
Edited by Rosemary S.L. Mills and Steve Duck
ISBN: 0-471-99880-X

Communication and Personal Relationships
Edited by Kathryn Dindia and Steve Duck
ISBN: 0-471-49133-0

Families as Relationships
Edited by Robert M. Milardo and Steve Duck
ISBN: 0-471-49152-7

Clinical and Community Psychology
Edited by Barbara Sarason and Steve Duck
ISBN: 0-471-49161-6

FAMILIES AS RELATIONSHIPS

Edited by

ROBERT M. MILARDO AND STEVE DUCK

JOHN WILEY & SONS, LTD

Chichester · New York · Weinheim · Brisbane · Singapore · Toronto

Other Wiley Editorial Offices

John Wiley & Sons, Inc., 605 Third Avenue,
New York, NY 10158-0012, USA

WILEY-VCH Verlag GmbH, Pappelallee 3,
D-69469 Weinheim, Germany

Jacaranda Wiley Ltd, 33 Park Road, Milton,
Queensland 4064, Australia

John Wiley & Sons (Asia) Pte Ltd, 2 Clementi Loop #02-01,
Jin Xing Distripark, Singapore 129809

John Wiley & Sons (Canada) Ltd, 22 Worcester Road,
Rexdale, Ontario M9W 1L1, Canada

Library of Congress Cataloging-in-Publication Data

Families as relationships / edited by Robert M. Milardo and Steve Duck.
       p. cm.
   Includes bibliographical references and index.
   ISBN0-471-49152-7 (pbk. : alk. paper)
     1. Family.   2. Family—Study and teaching.   3. Interpersonal relations.   I. Milardo,
   Robert M.   II. Duck, Steve.
   HQ518 .F2969 2000
   306.85—dc21
                                                                      00–021190

British Library Cataloguing in Publication Data

A catalogue record for this book is available from the British Library

ISBN 0-471-49152-7

Typeset in 10/12pt Times by Dorwyn Ltd, Rowlands Castle, Hants
Printed and bound in Great Britain by Redwood Books Ltd, Trowbridge, Wiltshire
This book is printed on acid-free paper responsibly manufactured from sustainable forestry,
in which at least two trees are planted for each one used for paper production.

CONTENTS

ABOUT THE EDITORS

Robert M. Milardo is Professor of Family Relationships at the University of Maine. He received his MS in social psychology and Ph.D. in Human Development and Family Studies with a minor in social psychology from the Pennsylvania State University. With a long-standing interest in developing models of social structure and their connections to the development of personal relationships, he edited *Families and Social Networks* (1988), the *Handbook of Personal Relationships* with Steve Duck (Wiley, 1997) and is currently the Editor of the *Journal of Marriage and the Family*.

Steve Duck is the Daniel and Amy Starch Distinguished Research Professor at the University of Iowa and has been a keen promotor of the field of personal relationships research since it was formed. He co-founded the first International Conference on Personal Relationships in 1982, and was founder and first editor of the *Journal of Social and Personal Relationships*, first President of the International Network on Personal Relationships, the professional organization for the research field, and editor of the first edition of the *Handbook of Personal Relationships*. The Steve Duck New Scholar Award was endowed and named in his honor by a group of independent scholars to recognize his promotion of the work of younger professionals and his dedication to developing the field.

ABOUT THE AUTHORS

Linda K. Acitelli is an Associate Professor in the Department of Psychology at the University of Houston. Her research on relationships has been funded by the National Institute of Mental Health. Her major research interests are cognition and communication in relationships, specifically thinking and talking about relationships and the factors that determine their impact on individual and relationship well-being. In 1995, the International Network on Personal Relationships awarded her the Gerald R. Miller Award for her early career achievements.

Graham Allan is Senior Lecturer in Sociology at the University of Southampton. He is the author of *Placing Friendship in Context* with Rebecca Adams (1998), *Friendship: Developing a Sociological Perspective* (1989), *Family Life: Domestic Roles and Social Organisation* (1985), and *A Sociology of Friendship and Kinship* (1979).

Katherine Allen is professor of Family Studies in the Department of Human Development at Virginia Polytechnic Institute and State University. She is a faculty affiliate of the Center for Gerontology, and a member of the Women's Studies faculty in the Center for Interdisciplinary Studies. In addition she chairs the Virginia Tech Academy of Teaching Excellence. She received her Ph.D. and MA in Child and Family Studies, with a Certificate in Gerontology, from Syracuse University, and her undergraduate degree from the University of Connecticut. Her research interests include family diversity over the life course, reflection in teaching and research, and feminist family studies.

Victoria Hilkevitch Bedford is Associate Professor of Psychology in the Department of Psychology at the University of Indianapolis. She received her Ph.D. from Rutgers University in developmental psychology with a concentration on life-span development. Recent publications include *Handbook of Aging and the Family* (with Rosemary Blieszner), "Memories of parental favoritism and the quality of parent-child ties in adulthood" (*Journal of Gerontology*), and several chapters on adult sibling relationships. Her primary research interests are in family relationships of middle-aged and old adults and life-span development.

Rosemary Blieszner is Professor of Gerontology and Family Studies in the Department of Family and Child Development and Associate Director of the

Center for Gerontology at Virginia Polytechnic Institute and State University. She received her Ph.D. from the Pennsylvania State University in human development-family studies with a concentration in adult development and aging. Her research focuses on family and friend relationships and well-being in old age. She is co-editor with V.H. Bedford of *Handbook of Aging and the Family*, co-author with R.G. Adams of *Adult Friendship*, and co-editor with R.G. Adams of *Older Adult Friendship: Structure and Process*. Her research has been published in gerontology and family studies journals, and the *Journal of Social and Personal Relationships*.

Heather Coon graduated from Mount Holyoke College in 1988 and subsequently worked as a research assistant for Teresa Amabile, conducting studies on creativity and intrinsic motivation at Brandeis University. She is finishing her doctorate in social psychology at the University of Michigan and is joining the faculty of North Central College as an assistant professor. Her recent work has investigated the consequences of endorsing cultural norms for Black and White couples in the USA, the cultural self, and North American individualism and collectivism.

Teresa M. Cooney received her doctorate in human development and family studies with a minor in demography from the Pennsylvania State University. Upon completion of her degree she was awarded an NICHD-funded postdoctoral research position studying family demography and the demography of aging at the Carolina Population Center, University of North Carolina, Chapel Hill. Currently, she is an Associate Professor in the Department of Human Development and Family Studies at the University of Missouri, where she has taught since 1997. Her research focuses primarily on the impact of socio-demographic changes on adult child–parent relationships. She recently completed a 5-year project, funded by an NIMH First Award, in which she examined the consequences of recent parental divorce for young adults' family and personal relationships, life-course transitions and mental health and well-being.

Ann C. Crouter is a Professor of Human Development at Pennsylvania State University, where she has served on the faculty since 1981. Her research focuses on the connections between parental work and family life, and the implications of these dynamics for the daily activities and family experiences of school-aged children and adolescents. Together with her colleague, Susan McHale, Professor Crouter is conducting two longitudinal studies of families, both funded by the National Institute of Child Health and Human Development. The first study focuses on gender role socialization in middle childhood. The second explores the linkages between parental work, family processes and adolescent development. A theme in both studies is "within-family variability" in the experiences and perceptions of family members–mother, fathers, brothers, sisters–as they interact and develop over time, as well as the implications of these differences for family members' developing competencies, interests and psychological well-being.

David H. Demo is Professor and Chair, Department of Human Development and Family Studies, The University of North Carolina at Greensboro. His research focuses on the influences of divorce, family structure, and family relationships on the well-being of children and parents. His recent publications include *Family Diversity and Well-being* (Sage, co-authored by Alan Acock) and *The Handbook of Family Diversity* (Oxford University Press, co-edited by Katherine Allen and Mark Fine).

Mark Fine received his doctorate in clinical psychology from The Ohio State University in 1983. He was assistant, associate, and full professor in the Department of Psychology at the University of Dayton from 1984 to 1994. Since 1994, he has been Professor and Chair of the Department of Human Development and Family Studies at the University of Missouri–Columbia. He was Editor of *Family Relations* from 1993 to 1996 and is currently Editor of the *Journal of Social and Personal Relationships*. His research interests lie in the areas of family transitions, such as divorce and remarriage; program evaluation; social cognition, and relationship stability. He is co-editor, along with David Demo and Katherine Allen, of the *Handbook of Family Diversity*, published in 2000 by Oxford University Press.

Heather Helms-Erikson received a MS degree in Family Studies with a specialization in marriage and family therapy from the University of Maryland in 1992, and a Ph.D. in 2000 from the Department of Human Development and Family Studies at the Pennsylvania State University. Her research interests encompass issues pertaining to the work–family interface as it relates to marital and family relationships, including gender-role issues in marriage, parenting and work concerns of dual-earner couples, and the gender-role socialization of children in dual-earner families.

Michael P. Johnson is Associate Professor of Sociology and Women's Studies at the Pennsylvania State University. He has published broadly in the area of close personal relationships, including work on commitment to relationships, relationships between networks and close personal relationships, gender issues in the structure of marriage, and domestic violence. His current work is focused on two areas: gender and commitment, and domestic violence.

Renate Klein is an assistant professor in family studies and women's studies at the University of Maine. She received her training in psychology at the University of Marburg, Germany, where she worked on altruism, personal relationships and the psychology of justice. In 1992 she came to the USA with a fellowship from the German Science Foundation to conduct research on conflict in couples' strategic preferences, the role of third parties, and the analysis of common ground and understanding between partners. She is the founder of the European Network on Family Violence and editor of *Multidisciplinary Perspectives on Family Violence* (Routledge, 1998).

Esther S. Kluwer is assistant professor of social psychology at the Free University in Amsterdam. She received her Ph.D. in psychology from the

University of Groningen in 1998. Her research focuses on marital conflict, justice processes in close relationships, the division of family work, and gender issues. Her research has been published in journals such as *Journal of Marriage and the Family*, *Journal of Social and Personal Relationships*, and *Social Justice Research*.

John Nicholson is Assistant Professor of Communication in the Department of Communication, Drama and Journalism Angelo State University, San Angelo, Texas. His main interest is in studying sibling alliances, a topic on which he received his Ph.D. from the University of Iowa in 1998.

Joseph Veroff is a social psychologist who holds a joint appointment at the University of Michigan as Professor in Psychology and Research Scientist at the Survey Research Center. With a BA from Wesleyan University in 1950 and a Ph.D. from the University of Michigan in 1955, he was first immersed in research on individual motivations, but soon became involved in social psychology as he focused on the problem of well-being and help-seeking in the American population. Discovering in *Americans View Their Mental Health* (1960) and in *The Inner American* (1981) that for most people the bases of general well-being centered on how well a person's marriage fared, in 1986 he turned to the study of marital well-being and stability. Since that time he has been helping direct a longitudinal study of 373 newlyweds, the results of which figure in the chapter he has co-authored in this volume. He is in the 42nd year of his own marriage to Joanne Bennet Veroff.

Alexis Walker holds the Jo Anne Leonard Petersen Chair in Gerontology and Family Studies at Oregon State University, where she is professor of Human Development and Family Sciences and Director of the Program on Gerontology. She is a faculty affiliate of the Women Studies and Difference, Power, and Discrimination Programs at OSU. She received her Ph.D. in human development and family studies from the Pennsylvania State University and her MS in child development and family life from Purdue University. Her research interests include women's inter-generational relationships, gender and family relationships, and feminist pedagogy.

Amy M. Young received her Ph.D. in personality psychology at the University of Michigan. She received her Bachelor's degree from Earlham College in human development and social relations and her Master's degree in psychology from the University of Michigan. Her current research focuses on the impact of relationship dynamics on self-descriptions, and feminism and marital relationships.

INTRODUCTION

Although the field of family studies has a long and rich academic history, it has only recently seen the development of a more specialized focus on the character of particular relationships. The nature of these relationships may take many forms but typically involves individuals who view themselves as a unit with a long-term commitment to continue their relationship. Traditionally, at least in western societies, families are defined in terms of two parents living together with responsibility for rearing their children. In fact, these so-called nuclear families are unique in many respects. For instance, in the United States the Bureau of the Census reported in 1998 that married couples living together with one or more children represented only 23% of all American families, married couples have declined as a proportion of all households from over 70% in 1970 to 53% in 1998, and approximately 25% of all white births, 41% of Hispanic births and 70% of African–American births occur outside of marriage (Teachman, Tedrow, & Crowder, in press). Single parent families, childless couples, lesbian or gay male couples with or without children are all represented in the broad mix of relations we may usefully refer to as families.

Families as Relationships is composed of ten chapters. Six of these chapters –originally appeared in the *Handbook of Personal Relationships* (Duck et al., 1997) although they have all been revised, some quite substantially, to take advantages of developments that have occurred since the initial publication of the *Handbook*. Three entirely new chapters (Chapters 1, 4 and 8) have been commissioned especially for this volume (those by Katherine Allen and Alexis Walker, Esther Kluwer, and Mark Fine and David Demo) and a substantially revised positioning chapter has been added (Chapter 10 by Duck, Acitelli and Nicholson). Our purpose in assembling this work is based on the belief that the dynamics of personal relationships are a key basis of social life and remain a central concern for students, now that courses on personal relationships are increasing in a variety of disciplines. What is lacking for such readers is an affordable source of high quality and theoretical breadth and strength that focuses on the particular contributions of specific disciplines. The main purpose of the present paperback book was to be not only a compendium of past achievements but a source of inspiration. We hope that it will prove a whetstone for the cutting edge and a stimulus for further work, while also offering a state-of-the-art survey of a particular field of scholarship about personal relationships. Authors were specifically requested to challenge rather than merely to report, to be selective and guiding rather than merely comprehensive, and to indicate future lines of promise. A major advantage of the book is that it will provide student readers with a terrific view of a focused and specific part of the field that interests them from their own academic viewpoint.

In the lead chapter, Katherine Allen and Alexis Walker start with the fundamentals, gender and diversity. They examine how gender is constructed in the ongoing, ordinary, and sometimes quite mundane interactions between family members. They begin with a series of narratives, each depicting a different constellation of members and relationships, while all are clearly recognizable as families. In this view, families are constructed within household units but they are unbounded by generation, gender, or traditional values. They remind us of the rich diversity in the ways people organize their personal relationships. Families sometimes consist of parents with children from that union, but they often include stepchildren, or grandparents. Families sometimes consist of single parents, or same-sex parents, adults without children, and they sometimes span multiple households. The common feature is that the members consider themselves a family bound by deeply personal relationships, and they act accordingly. Understanding this diversity has the effect of enriching the domain of study, leading to a field of inquiry that more faithfully represents how people actually organize their relationships.

In all of the diverse forms of families, gender is a dominant structural force, and consequently must be central to any understanding of their inner workings. Katherine and Alexis show how traditional views of gender represented in functionalist, socialization, or exchange perspectives are severely limited in how they come to understand and represent the daily construction of gender and the very inner workings of families. As an alternative, these authors turn to a social constructionist view of gender rooted in family relationships. The application of this perspective is illustrated by a series of detailed reviews of prototypical research. Although drawn from a wide range of topical areas (i.e., studies of household labor, marital status, family care giving, and marital conflict), these prototypes share a common understanding that gender is not functional, purely a matter of socialization, or available resources, but rather is a dynamic social construction where conditions like race, class, age and sexual orientation intersect and in doing so structure the ways in which we enact ourselves and our relationships.

Joe Veroff, Heather Coon and Amy Young (Chapter 2) discuss early marriage. They frame their work in a perennial question, one that has inspired family scholars since Ernest Burgess' work on marriage in the 1930s. How do young relationships become enduring relationships? Fortunately several longitudinal studies following couples through their early years of marriage are currently being conducted, and consequently provide an enriched source of material. Joe, Heather, and Amy examine how partners manage two broad sets of tasks, one concerning relations with external environments, and one concerning internal environments. They address questions regarding how partners begin to blend their networks of kith and kin, the demands of work, and the commitments of parenthood. They then move into the arena of couple dynamics and the fault lines where conflicts so frequently emerge with issues about creating a balance of responsibility for household labor, and a comfortable level of mutual gratification. In their analysis, these authors are as much interested in establishing an understanding of the pattern of successful entry into early marriage as they are in understanding the potential variability in that pattern. Hence they examine how African American and white non-Hispanic couples differ by virtue of their different cultural experiences. In doing so, they reiterate an important theme echoed in later chapters that social positions imply differential access to primary resources, like wealth and education, that in turn become important foundations for negotiations in marriage.

Terri Cooney, Chapter 3, turns to relationship between parents and their adult children. She begins with relations among parents and adolescents and argues quite reasonably that the task of growth in adolescence is not simply a matter of separation and individuation from parents but rather is far more richly textured. Here we find as well that the growth needs of parents are themselves influenced by those of the adolescent child and require a transformation of parental responsibilities that allows for their own separation and development as well as those of their children. The process of individual development is thus recast in terms of the modification of a relational bond. Separation is not an individual developmental task but a relational task requiring that parent and child come to view one another anew. The chapter continues these themes in an analysis of relations among adult children and parents, in addition to considering this study within a wider system of family relationships. Undoubtedly, the relations between adult children and parents are influenced by their relations with spouses, in-laws, and siblings. In her own work, Terri finds significant links between the expression of conflict among parents and reduced closeness reported by adult children, particularly with fathers.

Esther Kluwer's chapter (Chapter 4) examines the issue of marital quality. Few areas have engendered more interest in the family field, and in fact theory and research on marital quality dates back to the early part of this century, with measures of marital quality appearing in the work of Bernard (1933) and Burgess and Cottrell (1939). In retrospect this early work provided what became the essential frame of reference for much of the work that was to follow. These pioneering scholars anticipated the key issues that now so frequently command attention. For instance, the Locke–Wallace Marital Adjustment Test and the Spanier Dyadic Adjustment Survey, two of the more commonly used measures of marital quality, are essentially minor deviations of the theory and initial measures developed by Burgess and Cottrell.

There has been substantial progress in the study of marital quality and a surprising continuity to this progress. Esther reviews current advances in theory, including the commitment and adaptation models of marital quality and stability, two of the more promising theoretical models, recent advances in the measurement of marital quality, and the substantial accumulation of some very creative research, especially in the areas of behavioral observation of families, and in the analysis of social cognitions (e.g., how people understand the causes of their own and their partners' actions).

The theme of conflict is advanced further in a chapter by Renate Klein and Michael Johnson (Chapter 5). Here the authors draw on a wide variety of theory and research ranging from studies of organizational bargaining and strategic choice to important theoretical advances in the analysis of family violence and wife battering. An informative introduction defines key concepts and proceeds to analyze individual and situational factors that influence strategic choice. Three patterns of action common to close relationships are examined in depth: the demand/withdrawal pattern in asymmetrical conflict, negative reciprocity, and physical violence. Throughout Renate and Michael are careful to integrate their analysis of strategic choice with contemporary feminist analyses of gender and the asymmetries that result from the situated construction of gender. They explore, for example, how heterosexual relationships, and especially marriage, are assembled in ways that benefit husbands and disadvantage wives, which in turn result in distinct preferences for actions in conflict episodes. Their analysis is as provocative as it is penetrating.

Few areas in family studies have engendered more attention of late than the intersection of work and family. Ann Crouter and Heather Helms-Erikson (Chapter 6) examine the complexity of dual-earner families where wives and husbands each bring to the family their own work-related experiences. In doing so they wisely acknowledge that marital events must be understood in terms of the systematic differences in the circumstances of employment for men and women, circumstances that result from the gender stratification of work. Men and women generally work in distinctly different occupational sectors, with different opportunities for advancement, authority, job complexity, prestige, and pay. These variations in inequality become an appropriate backstage for the latest generation of research on work and family. Then too, in dual-earner families the implications of one spouse's experiences of work can be understood best relative to the other partner's work experience. From this distinctly dyadic perspective, Ann and Heather address three dimensions of wage labor and their implications for marital relationships. They examine spouses' access to work-related resources such as income and occupational prestige as these factors influence, for example, marital power or husband's contributions to household labor. They examine job complexity and the extent to which work encourages adults to value self-direction for themselves and others, and how this complexity influences the construction of stimulating home environments. Finally, they examine how the daily experience of work-related tensions spills over into home life. Their perspective is fresh and insightful, drawing on a rich array of contemporary theory and research in an area of central concern to any student of family relationships, and perhaps equally of concern to spouses and their children.

Graham Allan and Bob Milardo (Chapter 7) examine the social context in which marriages develop. They review nearly four decades of research addressing how the configuration of spouses' networks of personal associates influences the character of their marriages. They begin with an analysis of Elizabeth Bott's early hypotheses linking network configuration with the organization of conjugal roles (i.e., spouses' joint or separate participation in household labor, child care, and leisure pursuits). They critique the empirical studies directly testing her hypotheses as well as the literature on nonhuman primates, which is directly relevant to the linkage of network properties and relational (dyadic) outcomes. This analysis leads them to reframe Bott's original hypotheses into more general sociological terms by specifying how the structure of a network can be conceptualized in terms of the pattern of ties linking members, how the predictive power of this structural configuration is apt to be linked to the value consensus among members, and how configuration influences the conduct of a marriage. For instance, where network members know and interact with one another, a condition they refer to as structural interdependence, optimal conditions exist for the development, maintenance and enforcement of a consistent set of normative beliefs and expectations, and any deviations from those beliefs are most visible. Structure is thereby closely tied to the development of norms, the flow of information between members, and the sanctioning of individual behavior. Where networks are highly structured, spouses, like all other structurally equivalent members, will experience considerable influence to act in accord with those norms. They end the chapter by noting the considerable challenges that yet remain in the development of network theory, especially with regard to the very definition of a network and its membership.

Mark Fine and David Demo (Chapter 8) examine the consequences of divorce. The issue of whether divorce has profound effects on spouses or children is often contested. The available research is voluminous and varied, the topic central to all, and the fact that it is controversial is no surprise. The approach that Mark and David adopt is unique in that they center on the intersection of personal values and social research, which fuels public discourse and which in turn are influenced by that discourse. They focus on the key areas in which divorce has its potential for impact: relationships between parents and children, relations between former spouses, as well as the psychological and socioeconomic outcomes for all concerned. The available research in these areas is reviewed and carefully evaluated, but what is intriguing about their approach is the analysis of the construction of quite divergent conclusions regarding the aftermath of divorce. The authors are as much critiquing one field of inquiry as they are critiquing how social science is conducted, and as a result their recommendations are forward thinking and apply equally well to the broader enterprise of relationship studies.

The next contribution to this volume is a chapter by Victoria Bedford and Rosemary Blieszner (Chapter 9). They begin with a focus on relationships among family members where at least one member is old and how these bonds, most notable for their sheer longevity, are typically arranged. Some elderly families are composed of multiple generations, including children and grandchildren, while others live within families of single generations. Nearly one-third of all white Americans and nearly one-half of black Americans live without surviving children, for example. They then turn to several primary features of the family relationships of the elderly including their ascribed or non-voluntary status, persistence over time, their largely symbolic status, instability as the pool of constituents and the resources they offer one another declines during the course of old age, and finally their integration in a system of relations that span multiple generations with corresponding variety in the types of familial roles and normative expectations that each implies. This analysis extends the focus on marriage and friendship, which so typically defines the current study of personal relationships, into areas more germane to the actual experiences of the elderly and in this way enriches the full domain of inquiry.

Finally Steve Duck, Linda Acitelli and John Nicholson (Chapter 10) offer a proposal that focuses on the lived experience of family members in the variegated quilt of daily life in a chapter which poses some issues about the conduct of research about families and also the management of daily experience in those families.

Taken together the ten chapters in this book span a variety of theory and research sharpening our understanding as well as offering designs for future developments.

ROBERT M. MILARDO AND STEVE DUCK

Chapter 1

Constructing Gender in Families

Katherine R. Allen

Virginia Polytechnic Institute and State University, Blacksburg, VA, USA

and

Alexis J. Walker

Oregon State University, Corvallis, OR, USA

INTRODUCTION

In this chapter, we juxtapose gender and families because families are the primary arena in which gender is taught, learned, and transformed. By the age of 3 or 4, children understand that they are a boy or a girl, and those who do not are pressured by parents, teachers, relatives, and peers to conform (Bem, 1983). Parents are the primary agents for reinforcing gendered activities in families, particularly when children are young. Through influences as comprehensive as kin and friendship networks, religious and social organizations, and the media, children observe and parents teach how to reproduce ideological gender codes (Arendell, 1997). Families provide the key environment for social reproduction, by reproducing life on a daily basis, over time, and intergenerationally (Laslett & Brenner, 1989).

Examining how gender is constructed and reconstructed in families from a standpoint of diversity and change, it is clear that families cannot be imaged

Families as Relationships.
Edited by Robert M. Milardo and Steve Duck. © 2000 John Wiley & Sons Ltd.

around a central theme or unitary prototype. To illustrate family variability, consider the following narratives, drawn from past research we have conducted on family structures and intergenerational relationships over the life course. These examples show how different combinations of family relationships, structures, and households provide a fertile arena in which gender is transformed:

Mary and Sally are two women in a committed partnership and rearing two children together in the same household. Each woman is the biological mother of one child, and the nonbiological comother of the other child. The children are not biologically related; they consider themselves related by love. The children both have biological fathers who are involved in their family, though not what they consider to be their immediate family. One father lives with his new wife and their son; another father lives with his male partner. Others ask the children, who is in your family? Is this one family, two families, or three families? The children are not confused. They know their parents are the people who take care of them on a daily basis. Their view of family is expansive and capable of handling the structural ambiguity that others may perceive with discomfort.

John, a widower in his 80s, lives alone. He is visited daily by his brother, Jim, five years his junior. Both rely on Jim's daughter for transportation to the doctor and grocery store. When asked in an interview who is in his family, he says, "my brother and niece." Though the three maintain separate households, they are a family.

Pat is in her 40s and has recently re-evaluated her life. She has come to realize that she is not likely to marry or have children, but she is also tired of living alone and in an apartment. At the library, she notices a flyer inviting people to attend a group interested in starting a cohousing community. Intrigued, she researches the cohousing movement and discovers that it became popular in Scandinavian countries a few decades ago. She decides to join the local group, recognizing it as a way to retain her privacy and independence but still gain the security of community that comes from living around other adults and children.

George, age 19, is a sophomore in college. He is trying to decide what to do about Thanksgiving break. Should he go to his father's home and share the holiday with his father's new wife, her young son, and her parents? Or, should he go to his mother's home, where he grew up, and share the holiday with her boyfriend, a man only a few years older than he. Neither option feels comfortable to him. Maybe he will take his roommate up on her offer to have Thanksgiving dinner with her family.

Emma, age 12, is waiting for her new sibling to be born. She is at her mom's house, where she lives two weeks of each month. Emma, her mom, and her mom's partner, Nancy, share a home with their two dogs. Emma's father and his current wife, with whom Emma lives the other two weeks of the month, are expecting the baby. Although Emma's mom and dad were married when she was born, her biological father is a man with whom her mother had an extramarital relationship. Emma has two dads, three moms, and a sibling on the way.

Sharon is a 60-year-old great-grandmother. She lives with Jan, her 15-year-old granddaughter; Tom, Jan's 17-year-old boyfriend; and Jan and Tom's infant son. Also living with them is Sharon's 85-year-old aunt. Julie, Sharon's daughter and Jan's mother, is living in a rehabilitation center for recovering addicts. Sharon is the main source of support for all of the members of her family, including Julie.

These stories capture some of the complexity in structures and relationships characterizing families today. They reveal that family forms and processes are dynamic, and that there is no universal truth about how families look and what they do. Indeed, the history of families in Western society has always been complex and multidimensional (D'Emilio & Freedman, 1997; Mintz & Kellogg, 1988). Despite the legacy of diversity, however, media images and mainstream theories of how families exist and develop over time still privilege the view that families are composed of a husband, a wife, and their biological children; that the activities that occur within families are individually, relationally, uniquely, and independently devised; and that the resulting patterns of family structure, composition, and activities are functional for society.

In contrast, feminists have drawn attention to the mismatch between these presumptions about families and historical and contemporary variability in family structure and composition. In particular, feminists focus on the way the everyday lived experience in families is stratified by gender and generation. From a social constructionist perspective, most notably gender theory (e.g., Wilkie, Ferree, & Ratcliff, 1998), the standards for describing, studying, and evaluating family relationships and structures are critiqued as being tied to a false norm, based on two assumptions of universality: (a) families are assumed to be grounded in heterosexual lifelong marriage in which male gender is privileged, and (b) extended through intergenerational relationships, of which the parent–child relationship is given primacy. In fact, for some, there is no "family" without the presence of children. These assumptions about family structures and relationships posit the family of orientation, defined as the family into which one is born, and the family of procreation, defined as the family one establishes with the act of marriage and the subsequent birth of offspring (H. T. Christensen, 1964). Both of these ideas rely upon legal heterosexual marriage and biological parenthood as the functional foundations of family.

Hypothesizing separate roles for women and men in families is thus a persistent theme in both the popular imagination and the scholarly literature. Even though these roles are acknowledged to be historically variable, we still speak of and understand them as "gender roles," albeit changing gender roles. As Lopata and Thorne (1978) pointed out two decades ago, the language of "gender roles" obscures the complexities with which gender is reproduced in families and society. Despite a growing understanding that the abilities, capacities, and characteristics of women and men, girls and boys, overlap significantly, the belief in gender as fixed and inevitable is reinforced by a concomitant belief that gendered roles are "a choice," in part, due to socialization, and, in part, due to individual preference.

These twin ideas of socialization and individual choice enable not only individuals but also family and relationship scholars to focus almost exclusively on characteristics and processes internal to families, thereby ignoring the structural roots of gendered beliefs and practices. Social scientists who study family relationships often err by highlighting the trees but excluding the forest. In this manner, gendered patterns and processes that are similar across families are attributed to socialization and the freedom of individual choice. In contrast, feminists argue that family scientists need to step back so that they can examine the similarities in the ways individual trees are patterned within and across forests; to recognize that everything from who changes the baby's diaper, to who drives the family car, to who is paid for their labor, to what kind of partner a college student dates is marked by gender.

Feminists also argue that, although gender is a dominant structural force in families, it is constructed and reconstructed on a daily basis in the private relationships individuals have with one another. In this view, and under varying conditions, because of the dynamic quality of gender, individuals in relationship can be more or less gendered in their characteristics and interactional processes. Thus, in society in general and within families in particular, both old and new ideas about gender and old and new gender practices coexist (Coltrane, 1998; Risman, 1998; Schwartz & Rutter, 1998; Walker, 1999). In this chapter, we examine *how* gender is constructed and transformed in families today.

THEORETICAL PERSPECTIVES IN HISTORICAL CONTEXT

Functionalist Foundations

Current ideas about gender in families are, in part, a reaction to earlier functionalist ideas about "the family," which presupposed a rigid separation of labor between the sexes. Parsons (1964) gave the field the now famous terms, "instrumental and expressive functions," in which husbands inherited the legacy of providing financial support for their families and intervening between the private haven of their families and the cruel, outside world (Lasch, 1977); wives inherited the legacy of meeting the everyday needs of family members for nutrition, hygiene, and emotional support. The developmental approach to the family, still a mainstay of undergraduate marriage and family textbooks, reinforced these roles along gender and generational lines, and suggested a family life cycle rooted in the stages of marital and parental roles (Duvall, 1971; Hill & Rodgers, 1964). These roles—wife, husband; mother, father—are highly gendered.

When applied to studies of the division of family labor, this perspective has been described as the *specialization of tasks* view (e.g., Finley, 1989). This conceptualization, consistent with Parsons' perspective, is that the most efficient way to carry out the work required for family life is for the two adults present—note the underlying assumption of heterosexuality—to divide the tasks as "appropriate" to their respective roles. In fact, work has been a primary focus of feminists who study family. It is no accident that much of the feminist research on gender within families focuses on household labor. Work, both paid and unpaid, is at the center of gender, because the development of equality between women and men is stalled by the misalliance between wage labor and family life (Ferree, 1990, 1991; Hochschild, 1989; Osmond & Thorne, 1993). A more recent version of the specialization of tasks approach was proposed by Becker (1981). Because men usually earn higher wages, it makes sense and is efficient, in his view, for them to specialize in wage earning and for women to specialize in domestic or unpaid tasks. Thus, gender differences are reinforced as natural, functional, and normative.

A related perspective is the *socialization* view. According to this approach, throughout their childhoods, girls and boys learn to carry out and come to prefer the tasks that are consistent with a nurturing (i.e., female) or an instrumental (i.e., male) personality (Berardo, Shehan & Leslie, 1987). There is some debate over whether the functionalist and socialization perspectives essentialize ideas about gender. Some suggest these approaches assume that women, due to their unique genetic and biochemical makeup and their capacity to bear and breastfeed children, are inherently nurturant and passive; and that men, due to their unique genetic and biochemical makeup, are inherently strong, protective, and aggressive. These gender-specific personality traits pair neatly with the idea of the home and the workplace as separate spheres, one private and characterized by love and socioemotional support; the other public and characterized by aggressiveness and competition.

Mainstream theories of individual and family development presume that the separation of home and work is a functional imperative, halfway between a biological need and a social need, and thus universal. Critical and feminist theorists have exposed the separation of home and work as socially constructed, not biologically determined, growing out of the industrialization associated with modern capitalism (Agger, 1998; Cheal, 1991). Indeed, in the contemporary postindustrial era, on the verge of the 21st century, the small, privatized, gender-segregated, nuclear family consisting of a married couple with children comprises less than 25% of families in the United States (US Bureau of the Census, 1995). Compared to the first half of the 20th century, there are far more persons living alone, mother-only families, cohabiting couples, and stepfamilies . . . [and] "a child can no longer expect to live his or her childhood with both biological parents" (Teachman, 2000, p. 51). Considering how families themselves change over time, a much more flexible conceptualization is needed to define and explain family experience than the ideology of static, gender-specific roles. It is difficult to predict, based on its current configuration, any given family's future trajectory, due to the likelihood of cohabitation, divorce, remarriage, and singlehood that characterizes adult intimate relationships (Bumpass, Sweet & Cherlin, 1991).

Now that there is ample and sufficient evidence that women can function effectively, even masterfully, in the paid work force, and that men are capable of raising children well and of constructing a loving, protective environment without the companion presence of a woman, or, better yet, a biological mother, it is clear that functionalist and socialization perspectives reify presumed gender differences. Furthermore, historical evidence regarding immigrant families, families of color, and otherwise poor families reveals that these groups never had the luxury of dividing family tasks into two rigidly defined areas of responsibility (Dill, 1988; Stack, 1974). The inability to support oneself and one's dependents with a single wage necessitated women's contributions through visible (i.e., jobs outside the home) and invisible (i.e., taking in boarders, laundry, and mending) paid labor, forcing family members to rely on extrahousehold and fictive kin to meet their socioemotional needs (Dill, 1988; Hareven, 1991; Scott & Tilly, 1975).

What is so compelling about the separate spheres perspective to render functionalist views (now neofunctionalist) as popular as ever (e.g., Becker, 1981; Pittman, 1993; Scanzoni & Marsiglio, 1993)? Smith (1993) pointed out that the conceptualization of the "standard North American family" is an ideological code, as resilient as a genetic code in terms of its ability to transform itself in divergent discursive settings. Even in critiques of traditional views of "the family," the notion of gendered spheres survives. The focus on individual choice, as in, "I prefer taking care of the baby, and I'm better at it than he is," a view centered on the "trees," prevents social scientists from seeing the broader picture: a society stratified by gender (and race, ethnicity, class, and sexual orientation) such that the choices available to individuals are constrained.

Social Exchange Perspectives

Another perspective commonly employed to explain gendered patterns in families is the *time-availability* hypothesis (e.g., Berardo et al., 1987; Condran & Bode, 1882). According to this view, competing roles and time demands determine the time that family members have to devote to household work. Employed persons have less time to devote to unpaid family labor than nonemployed or part-time employed persons.

A related and more commonly used approach is the *resource* perspective, which is also rooted in social exchange theory (e.g., Blood & Wolfe, 1960; Homans, 1961; Sanchez, 1994). This view suggests that individuals make choices inside families based on the externally generated resources they bring to their marital and family relationships. According to resource theory, a spouse's education level, occupational status, and income shape the power dynamics and thus the choices made in families. Individuals with more education, a higher occupational status, and who have the ability to generate more income are believed to have more power inside families. Relatively more income, job status, and education enable a family member to forego less desirable activities (e.g., doing laundry, cleaning the bathroom), leaving them to family members with relatively less income, lower job status (or no job), and less education (Hochschild, 1983). As political theorist Tronto (1987) explained, subordination accompanies marginalized status, as in being female, black, poor, or any combination of the status of "other" in a society that dichotomizes gender, race, and class into oppositional categories across social institutions (Lorde, 1984). The majority of low-paid service jobs are filled by men of color and women of all social classes and races.

Strikingly, resources and even available time have been, at best, inadequate to explain such patterns as the gendered division of labor in households and caregiving for aging family members (e.g., Finley, 1989; Hochschild, 1989; Tichenor, 1999). Variability within gender in "feminine" and "masculine" personality traits and in preferences for activities defined as "sex-typed" calls into question beliefs that women are one way, men are another, ergo men work for pay and women mother. Feminists have documented and drawn attention to the fact that the division of family work is not a straightforward reflection of the distribution of resources and time demands. Feminists have also shown that élite white women, too, find other ways to carry out some aspects of family labor when they have the resources to do so (e.g., Oropesa, 1993), such as hiring other women, especially women of color, to provide child care services (Uttal, 1996) and other domestic help (Rollins, 1985).

There is no better predictor of the division of household labor than gender. Regardless of one's attitude about "gender" roles, the resources one brings to the relationship, and the time one has available, there is nothing that predicts who does what and how much one does in families than whether one is a woman or a man. Family work is best seen as a pattern of activities set forth by socially constructed boundaries between women and men (Wilkie et al., 1998). These patterns and boundaries are strengthened by the ways in which the culture assigns different tasks to women (e.g., finding appropriate child care) and men (e.g., deciding how much money to spend on a new car), and by attaching a different meaning to the same or similar behaviors (e.g., men who do housework are "helping" their wives; women who engage in paid labor are secondary or supplemental providers, regardless of the proportion of family income they earn). To challenge these gender boundaries, one must change both the behavior and the meanings we attach to them (Wilkie et al., 1998).

Gender and Families in the Late 20th Century: a Social Constructionist Lens

The discovery of the limitations of functionalist, socialization, time-available, and resource perspectives to explain the gendered nature of family work coincided with the development of a social constructionist view of gender and family life. A social constructionist view, with roots in critical, feminist, and life course theories, provides a better framework for understanding how adults and children—women and men, girls and boys—live in families.

In critiquing the functionalist framework, critical theorists (e.g., Agger, 1998; Cheal, 1991; Poster, 1978), feminist scholars (e.g., Collins, 1990; Glenn, 1987; Thorne, 1992) and social historians (e.g., Elder, 1981; Hareven, 1991; Scott & Tilly, 1975), have revealed that the functionalist framework is directed toward a family that never or rarely was (Coontz, 1992). Like other scholars examining gender today, we believe a social constructionist view provides a much broader framework for understanding gender and families.

The functionalist version of gendered family roles is ethnocentric. It projects the cultural ideal of élite, educated white men at mid-century onto others' realities (Mills, 1959). Ivory-towered theorists were free to pursue intellectual aims because wives, hired help, and students were doing the invisible labor that maintained their occupational work. The functionalist perspective is based on a narrow slice of history, indeed, a demographic anomaly, peaking in popularity in the 1890s, at the height of the industrial era, and decreasing in numerical strength by the 1960s (Gittins, 1993). The postwar era, roughly 1948 to 1958, brought a resurgence in the popularity of the functionalist view of gender-segregated roles in families (Skolnick, 1991; Stacey, 1990). With help from the GI bill, the military-industrial complex built to support the Cold War, and a corresponding economic boom, the quality of life for more privileged members of society improved, particularly in contrast to the sacrifices imposed by the two World Wars and the Great Depression. This image matched the experiences of élite members of society, upper-middle-class whites with access to education and occupations that enabled a husband and father to support himself and his dependents—a wife and children.

By 1960, it was apparent that the economic promise of prosperity for all citizens, regardless of occupation, would not be fulfilled. Working-class families, just beginning to realize the male breadwinner ideal actualized by white, middle-class families in the 20th century (Bernard, 1981; Hood, 1986), found that wives still had to work double shifts: for pay at work and without pay at home (L. B. Rubin, 1994; Skolnick, 1991). Immigrant families and families of color were never included in the promise of prosperity: because the Civil Rights Act was not signed into law until 1964 and major immigration laws were not changed until 1965, overt segregation and discrimination continued to structure inequality into their daily lives (Espiritu, 1997; Taylor, 1998; Youth of the Rural Organizing and Cultural Center, 1991). Feminist criticism of the segregated lives of women and men began with the publication of Friedan's (1963) *The Feminine Mystique*. In 1967, Mead referred to the so-called golden age of the 1950s with its glorification of isolated suburban homes as a "massive failure" (Mead, 1967); more recently, Coontz (1992) called the desire to compare present (1990s) to past times (1950s) a "nostalgia trap."

In contrast to earlier perspectives, the social constructionist view is informed by the critiques of feminists and scholars of color, who have pointed out the historical inaccuracies underlying dominant theories and argued for more realistic portrayals that do not rely on idealized images of neat gender roles (Baber & Allen, 1992; Collins, 1990; L. Thompson & Walker, 1989). The social constructionist perspective draws attention to the fact that the idealized dichotomy of dominant husband/supportive wife does not describe family life for the majority. As many scholars now argue, there is no universal family form (Allen & Demo, 1995; Scanzoni, 2000; Schwartz, 1994). The view of monogamous marriage as the cornerstone of family life is actually practiced by only 10% of the population world wide (Gittins, 1993). Rather than being separated, isolated, or protected from the broader society as in the separate-spheres approach to the nuclear, two-generation, gender-stratified family, the one constant about families is that, through their relationship processes, they reflect and transform the structural patterns of the sociohistorical context in which they are embedded (Elder, 1981; Gittins, 1993). Furthermore, in acknowledging that the stratification evident in society is recreated within families, this perspective highlights families as locations of both struggle and support (Baber & Allen, 1992; Hartmann, 1981, Thorne, 1992). Not every family is characterized by the loving interaction presumed in the romantic ideology of family life as a haven from the heartless world (Lasch, 1977). Stress and violence occur routinely within families, between men and women (see Johnson, 1995, on patriarchal terrorism), and parents and children (see Greven, 1992, and Straus, 1994, on corporal punishment and child abuse), and the patterns with which they do so reflect broader systems of stratification (e.g., Babcock, Waltz, Jacobson, & Gottman, 1993; Jacobson et al., 1994).

The postindustrial era of the late 20th century has brought unprecedented change in daily family life, reminding us that history and social structure generate unique circumstances that enable individuals and groups to transform both culture and everyday life (Daly, 1997; Gergen, 1991; Scanzoni, 2000). Currently, only 25% of the population has a college degree, and yet, a college education is increasingly necessary for the kinds of well-paid, highly technical jobs available today. There is a growing instability of jobs and even careers as new technologies render existing occupations and industries obsolete, yet require an increasingly educated and trained work force. Institutions of higher education, the last bastion of modern stability, are being changed by competitive markets and technological innovations. New generations of students reared with the Internet want at least some of their education easily accessible, and for-profit corporations now view "learning" as a lucrative business (Edgerton, 1997; Finkelstein, 1999).

The life span has elongated, particularly for whites. A male child born in 1900 could expect to live until age 48, and in 1990, until age 72. A female child born in 1900 could expect to live until age 51, and in 1990, until age 79 (Kinsella, 1996). The implications of increased longevity include shorter time spent by mothers in childbearing and rearing, longer periods for adults in a household without children, and more time spent alone in adulthood than ever before (Teachman, 2000). At the same time, late 20th century postindustrial society has brought with it new, and in some cases, more deadly diseases (e.g., AIDS, heart disease, breast cancer, stroke, chemical dependence) than before, affecting health, mortality, and the quality of individual and family life in unanticipated ways.

Same-sex couples are increasingly likely to see legal, or at least, public recognition of their relationships. Although not one state in the United States allows same-sex marriage, lawsuits have been filed in Hawaii, Vermont, and the District of Columbia, challenging state and district bans. The Hawaii case led to the Defense of Marriage Act (DOMA), signed by President Clinton in 1995, which allows individual states to decide if they will honor a marriage license offered from another state as valid in their own. As of this writing, only 12 states have not enacted a DOMA law. Nevertheless, with greater media coverage and a strong gay and lesbian civil rights movement, as well as research debunking myths about gay and lesbian people as partners, parents, and community members (Allen & Demo, 1995; Falk, 1989; Patterson, 1992; Stacey, 1996; Weston, 1991), public opinion is changing toward greater recognition of the discrimination and vulnerability experienced by members of gay and lesbian families.

LINKING A SOCIAL CONSTRUCTIVIST PERSPECTIVE WITH EMPIRICAL EVIDENCE OF GENDER IN FAMILIES

The critique of dominant conceptual approaches and the application of a social constructionist perspective to the nexus of gender and family life has facilitated the development of a rich reservoir of research on relationships and their variability. Here, we review examples from the interdisciplinary relationships literature to explode some of the persistent myths about how gender operates in family ties, emphasizing that gender is connected to broader social structures. Each of the studies we examine is an example of work published in traditional social science journals; all reveal that gender is neither functional, individual, nor socialized, nor is it about relative resources. These scholars give voice *and* empirical evidence to the conceptualization of gender as situated, variable, and changing. Thus, empirical evidence does exist for the socially constructed nature of gender. What intrigues us is how gender stereotypes persist in the literature despite this evidence. We draw attention to these studies to raise new questions about the validity of gender difference and individual choice models and to promote new insights about how to study gender transformations in families.

Household Labor and Gender: Variations among Heterosexual, Lesbian, and Gay Couples

Our first example is Kurdek's (1993b) research on the allocation of family labor in gay, lesbian, and heterosexual married couples. This work is novel not only for the inclusion of lesbian and gay couples, but because it positions gender as a central explanatory variable, separate from power, resources, and other dimensions typically intertwined with gender. Men generally have greater access than women to external resources (e.g., income, occupational status) that they bring to their relationships. This gendered access to resources may be a key variable in the relationships and interactions within heterosexual couples, but it will affect lesbian and gay couples in a different way. Gay couples are likely to have more income and other resources than are lesbian couples, but, within these pairs, there is less likely to be the same income disparity that exists within heterosexual pairs. Only if Parsons (1964) and Becker (1981) are right, would gay and lesbian couples structure their household tasks so that one carries out all the tasks defined as instrumental and the other carries out all the tasks defined as expressive.

In fact, in Kurdek's study of 145 heterosexual married couples, 95 gay couples, and 61 lesbian couples, most of whom were white, the distribution of household labor differed remarkably by relationship type. Married couples were highly segregated in their task allocation patterns; that is, one of the two partners—in this case, wives—performed the majority of household tasks. Except for buying groceries, performed by 55% of the wives, wives did at least two-thirds of the housework, cooking, cleaning the bathroom, laundry, and writing grocery lists in these married couples. This finding is similar to that of many other studies of the division of labor between wives and husbands (e.g., Berardo et al., 1987; Coltrane, 1998; Ferree, 1991; Sanchez, 1994). Gay couples distributed the family work more equitably, but they did so in a task-specialized way: they divided the tasks into what they described as halves, and then allocated the two halves on the basis of skill, interest, and available time. Although they followed a specialization model, the model was not consistent with a gendered pattern. Instead, it reflected an interest in equality. Lesbians also were more likely than married couples to allocate tasks equally, but, unlike gay men, lesbian women shared tasks by performing them together.

A striking supplemental finding was that the performance of household tasks was positively associated with psychological symptoms of depression and distress for wives, and negatively associated with such symptoms for lesbians. This pattern may have occurred both because wives did more household work than lesbians—wives consistently performed more than half of the household work—and because wives performed these tasks alone. Kurdek suggested that it was highly unlikely that lesbians enjoyed doing housework more than wives did, but the context in which they did the work—with their partners—rendered the tasks less problematic.

Mexican–American Marriages and Migration: Variations by Sociohistorical Context

Our second example demonstrates that allocation of household labor is related not only to gender composition in families, but also to sociohistorical context. Consider research on patterns of family work in immigrant, heterosexual, Mexican–American couples. Hondagneu-Sotelo (1992) compared the experiences of couples who migrated to the US prior to 1965 with those who migrated after. Each migration period was distinctive, as was life in the US during the period following migration. In both sets of pairs, families migrated in stages, with husbands coming first. In early-migrating couples, however, husbands preceded their wives and children by from 1 to 16 years. The average length of separation was 6 years. When the men arrived in the US, they typically lived as borders in communal settings with other men. Few women were present. Of necessity, men took on the responsibility of cooking, cleaning, shopping, and doing laundry. Back in Mexico, their wives earned income to support their families and made financial and other major decisions.

These patterns were in stark contrast to the traditional gendered pattern evident in their premigration households. Wives eventually followed their husbands, often on their own and with the assistance of other women—primarily in-laws and other kin, including their children—who helped them to obtain legal status. The long period of separation and the wives' confidence in earning incomes and managing financial affairs helped the women operate independently, sometimes even against their husbands' wishes. Once reunited, the pattern of household labor that emerged was more egalitarian than that in the premigration period. Men sometimes retained their interest in domestic skills, expressing pride, for example, in their ability to make tortillas. Their wives continued to be employed and had high expectations as well for their husbands' involvement in family labor. These wives were more independent and assertive than they had been before migration, and they exercised new power within their marriages.

Patterns in couples where migration occurred after 1965 were quite different. Although husbands typically preceded their wives in coming to the US, the periods of separation were much shorter, so wives did not have sufficient time to develop experience with and confidence in their abilities to support and manage their families on their own. The men who came alone to the US most often stayed in family settings, where women—other men's wives, mothers, and daughters—did the laundry, the shopping, the cooking, and the cleaning. There was no need for these husbands to learn how to perform "women's" work. When reunited, even though both husbands and wives were wage earners, husbands expected their wives to wait on them and to cook and clean for them, and wives expected to carry out these tasks as well as their waged work.

What is unique in Hondagneu-Sotelo's (1992) study is not the gender composition or marital status of the couples—all were heterosexual and married—but the sociohistorical conditions of migration. The migration patterns reflected patriarchal relations in that men migrated first and did so for reasons tied to family financial support, but the gendered patterns on couples' reunions in the US reflected the distinct nature of the respective activities of wives and husbands during the period of separation. These findings conflict both with the idea that Latino families are always patriarchal, and that immigrant families from a single culture are similar in the extent to which they assimilate into the dominant or mainstream pattern. The pattern of activities during and after migration set the context in which gender was constructed and reconstructed for these migrant, Latino couples, revealing that gender difference alone is not an adequate explanation for variations in family lives over time.

Social Attachments are Stronger Predictors of Well-being than Marriage: Variations by Marital Status

A third distinct contribution comes from the work of C. E. Ross (1995), who deconstructed the notion of marital status. Ross took issue with the underlying assumptions in decades of research linking marital status to psychological well-being. Why is it, she wondered, that researchers find married persons to be better off psychologically than persons who are divorced or never married? Ross reasoned that well-being could not possibly be higher for individuals in long-term, unhappy marital liaisons than it is for individuals with the benefits of marriage, but without its legal status. Is it not possible that unmarried people with socioeconomic support are just as likely to be well off psychologically as married people are? She considered the presumed benefits that derived from marriage: social integration (living with someone rather than alone), emotional support, and enhanced income. If one has access to these social attachment resources, even without being married, she argued, one should benefit psychologically.

Ross's (1995) findings, based on a national probability sample of US households, and controlling for gender, race, and age—each of which is associated with well-being—supported her view that it is not marriage per se that contributes to psychological well-being. Instead, it is the dimensions of social attachment that co-occur with marriage. Specifically, married persons had better psychological well-being than persons who had a partner, but only those whose partner lived outside the household. Individuals with live-in partners did not differ from married persons in well-being. Furthermore, never-married individuals who reported high levels of social attachment and support were not different from married persons in psychological well-being. When perceptions of economic support were added to the equation, even divorced persons were indistinguishable from married persons in well-being. In other words, much of the effect of marital status on well-being is explained by the underlying constructs of social attachment, social support, and economic resources.

Ross (1995) extended her findings by comparing the psychological well-being of persons without a partner to the well-being of persons in unhappy, moderately happy, and very happy relationships. Her findings revealed that people with no partner are better off psychologically than are people who have a partner but who are unhappy in their relationship; that is, "negative social attachments are worse for well-being than no social attachments" (p. 137). Significantly, Ross did not confine her interpretations to the patterns of support distributed within persons. She noted explicitly that, although the findings were the same for women and for men (i.e., the effects of integration,

attachment, support, and income were equally positive for both), these resources are not evenly distributed across the genders. In fact, although men
are as distressed as women by the absence of economic support, they have
lower levels of economic hardship than women do. Furthermore, although
women are as distressed as men by the absence of emotional support, they
have higher levels of emotional support than men do.

Reflecting on Ross's contribution, we observe that she embedded a finding
of no difference between women and men into the social context that positions women differently from men in relation to social resources. This strategy is an excellent example of pairing a social constructionist theoretical
model with quantitative evidence, thereby demonstrating that it is untenable
to dismiss gender even after demonstrating that gender is not a "significant"
predictor variable. Women and men may be similarly human, and may behave
and react in similarly human ways, but they are differentially positioned with
regard to social and psychological resources, and this structural positioning
works to shape and define the reality of their everyday lives.

Gender, Subordination, and Ambivalence: Variations in Family Care

In our fourth example, Dressel and Clark (1990) conducted a qualitative study
of diaries written by 26 women and 12 men, detailing activities of family care
they provided every hour during a 24-hour period. Using a social constructivist approach, the authors described the phenomenology of family care, notably that there are contradictions between the culture of family care (e.g.,
both men and women hold idealized views of caring), and the conduct of
family care (e.g., women, in particular, experience ambiguity in their feelings
about caregiving and diversity of motives, aspects linked to women's relative
subordination in marital and family relationships). Indeed, 75% of women
indicated emotive dissonance, defined as feelings of being at odds with their
care behaviors, while most of the men did not. To illustrate, one mother
expressed feeling positive emotions such as warmth, serenity, and tenderness
about the day's activities, and at the same time, she conveyed "feelings of
frustration, impatience, resentment, and being upset, often during the very
same activities that produce the positive affect" (p. 778). Women were ambivalent about doing things for family members that they could or should do
for themselves (e.g., running a husband's bath, picking up dirty clothes, hem-
ming trousers). Ambivalence is just one consequence of feeling pressure,
disguised as a "choice," to sacrifice personal time to provide care for other
family members. In contrast, men felt more rewarded when they participated
in family care, perhaps because, as Hochschild (1983) noted, they are not
expected to do so.

Dressel and Clark's (1990) findings challenge popular ideas about who
benefits from care. A diversity of motives for acts of care was more evident in
women's diaries than in men's. Women reported hugging their husbands just

to be near them, or calling relatives just to hear their voices. Men revealed motives that were more self-beneficial, such as a father agreeing to play with his daughter because he wanted to get outside. Instead of reinforcing these differences in their interpretation of findings, Dressel and Clark argued that men are not simply being instrumental and women are not simply being expressive in their acts of care. Rather, they suggested that what looks like expressive behaviors (e.g., hugging, phoning) may really be "instrumental ones in the service of having one's own needs met" (p. 776). Again, in keeping with a social-constructionist perspective, instead of gendered roles, the under-lying dynamics of relative status and power were revealed.

Gendered Meanings in the Demand–Withdraw Hypothesis: Variations by Power and Status

Our final example of empirical work that deconstructs gender as a fixed quantity is the study of the demand–withdraw hypothesis in wife–husband interaction during marital conflict (e.g., Christensen & Heavey, 1990; Heavey, Christensen, & Malamuth, 1995: Heavey, Christopher, & Christensen, 1993). In this pattern, one spouse exerts pressure by criticizing, complaining, or pressuring the other with emotional requests. The other responds by retreat-ing from the conflict through inaction or defensiveness. This is an important pattern in marital conflict because it is associated with unhappy marriages (Sullaway & Christensen, 1983).

Much of the research in this area has been conducted by observing married couples interacting in a laboratory (e.g., Christensen & Heavey, 1990). Typ-ically, couples are asked to act out real-life situations in which a wife expresses a desire for change in her husband, and this is the scenario that is observed. Thus, these laboratory studies have found that the demand–withdraw interac-tion pattern is common when wives want change in their husbands. Chris-tensen and Heavey (1990) demonstrated that when husbands make demands on wives, women also withdraw.

Several explanations have been posited for the demand–withdraw pattern. Gottman and his colleagues (e.g., Gottman & Levenson, 1988) connected the withdrawal reaction in men to stress which then leads to physiological arousal. They hypothesized that men find the arousal associated with conflict to be uncomfortable. This discomfort leads to their withdrawal from the interaction (e.g., Gottman, Coan, Carrere, & Swanson, 1998). Gottman et al. found that, in interaction, women are less likely to be aroused, more comfortable dealing with stress and conflict, and more likely to escalate negative patterns and conflict than to withdraw. This explanation thus relies on a gender difference approach rooted in biology.

In contrast, Christensen and Heavey (1990) situated their research on the demand–withdraw pattern on work by Jacobson (1989), who proposed a *structural* explanation. In Jacobson's view, men are the primary beneficiaries of traditional marriage because women, but not men, face a second shift of family work when they are in the paid labor force, and because marriage increases the likelihood of depression in women but decreases it in men. According to this perspective, the benefits of marriage lead men to strive to maintain the status quo and women to strive for change. This view hypothesizes that wives will seek change to improve their position. In contrast, men will avoid change to protect their position, thus withdrawing from any attempts to get them to change. Christensen and Heavey's (1990) innovation was to bring a structural approach to the demand–withdraw literature, thereby challenging the implicit gender stereotypes in the language of demand–withdraw. Instead of conceptualizing demand as associated with a "female" role or biology, and withdrawal as associated with a "male" gender role or biology, Christensen and Heavey (1990) observed that what matters more is a person's relative status in the relationship.

Consistent with Jacobson's (1989) view, Christensen and Heavey (1990) found that avoiding intimacy gives husbands more power in marital relationships. Because wives do not find the relationship they want, and because they have less power than their husbands, they resort to the means available to them: complaining and criticizing. Because husbands find a relationship more suited to their wishes, and because they have more power to resist their spouses' demands when asked to change, husbands choose not to act or to withdraw from the interaction. The structural approach is consistent with other discussions of the gendered distribution of marital power (e.g., Kelley, 1979; Peplau & Gordon, 1985; Raush, Barry, Hertel, & Swain, 1974).

Kluwer, Heesink, and Van De Vliert (1997) confirmed Christensen and Heavey's (1990) hypothesis that wives' dissatisfaction with the division of household labor leads to spouses' perceptions of interaction patterns consistent with the wife-demand/husband-withdraw type. Yet to be determined is why requests for change (including criticism, complaining, and emotional appeals), commonly from wives, have been labeled as "demands," and responses to such requests (including inaction, defensiveness, and avoidance), commonly from husbands, have been labeled "withdrawal." The very labels suggest underlying beliefs about gender.

The solution Gottman et al. (1998) proposed to deal with problematic interactions is grounded in the primacy of men's physiological response as the key ingredient in the demand–withdraw pattern. Wives should "soften their start-up" (p. 7), or begin conflict discussions without negative affect. This "solution" would be effective because, in unhappily married couples, husbands escalate the negative affect by responding with belligerence, defensiveness, or even contempt. A softened start-up would keep men in such marriages from experiencing the stress that leads to extensive physiological arousal. Couples could avoid this pattern by "soothing the male" (p. 17), thereby lowering his physiological symptoms.

Consider the full pattern, however. It involves negative start-up (e.g., complaints) by the wife, resistance from the husband or refusal to accept her influence, wife's reciprocation of the husband's low-intensity affect, and the husband's maintenance or escalation—but not de-escalation—of negative affect. The full picture of the conflict suggests that there are two ways to prevent this conflict pattern: the wife can soothe her husband (e.g., by using humor) or the husband can soothe himself (e.g., by de-escalating the negative affect or by responding with positive affect). These solutions are grounded in stereotypes of male and female differences consistent with functionalist and socialization accounts. More importantly, "soothing the male" as a solution shifts responsibility for men's behavior from men to women. A feminist interpretation would ask why are husbands aroused when wives seek change? A structural analysis of relative status in marriage suggests that challenges to male power are problematic for men.

DIRECTIONS FOR THE FUTURE

In the postindustrial, information age, old certainties that benefit the privileged (of whom there are few) are giving way to new understandings that women and men both inside and outside of families live contested and ambiguous lives. Increasingly, scholars are recognizing the benefits of using a "both/and" lens to view gender and families, a lens that is necessary for making sense of our own lives. A social constructionist view allows us to see the world from the perspective of those who are marginalized and vulnerable, shedding new light on all kinds of families, not just those who benefit by mirroring a cultural ideal. Viewing families in their diverse contexts means understanding how gender intersects with race, class, age, and sexual orientation to structure life chances and create its opportunities.

Our review of selected research reveals that the gendered patterns we observe in family relationships have structural, as opposed to biological or developmental, roots. The evidence is clear: traditional family patterns reinforce relationship processes and a division of labor that are unfair to women. By examining the sociohistorical context, we can identify equitable arrangements and the conditions under which they have emerged. There is no fixed or universal pattern; human behavior in relationships and families has the potential for infinite variety. As family and relationship scholars consider future directions, it is wise to remember the resilience with which outdated and inaccurate notions of gender and family survive, and to challenge rather than reinforce beliefs with little bearing in reality.

Chapter 2

The Early Years of Marriage

Joseph Veroff, Amy Young

and

Heather M. Coon

University of Michigan, Ann Arbor, MI, USA

After a blissful beginning to most marriages, couples commonly experience an erosion of their well-being in the initial years (Markman & Hahlweg, 1993), as the two partners in a couple confront the tasks and problems in blending their lives. For a third of all new marriages this erosion leads to divorce in the first 5 years (National Center for Health Statistics, 1991). Most family researchers have sought to illuminate why some young couples remain relatively satisfied while others find it difficult to maintain commitments to each other. Beyond exploring marital stability, these researchers have further assumed that even if divorce does not occur in the early years, reactions in early marriage set the style of adaptation that will characterize the trajectory of the marriage well into the future. Thus, there is considerable interest in understanding the dynamics of early marriage.

We examine situational circumstances as well as behaviors and attitudes that contribute to the stability of early marriages and to the sense of marital well-being in individual partners. Because the study of early marriage has focused more on problems inevitably confronting couples than on theoretical questions about interpersonal dynamics, we organize our chapter around critical problems of adaptation in marriage that have been highlighted in social research. These problems have been of interest to both sociologically and

Families as Relationships.
Edited by Robert M. Milardo and Steve Duck. © 2000 John Wiley & Sons Ltd.

psychologically minded family researchers. From the sociological emphases in the literature, the identified problems boil down to three: how couples weave their social networks (particularly their families of origin) into the fabric of their marriages, how couples negotiate the world of work and react to each other's commitments to work and earning money, and how couples react to becoming a family of procreation with the introduction of children into their lives. These are not totally independent externally demanding tasks, but they can be differentiated.

From the psychological emphases in the literature, we identify four major tasks that describe how couples must regulate their patterns of interaction with one another. Two tasks deal with the more overt activities of the couple: how to divide the labor of the household and how to manage inevitable conflicts. Two additional tasks deal with the covert meaning of their interactions: how couples develop a sense of being a collaborative unit, and how they promote the gratification of each other's affectional and esteem needs. Again, these tasks are interrelated but distinct.

The sections of this chapter are organized around the three external tasks (networks, work demands, demands of parenthood) and the four interactive tasks (dividing household labor, managing conflict, developing a collaborative unit, and promoting gratification of affectional and esteem needs). Because these tasks are not entirely differentiated from one another, with the interactive tasks often embedded in the external tasks (e.g., the need to divide household tasks often flows out of work demands, or the need to manage conflict is stimulated by the birth of a child or the provocation of networks), discussion of one task is often relevant to discussion of the other tasks. Nevertheless, each task is presented separately. For each, we will highlight major conclusions drawn about factors that affect how that task is negotiated, and the theoretical concepts that have been useful in understanding these factors. Furthermore, we identify how the tasks are different for men and women, and for different ethnic/class groups. At the end of the chapter we draw conclusions about the relative importance of outside vs. inside factors in affecting early marriage, as well as how outside and inside factors are interconnected. In addition, we bring together the findings about gender and ethnicity differences to make some general observations about how these factors affect early marital adaptation.

It is important to note that while we have attempted to draw strictly from research on the early years of marriage, for some marital processes it has not always been possible to do so because of the paucity of research. Although some marital issues change over the course of marriage, while others remain relatively consistent, certain marital processes may be only prominent during the early years of marriage when the partners are adjusting to their lives together. Thus, it is arguable whether general research findings on marital issues are applicable to the early years of marriage. Although we feel comfortable with this assumption, future research needs to address the extent to which processes of adaptation in early years of marriage are distinct from processes discovered about the later years. In order to allow our readers to make their own judgments, throughout this chapter we note when we are referring to data that specifically address the early years of marriage.

OUTSIDE FACTORS AFFECTING EARLY MARRIAGE

Social Network

During courtship, planning and arranging the wedding, and thinking through goals after the honeymoon, a couple's friends and family are very much part of the couple's lives (Surra & Milardo, 1991) The newlywed couple is traditionally permitted only a minimum period of withdrawal from its social networks in courtship and early marriage, a time unencumbered with social obligations. Slater (1963) and Johnson and Milardo (1984) argue that withdrawal, when it occurs, is selective, for the couple need to construct a joint network and clarify where circles of associates and kin should overlap and where they should be separate (for empirical work describing these processes, see Milardo, 1982, Johnson, Huston and Milardo, 1983, and Parks & Eggert, 1991). These negotiated networks in early marriage are important for they help define the norms of the marriage and lay the foundation for whether support experienced during difficult periods the couple may face will have positive or negative consequences.

Tallman, Burke and Gecas (1998) have studied the role socialization implicit in the models for marriage that newlywed couples get from their families of origin. For newlyweds the strains in the marriages of their parents can be particularly important in providing positive or negative models for the development of any trust that the couple has for one another. Tallman and his associates found that judgments about the family of origin affect the couple's expectations and trust, which in turn have an impact on what couples disagree about and how serious those disagreements are in the initial months of marriage. Thus, ongoing and past behaviors observed within families of origin, or even in married friends (Oliker, 1989), serve as models for marriage that individual spouses use to shape their newly formed marital dyads.

The implicit models spouses act upon vary in their permeability with some family systems having more closed boundaries to any newcomer, and others having more open boundaries (McGoldrick, 1980). The husband's family and the wife's family, as well as married friends, offer a variety of norms for how husbands and wives are to behave or what they should feel. One important task for newlywed couples is to learn to be selective within their networks about which norms will be primary, and which will be inappropriate. To date, few researchers have explored these adaptive and creative processes.

Social networks are significantly involved in the variables found to he predictive of marital instability (Veroff, Douvan & Hatchett, 1995). Using a representative urban sample of newlyweds, henceforth to be called the Early Years of Marriage (EYM) sample, Veroff, Douvan & Hatchett found that interferences felt from friends and family in the couples' lives the first 2 years of marriage were associated with marital instability 2 years later. On the positive side, feelings of closeness with family were predictive of relative stability among African–American couples, but were not significantly related to marital stability among white couples. Moreover, Timmer, Veroff and Hatchett (1996) found in the EYM study that various measures of a spouse's closeness with in-laws are positively associated with feelings of marital well-being, although measures of a spouse's closeness to his/her own family are less uniformly tied to feeling happy about that spouse's marriage. While these results from the EYM study cannot establish for a fact what the direction of causality is (unstable marriages can induce interferences from the network; stable marriages can promote closeness with in-laws), being longitudinal in its method, the results do support the interpretation that networks can affect the quality of the marital relationship.

Timmer and her colleagues may not have found a direct positive relationship between one's marital well-being and closeness to one's own family because: (1) some wives and husbands in the early years of marriage who feel particularly close to their own families may be just the ones that are having difficulties adjusting to the transition; and (2) extremely close ties can be signs of enmeshment in one's family of origin, which can preclude making strong commitments to new partners (Bott, 1971; Blood, 1969). Timmer, Veroff and Hatchett (1996) found that African–American women are particularly involved with their families of origin; they see their families of origin more than their husbands do, and more than white wives or husbands do. However, this strong connection is not correlated with strong feelings of support from family members that would help these women transact rough times in their marriage. Thus, one must distinguish between the kind of closeness with families that can be supportive of marriage bonds in the early years of marriage, and the kind of closeness that may he so strong that it prevents the formation of a strong new bond between spouses and the new family they are creating. Burger and Milardo (1995), for example, find in a sample of young married couples that the impact of strong connections on their marriages with perceived networks was generally positive for husbands and negative for wives. Furthermore, the particular identity of the family member determined whether there was a positive or negative effect of being particularly close to a member of a family.

Family closeness is not the only network variable that may play a significant role in affecting marital well-being in the early years. Vangelisti and Huston (1994) examined satisfaction with one's network as part of another longitudinal study of newlyweds, henceforth called the Project on Processes of Adaptation in Intimate Relationships (PAIR) (Huston, McHale and Crouter, 1986). Vangelisti and Huston found that satisfaction with network ties was correlated with the overall marital well-being of wives but not husbands when they were first married. Furthermore, network satisfaction did not affect the way wives feel about their marriage as the years progressed. These results suggest that network satisfaction plays only a minor direct role as a contributor to marital well-being in early marriage and only with women in the newlywed stage.

Work Demands

Most newlywed couples must financially support themselves, and working can affect couples' marriages in many ways. Satisfactions and stresses experienced at work have reverberations in the marriage. In addition, many couples today must deal with the additional challenge of being a dual-earner couple, and the employment of women outside the home has led to significant differences from traditional power dynamics within the marriage. Furthermore, the attitudes of both spouses regarding their roles as providers can have a significant impact on their marriage.

Crouter and Helms-Erikson (1997) provide a detailed overview of the effects of work on marriage. One of the major phenomena they cite is that stress and bad moods at work spill over to the marriage, following people home and affecting relationships with their spouse and family (Bolger et al., 1989). Unemployment has also been shown to have negative spillover (Vinokur & Van Ryn, 1993). Although the studies summarized by Crouter & Helms-Erikson do not focus on the early years of marriage, specifically, data from the EYM study indirectly support the spillover phenomenon for the early years. Veroff (1994) found in the EYM study that by the seventh year of marriage, spouses who were satisfied with their marital relationship were particularly happily married when they had outside satisfactions, including their jobs. These results were statistically significant for most working spouses, but were not for African–American working women. This pattern of results corroborates other research cited by Crouter and Helms-Erikson that indicates that the work–marriage spillover effect is less apparent for some women, but consistently present for men. It is also interesting to note that the EYM study found spillover not with regard to stress, but with regard to satisfaction, which has not been generally examined in work–family spillover research. Gratification at work thus potentially has positive consequences for a marriage, and vice versa, for some people.

Aside from spillover, some theorists have argued that the fact that a wife works may have another type of consequence for marriage. By working a woman increases her overall power within the household because she contributes more resources than she would if she were not employed, and the power gained should be proportional to the income and prestige associated with the job. However, women's employment has not resulted in a redistribution of power within the couple in a clear and straightforward manner (Hochschild, 1989; Kompter, 1989; Crouter & Helms-Erikson, 1997). Issues of power are never clear-cut, because there are so many different bases of power. Nevertheless, Sexton and Perlman (1989) found that dual-career couples were more likely to try to influence each other than single-career couples. At least at one level, therefore, wives in dual-career families were exhibiting more overt attempts to exert power than were women in single-career families.

The fact that wives work outside the home can have effects on power dynamics in another sense. Working can help engender interests outside the relationship. Kurdek (1998) suggests from a longitudinal study of early marriage that when wives value autonomy (e.g, having interests outside the relationship), they are less involved in being the traditional relationship re-pairers and in performing the roles of traditional nurturing. Kurdek finds that such values predict marital dissatisfaction over time for both husbands and wives. If the mere fact of working makes women value their autonomy more, then Kurdek's results can be read to mean that working women are less dependent on and less committed to their relationships, all other things being equal.

Furthermore, women may subtly transmit the power they experience in being employed in their interactions with their husbands. Ruvolo and Veroff (1997), using EYM data, measured the discrepancies between ideal charac-teristics wives would like their husbands to have and their appraisals of what their husbands were actually like. The researchers found that these discrepan-cies are correlated 2 years later with lower marital quality for both husbands and wives, but only if the women were employed. Ruvolo and Veroff inter-pret the findings to signify that, compared to full-time housewives, employed wives can more easily attend to the dissatisfactions with their husbands and communicate them to their husbands. The researchers argue that in being employed, women develop a sense of their own worth, which permits them to take their criticism of their husbands more seriously.

Finally, as Crouter and Helms-Erikson (1997) suggest, husbands' and wives' attitudes about their own roles as providers are related to their marital satisfaction. For instance, men who value the idea of being the main providers (or "breadwinners") tend to be very satisfied with their marriages if they do not participate in household work, while men who are ambivalent about being a main provider but at the same time do a lot of housework are less satisfied with their marriage (Perry-Jenkins & Crouter, 1990). It is important to realize that couples may continually redefine what it means for husbands and wives to be workers and providers, and these definitions may be particularly salient to young, newly married couples as they integrate their work and family lives, and compare their integrations with those from their valued networks.

The Transition to Parenthood

An exciting and challenging transition faced by many newly married couples is the birth of a child. Children not only require extensive attention but often they create disequilibrium within the couple as spouses learn to balance new responsibilities and attempt to maintain old ones (Cowan & Cowan, 1992) Changes in perceptions of one's own identity, as well as changes in couples' interactions and patterns of conflict, often lead to a drop in marital harmony that can indeed have long-term consequences. The division of labor often has to be reconsidered, both with and without the benefit of a parental leave from work. Revisions in household assignments require new collaborative agree-ments if transitions are to be handled smoothly. In juggling new and old tasks, adapting to disruptions in sleep and sexual patterns, couples must develop new ways to regulate their feelings, reapportion their time, and satisfy their esteem and relational needs. Outlined below is a discussion of these new demands as they have been highlighted in research about the transition to parenthood.

Dealing with Negative Affect Emerging from Conflict

The transition to parenthood involves a great change in the interaction patterns of the couple, creates conflict and thus induces a need to regulate affect. Positive affective interactions between spouses decrease after the birth of a child (Spanier, Rovine and Belsky, 1983; McHale & Huston, 1985) and levels of conflict increase (Cowan et al., 1991). These changes occur generally over the first years of marriage, but to a greater extent among new parents compared to childless couples. Although White and Booth (1985b) find the opposite effect (fewer conflicts in new parents), they did not control for length of marriage. With the increasing level of conflict in the transition to parenthood, a major task for many couples is how to deal with this new level of tension between them. Cowan et al. (1991) indicate that many new parents are at a loss for dealing with conflict at this point in their lives, and this difficulty affects the entire family unit. Cowan et al. propose that the solution involves learning how to regulate affect. Couples who do learn to regulate affect are thought to become secure models of attachment for their children (Cowan & Cowan, 1994).

Reapportionment of Time

In general, household division of labor after the birth of a child has been characterized as more traditional, with women assuming more of the burden for cooking and cleaning (Lang, Rovine and Belsky, 1985; McHale & Huston, 1985). However, other work by Cowan and Cowan (1988) suggests that the division of labor, and men's and women's roles, become both more traditional and more non-traditional, depending on the time of assessment relative to the birth of the child and the questions asked. In their longitudinal study, there was no general shift from one person to another in responsibility for household tasks; however, there was more role specialization, with each parent assuming more responsibility for certain tasks.

Cowan and Cowan (1988) also measured the level of spousal satisfaction with the division of labor. First, men's level of involvement in household tasks positively affected wives' satisfaction with the chores each was doing. However, husbands were doing less collaboration than their wives expected (Belsky, Ward & Rovine, 1986). Finally, for both spouses, satisfaction with the labor arrangements was related to self-esteem, parenting stress and marital quality after childbirth. Negotiating the division of labor is not a trivial affair. In several studies spouses reported that the division of family labor after the birth of a child was the issue most likely to cause arguments (Belsky, Ward & Rovine, 1986; Cowan et al., 1991).

In addition to reapportionment of household responsibilities, parenthood requires a reapportionment of leisure and sexual activities. It is quite easy to understand why parents of newborns have to alter their leisure activities and put constraints on their sexual lives. In fact, Spanier, Rovine and Belsky (1983) found a significant decrease in joint leisure activities of spouses for the third trimester of pregnancy, and through three months post-partum, with a leveling off at this lower level after that. McHale and Huston (1985) in the PAIR study observed a change in the kind of leisure activities in which the spouses engaged: they became more child-centered. It follows that with less joint leisure time and more child-centered leisure, there would be less time for sex.

Gratifying Self and Relational Needs

Being constantly responsible for another person brings many frustrations along with the gratifications. Parents are often called upon to make their own needs subservient to their infants' and therefore the parents experience frustration. With parenthood, wives and husbands see themselves less as lovers and more as partners (Spanier, Rovine and Belsky, 1983; Lang, Rovine and Belsky, 1985: Cowan et al., 1991). In addition, women's focus back to the home gives them a reduced sense of being workers or students. Coping with these psychological changes is one of the main difficulties that couples face in the transition to parenthood; they affect a person's whole sense of identity. Further, men and women change differently (Cowan et al., 1991), and depending on the directions each goes in, the changes can be bases for either couple estrangement or couple development. Generally, negative changes are experienced first by women. Men seem to experience change only after women. Perhaps because women are more relationship-oriented, they "pass on" the negativity they feel to their husbands.

While most of the results reported above document the difficulties associated with the transition to parenthood, it should be pointed out that the actual differences found between parents and non-parents were modest (Belsky and Pensky, 1988). In addition, marriages that were doing better before the child was born continue to look the same relative to other marriages after the birth of a child (Spanier, Rovine and Belsky, 1983; Belsky, Ward & Rovine, 1986; Cowan & Cowan, 1988; Cowan et al., 1991; McHale & Huston, 1985). Cowan et al. (1991) speculate that declines in marital satisfaction during the transition to parenthood will widen already existing differences between partners.

Furthermore, having and raising a child remain important sources of fulfillment for most couples. Thus, the increased stress associated with child-raising may not necessarily mean that there is a decrease in overall life satisfaction as people become parents, whatever challenges it may bring for marital functioning. In fact, parenthood may actually bring an increase in life satisfaction because parents see themselves as achieving important goals in their lives. When asked how their lives are changed by having children (Veroff, Douvan & Kulka, 1981), many parents answer in terms of the new meaning they find in their lives. Depner (1978) found that a measure of value fulfillment through parenthood related significantly to overall life satisfaction, while a measure of satisfaction felt in performing parental requirements did not. Depner's results suggest that the goals of being parents can play an important part in well-being independently of the dissatisfactions attendant to the role discovered in early marriage.

We should note the special case of step-parenting in its effects on early years of marriage. In our own society, due to the increasing permissibility of bearing children out of wedlock and the high divorce and remarriage rate, many couples come into marriage with children already born, either to the couple or to one or the other of the spouses from previous relationships or marriages. To these couples, parenthood is a given at the onset of marriage, and they need to deal immediately with the issues of these external matters as a part of becoming married (Coleman & Ganong, 1994).

By and large, step-parenthood decreases the stability and satisfaction of second marriages (White & Booth, 1985a). However, Kurdek (1989) suggests that among newlyweds who have both been married before, the presence of stepchildren has a positive association with reported marital quality. Thus the effects of stepchildren on the early years of a marriage are indeed complex, although most of the evidence points to the disruptive effects they have.

We should also note the not so uncommon case of entering a first marriage with a child of one's own conceived before marriage. Sutherland (1990) has shown that newlyweds who have never previously married but who enter marriage with a child (whether or not the child is from another relationship or the couple's own) find marriage more difficult than either having no children at entry or experiencing the transition to parenthood during the early years. In Sutherland's study, using the EYM data, couples who had experienced premarital children or pregnancies were especially economically disadvantaged and suffered the most inadequate network supports in the first year of marriage. This was true for both white couples and African–American couples. When income and education were controlled, the negative relationship between premarital pregnancy/birth and marital stability disappeared. Interestingly, white women who married the father of their premaritally conceived or delivered child indicated the greatest marital happiness in the first year.

INTERNAL FACTORS AFFECTING EARLY MARRIAGE

All the external factors affecting early marriage we have discussed reverberate in the psychological responses of the couples. Networks, jobs and having children are structural phenomena that couples adapt to more or less by finding a compatible way of regulating their lives, relations and the demands of others. We limit ourselves to discussing four broad issues. Two are quite salient to the couple's own conscious appraisal of their lives and include the division of labor in the household and the management of conflict. Two represent more non-conscious processes and include how couples define their collaborative working unit and how spouses satisfy each other's esteem and relational needs.

Division of Labor in the Household

Each couple would like to seek out the optimal division of labor in the household so that the work gets done efficiently and well. Changing gender roles in our society, however, have complicated what had been the traditionally simple set of expectations in modern industrial America: men should work outside the home for money and women should do the inside household work. The division of household labor is affected in many ways by who works outside the home and how spouses perceive their roles as providers.

Equity with regard to household labor is difficult for most couples to achieve. The clearest finding in many studies is that regardless of any advances in equality that women have made in the workplace, within the home women continue to carry the burden of the workload (Hochschild, 1989). Furthermore, the work that women do out of the home does not influence the amount that husbands do within the home (Pleck, 1985; Baxter, 1992). Thus, for women, work outside of the home simply means more work rather than an exchange of outside-the-home labor for inside-the-home labor. Interestingly, this is not the case for husbands. The more work that they perform outside the home, the less work they perform within the home (Baxter, 1992). However, some data suggest that among many African–American couples, for whom the dual-earner norm has been prevalent for decades, there has been some movement towards egalitarian roles in the household, and with some success. For example, it has been estimated that African–American wives perform 60% of the household work (Wilson et al., 1990), whereas white wives perform 70% (Berk, 1985: Demo & Acock, 1993).

Regardless of behaviors, attitudes about household work at least are changing, although the traditional attitudes are hard to erase. With these changing norms for husband and wives, newly married couples have a greater task before them and it becomes exaggerated during the transition to parenthood, as noted in our discussion of parenthood demands. Child care can clearly be seen as an interruption of individual pursuits (Crawford & Huston, 1993), and thus the allocation of household labors can be a source of considerable negotiation during the transition to parenthood.

The division of labor in the household thus requires more negotiating within the couple than it once did. Conflicts about household labor are the most common source of tension reported by newlyweds (Tallman, Burke & Gecas, 1998). How then do couples negotiate the allocation of tasks? Many researchers have noted that this negotiation depends on the power distribution within the couple (Ross, 1987; Hartmann. 1981). According to this argument, men's and women's relative earning power outside the home provides the leverage in negotiating the allocation of household labor. However. research on power distribution and household labor fails to provide conclusive support for this claim (Crouter & Helms-Erikson, 1997).

Dissatisfaction with the distribution of household labor is related to incongruencies between gender role attitudes and actual division of labor. McHale and Crouter (1992) have found that newly married women rated their marriage more negatively if they had traditional household roles and egalitarian attitudes. Men, on the other hand, rated their marriage negatively if they had traditional attitudes but egalitarian roles. Thus, not all women are unhappy with the unequal distribution of household labor, and not all men are unhappy about equality in household labor. Although both partners agree that this inequality exists, they do not always view this differential as unfair (Thompson, 1991). It is only when wives expect their husbands to share the housework equally that they become unhappy. Thus, women's expectations about men's involvement, and the meaning that they attribute to their contribution to household labor, play a significant moderating role in the relationship between division of labor and marital and personal well-being (Pina & Bengston, 1993).

There is, no doubt, some resistance by many men to changing their participation in household labor. In fact, one study suggests that the optimization of marital happiness, especially for men, occurs when women profess traditional household attitudes. Vangelisti and Huston (1994) have shown that more traditional ways of dealing with household tasks increases men's loving feelings towards their wives in the PAIR sample, which is heavily working-class. These positive feelings then have positive repercussions on their wives' feelings about their marriages. Tallman & Riley (1995), in an analysis of feelings about and actual participation in household labor in their sample of newlyweds in Washington State, speak of a cultural lag that reinforces both men and women seeing the traditional division of labor with regard to household chores as more comfortable. Orbuch and Custer's (1995) analysis of the EYM data indicates that white males whose wives work felt particularly distressed if they were sharing in household chores.

The pattern of results in the Orbuch and Custer analysis was not true for the African–American males. It is important to realize that for African–American couples the expectation that wives work has been more normative for a longer period of time. This suggests that as it becomes more common for women to work, "traditional" gender expectations about the division of labor in the household will erode. If this trend continues, in the 21st century young dual-earner couples will gravitate more easily to an equitable division of labor. Already some couples are willing and perhaps eager to take on "peer marriages" (Schwartz, 1994), sharing equally in household responsibilities among other things. Schwartz finds that there are potential costs to such an arrangement, but argues that the collaboration involved in such marriages undergirds a solid marital structure with intense personal fulfillment.

Managing Conflict

All married couples find themselves engaged in some kind of conflict throughout their marriage. However, conflict does not necessarily lead to marital distress and destruction. Instead, conflict can intensify spouses' intimacy (P. C. Miller et al., 1986) and can be indicative of positive functioning (Markman, 1991). Although newlyweds may experience an initial "honeymoon" phase with few conflicts, they have to learn continuously how to manage the conflicts that occur, a task that began in courtship. Indeed Noller and Feeney (1998) have found that premarital conflict patterns are highly predictive of marital quality in early marriage, and what is more, do not change much in the early years. The processes of conflict management may be more critical for marital satisfaction than the actual conflict, although successful management should reduce the sheer number of conflicts (Klein & Johnson, 1997).

Several approaches of marital conflict management have been extensively studied: *constructive engagement*, characterized by open, direct communication; *destructive engagement*—"attacks" toward a partner involving criticism and hostility: and *avoidance* (withdrawal), evidenced by ignoring or denying the problem (P. C. Miller et al., 1986; Raush et al., 1974). Raush et al. (1974) demonstrated that compatibility of conflict styles is critical to marital harmony for newlyweds. Generally, constructive engagement in conflict leads to new understandings of the relationship. In contrast, avoidance tends to stifle relationship growth. However, Raush and his colleagues also showed that conflict avoidance within the context of a bond of mutual affection does not necessarily steer couples to an unhappy marriage, especially if it is normative for the couple. This suggests that it is not conflict behaviors *per se* that lead to distress but rather how spouses think about them.

Crohan (1988, 1992) studied the moderating role of conflict beliefs in the relationship between conflict behaviors and marital satisfaction with the EYM sample. She found that one configuration of conflict styles was especially important to well-being. Marriages where both partners believe disagreements can be settled through discussion had higher levels of marital happiness than marriages where both spouses believe that disagreements cannot always be solved, and where the spouses disagreed about their beliefs. Moreover, moderately attacking (but not severely attacking) behaviors were positively related to marital well-being among spouses who believe disagreements are healthy. Such was not the case for spouses who did not hold these beliefs.

In examining the aforementioned results separately for African–Americans and whites, Crohan (1988) pointed to patterns that may be different for African–American newlyweds. Most notably, African–American women were more likely than white women to believe that disagreements can always be settled, that people should try to control their anger, and that conflict should be avoided. Furthermore, avoiding conflict had more negative consequences for the well-being of white couples than African–American couples. Some sex differences were observed in Crohan's analysis as well. Men and women did not, in general, hold different beliefs about conflict. However, the use of constructive engagement was more important for the well-being of men than it was for women. Women who believed in confronting conflicts reported being happier when negative behaviors were exhibited in a conflict resolution task; such was not the case for men. Women used constructive behaviors less frequently than men did, and these behaviors did not predict happiness as well for women as they did for men.

In addition to conflict beliefs, the attributions that spouses make about each other during fights are related to the successful management of conflict. Fincham and Bradbury (1987, 1993) find that dissatisfied spouses compared with satisfied spouses make negative attributions about their partner's behavior. When conflicts occur, distressed spouses tend to view their partners as selfishly motivated and behaving with negative intent. This suggests that attributions about conflict can exert some causal influence on judgments of relationship quality.

There is no single ideal style of conflict management. Instead, couples can confront conflict in different ways and still maintain high levels of marital satisfaction. Conflict beliefs and attributions regarding negative behavior play a central role in successful conflict resolution. Rusbult et al. (1998) also found how much commitment to marriage mediated the effects of conflict styles on early marital well-being.

Nevertheless, there are certain behaviors that occur in the context of conflict that are in themselves indicative of marital distress and dissatisfaction. Problem drinking associated with conflicts has been identified as a strong negative influence in changes in marital quality during the first year (Leonard & Roberts, 1998). Another pattern identified by a number of researchers (Christensen & Heavey, 1990: Gottman & Krokoff, 1989; Gray-Little & Burks, 1983; Lane, Christensen and Heavey, 1993; Renick, Floyd & Markman, 1993) is male withdrawal from conflict in conjunction with demanding behaviors by females (i.e., emotional engagement in the conversation, blaming, and pressures for change). Couples with these highly stereotypic interactions were found to be most at risk for marital dissatisfaction. Lane, Christensen and Heavey (1993) found that this conflict pattern was most likely to occur when couples were discussing issues in the husband's behavior that the wife wanted to change. In contrast, when couples discussed behaviors that the husband wanted to change, there was no distinction in the roles each spouse took in conflict management. Lane, Christensen and Heavey hypothesize that men's higher status in society allows them generally to structure the relationship more to their liking and that, as a result, they have less need to change what is happening in a marriage. Conflicts are thus usually about wives' complaints, which induce the stereotyped and often dysfunctional conflict management styles.

Negativity also plays a central role in managing conflict. Gottman (1979) found that the proportion of positive behaviors exhibited during conflict resolution was less indicative of relationship distress than was the proportion of negative behaviors. Over time negativity becomes a good predictor of marital dissatisfaction. Huston and Chorost (1994) support macroanalytically what Gottman found microanalytically. In their PAIR project, Huston and Chorost found that negativity had adverse effects on marital satisfaction because the marriage becomes less affectionate in the early years. However, negativity does not always sharply affect marital quality. Affective expression, the level of affection spouses express toward each other, and substantial effort on relationship maintenance buffer the effect of negativity on women's marital quality. Huston and Chorost found that when husbands exhibit high levels of affective expression toward their wives, their negativity is less associated with a drop in wives' satisfaction over time. However, no such buffering occurs when examining the effects of wives' negativity on husbands' satisfaction. Because women's affective expression is more taken for granted by men than men's affective expression is by women, women's affective expression may not serve any buffering function for men.

So how can this pattern of negativity and withdrawal be reversed? Markman and his colleagues (Renick, Floyd & Markman, 1993) have developed interventions to predict and prevent "erosion" in couples' satisfaction and, like Cowan and Cowan (1992), state that affective regulation is a key to understanding how conflict can be managed. Spouses need to support one another during conflict resolution by validating each other and summarizing each other's distress rather than by cross-complaining and summarizing one's own position. Support during conflict management occurs more often in non-distressed couples than in distressed couples, perhaps because support prevents withdrawal/avoidance in conflicts and prevents the escalation of conflict. Cutrona and Suhr (1994) have presented experimental evidence for this effect in young married couples. The results of the Huston and Chorost (1994) study would suggest that support from men can be found simply in expressing positive feelings towards their wives in the context of conflict, but support from women in ongoing conflict interactions may have to go beyond simple expression of feelings towards their husbands and entail complex affirmation of their husbands' ideas and positions.

In summary, learning to manage conflict and avoiding certain patterns of conflict behavior in the early years of marriage may be critical for the long-term survival of the marriage. Markman (1991) suggests that expressing conflict may be related to dissatisfaction in the early years of marriage as couples struggle to determine their conflict style, but ultimately, expressing conflict early on seems to be positively related to satisfaction with marriage, especially if it occurs in the context of general support or with a clear problem-solving orientation (Conger & Elder, 1994).

Defining the Collaborative Unit

Getting married is a public commitment. The new legal status emerging from that commitment enjoins a man and a woman to shift their focus of concerns from themselves as individuals to the collective. For partners who already thought of themselves as a collective, especially among those who had co-habited, this is a minor transition. For others who had not psychologically emphasized being a couple, it is a major transition. Living together in marriage is supposed to require each partner to coordinate with his/her spouse's concerns. Money, work, eating, housework, sexual needs and leisure activities are now to be transacted in a collaborative system. How seriously individuals take these implicit rules for collaboration that becoming married brings, and how far partners go in enacting ideals of collaboration, are questions that couples face when first married. Should spouses give up their private life space entirely to the collective life space or preserve a large territory of their private space? This question defines a major task of the early years of marriage, one that can be assessed only indirectly. A couple's success at this task is related to their shared perceptions of marriage and of each other (see Berger & Kellner, 1964).

Whether partners share attitudes and values can affect the ease of collaboration in marriage. Creamer and Campbell (1988) have found that well-adjusted couples describe themselves as being more similar in beliefs and preferences than do poorly adjusted couples. Such findings do not implicate collaboration directly, but only suggest that similarity between spouses can pave the way for greater collaboration. More direct evidence comes in Kurdek's (1993a) 5-year longitudinal study of newlyweds, which finds that discrepancies in husbands' and wives' perceptions of the reasons for entering the marital union are good predictors of marital dissolution. Having similar motives for marriage helps the couple collaborate and regulate each others' lives without elaborate discussion or working through conflicts about goals and means for arriving at goals. Cowan et al. (1991) also found that smaller discrepancies in partners' relationship values were predictive of how well they dealt with the transition to parenthood. Again, shared meaning, more covert than overt, helps regulate how a couple together might approach a momentous event in their lives.

Tallman, Burke and Gecas (1998) likewise reason that early marriage represents a negotiation of roles based on the individual socialization experiences of each partner and the resources they bring to marriage. A collective identity is required. Veroff, Sutherland, Chadiha and Ortega (1993) also show that a jointly derived positive reconstruction of the couple's courtship in a narrative of their relationship is predictive of their happiness. These findings and others (Veroff, Douvan & Hatchett, 1995) about joint narratives suggest that a collaborative orientation to their affective life is important to couples' well-being in early marriage.

The importance of collaboration in early marriage can also be found in Aron, Aron and Smollan's (1992) work on the degree to which the self and other are perceived as being connected or merged in good relationships. They use a series of two circles that are depicted as being non-overlapping at one extreme, and almost completely overlapping at the other extreme. Men and women are asked to pick the two circles that best describes their marital relationship. These authors find that selecting the two circles that depict more perceived merging rather than independence is correlated with happier marriages, a result that was repeated by Veroff (1994). There is a hint in Aron, Aron and Smollan's work that over-merging may be a problem for women, who interpret the extreme of the perceptual measure used by the researchers (highly overlapping circles) as representing a submergence of self, which can be negatively experienced. For those women, over-emphasis on collaboration disrupt their ideals for marriage, and may mean subjugating their wishes to a husband who is seen by some to have more power in the unit.

With that note of caution, that collaboration can mean an unequal submergence of the self on women's part, we would still suggest that embracing marriage in the early years as a collaborative enterprise can subtly set that stage for a strong sense of well-being and commitment to the marriage. Collaboration is difficult to teach but may be subtly generated when partners have similar goals and values as well as a commitment to the collective rather than to individual needs. The transition to parenthood may be the severest test of the collaborative capacity of the couple in the early years.

Gratifying Each Other's Affectional and Esteem Needs

There is considerable evidence for a general proposition that to find marriage satisfying, partners have to learn to balance their needs for relating affectionately to each other with their needs for appreciation of their individual worth, to balance giving and receiving love, to accommodate to one another without losing a sense of self. Such positions are explicit in various dialectical theories (e.g., May, 1973; Veroff & Veroff, 1980) and can be found implicitly in Askham's (1984) views of social identity in marriage, Rusbult and Buunk's (1993) application of theories of interdependence to relationships, Fromm's (1956) views of the nature of love, and Malley's (1989) application of Bakan's (1966) dualistic theory of agency and communion to marriage. Two themes run through these theoretical views. First, for gratifying relationships, couples need to accommodate to one another. Second, couples need to feel affirmed as individuals. Such affirmation and accommodation may be difficult to achieve as couples adjust to the inevitable flaws that crop up when two people, however well-intentioned they may be, stake out their lives together. Under what conditions do affirmation by and accommodation to one's spouse take place in a gratifying way?

It is suggested that men and women will attempt to maintain illusions to accommodate to difficulties in the way their spouse acts towards them. Murray, Holmes and Griffin (1996) find that young married couples project their ideals onto their partners, over and above any tendencies they may have to see people in a "pollyanna" way. These evaluations are more positive than their partners' own view of themselves. This type of illusion seems to have positive consequences for their partners, perhaps helping to maintain both affectional and esteem needs and inoculating them against life's inevitable difficulties.

It has also been found that happily married couples partially maintain their idealization of each other by attributing partners' negative behaviors to situational forces, rather than to anything dispositional about the partner (Bradbury & Fincham, 1990). Kayser's (1993) remarkable retrospective study of how men and women retell the stories of their disaffection in marriage indicates the implications of focusing on the negative features of one's spouse. Doing so can contribute to further hurt, alienation and anger during conflicts, which in turn create a spiraling, potentially unchangeable disaffection process. In contrast, Murray, Holmes and Griffin (1996) present evidence that couples can fend off doubts raised about each other by turning apparent flaws into virtues and highlighting something positive in spite of a flaw. Again these processes are cognitive construals that help maintain affirming attitudes towards one's partner. Such affirmation can positively influence one's partner who, in turn, may reduce the frequency of the negative behaviors that originally induced the concerns.

Veroff, Douvan and Hatchett (1995) have found that communicating affirmation of one's partner is a central subtle process that undergirds stable marriages in the early years. Does a husband believe his wife makes him feel good about having his own ideas and ways of doing things? Or, does a wife think her husband feels especially caring towards her and makes her life especially interesting and exciting? Positive answers to these questions make up a scale of "affective affirmation", which in the EYM study has been a strong correlate of marital stability and well-being. A surprising finding was that affective affirmation by wives was especially important for men, which is interpreted to mean that men's affirmation through their spouse may be the major or only source of affirmation they experience, while women may more readily find affirmation through friends and other family members.

Among white males in our society, one strong basis of affirmation seems to occur by establishing a particularly satisfying sexual relationship with their wives. Veroff et al. (1998) examined the bases of especially happy marriages among couples in their third year of marriage who were very committed to the marriage, and found that sexual satisfaction in white men is a clear marker of these happy marriages. From these results one might infer that white men feel particularly affirmed in their marriages if they can give and receive sexual pleasure. These results were not apparent among African–American couples. White males evidently have considerable self-esteem tied up in their sexual lives in marriage.

Affirmation processes take many forms and seem to be different for men and women. For women, the expression of affection, rather than sexual gratification, seems to be paramount for maintaining good feelings about marriage. Newly married husbands' affection expressed towards their wives may serve as cushion for the bad effects that nasty encounters have on their wives' evaluation of their marriage (Huston & Chorost, 1994).

Once discrepancies between marital expectations and reality are found, another process that can help preserve the partner's feelings in a relationship is to accommodate to what is actually present in the relationship. Rusbult and Buunk (1993), conceptualizing accommodation in a theory of interdependence and commitment, highlight a number of strategies that spouses use:

downplaying alternative partners' attractiveness, focusing on comparisons to other marriages where things appear worse, being willing to sacrifice, and establishing rules controlling extradyadic involvement.

A different kind of accommodation is to change oneself in the direction of the goals set by one's partner. Using EYM data, Ruvolo (1990) designed such a measure, and Veroff, Douvan and Hatchett (1995) found that measure in men *negatively* related to marital stability. Evidently, men may accommodate in the sense of changing to please their wives only in faltering marriages; women may accommodate as part of their expected way of operating in marriage, whether the relationship is good or bad.

This differential basis of accommodation in men and women undoubtedly reflects the societally supported greater power that men have in the commitment process in marriage. It is perceived, at least within the dominant culture, that most men can initiate alternative relationships if a marriage goes sour and that men generally have fewer risks with regard to employment and less responsibility for children if the relationship were to dissolve. Among African–American couples the picture may be different. Ending a marriage may be an easier alternative for women, because African–American women have had many models of women who are self-reliant economically and have turned easily to family for assistance with children.

SOME GENERAL OBSERVATIONS

We have organized our thinking about early marriage into external factors and internal factors, and along the way we have suggested how these categories affect each other. We have not specified any ordering of the importance of these sets of factors in couples' experience, either within or across these broad categories. Our guess is that within certain ethnic groups and socio-economic statuses some categories are dominant over others.

One way to focus on factors that determine marital quality and stability in the early years is through the ethnicity lens. Veroff, Douvan and Hatchett (1995) present a wealth of data to capture many kinds of determinants of stability. One clear finding is that factors "outside the couple" seem to govern the stability of African–American couples more than they do white couples, and that internal determinants seem to govern the stability of white couples more than African–American couples. For example, husbands' concern about financial security is related to marital instability among African–American couples but not white couples, and a sense of closeness to family and friends is also more important in the African–American couples. In contrast, factors of sexual life and interpersonal perceptions are more prominent in understanding well-being among white couples than among African–American couples. Thus, a couple's position in the larger society can determine what factors will take over as primary for understanding their marriage relationship. Different social positions imply different access to resources, which becomes the basis for role negotiation in marriage (Tallman, Burke & Gecas, 1998). This might be particularly so in the early years as couples establish themselves in the economic structure. We suggest that a young married person of a non-dominant social or ethnic group in our society is more conscious of the salience of power in society and focuses on external regulations of married life (i.e., work demands, parenting and networks). These factors should be the prime regulators of the adaptation that couples from minority groups or lower status groups experience. In contrast, a person from a dominant social group may tend to focus on the internal workings of the marriage. We suggest that this interpretation may also be useful in comparing marriages from different class positions, but it is particularly useful in thinking about African–Americans who, in addition to being generally lower in economic status, have been disadvantaged for so many years in accessing the resources of the society, because of institutional racism.

Gender is another important lens for viewing the determinants of marital quality. Women and men may ask different questions as they evaluate their marriages because their assumptions about their lives and their selves are so different (Lykes, 1985). Women as a group have also been deprived of power in society. That fact alone could determine how men and women look at their marriages, particularly the power inherent in their relationships with their partners. Kompter (1989), however, has suggested that the amount of power that women have in marriage is not just related to whether they work and how much money they earn in relation to their husbands. She argues that there may be latent power and invisible power in the marital relationship, both of which favor men. Latent power is the ability of husbands to keep their wives silent about their desires. Invisible power comes in perceptual biases that permit men to exaggerate the amount of effort they expend towards the household or towards meeting their wives affectional needs (for a more detailed examination of feminist views of marital power, see Osmond & Thorne, 1993). Because of their long history of competing relatively well compared to their husbands in the economic arena, African–American women may experience more overt power in their marriages than their white counterparts. However, they still may be overshadowed by their husbands with regard to latent power. To the degree that African–American men have been deprived of a dignified position in the economic structure, and to the degree that their wives have been able to gain some access to steady work, African–American men may be especially eager to hold on to the latent and invisible power afforded them in our society. We should at least be aware that the dynamics of power differential for husbands and wives in their marriages may be different for African–American couples than for white couples.

In addition to considerations of power, we should also consider the differential meanings social relationships have for men and women and specifically the role that marriage plays for self-definition in the matrix of other relationships. The intimate social support provided in marriage is typically more critical for men than women; women tend to be more generally relationship-minded than men, making their friends, family of origin, and family of procreation all important facets of their selves (Antonucci, 1994).

Women more than men rely on and invest in relationships in addition to marriage for defining themselves. These networks of relationships are engaged by women to compensate for their reduced power in marriage and in society at large, at least compared to men. For women marriage may be important, but it is only one of many supports available to them (Argyle & Furnham, 1983; Oliker, 1989; Fowers, 1991). However, for men the marital bond is the major relationship in their lives. Therefore, compared to women, the intimacy of marriage through love and sex becomes the critical basis of support for men's self-definition.

Women are still more aware than men about problems in their relationships (Markman & Kraft, 1989; Notarius & Pellegrini, 1987), but in one sense men are more love-dependent on marriage than women. The pattern may be especially striking for African–American men in the early years of their marriage. Among African–American men there may be some special sensitivity to being accepted as men by their wives. Deprived of status in the outside, they may be particularly eager to seek status in the *inner* dynamics of their marriage. Some of the results from the EYM study support this hypothesis, especially showing that affective affirmation is so critical to the marital well-being of African–American men.

Although different groups may emphasize either the external or the internal factors that we have selected to review for this chapter, it is the case that all groups are affected by both external and internal factors determining how couples adapt to the early years of marriage. Furthermore, external and internal factors clearly interact, and in the approach we have taken it is hard to assert simply that external factors or internal factors shape the nature of marital well-being in the early years. Networks matter; work matters; becoming parents matters, but each of these external contexts implicate the internal dynamics of a marriage. These include arranging the division of labor in the home, managing conflicts, building collaborative efforts as a couple, and gratifying each others' relational and esteem needs. We particularly highlighted how gender differences in external factors affect the way couples consider internal aspects of their marriage. We have also examined differences between African–American couples and white couples in their access to external power in the society and how that might shape their differential reactions to internal issues in marriage. We have relied heavily on the EYM study which permits comparisons of these groups. As more data accumulate about gender and ethnicity effects among African–American couples and among couples from other ethnic groups, researchers will be in a better position to spell out more fully the complexity that a contextual approach to the study of marriage in the early years engenders.

Chapter 3

Parent–Child Relations across Adulthood

Teresa M. Cooney

Department of Human Development and Family Studies, University of Missouri, Columbia, USA

PARENT–CHILD RELATIONS IN YOUNG AND OLDER ADULTHOOD

The bulk of the parent–child relationship today is situated in the adult years for both generations; with average life expectancy currently exceeding 75 years, we are expected to live over 40 years as adults with at least one surviving parent (Watkins, Menken & Bongaarts, 1987). Yet, much of research and theorizing about normative parent–child relationships focuses on the relationship as it exists early in the child's life. Then, as noted by Hagestad (1981), researchers "seem to drop the relationship and not pick it up again until parents are old and the children are middle-aged" (p. 33). At that point, research attends primarily to the relationship during non-normative crises, as evidenced by the voluminous caregiving literature (Zarit & Eggebeen, 1995). In contrast, little attention is paid to the relationship between adult daughters and mothers in the absence of maternal frailty and ill-health (Barnett, Kibria, Baruch & Pleck, 1991). Consideration of adult males in their roles and relationships as sons is even more limited (Barnett, Marshall & Pleck, 1992).

This chapter presents an overview of the literature from the past two decades that deals with adult child–parent relationships, in the absence of

Families as Relationships.
Edited by Robert M. Milardo and Steve Duck. © 2000 John Wiley & Sons Ltd.

caregiving. It begins with an overview and critique of a few of the recent, popular frameworks for conceptualizing young adult child–parent relationships. Next, the chapter considers some of the processes involved in the transformation of parent–child relationships between adolescence and later adulthood. Current, popular views on mid- to later-life parent–child relationships are described next, followed by a final section identifying key challenges for researchers working in this area today.

THE YOUNG ADULT YEARS

Whereas in later adulthood, researchers study parent–child relationships primarily for their inherent interest in interpersonal relationships and family life (Fischer, 1986; Hagestad, 1984; Rossi & Rossi, 1990), in late adolescence and early adulthood parent–child bonds are viewed almost exclusively in terms of their implications for individual development—and then for the younger generation only. With this in mind, two dramatically different views of parent–child relationships as they pertain to individual development during late adolescence and early adulthood are presented below.

Detachment from Parents: Separation–Individuation Theories

The central task of adolescence, according to the "new" developmental psychology (Josselson, 1988), is the formation of a unique identity distinct from that of one's parents. Separation and individuation from parents are viewed as key prerequisites to identity formation. Supposedly, physical and emotional detachment from their parents contributes to adolescents' ability to clearly differentiate between self and other. To theorists who support such notions "separation of the self out of the more or less enmeshed child–parent web is what adolescence is all about" (Josselson, 1988, p. 94).

Measuring Adolescent Separation–Individuation

One widely used empirical formulation based on this separation–individuation theory of parent–child relations is Hoffman's (1984; Hoffman & Weiss, 1987) Psychological Separation Inventory (PSI). This inventory assesses the degree to which late adolescents have separated and individuated from their parents in four domains originally laid out by Blos (1979) as central to the adolescent separation–individuation process. Specifically, emotional independence emphasizes "freedom from an excessive need for approval, closeness, togetherness and emotional support" (Hoffman, 1984, p. 171) from parents. Attitudinal independence addresses value and attitudinal differences between oneself and one's parents. Conflictual independence denotes the absence of negative feelings toward parents, such as mistrust, inhibition, and anger. Finally, functional independence refers to managing the practical matters of one's day-to-day personal life without parental involvement (Hoffman, 1984).

In developing the PSI, Hoffman recommended that the measure be applied separately to mother–child and father–child relationships. In so doing, Hoffman recognized the uniqueness of adolescents' relationships with mothers versus fathers, and, as a consequence, the distinctiveness of the separation process in relation to each parent. Lopez, Campbell, and Watkins (1986, 1989) demonstrate the reality of this distinction for adolescents by reporting greater independence from fathers than mothers for adolescents with divorced as well as married parents.

Sex Differences in Adolescent Separation–Individuation

Not only is the sex of the parent potentially important in examining levels of adolescent separation, but so too is the sex of the younger generation. Studies comparing average PSI scores for males and females note lower levels of separation from parents for daughters than sons, at least on some of the four dimensions (Lapsley, Rice & Shadid, 1989; Lopez, Campbell & Watkins, 1986). Subscale scores on various PSI dimensions also correlate negatively with young women's college adjustment (Kenny & Donaldson, 1992; Lopez, Campbell & Watkins, 1986). This finding is critical given that, theoretically, greater separation–individuation is equated with healthy development and positive functioning among youth, and perhaps healthy marriages and adult relationships as well (Milardo & Allan, 1997).

While findings inconsistent with the theory are more often found for females than males, Hoffman (1984) reports significant negative associations between attitudinal independence and personal adjustment for both sexes, as do Lapsley et al. (1989). Hoffman (1984) provides *post hoc* speculation that attitudinal similarity may reflect internalization of the parental objects by the youth, which could be positive for the adolescent if it promotes higher-quality parent–child relations and subsequently better personal adjustment. This reasoning is noteworthy because it conflicts with most of the separation–individuation literature that largely dismisses parental input in the adolescent's individuation experience.

Limitations of Separation–Individuation Theories

Despite their popularity, separation–individuation theories present several problems. One criticism is that the separation–individuation process is discussed in an extremely individualistic fashion although it actually involves modifications in a relational bond. To illustrate, Hoffman's PSI appears to have no parallel "parent measure" of adolescent–parent separation. Without parental reports of the process, it is difficult to understand the relational interplay involved in this process. Moreover, separation–individuation is viewed as a personal characteristic of the adolescent, rather than as a property of a given relationship, even though Hoffman requires that relations with each parent be assessed separately. Finally, in largely overlooking the parents' contribution to separation–individuation, this perspective fails to address what role behaviors are expected of parents during the process. The relationship of the parents' own development to this process is also totally ignored. Indeed, Youniss (1983) notes that in the conventional view of adolescent development, the process is totally self-instigated and self-guided on the part of the adolescent.

When the interplay of the adolescent's and the parents' development has been recognized, the discussion has been based on anecdotal impressions or small case-study approaches (Colarusso & Nemiroff, 1982; Farrell & Rosenberg, 1981; Kidwell, Fischer, Dunham, & Baranowski, 1983). Kidwell et al. (1983) claim, for example, that the parents' development contributes to changes in relations with their developing adolescents, without explicitly examining the impact of parental development on the relationship or vice versa. Colarusso and Nemiroff (1982) more specifically argue that parental (in this case paternal) support and encouragement of adolescent independence may be instrumental in the parents' own successful resolution of the generativity-stagnation task (Erikson, 1968) in mid- to late-adulthood. Still, they too present no data to support their claim.

One published study that links parent and adolescent development is a cross-sectional investigation of early adolescents and their parents by Silverberg and Steinberg (1987). They report significant correlations between various measures of parents' development and well-being at mid-life and their offsprings' levels of independence, as well as parent–adolescent conflict. Greater emotional autonomy among adolescent boys is associated with both heightened levels of mid-life concerns among fathers as well as reduced life satisfaction. For mothers, reduced life satisfaction is linked to greater conflict with adolescents of both sexes. These authors primarily cast their findings in terms of psychoanalytic theory, claiming that individuals' mid-life reappraisal, self-questioning and doubt (elements of what Silverberg and Steinberg refer to as mid-life concerns), may be triggered by the increasing independence and identity formation of adolescent offspring (which includes de-idealization of parents, questioning of parental choices and views, etc.). This is just one example of how the literature is largely biased toward the view that the adolescent is the driving force behind parent–child relationship changes during the child's adolescence.

Finally, severe criticism of this perspective deals with its perceived lack of applicability and validity for female development (Gilligan, 1982; Josselson, 1988). As noted, several studies have reported sex differences in measures of separation–individuation from parents. In response, critics have charged that to merely interpret these sex differences as illustrative of females' more problematic or stalled development is invalid because male and female development may not necessarily proceed along the same track. Indeed, as Josselson (1988) notes, several perspectives suggest that unlike the male developmental trajectory that is characterized by increasing levels of autonomy and self attainment, "female development proceeds on an interpersonal track" (p. 99) and is embedded "in the context of ongoing connection" (p. 95). Therefore, adolescence, at least for females, requires balancing of an enhanced need for autonomy and self-expression and continued need for relationship.

In sum, conventional approaches to adolescent development, such as Hoffman's (1984), assume "that the adolescent develops as an individual precisely by moving outside the relation with parents" (Youniss, 1983, p. 95). Speaking of the fate of the parent–child relationship during this period, Josselson (1988) contends that to developmentalists like Blos (1967, 1979) Mahler (1968) and Anna Freud (1969), "Once it has served its presumed developmental function, the relationship that was separated from has no further interest" (p. 94). Gaining attention and popularity, however, is a school of thought grounded largely in feminist revisions of development. In this view, adolescent individuation occurs within an ongoing relationship with parents, where parent–child relations, for both sexes and generations, are merely transformed during the transition to adulthood and thereafter, rather than being totally eliminated. Conceptualizations of this type are considered next.

Bringing Parents Back In: New Views on Parent–Adolescent Relations

Recent conceptualizations of parent–child relations in late adolescence and early adulthood emphasize an ongoing connection between the generations. Although this position holds that the parent–child relationship remains intact during this period, it is not viewed as static. Supposedly, as offspring confront their increasing need for individuality, they revise their connections to their parents. Through the rebalancing of individuality and connectedness, truly individuated relations are achieved (Cooper, Grotevant & Condon, 1983).

Adolescent individuation, according to Cooper et al. (1983), is not an absolute psychological characteristic achieved by an individual (as Hoffman and others seem to assume), but instead applies to specific relational contexts. For example, the level of individuation an adolescent has achieved may vary in regard to each parent. For this reason, I refer to these theories as contextual theories whereas those reviewed in the former section will be called theories of absolute separation–individuation.

The process of individuation within a context of connection entails four distinct sets of behaviors (Grotevant & Cooper, 1982). Two of these—the adolescent's ability to recognize differences between self and other (labeled separateness), and the ability to assert one's own point of view, comprise the individuation component. The connection aspect of the process involves permeability—the ability to be open and responsive to another's point of view, and mutuality, which is demonstrating respect for alternative viewpoints (Cooper, Grotevant & Condon, 1983). The individuation part of the process largely involves the relinquishment of over-identification with parental beliefs and recognition of one's own uniqueness, whereas the connection aspect involves the maintenance of relationships despite recognized differences.

A unique aspect of these contextual perspectives, in contrast to views of absolute individuation–separation, is that connection to parents is considered beneficial, if not necessary, to the individuation process. Bell and Bell (1983) contend that the maintenance of parental bonds is necessary for adolescents to obtain validation of their new, unique selves in the process of individuation. Family bonds also provide adolescents a secure base from which to explore the world and the divergent views it holds en route to achieving an individuated identity (Cooper et al., 1983).

Assessing Relationship Transformations of Parents and Offspring

The transformation of parent–child relations during late adolescence is discussed in terms of achieving more peer-like ties based on interdependence and interrelatedness instead of dependence, submission, and rebellion (Josselson, 1988). K. M. White, Speisman and Costos (1983) provide a framework for viewing this relationship transformation, using adolescent individuation as an initial stage in a series of six stages involving relational changes for both generations. Theoretically, the end goal of this process is a symmetrical relationship based on mutuality and a broadened sense of perspective-taking between the generations. Yet, White et al. (1983) report that most offspring in their twenties do not achieve the final stage characterized by "full peer-like mutuality" in relation to their parents—in this case their mothers.

Still, their framework is appealing because it considers individuation in the context of relationships and it specifies changes that both generations must make in this process. Both generations, for example, are expected to increasingly recognize the other as individuated persons apart from their respective family roles. Although not articulated by White, Spiesman and Costos (1983), it is likely that the individuation process of adolescence also entails some redefining of self by the parents. Colarusso and Nemiroff (1982) mention identity changes fathers must make, for example, as their offspring move through adolescence—shifting from role of protector and caretaker to one of interested facilitator of their children's development.

In recognizing the interactive, reciprocal nature of parent–child relationships, the contextual theories (in contrast to the absolute separation–individuation theories) present the possibility that individuation from parents may be initiated and directed by alterations in the behavior and thinking of both generations. Parents may consciously or inadvertently control the pace of the individuation process, perhaps in response to their own developmental needs. Additionally, family structure and situations may influence how parents approach their adolescents' individuation. Greene and Boxer (1986) speculate that the developmental stake posed by Bengtson and Kuypers (1971) may have different meaning, for example, as a result of family size and birth order. The developmental press may be less urgent for parents in larger families or in reference to the youngest child, therefore the psychological need to maximize closeness to and similarity with a particular child—and perhaps to stall or interfere with individuation may be attenuated (Greene &

Boxer, 1986). Similarly, Silverberg (1996) reflects on earlier findings (Silver-berg & Steinberg, 1987) that linked adolescents' involvement with mixed-sex peers and dating with heightened mid-life concerns, reduced self-esteem, and lower life satisfaction for parents, except those who had relatively high work-role investments. In interpreting these findings, Silverberg acknowledges that the association may indicate that parents with a strong work orientation were better able to psychologically protect themselves from feelings of loss as their adolescents matured and moved beyond the family (Steinberg & Steinberg, 1994), or, that the parents' situations actually influenced the adolescents' development.

> . . . early adolescent maturation may be influenced by parental well-being—rather than the reverse—and that this effect may depend on level of parental work-role orientation. It is conceivable, for example, that when mothers or fathers are less psychologically involved in work and are low in well-being (a combination that is perhaps a sign of general discontent), early adolescents begin to look elsewhere for close, intimate relationships and become more involved in heterosexual activities. (Silverberg, 1996, p. 232–233).

Regardless of the scenario one draws, the key point is that contextual theories of parent–young adult relations recognize the possibility of parental influence on parent–child relationship transformations in adolescence and early adult-hood, although the data at hand may not address it.

Sex Differences in Applying the Contextual Perspective

Employing their six-stage model, White, Spiesman, and Costos (1983) find greater progression through the stages of parent–child relationship transfor-mation for females than males. This finding may demonstrate valid sex dif-ferences in relational maturation in young adulthood or it could be an artifact of the research method. Males might have shown greater progression in this process than females if relations with fathers rather than mothers had been considered, as others (Youniss & Ketterlinus, 1987) report greater differentia-tion favoring relations with mothers over fathers by daughters than sons. Also, because White's model emphasizes relatedness in the form of verbal sharing and expressivity, females may actually be favored in scoring over males, given that feminine socialization is verbally oriented with an emphasis on talk about relational issues and feelings (Wood, 1993). Thus, whereas absolute separation–individuation frameworks may have an underlying male bias, these contextual perspectives may be biased in favor of female socialization.

Strengths and Limitations of Contextual Perspectives

Frameworks like that posed by White, Speisman, and Costos (1983) are ap-pealing because they conceptualize the process of adolescent individuation within a dynamic, bidirectional parent–child relationship. They also appear more grounded in reality than do absolute separation-individuation theories; that is, rather than disregarding the actual way in which parents and children are known to live and interact in adolescence and adulthood (Youniss, 1983), the contextual theories support the empirical findings showing interdependence between parents and offspring across adulthood (Cooney & Uhlenberg, 1992; Eggebeen & Hogan, 1990; Spitze & Logan, 1992).

Although these frameworks demonstrate strong theoretical promise, their empirical application to date remains limited. One problem is that the literature is based almost entirely on the perspective of the younger generation. If models such as this are to be relational in nature and sensitive to dyadic issues, more research is needed where multiple perspectives are gathered and analyzed. Such work will enhance our theoretical understanding of the relational changes each generation experiences during these middle years.

In summary, at least two schools of thought exist regarding parent–child relations in young adulthood. Absolute separation–individuation theories emphasize detachment and emancipation from parental influence and connections, whereas contextual theories recognize the ongoing relationships between parents and children and concentrate on the transformation of these bonds during the offspring's late adolescent and young adult years. The next section briefly describes how such relationship transformations are initiated and proceed in the middle years of family life.

PROCESSES OF RELATIONSHIP TRANSFORMATION IN ADULTHOOD

As offspring become more psychologically mature and complete the social transitions associated with adulthood in our culture (e.g. leaving home, completing school, getting married—see Hogan & Astone, 1986), they expect new rights within the family, particularly in relation to their parents. As argued, perhaps the most accurate description of what happens to parent–child ties at this point is movement of the child away from dependence on the parent to a situation of interdependence between the generations—an outcome quite different from the isolated independence posed in Hoffman's (1984) model. Viewed within a context of transformation, the parent–child relationship in early to mid-adulthood involves the "renegotiation of the interdependencies that bond and bind" (Greene & Boxer, 1986, p. 138) the two generations.

Central to this renegotiation process is the establishment of clear boundaries—recognized distinctions—between maturing children and their parents. The most obvious boundaries are physical, where adult children establish a residence apart from their parents. But other boundaries, such as psychological (e.g. value differences between parent and child) and behavioral ones (e.g. grandparents avoiding interference in the rearing of the grandchildren) are equally important to negotiate. Specific strategies for re-establishing boundaries between parents and children are discussed below.

Developing Privacy Rights

The development of privacy rights is central to the individuation process of adult offspring and involves behavioral changes by both parent and child (Petronio, 1994). Some of the issues that demand renegotiation in adulthood are the ownership of space, belongings, and information. According to Petronio (1994), by regulating privacy, offspring and parents can more effectively coordinate separateness while maintaining closeness in their relationship—a view that is consistent with the contextual theories discussed earlier. Clearly, the issue of privacy is a salient one during young adulthood. A lack of privacy is one problem young adults anticipate when they consider residing with their parents (Shehan & Dwyer, 1989).

Most of the literature on privacy issues and boundary conflicts in the family during late adolescence and early adulthood (see Petronio, 1994) considers how parents deny maturing children adequate privacy by interfering in their lives (e.g. asking too many questions, demanding to know more than the child wants to share). What is considered less often, except perhaps by clinicians, are situations where parents threaten boundaries by offering too much about their own personal lives to the child, or expecting their adult children's input on issues that may create stress for them.

Triangulation, as referred to by clinicians, is when parents overextend their relationships with their children, expecting more peer-like interaction with them (e.g. getting advise and emotional support), at the cost of failing to meet the children's needs (see Fullinwider-Bush & Jacobvitz, 1993). Generally, triangulation involves daughters who are promoted to the level of a parental peer by their mothers—often their divorced mothers (Silverberg, Jacobs & Raymond, 1998). Such cases also may involve high levels of inter-parental conflict (Fullinwider-Bush & Jacobvitz, 1993), which may partially explain why one of the parents turns to the children for support, comfort and advice rather than to the more appropriate choice—the marital partner. The discussion of triangulation is relevant here because it suggests that while the development of mutual relationships between parents and adult offspring is important (White et al., 1983), there are still boundary distinctions between the generations that need to be recognized for healthy individual development and interpersonal relationships (Silverberg et al., 1998). These boundaries pertain to issues that are of a personal nature to parents as well as their adult offspring.

Intrafamilial Strategies for Establishing Boundaries

Many of the strategies used to establish intergenerational boundaries revolve around the issue of how maturing offspring and their parents manage divergent viewpoints and lifestyles in relating to one another. One approach, represented by Hagestad's (1979) concept of demilitarized zones (DMZs), is that of avoidance, in which potentially conflictual topical areas are mutually and knowingly omitted from family discussions.

Boundary recognition is another less conflict-oriented strategy used to facilitate relationship maintenance between adult children and parents (Greene & Boxer, 1986). With boundary recognition, parents and children may disagree and differ in such things as behaviors, attitudes, and values, yet these differences are openly accepted as a valid part of each person. Greene and Boxer (1986) theorize that as children mature, an increasing number of issues in their lives become protected from parental input and criticism as a result of this process. Their proposition is consistent with speculation raised by Shehan and Dwyer (1989) that children's autonomy from parents may be reflected in the number and/or proportion of personal decision areas that are not open to negotiation with parents.

Extrafamilial Influences on Boundary Establishment

The status and roles adult offspring possess outside the family are major determinants of the extent to which boundaries are recognized in the adult child–parent relationship. Boundary facilitators are status and role changes beyond the family of origin that promote increased recognition of intergenerational boundaries (Greene & Boxer, 1986) and which may result in greater mutual respect, understanding, and other positive interpersonal factors. Young women's marriage, for example, is associated with improved relations with their mothers (Frank, Avery & Laman, 1988; Kaufman & Uhlenberg, 1998) and fathers (Kaufman & Uhlenberg, 1998), as is parenthood (Fischer, 1981). Yet, some studies fail to find effects of children's marital and/or parental status on relations with parents (Barnett et al., 1991; Baruch & Barnett, 1983), and some even report negative outcomes as a result of these status transitions (Baruch & Barnett, 1983; Frank et al., 1988).

Research on fathers and children also links the assumption of adult roles by sons with enhanced father–son understanding and empathy, whereas fathers' increased understanding with daughters appears more closely linked to daughters' assuming nontraditional roles, particularly in the work sphere (Nydegger & Mitteness, 1991). Nydegger (1991) claims that the adoption of roles similar to those of one's parents fosters the development of "filial comprehending" by offspring, where they begin to view their parents as individuals rather than just parents. She proposes that this ability is one of two essential requirements of filial maturity—the other being filial distancing. This latter concept refers to the emotional distancing from parents that is necessary for maturing children to gain greater objectivity about themselves and their parents.

Attending to the dyadic nature of relationship transformations, Nydegger (1991) argues that a parallel process of parental maturity also occurs. This entails the need for parents to facilitate their children's development by encouraging their distancing efforts; moreover, by distancing themselves from their children, parents begin to reshape a self-definition based on something other than parenting, which is critical as the centrality of this part of their lives wanes. In addition, parents must comprehend how their children are developing within their own distinct social worlds if they wish to maintain close, positive relations with them and facilitate their development.

Intergenerational boundaries also are altered in response to the loss of extrafamilial social status or roles, as these transitions typically contribute to the weakening of parent–child boundaries (Greene & Boxer, 1986). When roles typically linked to adulthood are lost, the rights adult children have in relation to their parents seem threatened. For example, in a study of parents with coresident adult offspring, Aquilino and Supple (1991) note greater relationship negativity and parental dissatisfaction with the situation when the offspring are unemployed, divorced or financially dependent. Kaufman and Uhlenberg's (1998) findings are even more illustrative of the power of status loss on parent–child relationships, as they show with longitudinal data that daughters' transitions from being married to divorced are associated with reductions in the quality of parent–child relations over the same period. Finally, the process of boundary disruption is illustrated in Hetherington's (1989) work as well. She finds that divorced women who reside with their parents feel "infantilized" by them, as evidenced by conflicts with their parents regarding their independence and social lives, and parenting of their own children (the grandchildren).

In sum, role and status markers outside the family drive role renegotiations inside the family (Greene & Boxer, 1986). Who has greater leverage in establishing relationship boundaries—the adult child or the parents, is determined largely by whether adult social roles are gained or lost by the offspring. These processes are key determinants of the nature of parent–child relationships that evolve in mid- to late-adulthood. Current conceptualizations of these relationships are considered next.

PARENT–CHILD RELATIONS IN THE MIDDLE YEARS

While much of the literature on parent–child relationships during mid- to later-life takes a problem-oriented rather than theoretical approach to the issues under study (Hagestad, 1982; Lye, 1996), a substantial body of work (Bengtson, Olander & Haddad, 1976; Bengtson & Roberts, 1991; Glass, Bengtson & Dunham, 1986; Roberts & Bengtson, 1990; Rossi & Rossi, 1990; Silverstein & Bengtson, 1997) is grounded in the theoretical perspective known as family solidarity. Bengtson's notion of family solidarity is derived from Durkheim's (1893) conceptualization of mechanical solidarity at the societal level, which depicts individuals as similar and undifferentiated as a result of shared norms and values. As a result of such similarity, persons can supposedly occupy a number of positions and serve a wide variety of functions within a social system. Moreover, shared experiences and perspectives bond persons together.

Measurement of Family Solidarity

Just as Durkheim emphasized that societal cohesiveness is partly a result of similarity in norms, values and experiences, Bengtson et al. (1976) originally viewed family unity or cohesiveness—what they called *solidarity*—as primarily based on congruence in sentiment and attitudes, and association among family members. While the proposed number of dimensions that contribute to family solidarity has varied over time with the development of the concept, the latest conceptualization includes six constructs: intergenerational family structure, and associational, affectional, consensual, functional and normative solidarity (Bengtson & Schrader, 1982). Structure refers to the size, type and geographic distribution of the family. Associational, affectional and consensual solidarity refer to the degree to which family members interact, feel positively toward one another and agree on values and issues, respectively. Functional solidarity is the extent to which services and aid are exchanged between the generations, and normative solidarity pertains to expressed levels of familial obligation (Bengtson & Schrader, 1982). It is assumed that high levels of familial obligation, mutual assistance, association, consensus, and positive regard are desirable, as they, along with heightened opportunities for interaction (an aspect of family structure), contribute to a higher-order construct of family solidarity.

How these observable dimensions contribute to a more abstract concept of family solidarity is still under study. Results from recent empirical tests of propositions dealing with family solidarity suggest that a simple linear addition of the various dimensions is not valid. Silverstein and Bengtson (1997) submitted indicators of five of the six (omitting normative obligations) types of solidarity to factor analysis to determine if these aspects of solidarity could be simplified into fewer core, underlying dimensions of intergenerational relations. What resulted were three clusters of relationship elements, which they labeled affinity (emotional closeness and attitudinal consensus), opportunity structure (geographic proximity and contact), and functional exchange (receiving and giving assistance). Furthermore, their analysis of data for non-resident adult offspring and parents found evidence of five "types" of parent–child relationships (i.e. tight-knit, sociable, obligatory, intimate but distant, and detached) based on varying levels of these three relationship clusters. They go on to show that the distribution of father–child and mother–child relationships across these types clearly differs, as do the individual characteristics of parent and adult child that predict classification into a given type of relationship. Their analysis is noteworthy for its efforts to move beyond single-variable relationship outcomes to more complex and complete classifications of intergenerational relationships.

Criticism of the Solidarity Framework

Criticism of the solidarity perspective stands in interesting juxtaposition to that of the absolute separation–individuation perspective of young adulthood.

As noted, models like Hoffman's (1984) have been faulted for their narrow emphasis on separation and independence from parents, despite overwhelming empirical evidence of intergenerational interdependence in adulthood. In sharp contrast is Bengtson's view that interdependence and similarity between parent and child are what are valued in adulthood; virtually no mention is made of a need to maintain any independence within relationships after young adulthood or whether too much attitudinal similarity or association, for example, may be maladaptive. This contrast in perspectives is evident in Table 3.1, where sample items used to assess four of the relational dimensions in Bengtson's model are shown along with sample items from the four dimensions of Hoffman's independence model. A key point to reiterate is that in the solidarity model it is high solidarity that is viewed positively, whereas in Hoffman's independence framework low levels of similarity and connection are valued.

Table 3.1   Sample items used to assess parent–child relations in Bengtson's measure of family solidarity and Hoffman's psychological separation inventory

Bengtson's dimension	Sample items	Hoffman's dimensions	Sample items
Functional solidarity	In the past month, how often have you turned to your mother/father for advice on child rearing?	Functional independence	I ask for my mother's/ father's advice when I am planning my vacation time
Affectual solidarity	How is communication between yourself and your mother/father— how well can you exchange ideas and talk about things that really concern you?	Emotional independence	I sometimes call home just to hear my mother's/father's voice
Consensual/ attitudinal solidarity	In the past year, how often have you and your mother/father argued about politics and political candidates?	Attitudinal independence	My beliefs regarding national defense are similar to my mother's/ father's
Associational solidarity	How often do you do things together with this parent?	Conflictual independence	When I don't write my mother/father often enough I feel guilty

The lack of attention to boundary maintenance and some degree of separateness in the solidarity literature is particularly interesting given the extensive discussion in the adolescent/young adulthood literature on the renegotiation of boundaries between adult children and parents. Indeed, Atkinson (1989) criticizes Bengtson's conceptualization for over-reliance on mechanical solidarity and neglect of what Durkheim (1893) labeled organic solidarity. This latter form of solidarity results from differentiation between persons and the division of labor within a social system, with individuals becoming interdependent with others in order to manage all of the functions of daily life. In sum, mechanical solidarity poses similarity as the driving force behind the formation and maintenance of social bonds, whereas organic solidarity emphasizes differentiation between persons as the factor that draws them together based on a need to rely on one another.

Empirical findings indicate the value of both similarity and difference in the bonding of parents and adult children. In support of the similarity view, studies indicate that when parents and children occupy similar social and family positions (e.g., spouse, parent, worker) they report stronger family ties (Fischer, 1981; Frank et al., 1988) and attitude similarity (Glass et al., 1986). Yet, evidence conflicting with the similarity emphasis is presented by Bengtson himself, as his work with Roberts (Roberts and Bengtson, 1990) fails to find a link between attitude similarity and emotional closeness. In addition, studies like that of Aquilino and Supple (1991) reveal that excessive dependence and contact may contribute to strained intergenerational relationships. Thus, mixed evidence suggests that both similarity and difference are important to parent–adult child relationships, supporting Atkinson's (1989) view that organic solidarity deserves more attention in theorizing and research on intergenerational relationships in adulthood.

The concept of family solidarity also is criticized for downplaying the value of conflict and negotiation (Luescher & Pillemer, 1998; Marshall, Matthews & Rosenthal, 1993) and considering only positive affect between adult children and parents. This practice, which is evident in the literature on middle-aged children and their parents more generally (Mancini & Blieszner, 1989), fails to address the multidimensional nature of familial affect, thereby overlooking the possibility that positive and negative affect and behavior may independently exist within a given relationship, each having its own set of predictors and outcomes. In addition, the potentially beneficial aspects of conflict, such as promoting positive family change (Petronio, 1994) are ignored. Finally, the lack of attention to conflict, or viewing it as merely the polar opposite of positive affect on a unidimensional scale, raises serious methodological consequences (Bengtson & Mangen, 1988; Landry & Martin, 1988).

In response to these issues, Luescher and Pillemer (1998) propose the notion of intergenerational ambivalence. This concept captures the relational dynamic in parent–child relationships where negative and positive evaluations of the relationship co-exist simultaneously, or structural conditions surrounding parent or child roles create contradictions. According to Luescher and Pillemer, intergenerational ambivalence is likely to be exacerbated when either dyad member is experiencing a status transition because such changes usually result in both losses and gains for individuals. This idea is sure to stimulate new approaches to the measurement of intergenerational relationships that are more sensitive to the multidimensional, dynamic nature of close family relationships.

In summary, a review of the recent literature on parent–child relations in adulthood reveals a need for a unified lifespan perspective for conceptualizing this relationship. While the domains of relevance to the relationship appear consistent across early and later adulthood (e.g. functional and affective issues), how researchers conceptualize relationship dynamics during these two life phases is dramatically different. It is possible that a need for distinctiveness and relative independence is a valid characterization of the relationship early in adulthood, whereas similarity and dependence predominate later in life. Indeed, Newman and Newman (1975) claim that strong individuation is necessary and may actually alienate adolescents from their parents, temporarily. Yet, after establishing a necessary level of individuation and autonomy young people are ready to rebuild connections with their families. The fact that adult offspring report an increase in the likelihood of receiving advice from their parents between their early and late twenties is one piece of empirical support for this notion (Cooney & Uhlenberg, 1992). It may be that establishing independence—in this case functional independence (Hoffman, 1984)—is particularly critical early in adulthood, but once individuation is achieved, offspring are more receptive to parental input in a context of mutuality and reciprocity. If this is the case, much more interdisciplinary, psychosocial research is needed to explain how this dramatic shift in emphasis comes about and the role of each generation in the process. This problem clearly requires some added thought from researchers who assume a lifespan orientation as do a few other theoretical and methodological issues discussed next.

ADULT CHILD–PARENT RELATIONSHIPS WITHIN A WIDER FAMILY SYSTEM

The study of parent–child relationships in adulthood is based almost exclusively on the perspective of only one member of the dyad. The problems inherent in this approach are somewhat avoided in the few well-known multi-generational studies (Bengtson and Mangen, 1988; Hagestad, 1984; Rossi & Rossi, 1990). Still, these and most studies generally fail to address how the adult child–parent relationship operates within the various relational sub-systems of the larger family unit (Sprey, 1991). Little is known about how relations between adult children and parents are influenced by the involvement of each party in other relational sub-systems of the family, such as sibling, marital, and other parent–child relationships.

When family scholars have examined the impact of other family subsystems on parent–child relations they have concentrated on the parents' marital relationship. Belsky's model (Belsky, 1984) of the determinants of parenting is a popular example of this; he considers how the parents' marital relationship (along with such factors as work and personality) may influence children's development via its impact on parenting practices. Until very recently, research on adult child–parent relationships was primarily limited to examining how the parents' marital status (typically widowed versus married) affected intergenerational relationships (Bulcroft & Bulcroft, 1991; Cooney, 1989;

Cooney & Uhlenberg, 1992; Eggebeen, 1992). Only in the past few years have researchers linked parental marital interaction with adult child–parent relationships.

Recent studies fairly consistently document a significant connection between parental marital problems and reduced parent–child closeness, particularly with fathers (Cooney, 1994; Rossi & Rossi, 1990; Webster & Herzog, 1995). Webster and Herzog (1995) examined adults' ratings of their relations with parents along both positive and negative dimensions and found that childhood family structure and marital problems were correlated with the positive but not the negative relationship dimensions. Parental divorce and marital conflict predicted lower scores on measures of feeling loved and listened to by one's father. Thus, past interparental conflict did not result in a negative, acrimonious bond with one's aging father, but instead led to somewhat empty, distant relations.

Cooney (1994) considered the interplay of relational subsystems in the family by analyzing the correlation between father–child and mother–child relationship quality for young adult offspring. Interestingly, in intact two-parent families, relationships with mothers versus fathers were highly correlated for young adults of both sexes. Yet, relationships with fathers and mothers were not correlated in families where parents had divorced within the past three years. Cooney concludes that "parent–child relations in intact families appear to operate as a system of relationships—highly interdependent on one another—while those in divorced families exist virtually apart from each other" (p. 52).

Others have considered the interaction of family subsystems as they relate to individual outcomes. Hoffman and Weiss (1987) examined how the connection between interparental problems and daughter–mother relations affected the personal adjustment of college-aged females. Their rather complex findings showed that daughters who reported greater hostility and conflict with their mothers appeared to be less affected by their parents' marital problems than did young women reporting lower levels of conflict in relation to their mothers. Perhaps daughters in close, nonconflictual relationships with their mothers responded more empathically to parental marital problems because of the confiding their mothers were likely to be doing with them (Cooney, Smyer, Hagestad, & Klock, 1986). But, when marital problems existed in a context of poor mother–child relations, daughters may have distanced themselves from those problems. Additionally, the negative impact of parental marital problems may be more evident in offspring who are not also reacting to conflict in the parent–child relationship.

How the marriages of adult children affect their relationships with parents has been studied much less than the influence of the parents' marriage on these relationships. While we know that the marital status of adult children affects ties to aging parents (Baruch & Barnett, 1983; Fischer, 1981; Frank et al., 1988), and that adult children in poorer-quality marriages report less positive relationships with their own parents (Kaufman & Uhlenberg, 1998), the relational mechanisms operating in these associations are unknown.

The interplay of the sibling and parent–child subsystems also requires further attention. In one of the few studies in the adult child–parent literature to consider sibling configurations, Barnett et al. (1992) speculate that men's emotional connection to their parents may be enhanced when they have sisters. It is the consideration of these types of systemic interactions within the family that Sprey (1991) argues is necessary for a deeper understanding of multigenerational family life.

METHODOLOGICAL CONCERNS

A number of methodological limitations exist in the literature on adult parent–child relations, some of which have been discussed above. Very briefly, this section will identify issues of concern in the areas of sampling, units of observation and analyses, and data gathering and measurement.

Transformations in parent–child relations across adulthood and the intergenerational ties that exist during this period are certainly likely to vary for persons of different racial and economic groups given subcultural variations in familial norms, family needs and resources. Indeed, several investigations reveal differences in patterns of intergenerational exchange based on race, ethnicity and social class (Cooney & Uhlenberg, 1992; Eggebeen & Hogan, 1990; Spitze & Logan, 1992). Yet, studies consist primarily of white, middle class samples. This is especially the case in research on young adulthood, where data are drawn heavily from college students (Boxer, Cook & Cohler, 1986; Frank et al., 1988; Hoffman, 1984). The process of young adults' identity achievement and expected changes in relation to parents and family, as posed by the new developmentalists, also may differ significantly for ethnic and racial groups, such as Mexican–Americans (Williams, 1990), who adhere to strong norms of familism. Similarly, how parents figure into the process of identity achievement in young adulthood and how family roles are renegotiated during this period may differ in populations where the role of biological parents is less central in the lives of children, and the "parenting" role of extended kin and pseudo-kin is intensified due to the absence of the father, and/or to problems with the parents, or their young age (Burton, 1992, 1996).

The wide-spread use of college student samples to study relations between young adults and their parents also may compromise the validity of findings on relationship transformations during early adulthood. The college experience may constitute a unique experience for youth (Murphey, Silber, Coelho, Hamburg & Greenberg, 1963), affecting how young people view themselves (Karp, Holmstrom, & Gray, 1998) and their families. Moreover, youth who choose to go away to college may already differ from those who continue to reside with their parents in terms of their progress on tasks of identity development and in relationships with their parents. Possible selection effects of this type also exist in some of the multigenerational studies, such of that of Rossi and Rossi (1990), where sampling was restricted to parents and adult children who resided in the same geographic region. Living in close geographic proximity to one's parents or children may be a result of some unique relationship property, as well as a predictor of other relationship dimensions.

The literature on parent–child relations between adults also is limited by its nearly exclusive focus on individuals as the unit of observation and analyses. Some of the conceptual problems with this emphasis were already discussed. Another issue in studies that include multiple generations in the family is that divergent perspectives may be given by different family members. To illustrate, Boxer, Cook and Cohler (1986) found little intergenerational agreement between grandfathers, fathers and sons concerning the topics that created conflict between them, how conflict was handled, and whether it was ever resolved. These findings raise the critical question of whether there are indeed "family experiences" or properties to be studied and understood. These findings also present difficult analytic choices about how to handle divergent perspectives from family members.

In sum, work on parent–child relations in adulthood calls for greater attention to sampling and measurement issues to advance our understanding of the true relational aspects of this bond as it exists in a wider family system and as part of a broader cultural context. Another critical issue that has methodological implications is the search for sex-specific effects in parent–child relations.

UNDERSTANDING GENDER IN ADULT CHILD–PARENT RELATIONS

Whether one assumes an individualistic or more relational approach to gathering data on adult children and their parents, it is increasingly evident that research questions and methods must be framed in terms of both the gender of the parent and the adult child. Indeed, in nearly all of the literature cited herein, it was necessary to specify which parent–child relationships revealed particular effects, as findings that apply equally to mother–daughter, mother–son, father–daughter and father–son relations are rare. Thus, to speak sweepingly of parent–child relations in adulthood oversimplifies family bonds that are heavily gendered as a result of biology and the fact that "gender is a central organizing principle for social life" (Wood, 1993, p.31).

Gender-sensitive research requires more than merely asking the same standardized questions in reference to the four possible dyads of parent and child. Such an approach can error in at least two ways. First, certain topics or questions about the parent–child relationship may possess a gender bias. Using items that only tap interpersonal sharing and expression of emotion to measure parent–child closeness and intimacy, for example, may force men's family experiences into what is actually a female model of interpersonal relationships (Boxer et al., 1986; Wood, 1993). A typical result is that family relationships involving men end up looking deficient (Boxer et al., 1986).

A second problem with applying the same questions across all four parent–child dyads is that specific dyads may fail to display quantitative differences on a particular question or item, yet the underlying relationship may actually be qualitatively different across dyads. Nydegger and Mitteness (1991) asked fathers about the degree of difficulty they experienced in raising their adult offspring. Although fathers reported no differences in level of difficulty based on the child's sex, raising sons and daughters posed qualitatively different struggles for them. Fathers noted difficulty handling their sons' attempts at independence, whereas they found their daughters' emotional reactions to situations to be especially challenging (Nydegger & Mitteness, 1991).

It is unlikely that such sharp qualitative differences would have emerged from highly structured survey questions where no interviewer probing occurs. Thus, to better understand how male bonds are displayed in families (where female models of relationships have dominated) may require, at least initially, greater dependence on qualitative methods where the research subjects are granted more freedom to report on their social reality (L. Thompson, 1992). Once the domains of relevance are identified, quantitative methods may be more appropriate.

Finally, to advance our understanding of gender in family relationships more studies must examine the role of socially constructed gender characteristics in parent–child relations, in addition to the role of the sex of the parent and child (Rossi & Rossi, 1990; Wood, 1993). The value of such work is evident in Rossi and Rossi's research where they find that expressivity, a gendered characteristic, explains more of the variance in parent–child intimacy and exchange than does the sex of either dyad member. Highly expressive men are more intimate and involved with their parents (Rossi & Rossi, 1990). Apparently, a much deeper understanding of gender and its role in parent–child relations can be gained with approaches that go beyond simple comparisons of males and females.

SUMMARY

This chapter has reviewed the literature on parent–child relations across adulthood in an effort to demonstrate conceptual problems and methodological limitations that exist in this body of work. An apparent problem is the lack of a lifespan view of parent–child connections. As noted, the popular conceptualizations of the relationship in adolescence and early adulthood emphasize independence and distinctiveness between the generations, whereas frameworks used to study the relationship in the middle and later years of adulthood focus heavily on interdependence and similarity. How parents and adult children make this relational shift, if indeed they do, is not clear from the theoretical or empirical literature. Finally, the need for dyadic studies that consider parent-adult child relations within a broader family system and diverse cultural contexts was identified, as was greater consideration of the meaning of gender within adult parent–child relations.

ACKNOWLEDGEMENT

Work on the original version of this chapter was supported by a First Award from the National Institute of Mental Health (#1 R29 MH46946).

Chapter 4

Marital Quality

Esther S. Kluwer

Free University, Amsterdam, The Netherlands

One of the things we are most concerned with in life is the quality of our close relationships. As soon as we are involved in a close relationship, we regularly and carefully monitor our own and our partner's feelings about the relationship. We spend considerable amounts of time, energy, and even money on relationship maintenance by thinking and talking about our relationship, dealing with relationship conflict and distress, and some of us seek marital therapy and counseling. In addition, the quality of our relationship has far-reaching consequences for our psychological well-being (e.g., Gove, Hughes & Style, 1983), physical and mental health (e.g., Burman & Margolin, 1992; Fowers, 1991), parenting (e.g., Erel & Burman, 1995), and children's adjustment (e.g., Grych & Fincham, 1990). Not surprisingly, marital quality—also labeled "marital satisfaction", "marital happiness", "marital adjustment", and "marital success"—continues to be the most widely studied topic in the area of close relationships.

In this chapter, I will give an overview of theoretical considerations, conceptual and methodological issues, and empirical findings that have dominated the literature on marital quality until now. First, I will explain what is meant by marital quality and address conceptual and methodological issues. Second, two theoretical models of marital quality will be presented: the first is known as the *investment model of relationship commitment and stability* (Rusbult, 1983); the second and more recent one is the *vulnerability–stress–adaptation model* of marriage (Karney & Bradbury, 1995). Third, I will review research on the determinants and correlates of marital quality. The focus will

Families as Relationships.
Edited by Robert M. Milardo and Steve Duck. © 2000 John Wiley & Sons Ltd.

be on research published in the 1990s (for reviews of earlier work, see Glenn, 1990; Hicks & Platt, 1970; Spanier & Lewis, 1980). I will address three domains that have received considerable attention: behavior and cognition, individual differences, and coping with stressful events. I will conclude with directions for future research and summarize the main conclusions of the chapter.

DEFINING MARITAL QUALITY: CONCEPTUAL AND METHODOLOGICAL ISSUES

What is marital quality? Is it some multidimensional characteristic of relationships or is it simply how satisfied spouses feel in their relationship? Who decides what is a "good" relationship and what are the ingredients of such a relationship? These questions bear the essence of the conceptual confusion and disagreement about measurement that have characterized the literature on marital quality during the past decades (see Fincham, Beach & Kemp-Fincham, 1997; Glenn, 1990; Spanier & Lewis, 1980). When talking about marital quality, one is not merely *describing* but also *evaluating* marriage. The quality of a marriage can be high or low, some marriages are good and others are not, some relationships "work" and others don't. Accordingly, two questions come to mind: (1) what *criteria* are commonly used to describe and evaluate marital quality, and (2) *who* is asked to describe and evaluate the quality of a marriage—the individual, the marital dyad, or an outside observer? In the following discussion, it is important to realize that what is generally considered "high" and "low" marital quality is not only affected by the views and feelings of the intimate partners themselves, but also by the views of scientists (Duck, 1990; Duck, West & Acitelli, 1997), and, at a larger scale, by social norms and cultural standards (Montgomery, 1988).

Evaluation Criteria

The criteria that are used to evaluate marriage have received ample attention. In the past, two main approaches have emerged. The first approach dominated the 1970s and defined marital quality as a multidimensional characteristic of the relationship (e.g., Snyder, 1979). These researchers favored measures of *marital adjustment* that included both descriptive measures of marital interaction and evaluative measures of relationship satisfaction or happiness. Marital adjustment was defined as "a process, the outcome of which is determined by the degree of (1) troublesome marital differences, (2) interspousal tensions and personal anxiety, (3) marital satisfaction, (4) dyadic cohesion, and (5) consensus on matters of importance to marital functioning" (Spanier, 1976, p.17). The most frequently used measures of marital quality that sprung from this approach were the Marital Adjustment Test (MAT;

Locke & Wallace, 1959) and the Dyadic Adjustment Scale (DAS; Spanier, 1976). For example, the DAS includes the assessment of the degree of (dis)agreement on various issues (e.g., handling family finances, sexual relations, friends and family, career decisions), the frequency of various acts and activities (e.g., laughing together, kissing, confiding in each other, discussing something, quarreling), and the overall degree of happiness in the relationship.

Although these measures are still widely used, the marital adjustment approach has been criticized during the 1980s by researchers who objected to including in one scale both global evaluations of the relationship and measures of micro processes such as communication and conflict (e.g., Fincham & Bradbury, 1987; Norton, 1983; see also Huston & Robins, 1982; Sabatelli, 1988). They argued that the global measure of marital satisfaction or happiness affects or is affected by variables like marital interaction and conflict and that these variables should therefore not be included in one single scale. Put differently, measures of marital adjustment are confounded because they include process variables. For example, the DAS includes a measure of the frequency of marital disagreements as an indicator of marital quality, whereas one could just as well argue that the frequency of conflict serves as a determinant or as a consequence of marital quality. Instead, critics of the marital adjustment approach defined marital quality as the global evaluation of one's relationship and measured marital quality through self-report data that exclusively evaluated the relationship as a whole. Examples of measures are the Quality of Marriage Index (QMI; Norton, 1983) and the Kansas Marital Satisfaction Scale (KMSS; Schumm, Paff-Bergen, Hatch, Obiovah, Copeland, Meens and Bugaighis, 1986). For example, the QMI assesses marital quality by having spouses rate the degree of agreement with five statements (e.g., "We have a good marriage", "My relationship with my partner makes me happy") and have them rate their overall degree of happiness in their marriage. The strength of this second main approach is its conceptual simplicity as it avoids problems of interpretation that arise in the multidimensional scales (Fincham et al., 1997). The danger of unidimensional global scales, however, is that they do not provide much more information beyond the fact that spouses feel happy or distressed in their relationship.

Recently, Fincham et al. (1997) proposed a new theoretical perspective on marital quality. They argued that spouses can have both good and bad feelings about the marriage and can evaluate both positive and negative qualities of the spouse. For example, a couple may frequently get into serious fights while, at the same time, they feel intense love for each other and experience great companionship together. Building on the conception of marital quality as spouses' global, evaluative judgments of the relationship, Fincham et al. (1997) suggested that these evaluative judgments are two-dimensional, comprising positive marital quality (PMQ) and negative marital quality (NMQ) dimensions. The two dimensions can be crossed to produce a fourfold typology: those high on PMQ and low on NMQ are categorized as "happy" spouses and those low on PMQ and high on NMQ are categorized as "distressed". Spouses in the "ambivalent" category score high on both PMQ and NMQ dimensions, whereas "indifferent" spouses score low on both dimensions. Fincham and Linfield (1997) presented data that support this two-dimensional model of marital quality.

Using a global six-item assessment of positive marital quality (i.e., positive qualities of the spouse, positive feelings toward the spouse, good feelings about the marriage) and negative marital quality (i.e., negative qualities of the spouse, negative feelings toward the spouse, bad feelings about the marriage), they showed that the two dimensions accounted for unique variance in reported marital behavior and attributions beyond that explained by a conventional measure of marital quality.

Unit of Analysis

The question of *who* is asked to evaluate the quality of a marriage taps into the issue of unit of analysis and response bias. Should marital quality be assessed and analyzed individually or dyadically and to what extent are spouses' reports (in)dependent? In addition, are partners good evaluators of their own relationship or are their self-reports of marital quality influenced by impression management biases?

Most measures of marital quality are self-report measures that assess marital quality at the individual level. An exception is the ENRICH Marital Satisfaction Scale (Fowers & Olson, 1993) that provides a means to obtain both dyadic and individual satisfaction scores. The individual assessment of the quality of a dyadic relationship has implications for the statistical analysis of the data. In the past years, there has been increasing attention for the treatment of couple data and models of non-independence in dyadic research (e.g., Acitelli, 1996; Gonzales & Griffin, 1997; Kenny, 1996; Maguire, 1999). An important assumption in regular parametric statistics is that the observations are independent. However, the responses of married spouses are not independent: married couples are not randomly paired and they will be similar or at least influence each other on various dimensions. Therefore, we cannot simply perform statistical analyses on groups of husbands and wives because this violates the assumption of independent observations.

Kenny (1996) presents three models of non-independence that may be considered when choosing a strategy for the statistical analysis of couple data. The first assumes a *partner effect:* a characteristic of partner A influences another characteristic of partner B. For example, partner A's conflict behavior influences partner B's report of marital quality (and partner B's conflict behavior influences partner A's report of marital quality). The second model assumes *mutual influence:* a characteristic of partner A influences the same characteristic of partner B and vice versa. For example, partner A's reported marital quality influences partner B's reported marital quality and vice versa. The third model assumes *common fate:* partner A and B are exposed to the same causal factor. For example, the mutual conflict behavior of the couple influences their mutual report of marital quality (see Kenny & LaVoie, 1985). The choice of the appropriate model depends on the theory that is used and the particular model determines the type of statistical analysis that is performed (Kenny, 1996).

The fact that most measures of marital quality rely on self-reports raises the question whether these self-reports are affected by spouses' impression management biases (i.e., the tendency to purposefully self-present in an overly positive manner). Some authors refer to this self-presentational strategy as *socially desirable responding* and have included scales to correct for this response bias (e.g., Fowers & Applegate, 1995; Fowers & Olson, 1993). Research on social desirability response bias in measures of marital quality has shown that social desirability did not affect wives' self-reports, whereas husbands' self-reports of marital quality were positively related to social desirability (Hunsley, Vito, Pinsent, James & Lefebvre, 1996; Russell & Wells, 1992). However, Hunsley et al. (1996) showed that the magnitude of the associations between marital quality measures and other relationship variables was not reduced when controlling for impression management biases. Hence, they conclude that spouses' accounts of marital life appear not to be unduly affected by impression management biases (cf. Fowers & Applegate, 1995). Researchers can generally trust spouses' self-reports of marital quality and the reason why many couples report high levels of marital quality appears to be that they are correct (Russell & Wells, 1992).

Summary

Within the domain of marital quality research, it is widely recognized that the literature is characterized by a conceptual struggle in defining marital quality (e.g., Fincham et al., 1997; Glenn, 1990). There has been little agreement on the use of concepts as quality, satisfaction, adjustment, and happiness (Spanier & Lewis, 1980). An ongoing discussion about the multidimensional assessment of marriage versus spouses' individual perceptions of their marriage further hampered both measurement and conceptualization. Various measures of marital quality have been proposed, developed, and used in the past decades of research. Although they all have some virtue, each measurement scale has been criticized on theoretical, methodological, or both grounds. This leaves current researchers and practitioners with the problem of how to choose the right measure. Essentially, it all depends on the purpose for which the measure is used. Therapists and counseling psychologists may be interested in brief measures that can be used for screening purposes or prefer a more diagnostic instrument that includes assessments of communication and problem-solving. Relationship and family researchers may look for a marital quality measure that reliably covaries with a certain variable they are interested in. They should foremost be concerned with avoiding overlapping item content between the marital quality measure and the variables that are examined in relation to marital quality as this will produce an inflation of associations between dependent and independent variables. Finally, they should consider models of non-independence in their statistical analyses of couple data.

THEORETICAL MODELS OF MARITAL QUALITY

One important way to foster conceptual clarity and avoid disagreement about measurement is to advance theoretical models of marital quality. However, in the past decades, research on marriage has become broader, but not deeper (Karney & Bradbury, 1995). More and more variables have been examined as predictors of marital quality, but the field has not advanced towards a more theoretical approach of marital quality nor towards an integration of the abundance of empirical findings. Several exceptions exist, however, including models proposed by Lewis and Spanier (1979) and Berscheid and Lopes (1997). This section reviews the models that have been proposed by Rusbult (1983) and by Karney and Bradbury (1995). Rusbult's (1983) model is discussed because of its usefulness for empirical purposes and because it recognizes that being satisfied with the relationship is not the only ingredient of a stable marriage. Karney and Bradbury (1995) provide an integrative framework for the study of marital quality and change that helps us understand and structure the large body of research on relationship processes and predictors of marital quality. Their model will be used as a general guideline for the review of research in the next section.

The dependent variable in both models is *marital stability* rather than marital quality *per se*. Marital stability refers to the status of the marriage (i.e., whether the marriage is continuing or spouses are separated or divorced). Karney and Bradbury (1995) argued that the defining feature of close relationships is that they evolve over time and that a theory of marriage should specify the mechanisms through which development and change in marriage come about. Marital quality is not a permanent state, but subject to constant change, which calls for a process orientation towards relationships (cf. Clark & Reis, 1988; Duck, 1990; Duck & Sants, 1983; Erbert & Duck, 1997; Glenn, 1990). Rusbult's (1983) model has recognized that although satisfaction and stability are often positively associated, satisfaction does not necessarily predict stability and vice versa. Accordingly, instead of predicting marital quality as an outcome state, both models view marital stability or marital change as the criterion for marital quality.

The Investment Model of Relationship Commitment and Stability

Building on interdependence theory (Kelley, 1979; Kelley & Thibaut, 1978), Rusbult (1983) advanced a model of commitment and relationship maintenance mechanisms in close relationships. It suggests that *commitment level* is central to the functioning of couples, their adjustment processes, and the probability that a relationship will persist. Commitment is the internal representation of a long-term orientation, the intention of staying in the relationship for better or worse (Rusbult, 1983) and it is conceived of as the immediate predictor of marital stability. Commitment results from three factors: relationship satisfaction, investments in the relationship, and the quality of alternatives to the relationship. To start with the last, the quality of alternatives represents the expected costs and rewards of the best available alternative to the current relationship (e.g., being alone or being in another relationship). For example, a wife may stay in an abusive marriage because she has no viable economic alternatives (e.g., she depends on her husband's salary; Rusbult & Martz, 1995) and sometimes partners break up a relatively satisfying marriage because another partner or a different lifestyle appears more attractive.

Investments yield the number and magnitude of resources that are linked to the relationship (e.g., time, self-disclosures, shared possessions and friends). For example, distressed spouses may maintain the relationship because they have children together or because they have been together for many years. According to the model, investments have a major impact on commitment— hence, the model is often called the "investment model of commitment". Finally, satisfaction is operationalized as the individual's subjective evaluation of the relationship. It depends on the costs and rewards provided by the relationship and on the subjective standard against which the attractiveness of the relationship is evaluated (i.e., comparison level). This comparison level can be based on past experiences with relationships or on comparisons with the relationships of similar others. In sum, the model predicts spouses to feel committed to the relationship, which is the main ingredient of relationship stability, to the extent that they are highly satisfied with the relationship, have poor alternatives, and have made substantial investments in the relationship. Accordingly, commitment mediates the relationship between satisfaction, investments, and the quality of alternatives on the one hand and relationship stability on the other hand.

The model has received considerable empirical support from both cross-sectional and longitudinal studies using self-report measures. This research generally supported the predicted effects of satisfaction, investments, and the quality of alternatives on commitment and the theory successfully predicts long-term relationship stability (e.g., Bui, Peplau, & Hill, 1996; Rusbult, 1983; Rusbult & Martz, 1995; Rusbult, Martz, & Agnew, 1998). The variables in the model can be measured with the Investment Model Scale, which provides a valid and reliable self-report measure of commitment, satisfaction, investments and the quality of alternatives (Rusbult, Martz & Agnew, 1998). However, less clear support has been found for the mediational components of the model, namely that commitment mediates the effects of satisfaction, investments, and the quality of alternatives on relationship stability (Rusbult & Martz, 1995). The model is a useful tool in explaining how couples have different thresholds for separation and divorce. However, it is limited to the extent that it does not consider the effects of external stressors and individual differences. According to the model that is discussed next, these elements play an important role in marital quality and stability.

The Vulnerability–Stress–Adaptation Model of Marriage

In their *vulnerability–stress–adaptation model* of marriage, Karney and Bradbury (1995) identify three basic elements in an integrative framework for research on marital quality and marital stability: Adaptive processes, stressful events, and enduring vulnerabilities. The main dependent variable, marital stability, is unilaterally predicted by marital quality. The model further proposes a reciprocal relationship between adaptive processes and marital quality.

Adaptive processes refer to the ways couples deal with conflict and individual or marital difficulties. Marital quality changes as a function of the partners' behavioral patterns and judgments of marital quality in turn affect how spouses deal with conflict and marital difficulties. The model further proposes a reciprocal relationship between adaptive processes and *stressful events:* Marital interactions are partly determined by the stressors that couples are confronted with and the nature of how couples deal with these stressful events can exacerbate or alleviate the event. Examples of stressors are serious health problems, unemployment, financial problems, and the birth of a child. Finally, the model claims that stable intrapersonal characteristics or *enduring vulnerabilities*, such as attachment style and personality, can both contribute to stressful events and affect how couples adapt to individual and marital difficulties.

The model hypothesizes a positive relationship between marital quality and adaptive processes: good marital outcomes are more likely when couples are better at dealing with conflict and marital problems in constructive ways and poor marital outcomes are more likely when adaptive processes are poor (Bradbury, Cohan & Karney, 1998). In addition, the model hypothesizes negative relationships between marital quality and enduring vulnerabilities and stress: good marital outcomes are more likely when enduring vulnerabilities and stress are low and poor marital outcomes are more likely when enduring vulnerabilities and stress are high. Adaptive processes play a critical role in the model because they moderate the associations between marital quality and enduring vulnerabilities and stress. Couples with an average level of enduring vulnerabilities and stress will be unstable if adaptive processes are poor, less unstable if adaptive processes are average, and stable if adaptive processes are good. For example, a husband's unexpected lay-off (i.e., stressful event) and the subsequent depression that he suffers from (i.e., enduring vulnerability) will negatively affect the quality and stability of the relationship when his wife is not able to support him (i.e., adaptive process). However, the same event, combined with his depression, will affect the quality and stability of the relationship much less when his wife is able to show supportive behaviors.

A strength of the *vulnerability–stress–adaptation model* is that it provides an integrative framework for the mass of empirical findings on marital quality (see the next section for a review). The model successfully integrates previous theories of marriage, including social exchange theory (e.g., Levinger, 1976; Thibaut & Kelley, 1959), behavioral theory (e.g., Gottman, 1979), attachment theory (e.g., Bowlby, 1969), and crisis theory (e.g., R. Hill, 1949). It adds to behavioral theory, that views marital interactions as the core of marital quality, by considering the role of adaptive processes in enabling couples to adapt to new circumstances and situations. Stressful events frequently function as a test case of marriage. Spouses often find out the true value of their marriage when they are confronted with a stressful event and have to deal with it. A limitation of the model may be that its comprehensiveness makes a formal empirical test of the model quite difficult. Although general hypotheses follow from the paths in the model, the model appears less suitable for the description and explanation of more detailed processes. For example, it tends to ignore important differences, such as gender differences in particular paths in the model, discrepancies between spouses on particular variables, or differences in types of stressors, such as controllable versus uncontrollable or chronic versus acute stressors (Bradbury et al., 1998; Karney & Bradbury, 1995).

REVIEW OF RESEARCH ON MARITAL QUALITY

This section focuses on recent developments in research (i.e., in the 1990s). Following Karney and Bradbury's (1995) model, I will discuss three areas of research that have dominated the literature on marital quality: behavior and cognition, individual differences, and coping with stressful events. Although the studies that are reviewed have used divergent measures of marital quality (i.e., marital satisfaction, marital adjustment, marital distress, etc.), I will use the term "marital quality" as a general term for spouses' evaluations of the relationship.

Behavior and Cognition

One of the earliest attempts to explain why some marriages work and others don't focused on the behaviors that are exchanged during marital interactions (e.g., Gottman, 1979; Raush, Barry, Hertel & Swain, 1974). Research in this behavioral tradition has concentrated on conflict and problem-solving behaviors and the way couples interact and handle their conflicts was seen as one of the most important determinants of marital quality (e.g., Gottman, 1994). Indeed, conflict and problem-solving behaviors (i.e., adaptive processes) form one of the core elements of the *vulnerability–stress–adaptation model*. Research further suggests that cognitive responses affect marriage through their influence on marital interaction and conflict (e.g., Baucom, Epstein, Burnett & Rankin, 1993; Bradbury & Fincham, 1992).

Conflict and Communication

The guiding premise of the behavioral approach to marital quality is that positive and constructive behaviors enhance marital quality and negative or destructive behaviors are harmful. Indeed, distressed and non-distressed couples differ systematically with respect to the frequency of marital conflict and conflict behaviors and outcomes: distressed couples tend to report higher frequencies of conflict, more destructive conflict styles, and more negative outcomes than non-distressed couples (e.g., Canary, Cupach & Messman, 1995; Christensen & Schenk, 1991; Gottman & Levenson, 1992; McGonagle, Kessler & Gotlib, 1993). In addition, marital conflict has a profound impact on mental well-being, physical health, and family functioning (for a review, see Fincham & Beach, 1999).

Interestingly, it appears that it is not so much the constructive behaviors that are exhibited but rather partners' destructive conflict behaviors that determine the quality of the relationship. Destructive conflict behaviors, such as separating, ignoring the partner, or refusing to discuss the problem, were found more powerful determinants of couple distress/non-distress than constructive conflict behaviors, such as discussing the problem, suggesting solutions, or waiting and hoping for things to get better (Rusbult, Johnson & Morrow, 1986; see also Kluwer, Heesink & Van de Vliert, 1997). An explanation may be that constructive behaviors are "taken for granted" because they are what spouses expect from their partner in a close relationship. Destructive behaviors are generally less expected and may therefore have greater impact on spouses' evaluations of the relationship (Rusbult et al., 1986). A cognitive explanation is that other people's negative features, traits, and behaviors are generally more diagnostic and cognitively salient than other people's positive features, traits, and behaviors (Taylor, 1991). Hence, the partner's negative behavior may have a larger impact and cause more negative affect than the partner's positive behavior causes positive affect.

One particularly destructive marital interaction pattern is the *demand/withdraw interaction* pattern, in which one spouse attempts to engage in a discussion, resorting to pressures and demands, while the other spouse tries to avoid conflict and withdraws from the interaction (see also Chapter 5). Research has shown that wives tend to demand and husbands)tend to withdraw during marital conflict and that this wife-demand/husband-withdraw pattern generally occurs in conflict situations where the wife desires a change in her spouse's behavior while the husband wants to maintain the status quo (e.g., Christensen & Heavey, 1990; Heavey, Layne, & Christensen, 1993; Kluwer, 1998; Kluwer et al., 1997; in press). Wife-demand/husband-withdraw interaction is related to long-term declines in marital satisfaction among wives (Heavey et al., 1993, 1995) and distressed couples tend to report more demand/withdraw communication than non-distressed couples (Christensen & Schenk, 1991; Holtzworth-Munroe, Smutzler & Stuart, 1998). In addition, research showed that domestically violent couples are more likely to show demand/withdraw interactions (Babcock, Waltz, Jacobson & Gottman, 1991; Holtzworth-Munroe et al., 1998).

A conflict behavior that is particularly enhancing for the relationship is *accommodation:* An individual's willingness to inhibit impulses to reciprocate the partner's real or perceived tendency to behave destructively, and instead react constructively (Rusbult, Bissonnette, Arriaga & Cox, 1998). Although accommodative behavior can be costly for the accommodating partner, it has been found to be related to greater marital quality. Specifically, it was found to partially mediate the effect of commitment on marital quality that is predicted in the *investment model of relationship commitment* (Rusbult et al., 1998). Interestingly, the effect on marital quality was stronger for the perception of the partner's willingness to accommodate than for the individual's own accommodation. The perception of the partner's willingness to accommodate may enhance trust, which is thought to represent confidence in the partner's commitment and therefore foster relationship quality (Rusbult et al., 1998). A much broader, yet related, concept is the *willingness to sacrifice:* the propensity to forego immediate self-interest and sacrifice own needs for the needs of the partner or the well-being of the relationship (Van Lange, Rusbult, Drigotas, Arriaga, Witcher & Cox, 1997). Research showed that the willingness to sacrifice was positively associated with marital quality (Van Lange et al., 1997).

Cognition

The past decade has shown increasing interest in the role of cognitive factors in marital dysfunction (for a review, see Bradbury & Fincham, 1990). The most frequently studied cognitions are attributions that spouses make for events and behaviors that occur in their relationship (i.e., why did an event or behavior occur and who is accountable for the event or behavior?). Distressed spouses tend to attribute their spouse's behaviors to stable, dispositional factors and offer attributions that accentuate the impact of negative events, whereas non-distressed spouses tend to make attributions that minimize the impact of negative events (Bradbury & Fincham, 1990). For example, imagine a husband who has not done the dishes that he was supposed to do. A distressed wife might attribute her husband's behavior to neglectfulness or lack of interest for her needs, whereas a non-distressed wife might attribute this same behavior to a busy day at work. Distressed spouses tend to interpret their partner's negative behavior in terms of global and stable causes (e.g., "he is always so neglectful") instead of specific and transient causes (e.g., "he just had a busy day at work today"). Clearly, the first interpretation fortifies the impact of the negative behavior which can be detrimental to the relationship.

In addition, distressed spouses diminish the value of their spouse's positive behaviors and accentuate their spouse's negative behaviors in a way that maintains their feelings of distress (Holmes, 1991; Holmes & Boon, 1990). Distressed spouses tend to be reluctant to grant credit to their partner's positive behaviors or view them as intentional and motivated by unselfish concerns, whereas they tend to show the opposite pattern for their partner's negative behaviors. Bradbury and Fincham (1992) further showed that spouses' maladaptive attributions were related to less effective problem-solving behaviors and higher rates of negative behaviors, especially among distressed couples. For example, responsibility attributions (i.e., the extent to which the partner is thought to act with negative intent, to be motivated by selfish concerns, and is blamed for the event or behavior) moderated the relationship between marital quality and aggression among wives. Marital quality and physical aggression were significantly related for wives high in responsibility attributions (Byrne & Arias, 1997; see also Fincham, Bradbury, Arias, Byrne & Karney, 1997).

By contrast, happy couples tend to distort their appraisal of their relationship in positive ways, which has been found to relate to increases in marital satisfaction (Murray, Holmes & Griffin, 1996). This area of research on cognitions in marriage deals with the effects of social comparison on marital quality. People tend to hold more positive and fewer negative beliefs about their own relationships than about other relationships (Van Lange & Rusbult, 1995) and these positive illusions about marriage are associated with higher marital quality (Buunk & Van der Eijnden, 1997; Fowers, Lyons & Montel, 1996). Cognitive downward comparison (i.e., thinking that your relationship is *better* than others) is positively related to relationship satisfaction and commitment and especially affects distressed couples (Oldersma, Buunk & De Dreu, 1998; cf. Buunk, Collins, Taylor, VanYperen & Dakof, 1990). Although these illusions that result from comparisons at the dyadic level (i.e., own versus others' relationships) have positive effects, individual within-dyad comparisons (i.e., self versus partner) may have quite negative effects for the relationship. For example, individuals involved in relationship conflict tend to judge themselves as more cooperative and less competitive than their partner (Kluwer, De Dreu & Buunk, 1998) and such self-enhancing judgements are associated with conflict escalation, stalemate, and future conflict (De Dreu, Nauta & Van de Vliert, 1995), processes that can be quite detrimental to the relationship.

To summarize, the behavioral approach has illuminated important aspects of marital functioning. At the same time, it has been criticized for having little consideration for intrapersonal factors that may explain the link between conflict behavior and marital quality (e.g., Bradbury & Fincham, 1992). Hence, research on the effects of cognitions on marital quality and marital interaction complements the behavioral account of marital quality because it helps to explain *why* distressed partners exhibit and reciprocate destructive conflict behaviors. Together, the cognitive–behavioral approach offers a fruitful avenue for understanding the mechanisms by which relationships become more or less satisfying and stable over time.

Coping with Stressful Events

At some point in their relationship, most couples are bound to encounter events and transitions that are stressful and that require adaptation. Negative or stressful events can be related to, for example, health, children, housing, finances and work. A considerable amount of research has addressed how couples deal with stressful events and transitions and how this affects their relationship. In this section, I will discuss research on how coping styles in general affect marital quality and specifically focus on coping with a serious illness and on the transition to parenthood.

Stress and Coping

When spouses experience major stressors, it depends on their coping abilities whether their stress-related emotions and behaviors have a negative impact on their relationship. Coping can be defined as an individual's cognitive and behavioral efforts to manage negative or stressful events. Three major types of coping strategies are generally distinguished (e.g., Endler & Parker, 1994; Folkman & Lazarus, 1988; Lussier, Sabourin and Turgeon, 1997): Emotion-focused coping entails regulating emotions (e.g., worrying, wishful thinking, seeking social support, blaming), task- or problem-focused coping means trying to change the circumstances that cause the stress (e.g., analyzing the problem, seeking solutions), and avoidance-oriented coping is a way of trying to change the significance of the stressful event through avoidance (e.g., withdrawal, taking a vacation, eating, sleeping).

In general, spouses' task- or problem-focused coping tends to be positively related to marital quality, whereas avoidance-oriented coping strategies are negatively related to marital quality (Bouchard, Sabourin, Lussier, Wright & Richer, 1998; Bowman, 1990; Lussier et al., 1997). The findings on emotion-focused coping have offered mixed results, depending largely on the constructs that are used to assess the coping style. Some studies stress emotion-focused coping strategies that are positively oriented, such as seeking social support and positive reinterpretation, and have found positive relationships with marital quality (Ptacek & Dodge, 1995; Stanton, Tennen, Affleck & Mendola, 1992; Unger, Jacobs & Cannon, 1996). Other studies have emphasized negatively oriented strategies, such as worrying and self-blame, and found that these strategies negatively affect marital quality (Bowman, 1990; Cohan & Bradbury, 1994; Lussier et al., 1997). In sum, when a couple lacks the capacity to engage in adaptive coping (e.g., trying to change the circumstances that cause the stress, analyzing the problem, seeking solutions, and seeking social support), but rather engages in dysfunctional coping styles (e.g., worrying, blaming, and avoiding dealing with the situation), their stress-related reactions will negatively affect their interactions and, consequently, the quality of their relationship.

Major Health Problems

The diagnosis and treatment of a serious illness is extremely stressful for couples. Both patients and partners experience higher levels of psychological distress and have to cope with changing physical conditions and the negative side effects of medical treatments. In general, decrements in health seem to have a negative effect on marital quality. Changes in financial circumstances, shifts in the division of labor, declines in marital interaction, and changes in the balance of equity between patient and partner account for this effect (Booth & Johnson, 1994, Cutrona, 1996; S. C. Thompson & Pitts, 1992).

Coping with a serious illness can be seen as having three competing functions (Coyne & Smith, 1991): managing one's own distress (i.e., emotion-focused coping), dealing with various instrumental problems (i.e., task-focused coping), and coming to terms with each other's emotional needs. The latter is known as relationship-focused coping and entails either *active engagement*, involving the partner in discussions, inquiring how the partner feels and other constructive problem solving, or *protective buffering* which refers to hiding concerns, denying worries, and yielding to the partner to avoid disagreements (Coyne & Smith, 1991). A third way of relationship-focused coping is *overprotection*, referring to the underestimation of the patient's capabilities, resulting in unnecessary help or attempts to restrict activities. Kuijer et al. (in press) have shown that patients' evaluations of marital quality were positively related to the amount of active engagement by their spouse. Overprotection is generally seen as harmful for the patient's well-being, because it undermines the patient's feelings of control and motivation to initiate activities (S. C. Thompson & Pitts, 1992). Protective buffering seemed to have neither positive or negative effects (e.g. Kuijer et al., in press).

Transition to Parenthood

Since the 1970s, many have addressed the impact of the transition to parenthood on marital quality (e.g., Belsky, Spanier & Rovine, 1983; C. S. Russell, 1974; see also Chapter 2). Most studies on the marital career have claimed to find a U-shaped pattern for marital quality over the family life cycle with the average marital quality being higher in the pre- and postparental stages (e.g., Rollins & Feldman, 1970), but this appears to be a rather modest effect. Nevertheless, the transition to first-time parenthood is generally known as a challenging and difficult event in couples' lives. Adding a third member to the marital dyad implies drastic changes for couples' relationships. Spouses spend less time on leisure and joint activities, sexual satisfaction tends to decline, and patterns of communication change due to time constraints and the demands of the child (e.g., Crohan, 1996; Kluwer, Heesink & Van de Vliert, 1996, 1999). Although a decline in marital satisfaction over time is not necessarily unique to couples having their first child (MacDermid, Huston & McHale, 1990; McHale & Huston, 1985) and some couples experience no change or positive marital changes across the transition to parenthood (e.g., Belsky & Kelly, 1994), most studies show a small but significant decrease in marital satisfaction that is related to first-time parenthood, primarily among wives (see Belsky & Kelly, 1994, for an overview).

The transition to parenthood is accompanied by stress, which increases the risk of distress in parents and children, even in relatively well-functioning families (Cowan & Cowan, 1997). For example, an often replicated finding is that the division of labor between spouses becomes more traditional after the birth of the first child, with wives doing most of the family work and reducing their working hours. The division of labor generally becomes more traditional than was expected before childbirth and this disconfirmation of expectancies adds to the decline in marital satisfaction, especially among wives (e.g., Hackel & Ruble, 1992; Kalmuss, Davidson & Cushman, 1992; Ruble, Fleming, Hackel & Stangor, 1988; cf. Kluwer et al., 1999).

In sum, research on stressful events has focussed on "external" life stressors that may disrupt the quality and stability of the marriage. Extradyadic stressors have largely been neglected in the cognitive/behavioral tradition, but nevertheless are an important cause of marital instability. As suggested by the *vulnerability–stress–adaptation model*, they challenge a couple's capacity to adapt, which may alleviate or worsen the event (Karney & Bradbury, 1995).

Individual Differences

The third and last section of this review draws attention to the role of personal factors and individual differences in marriage. In the past decade, a substantial amount of research has focussed on the role of attachment style. Attachment theory suggests that the nature of the first close relationship in life— between infant and primary caregiver—determines the internal working model of what relationships are like and therefore determines the nature of an individual's close relationships later in life (e.g., Bowlby, 1969). Other personal factors that will be discussed are personality and background variables.

Attachment

Since Hazan and Shaver (1987) applied attachment theory to marital relationships, consistent empirical support has been found for the relationship between spouses' attachment style and marital quality. Secure individuals, who feel comfortable with closeness and intimacy, report more marital quality, intimacy, trust, and commitment in their relationships than avoidant individuals—those uncomfortable with closeness and intimacy—and anxious– ambivalent individuals—those who fear their partner will leave them and desire excessive closeness (e.g., Brennan & Shaver, 1993; Carnelley, Pietromonaco & Jaffe, 1994; Collins & Read, 1990; Feeney & Noller, 1990; Tucker & Anders, 1999). In addition, the attachment style of the partner influences the reported quality of the relationship. Individuals married to a securely attached partner report higher marital quality than those married to an insecure partner (e.g., Feeney, 1994; Kobak & Hazan, 1991; Senchak & Leonard, 1992; Simpson, 1990).

In a 31-year longitudinal study, Klohnen and Bera (1998) showed that avoidant compared with secure women experienced relationship trajectories that were less happy and less steady, and showed a consistent pattern of behavioral and personality characteristics, including interpersonal distance, defensiveness, and vulnerability (cf. Kirkpatrick & Davis, 1994). This research highlights the powerful effects of early life experiences and attachment processes in relationship functioning over the life span. However, it should be noted that attachment style is not a rigid and invariable determinant of close relationships. Attachment styles can be revised on the basis of experiences later in life, such as the loss of a parent. However, more research is needed to determine under what circumstances attachment styles change later in life (cf. Klohnen & Bera, 1998; Kirkpatrick & Davis, 1994).

Personality

Research on the role of personality is more scarce in the domain of marital quality. However, a few generalizations can be made. Neuroticism—the disposition to experience anxiety, anger, depression and emotional lability (Eysenck & Eysenck, 1985)—tends to have a detrimental effect on marital quality (e.g., Leonard & Roberts, 1998; Russell & Wells, 1994; Thomsen & Gilbert, 1998). For example, neurotic partners are more likely to overreact emotionally to conflict and engage in potentially destructive conflict behaviors, such as coercion and avoidance. Kurdek (1991) showed that large overall discrepancies between husbands' and wives' personality scores were negatively related to marital quality. Large discrepancies in personality may lead to marital conflict and, eventually, to marital distress. Botwin, Buss and Shackelford (1997) examined the personality characteristics that individuals want in a partner. Most people preferred partners who scored high on agreeableness (lenient, flexible, fair, generous), emotional stability (i.e., relaxed, even-tempered, secure), and intellect-openness (i.e., intelligent, creative, curious, analytical). They further showed that the personality characteristics of one's spouse significantly predicted marital dissatisfaction, especially when the spouse scored lower on these traits than desired.

Background Variables

Although background variables are often included in research on marital quality, few studies explicitly focussed on the effects of these variables on marital quality. Because many different background variables have been examined, I confine myself to reviewing only a few findings in detail. For example, several authors have examined the impact of employment and retirement on relationship functioning (see also Chapter 6). Retirement appears to have a powerful and pervasive influence on marital quality. Orbuch, House, Mero & Webster (1996) showed that reduced work and parental responsibilities in later life explained much of the later-life increase in marital quality. At the same time, changes that accompany retirement, such as role-reversals and decreased social support, may lower marital quality (Myers & Booth, 1996). Wives' employment is another topic that has received attention. This research is often based on the assumption that wives' employment has a negative effect on marital quality because her work decreases her availability at home, threatens spouses' role complementarity (i.e., the traditional division of labor), and challenges the husband's prerogative as the primary breadwinner (see Rogers, 1999). However, research indicates that neither the wife's work nor her time devoted to work nor her income appears to have the expected negative impact on marital functioning (e.g., Barling, 1990; Blair, 1993; Rogers, 1999).

Other research that addressed associations between marital quality and background variables has examined the influence of childhood family background (Webster, Orbuch & House, 1995), premarital predictors (C. T. Hill & Peplau, 1998), age (e.g., Levenson, Carstensen & Gottman, 1993), age at marriage (Wilson, Larson, McCulloch & Stone, 1997), religion and polygyny (Gwanfogbe, Schumm, Smith & Furrow, 1997), and (over)weight (Sobal, Rauschenbach & Frongillo, 1995). Although the vast majority of marital quality research in the past decades has been focussed on Western, particularly North American, marriages, the attention for cross-cultural and ethnical differences is growing. For example, research has investigated the relationships of African-american (e.g., Crohan, 1996; Timmer, Veroff & Hatchett, 1996), Hispanic (e.g., Contreras, Hendrick & Hendrick, 1996), Dutch (e.g., Buunk & Van der Eijnden, 1997; Kluwer et al., 1997, 1999, in press; Oldersma et al., 1998), Austrian (e.g., Mikula et al., 1998), Swedish (e.g., Kaslow, Hansson & Lundblad, 1994), Chinese (e.g., Shek, 1995), Cameroon (Gwanfogbe et al., 1997), and Israeli (Rabin & Shapira-Berman, 1997) couples.

To summarize, a fair amount of research has focussed on the role of intrapersonal factors in marriage. In the past years, the primary approach has been to study the role of attachment style. A second body of research has, directly or indirectly, studied the role of personality and background variables. Contrary to the work on attachment, however, research on background variables appears much less driven by theoretical considerations and often comprises scattered bits of knowledge. In addition, studies on the role of personality have accounted for relatively small proportions of variance in marital quality (Russell & Wells, 1994). Nevertheless, attachment style, personality, and background variables are important because, together, they provide a psychological context for spouses' behaviors and interactions which further predicts marital quality and stability (cf. Karney & Bradbury, 1995).

DIRECTIONS FOR THE FUTURE

The preceding review shows that, over the past decades, the empirical findings have accumulated to an impressive body of research on marital quality. Nonetheless, economical and social environments are subject to constant change and, as a result, couples have to adapt to new circumstances and deal with new relationship issues and events. For example, think about the effects of infertility and childlessness (e.g., Morrow, Thoreson & Penney, 1995), the impact of war and criminality, alcohol and drug abuse (e.g., Brennan, Moos & Kelly, 1994), and marital aggression and violence (e.g., Milardo, 1998).

Three social developments call for specific attention. First, with the number of women entering the labor market still increasing and relationships becoming more egalitarian, gender issues in the family—the division of labor (e.g. Kluwer et al., 1996, 1997), work–family conflict (e.g., Matthews, Conger & Wickrama, 1996), and the role of husbands in family work—continue to be important issues for research (see Chapter 1). Second, as our western society is becoming truly multicultural, the attention in research for the role of culture and ethnicity in relationships should continue to grow in the next decades. Finally, it is surprising to find that there is still very little attention for homo- and bisexual relationships (e.g., Kurdek, 1993a). The bulk of research on relationship quality is on heterosexual relationships. However, as the social and legal acceptance of homosexual relationships is slowly increasing—in the US, homosexual couples can adopt a child and The Netherlands is now the first country in the world that legally accepts gay and lesbian marriage—relationship research should start to pay more attention to non-heterosexual relationships. These are just a few examples of issues that will undoubtedly continue to be "hot issues" in the next decades.

Despite the importance of these issues, however, exploring the predictive effects of yet another set of variables is not what the field of marital quality research needs most. Rather, we need to further develop theoretical frameworks of marital quality that combine the contributions and empirical findings of past research. As several authors have acknowledged (e.g., Fincham et al., 1997; Glenn, 1990; Karney & Bradbury, 1995), much of the research on marital quality suffers from a lack of theory. The tendency is, still, to examine idiosyncratic groups of variables for their effects on marital quality instead of building theory. Specifically, it is necessary to develop and test models that explain the mechanisms by which marriages become more or less satisfying and (un)stable over time, instead of merely predicting marital stability and satisfaction. A promising development in this regard is the increased use of longitudinal research designs (see Karney & Bradbury, 1995), which is the best way to examine how marriages develop and change over time (cf. Duck, 1990). Part of building theory may be to conduct *meta analyses* of the predictors of marital quality and marital change, in order to examine the overall effect sizes of various predictors and models. Given the amount of research, it is truly surprising to find *no* meta analyses in the literature on marital quality so far. This is an interesting domain that has yet to be explored.

Attempts to develop a theory of marital quality and stability should build on and extend existing models such as the ones discussed in this chapter. For example, both the *investment model of relationship commitment* and the *vulnerability–stress–adaptation model* would gain from exploring the dyadic associations between partners' responses (see Bui et al., 1996). After all, relationships consist of two individuals and spouses constantly affect and influence each other. In addition, a formal empirical test of the *vulnerability–stress–adaptation model* is needed to further enhance this model. For example, it assumes intrapersonal factors to have an indirect effect on marital quality, via adaptive processes and stressful events. However, most of the reviewed research has considered direct relationships between individual differences and marital quality. Further research should explore whether these direct effects are in fact mediated by adaptive processes and stressful events, because this would shed light on the processes that cause certain individual differences (such as neuroticism) to have detrimental effects on marital quality. Finally, it is important for future research on marital quality to explore links between various models of marital quality and stability. For example, the *investment model of relationship commitment* would gain from considering the effects of external stressors and individual differences that are central to the *vulnerability–stress–adaptation model.*

SUMMARY AND CONCLUSION

Marital quality continues to be the most widely studied topic in the area of close relationships and has been studied from various perspectives and in different disciplines (e.g., sociology, family studies, communication, social and clinical psychology). In this chapter, I attempted to give an overview of current knowledge about marital quality. First, I discussed the concept of marital quality and issues of measurement. I illuminated what appears to be common knowledge among relationship researchers, namely that research on marital quality has suffered from conceptual and methodological confusion (e.g., Fincham et al., 1997; Glenn, 1990; Karney & Bradbury, 1995). This is caused mostly by disagreement on (1) the differential use of concepts as quality, satisfaction, adjustment, and happiness, and (2) the multidimensional assessment of the marriage versus spouses' individual perceptions of the marriage. It was concluded that researchers should most importantly avoid overlapping item content between their marital quality measure and the variables that are examined in relation to marital quality and they should consider models of non-independence in their statistical analyses of couple data.

Second, I presented two theoretical models of marital quality and stability: The well-known *investment model of relationship commitment and stability* (Rusbult, 1983) and the more recent *vulnerability–stress–adaptation model* of marriage (Karney & Bradbury, 1995). Rusbult's model is acknowledged for providing a sound theoretical perspective on marital stability and for its empirical usefulness. Her model has received considerable empirical support and it is widely used to predict relationship outcomes. Karney and Bradbury's model can be praised for its successful attempt to integrate previous theories and empirical findings on marital quality. It is among the first to provide a truly integrative framework for the study of marital quality and stability that helps us understand how relationships develop and change over time.

Third, I reviewed recent research that explored variables that affect marital quality. Following the *vulnerability–stress–adaptation model*, three main areas of research were discussed: behavior and cognition, individual differences, and coping with stressful events. Although the entire model has not yet received empirical support, the hypothesized relationships are generally supported by the research that was reviewed in this chapter. Conflict and problem-solving behaviors form the heart of marital quality and stability and are influenced by cognitive processes, such as attributions and social comparisons. Conflict and problem-solving behaviors become critical when they concern a stressful event, such as major health problems or the transition to parenthood, that requires coping and adaptation. Finally, individual differences in attachment style, personality, and background variables affect the quality of relationships.

A few limitations require mention. First of all, I concentrated on the determinants of marital quality, while there are also important consequences to consider. Research should further our understanding of the impact of marital quality on various individual outcomes such as psychological well-being (e.g., Gove et al., 1983) and physical and mental health (e.g., Burman & Margolin, 1992). In addition, a topic that has received increasing attention in the past deals with the impact of the quality of relationships on parenting (e.g., Erel & Burman, 1995) and child adjustment (e.g., Grych & Fincham, 1990). Second, an important field of research that I did not include in my review is the prevention and treatment of marital distress (e.g., Kaiser, Hahlweg, Fehm-Wolfsdorf & Groth, 1998; Markman & Hahlweg, 1993). Finally, my discussion of theoretical models is obviously limited and there are other attempts to develop a theory of marital quality that are left undiscussed.

To conclude, over the past decades, marital quality has proved to be an interesting, important, diverse, and at the same time difficult topic of research. Many social and behavioral scientists have contributed to our understanding of what makes some relationships work and what makes others fail. Considering the current host of findings, it is safe to state that the field of research on marital quality is ready for integration and building theory. It would benefit most from developing and testing models that integrate prior findings and theories, conducting longitudinal research, and doing meta analyses on the determinants and correlates of marital quality. Although these are all highly demanding scientific activities, they are indispensable for the advancement of marital quality research in the new millenium.

ACKNOWLEDGEMENT

I am grateful for the constructive comments and suggestions offered by Carsten de Dreu on an earlier version of this chapter.

Chapter 5

Strategies of Couple Conflict

Renate C. A. Klein

University of Maine, USA

and

Michael P. Johnson

Pennsylvania State University, USA

OVERVIEW

This chapter is about couple conflict in family relationships (for discussions of intergenerational conflict in families see Fincham & Osborne, 1993; Halpern, 1994; and Osborne & Fincham, 1994). Our focus is on conflict strategies and more specifically on an analysis of the factors that shape partners' choices among different strategies. The chapter is organized around the concept of strategic choice, which we borrow from negotiation research (Carnevale & Pruitt, 1992).

The chapter is composed of five sections. In the introduction we explicate the terms family, conflict, conflict strategies, and strategic choice. In the second section we discuss individual and situational factors in strategic choice and focus on three response patterns in couple conflict that have received considerable attention recently: the demand/withdraw pattern in asymmetrical conflict, negative reciprocity, and physical violence. The third section focuses on the role of third parties in strategic choice, an important field that, we believe, will receive more attention in the future. The fourth section has a

Families as Relationships.
Edited by Robert M. Milardo and Steve Duck. © 2000 John Wiley & Sons Ltd.

theoretical focus and presents a discussion of strategic choice from a situated sense-making perspective that takes into consideration the balance of inter-personal, social, and economic power between partners. In the final section we briefly summarize the chapter and point to our main conclusion about the importance of social context in couple conflict.

INTRODUCTION OF CONCEPTS

Family

Although this chapter is about couple conflict in family relationships, we would like to be clear at the beginning that we intend to focus on couple conflict in "families" broadly defined. Recent debates in the field of family studies (Burr, Herrin, Day, Beutler & Leigh, 1987; Marks, 1987; Beutler, Burr, Barr & Herrin, 1989a,b) have persuaded us and many other scholars that a narrow focus of the field on the traditional biological family is not conducive to the development of adequate theory. We find the arguments of Marks (1987) and Scanzoni, Polonko, Teachman & Thompson (1989) quite persuasive, that a broader focus on units that are organized around a sexual bond (Scanzoni et al., 1989) drawing upon broad theories of personal relation-ships (as exemplified in this volume) will be much more productive than would a narrower focus on the "traditional" family (cf. Chapter 9).

We think that such a broader concept of the family draws attention to the fact that similar conflict issues may play out differently in different family "types". For example, spouses in traditional, male bread-winner families are likely to debate issues around household chores differently than spouses in "peer marriages" (Schwartz, 1994). Similarly, arguments over household chores may play out differently for lesbian than for gay male couples because lesbian couples on average have a lower expendable household income than gay couples and are therefore less able to resolve chore conflicts by "expand-ing the pie" (J. Z. Rubin, Pruitt & Kim, 1994), in this case, by buying more free time for both partners. In addition, because most domestic workers are female, for many lesbian couples hiring household help may take on an un-welcome ideological meaning: by hiring female domestic servants they con-tribute to women's confinement to low-wage, part-time jobs (Patterson & Schwartz, 1994).

Conflict

While conflict can be perceived and defined in different ways (e.g., Baxter, Wilmot, Simmons & Swartz, 1993; Lloyd, 1987; Peterson, 1983) we are concerned with conflicts that arise when partners believe their needs and interests are incompatible. Similar notions of conflict have been adopted in a variety of disciplines. For example, Margolin (1988) defined marital conflict as the "incompatibilities or antagonisms of ideas, desires, and actions between the two parties" (p. 195). Similarly, in their discussion of social conflict, Rubin et al. (1994) understand conflict as the "perceived divergence of interest, or a belief that the parties' current aspirations cannot be achieved simultaneously" (p. 5).

Conflict strategies

We define conflict strategies as behaviors intended to manage or resolve conflict, which includes everything partners do and do not do in response to perceived or actual disagreement, from humorous and thoughtful discussions of each other's needs and interests to fierce and violent battles for power and control. Conflict strategies have been assessed through self-reports (e.g., Kurdek, 1994) and behavior observation (e.g., Gottman, 1979; Hahlweg, Reisner, Kohli, Vollmer, Schindler & Revenstorf, 1984; Prager, 1991), cross-sectionally and longitudinally (Gottman & Krokoff, 1989; Noller, Feeney, Bonnell & Callan 1994; McGonagle, Kessler & Gotlib, 1993; for a discussion of different methodologies see Bradbury & Karney, 1993; and R. L. Weiss & Heyman, 1990).

Many research areas are related to strategic choice but cannot be covered within a single chapter. The reader is referred to other sources on blue-collar and white-collar marriages (Krokoff, Gottman & Roy, 1988), influence and control tactics (Falbo & Peplau, 1980; Howard, Blumstein & Schwartz, 1986; Stets & Pirog-Good, 1990; Christopher & Frandsen, 1990), coping with unsettled disagreements (Bowman, 1990), relationship maintenance (Baxter & Dindia, 1990; Dindia & Canary, 1993; Stafford & Canary, 1991), and commitment processes (M. P. Johnson, 1991; Rusbult, Verette, Whitney, Slovik & Lipkus, 1991).

Conflict strategies constitute the course of conflict over time (Lloyd & Cate, 1985). Although we know that some conflict strategies reduce conflict and strengthen the bond between partners, whereas other conflict strategies escalate conflict and antagonize partners (Jacobson & Holtzworth-Munroe, 1986; Markman & Hahlweg, 1993; Markman, Renick, Floyd, Stanley & Clements, 1993), we are still far from fully understanding partners' choices in couple conflict (Jacobson & Addis, 1993). Therefore, we organize our review of couples' conflict strategies around the concept of strategic choice.

Strategic Choice

We organize our discussion of conflict strategies around the concept of choice for two reasons. First, we do so because we believe that partners do have a choice in how they respond to conflict and are not confined to "inevitable" developments of their disagreements. This does not mean each partner is capable and free to act as he or she pleases, nor are we implying that each choice involves a careful analysis of the consequences of different strategies. Although some choices may be the result of informed foresight, other choices may be the result of guesswork, mindlessness, or years of habit.

Second, the concept of strategic choice draws our attention to factors that may explain why partners choose one strategy rather than another. While there can be important internal or dispositional factors such as the effects of socialization, personality, or temperament (Gilligan, 1982; Seltzer & Kalmuss, 1988; Smith, 1990), we will focus on situational factors in strategic choice, using "situational" in a broad sense. On a micro-level, situational factors may include the structure of conflict within the dyad and the behavior of one's partner. On a macro-level, situational factors may include structural arrangements of intimate relationships (e.g., marriage) or the influence of third parties. In short, we will examine to what extent partners' strategic choices are situationally constructed and review empirical evidence on the demand/withdraw pattern, negative reciprocity, and physical violence. In the theoretical section we will take a step back and discuss strategic choices in terms of "sense-making" and the subjective meaning imposed by partners on confusing interaction sequences (Duck, 1994), and in terms of "differential advantage" and the constellation of power between self, partner, and third parties at any given point in the relationship.

STRATEGIC CHOICES IN COUPLE CONFLICT

Dual-concern Model

Our concept of strategic choice is borrowed from negotiation research where it has been researched and represented in the heuristic framework of the dual-concern model (see Pruitt & Carnevale, 1993, for a detailed description). Developed from work on managerial decision-making (Blake & Mouton, 1964) the dual-concern model has been used increasingly to analyze strategic choice in couple and family conflict as well (See Buunk's 1980 paper, cited in Schaap, Buunk & Kerkstra, 1988; Fry, Firestone & Williams, 1983; Rahim, 1983; Syna, 1984; Galvin & Brommel, 1986; Levinger & Pietromonaco, 1989; Rinehart, 1992; Spitzberg, Canary & Cupach, 1994; Klein, 1995).

The dual-concern model distinguishes between four basic conflict strategies (Pruitt & Carnevale, 1993): *contending* (e.g., being competitive, aggressive), *problem-solving* (e.g., being cooperative, talking things through, being creative), *yielding* (e.g., being conciliatory, giving in), and *inaction* (e.g., being passive, avoiding confrontation). There are several conceptual issues with such a typology. For one, the negotiation literature does not address critically the connotations of the terms used to label the four conflict strategies. For example, "yielding" carries connotations of not being able to defend oneself, although it may contribute successfully to conflict resolution. Second, the connotations vary with the power relations between the conflict parties. For example, for the more powerful party, "yielding" to the less powerful party, is a choice that may convey respect. In contrast, for the less powerful party, "yielding" to the more powerful party more likely expresses lack of choice and powerlessness. Third, gender adds an additional layer of meaning to the power relations between both sides. For example, in a heterosexual battering relationship, for the woman who is the target of her partner's abuse, "yielding" to the batterer probably is a survival strategy judged least risky under the circumstances. In contrast, for the batterer, "yielding", if it occurs at all, takes on connotations of a "special favor" that he grants and she will have to repay. With little attention to the structural significance of gender and power, researchers have measured the dual-concern strategies in a variety of settings (Putnam, 1994; van de Vliert, 1990) including couples' responses to conflict and disagreement (Rahim, Kaufman & Magner, 1993).

The dual-concern model attributes strategic choices to the blend of partners' egoistic and altruistic motivations: concern about one's own interests and concern about the other's interests (see Figure 5.1). Contending is interpreted as evidence of high self-concern combined with low other-concern, whereas problem-solving is interpreted as evidence of high self-concern combined with high other-concern. Yielding indicates low self- and high other-concern, whereas inaction indicates low self- and low other-concern (for experimental evidence supporting these links see Ben-Yoav & Pruitt, 1984a,b; Pruitt & Carnevale, 1993).

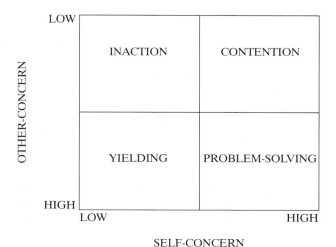

Figure 5.1 Dual concern model

We present the dual-concern model in some depth for several reasons. First, because it parsimoniously relates a broad range of conflict strategies to few underlying factors (for alternative models see Kelley, 1979; Rusbult,

1987). Secondly, what makes the dual-concern notion appealing to conflict management is the idea that opponents are not limited to a zero-sum approach to conflict in which they can choose only between a self-serving and a self-sacrificing approach. Instead, opponents can approach conflict in a way that integrates the interests of both self and other to their mutual benefit. Finally, the dual-concern model provides a focal point from which to examine factors that may shape concern and strategic choice.

Dispositional and Situational Factors in Concern

Feminist scholars such as J. B. Miller (1976) and Gilligan (1982) have argued that women tend to pursue a dual agenda in their social interactions, taking their own interests as well as those of the other party into consideration. More recent work locates evidence in support of such a dual agenda in "enabling" interaction styles (see Maccoby, 1990) or the "double-voice discourse" of young girls (Sheldon, 1992). Notions such as double-voice discourse or "self in relation to other" (J. B. Miller, 1976) capture the same idea as the combination of high self-concern and high other-concern in the dual-concern model: that it is possible to resolve interpersonal conflict constructively by attending to both sides simultaneously. For couple conflict in particular this would mean that, to the extent that women practice a dual agenda, they have the potential to be successful relationship diplomats and peace-makers. Yet, it is evidently not the case that relationships in which women are involved are automatically peaceful (e.g., Straus & Gelles, 1990). Women as peace-makers aside, it is important to realize that couple conflicts bear this contradiction: on the one side there is tremendous potential for constructive conflict management, on the other side couples are facing destructive negativity, deadlock, and violence. This contradiction suggests that the course of conflict reflects complex constraints on strategic choice.

While dispositional constraints are important, such as a socialization-based preference for compromising strategies, situational constraints such as the behavior of the partner can be extremely powerful. Referring to social interaction in general, Maccoby (1990) had argued that women can realize a dual agenda most successfully when interacting with other women but not with men, while men can pursue a self-concerned agenda most successfully when interacting with women rather than with other men. The argument that the viability of self-concerned or dual-concerned strategies is contingent on the interaction partner implies that strategic choice to some extent is constructed situationally and arises from the constraints and options each partner encounters during a particular conflict (see J. Z. Rubin et al., 1994, for the notion of feasible strategies). As observers of conflict we are prone to explain couples' strategic choices in dispositional terms and to underestimate the impact of situational factors (Ross, 1977). Consequently, we will focus on important situational constraints and options, beginning with the structure of conflict.

Conflict Structure and the Demand/Withdraw Pattern

The structure of conflict refers to the distinction between symmetrical and asymmetrical conflicts (Pruitt, 1991). In symmetrical conflicts opponents have incompatible interests but play similar roles. For instance, a young couple argues about how to spend the evening: he wants to spend it on his hobby, she wants to spend it together. In asymmetrical conflicts this issue takes on a different twist: one partner is now in the role of a complainant who wants to change the status quo, while the other partner is in the role of a respondent who is resisting change. Imagine the couple again, after another three years during which they have ended up spending most of their evenings individually. When she raises the issue again, she is now in the complainant's position and needs to overcome years of habit. In contrast, he is now in the respondent's position and wants to maintain cherished habits. Even if we assume that with regard to spending their evenings both partners are self-concerned and try to advance their own interests, the asymmetry of the conflict suggests different strategic choices (Peirce, Pruitt & Czaja, 1991). If she wants to advance her interest in time together, she has to come forward and take an active approach because otherwise things will remain the same (i.e., he will disappear into the den). If he wants to advance his interests in time spent on his hobby, he needs to remain as passive and withdrawn as possible because then things will remain the same (i.e., he will disappear into the den).

Such a conflict may result in what has been termed the "demand/withdraw" pattern, in which one partner "attempts to engage in a problem-solving discussion, often resorting to pressure and demands, while the other partner attempts to avoid or withdraw from the discussion" (Heavey, Layne & Christensen, 1993, p. 16). Observations that women seem to be more often in the role of the pursuer than men (A. Christensen, 1988; Heavey et al., 1993) gave rise to different explanations of this gender pattern. One dispositional explanation emphasizes the differential socialization of men and women. According to this explanation, women engage in conflict because they have been socialized to take care of relationships (Rubin, 1983). An alternative dispositional explanation suggests that men try not to engage in conflict because they find the accompanying physiological arousal more aversive than women (Gottman & Levenson, 1986). However, dispositional explanations overlook potential situational constraints on strategic choice such as the structure of the conflict (Christensen & Heavey, 1990), and neglect strategic aspects of gender differences in reactions to conflict.

With regard to strategic aspects of gender differences in conflict strategies, Sattell (1976), in response to the heavy socialization emphasis in the early literature on "the inexpressive male", has explicated the strategic advantages to men of avoiding or withdrawing from conflict, because such a tactic serves to maintain the status quo. Similarly, Zvoncovic, Greaves, Schmiege & Hall (1996) found that "passive contention" (p. 97) was used by husbands as an effective strategy to pursue their own interests in seemingly consensual family decisions. More recently, feminist scholars have moved away from a heavy emphasis on gender as socialized, to a more balanced focus on the situated construction of gender (West & Fenstermaker, 1993). To the extent that the roles of complainant and respondent are related to a gendered organization of partnership, marriage, or family life, the gender difference in the demand/ withdraw pattern could be constructed situationally.

In fact, several authors have argued that heterosexual relationships, most notably marriage, are set up in a way that benefits the husband and puts the wife at a disadvantage (e.g., Bernard, 1982; Delphy & Leonard, 1992; Jacobson, 1990). In heterosexual relationships, women seem to desire change more often than men (Gottman, 1994). For example, one study of couple conflict (Klein, 1995) found that in 70% of the couples the woman had confronted the issue first. To the extent that the male partner benefits from the arrangement he should resist change. To the extent that the female partner is unsatisfied with the status quo she should desire change and hence find herself more often in the complainant's role facing the difficult task of bringing about change.

In a study to compare dispositional (i.e., gender socialization) and situational (i.e., conflict structure) constraints on strategic choice, Christensen & Heavey (1990) found no gender asymmetry in the demand/withdraw pattern when the husband was the complainant; however, when the wife was the complainant, there was a pronounced gender asymmetry with the wife being in the demanding role more often than the husband. We wonder whether this finding, which was replicated by Heavey et al. (1993), reflects an interaction between conflict structure and dual-concern thinking. A simple conflict structure explanation assumes that all respondents are alike and will stubbornly resist change. However, if we argue that women are more likely than men to entertain a dual-concern agenda, then a wife-respondent should be more likely to consider a husband-complainant, making excessive demands by the husband unnecessary. In contrast, the resistance of a husband-respondent would be amplified by a self-concern agenda, making withdrawal a top priority for the husband and forcing the wife into the demanding position.

Future observations of the demand/withdraw pattern in same-sex couples might shed some light on this issue. Assuming that women import the dual-concern agenda into lesbian relationships and men import the self-concern agenda into gay male relationships, we would suspect that lesbian couples would be less likely to get caught in the demand/withdraw pattern because the complainant would be likely to be interacting with a considerate respondent. In contrast, the demand/withdraw pattern would pose a serious threat to gay male couples because the complainant would more frequently be interacting with a stubborn respondent, resulting in a strong demand/withdraw asymmetry with the complainant forced to pursue vigorously.

We used the demand/withdraw pattern to illustrate our notion that strategic choice is situated in the complex web of partners' general orientations toward self and other and situation-specific constraints in asymmetrical conflict. The demand/withdraw pattern is important because it has been linked to destructive conflict-management and relationship distress (Schaap, Buunk &

Kerkstra, 1988), and may be a precursor of eventual relationship dissolution. For instance, Gottman and his associates argue that withdrawal (or "stone-walling") is a sign of serious communication breakdown and foreshadows relationship dissolution (see Gottman, 1994, for details). Another pattern that has been linked to destructive conflict-management is "negative reciprocity", which we will discuss next.

Negative Reciprocity

Negative reciprocity has been termed a "hallmark of marital conflict" and denotes "the increased tendency to respond to a negative communication from the partner with one's own negative communication" (Epstein, Baucom & Rankin, 1993, p. 51; see also Margolin & Wampold, 1981; Revenstorf, Hahlweg, Schindler & Vogel, 1984). Distressed couples reciprocate negative behavior more often than non-distressed couples (Gottman, Markman & Notarius, 1977) thus demonstrating how difficult it can be to back out of a spiral of angry accusations and sniping remarks (Rubin & Rubin, 1993). Nonetheless, non-distressed couples, although not immune to negative interaction cycles, are able to exit them more quickly than distressed couples, such as physically aggressive couples (Burman, Margolin & John, 1993).

In addition to these differences in negative reciprocity between distressed and non-distressed couples, research on heterosexual married couples suggests gender differences in the likelihood to reciprocate negative behavior. For instance, Gottman et al. (1977) found that nondistressed wives were least likely to reciprocate negative behavior and thus were instrumental in terminating a negative interaction cycle. Similarly, Notarius, Benson, Sloane, Vanzetti & Hornyak (1989) report that distressed wives were least likely to respond with positive behavior. Although these findings suggest that women can be relationship "peace-makers", it is unclear under what conditions women's peace-making develops successfully.

Considering women's dual agenda we can argue that non-distressed wives are better able to integrate their husband's agenda and generate positive responses, whereas distressed wives are less able to do so, presumably because "genuine concern about the other party is enhanced by positive feelings and a perception of common group identity with that party" (Pruitt & Carnevale, 1993, p. 108) both of which may be questionable or even absent in distressed marriages. Genuine concern, and its absence, may also influence how partners interpret a negative exchange. While both partners are more likely to reciprocate the other's negative behavior if they attribute it to negative intent (see Fincham, Bradbury & Scott, 1990; Noller & Ruzzene, 1991), concern for the other may encourage a partner to mistakenly assume a positive intention where there was none (giving the partner the benefit of the doubt), whereas the absence of such concern may encourage partners to mistakenly assume a negative intention (Gaelick, Bodenhausen & Wyer, 1985).

Although negative reciprocity is considered a destructive approach to conflict-management, conflict-engagement (which often includes negative remarks about the partner) can improve relationship satisfaction in the long-run (Gottman & Krokoff, 1989). Yet, constructive conflict-engagement is contingent on the cooperation of both partners (Gottman, 1994). This poses a very real dilemma to the partner who wants to engage in conflict in order to make changes in the relationship. To the extent that cooperation from the respondent in asymmetrical conflict is not very likely, partners who strongly desire change may find themselves caught between a rock and a hard place because the conflict-engagement necessary to improve a relationship can contribute to its very decline.

Faced with the dilemma of trying to engage an unwilling partner to change a relationship he or she is not motivated to change, the complainant could consider two more options: not trying to change the relationship from within but instead leaving it ("exiting" in Hirschman's terminology, 1970; see also Rusbult et al., 1991), or trying to increase the respondent's motivation to collaborate by threatening to leave. These options are generally not viable for a complainant who is very committed to the relationship, and here we find that it is often wives whose various commitments preclude both options, and deepen the dilemma (Oliker, 1989). Wives are in many ways more personally, morally and structurally committed to the relationship than are husbands (M. P. Johnson & Kapinus, 1995). Lennon and Rosenfield (1994) have recently demonstrated that women's economic dependence on a relationship (an aspect of structural commitment) inhibits the development of dissatisfaction with an inequitable division of labor, a dissatisfaction that can be nothing but painful when one is relatively powerless.

To sum up, we think that women are often cast into the role of pursuer as well as primary peacemaker because they more often desire change while social and moral obligations, not to mention economic necessity, force them to change relationships from within. More generally, it appears to us that the social arrangements of intimate relationships exert a powerful influence on the strategic choices partners can make. Taking heterosexual marriage as an example, we wonder to what extent this institutionalized arrangement of male–female relations (Delphy & Leonard, 1992) shapes spouses' strategic choices, such as by putting women into the complainant's position, but generally providing little in the way of resources to bring about change.

As the final part in our discussion of situated constraints on partners' strategic choices we will now consider aggressive and physically violent conflict strategies.

Aggression and Physical Violence

It is unfortunately the case that responses to conflict sometimes involve the use of violence, a "resource" too often ignored in resource theories of power, which tend to draw upon an imagery of civilized exchange between relative equals, one of whom brings a bit more to the relationship than does the other, and thereby gets his or her way more often (Blood & Wolfe, 1960; Frieze & McHugh, 1992; McDonald, 1981; Sabatelli & Shehan, 1993). The authors of the National Family Violence Surveys (Straus & Gelles, 1990) have estimated that conflict strategies involve occasional violence in as many as 50% of American couples. In this connection, we would like to make a distinction between what we have elsewhere called "common couple violence" and "patriarchal terrorism" (M. P. Johnson, 1995).

Common couple violence is the occasional violence that arises out of strong reactions to the escalation of a particular disagreement. It is occasional in two senses: (1) it is situated in the interpersonal dynamics of a particular occasion rather than in a general pattern of power and control; and (2) it happens only occasionally in most families in which it occurs. M. P. Johnson (1995) has argued that this is the type of violence that is tapped by large sample survey research, and the type, therefore, which is the source of the much-quoted 50% estimate alluded to above. The violence identified in the National Family Violence Surveys occurs on average about once every two months, does not seem to escalate, involves both partners in two thirds of the families in which it occurs, and is almost perfectly gender-balanced. This sort of violence is probably best explained by means of theories that focus on the interpersonal dynamics of escalation in conflict situations, on the privatized nature of family life that protects such incidents from public scrutiny, and on a normative context that may accept the "unfortunate" possibility or even likelihood that family conflict will occasionally erupt into "minor" violence.

For obvious ethical reasons, there is no research, at least to our knowledge, that documents the escalation of a heated argument into a physical fight. The escalation explanation implies that violence is a last resort response "at the end" of a sequence of increasingly hostile, aggressive, and desperate exchanges. Minor physical violence, then, should be correlated with other instances of aggressive or desperate behavior. Moreover, those individuals who lack alternative coping skills should be more likely to resort to minor physical violence. In fact, Hammock & Richardson (1992) found moderate but consistent correlations between contentious and physically aggressive conflict strategies. Moreover, during marital interactions in the laboratory, husbands in physically violent relationships displayed more nonverbal signs of irritation and frustration as well as more attacking, defensive and patronizing behaviors than husbands from other distressed but not violent relationships (Margolin, John & Gleberman, 1988; Margolin, Burman & John, 1989). However, wives did not differ across relationships. Margolin et al. (1989) also report that physically aggressive couples lack alternative problem-solving skills. Also, O'Leary & Vivian (1990) report that in abusive couples, problem-solving is characterized by anger and the reciprocation of negative affect; and Murphy and O'Leary (1989, cited in O'Leary & Vivian, 1990) found that verbal abuse predicted the onset to the first instance of physical abuse. Taken together, these findings suggest that occasional violence could result from prolonged, unsuccessful attempts to resolve conflict.

There is another form of family violence that is embedded in a general pattern of power and control rooted in the patriarchal traditions of the family (Dobash & Dobash, 1992). This "patriarchal terrorism" is the sort of violence that is missed almost entirely by large sample surveys, with their 40% non-response rates (M. P. Johnson, 1995), but which shows up clearly in research that draws its data from agencies such as the police, the courts, hospitals and women's shelters. This violence happens frequently in those families in which it occurs (more than once a week on average for the women in shelters), it almost inevitably escalates, and it is initiated almost exclusively by men. The pattern is one of general power and control exercised by means of a variety of control tactics, ranging from economic control and purposeful social isolation to the use of sexual and non-sexual violence (Pence & Paymar, 1993). This sort of violence may not be so easily explained by general theories that focus on the interpersonal dynamics involved in attempts to resolve incompatibilities. The men involved have a need to exercise and to display control as a feature of "ownership" that may have little to do with particular incompatibilities or their partners' responses to them.

The analyses of physical violence in couple conflict serve as an unavoidable reminder of the central role of the cultural and social context in what at times may appear to be a very personal and private matter. Couple conflict can be private in the sense that it often occurs in the privacy of couples' homes and eludes public scrutiny. However, even if conflict occurs in the isolation of anonymous urban apartment blocks or remote rural homes, we think that, in a different sense, the enactment of conflict strategies is not isolated from the wider social context. For instance, norms that legitimize certain conflict strategies and outlaw others (Milardo & Klein, 1992) are likely to influence strategic choices of even geographically isolated couples. While the cultural and social context in which conflict strategies are enacted can be analyzed from various angles, we will in the next section focus on social context in terms of third parties, such as partners' kin and friends.

STRATEGIC CHOICE AND THIRD PARTIES

Although the term third party is most often used to denote a formal role, such as mediator, attorney, counselor, or consultant we use it in a broader sense that includes informal advice and intervention from friends, kin, and other members of partners' social networks (Klein & Milardo, 1993). The following discussion will focus on how informal third parties can shape partners' strategic choices (for a discussion of formal third parties in family conflict see Blades, 1985). This does not mean that third-party influence is unidirectional. To some extent partners grant influence to third parties by deciding with whom they will associate and whom they will ask for advice.

An important aspect of third parties, which we will mention only briefly, is the extent to which third parties are available to each partner. For example, is one partner cut off from his or her family, while the other is living amidst them? Do both partners, or just one of them, have close friends? We think it is important to consider the availability of third parties for each partner separately, not just for the couple as a whole, because separate third parties may exert different types of influence (e.g., partisan support, see Black, 1993) than joint third parties (Klein & Milardo, 1993, 1995).

In this section we will discuss primarily the different ways in which third parties can shape partners' strategic choices, such as by influencing partners' interpretations of the conflict, by providing approval or disapproval for strategic choices, and by providing or withholding necessary resources.

Conflict Interpretation

Several lines of research across different disciplines suggest that third parties can influence how opponents view the conflict (Black, 1993; Donohue, Lyles & Rogan, 1989; Mather & Yngvesson, 1981; Thomas, Schankster & Mathieu, 1994). For example, there is evidence that support and criticism by network members are related to the perceived legitimacy of partners' interests (Klein & Lamm, 1996).

The contribution of best friends to wives' "marriage work" (Oliker, 1989) illustrates the role of informal third parties in conflict interpretation. Marriage work denotes the active involvement of friends in efforts to "achieve or sustain the stability of a marriage or a sense of its adequacy" (Oliker, 1989, p. 123). Best friends helped with the marriage work in several ways. For example, they tried to make the wife see her husband in a rosier light, by generating positive feelings for him ("You know, he's probably feeling real insecure and angry." p. 125), ennobling him ("Doreen tells me, 'Jesse loves you'. And he's this and he's that. She tells me his fine points and puts me in good spirits about him." p. 126), and turning anger directed at the husband into a more "appropriate emotional response" (p. 126).

Anger is inappropriate because the purpose of marriage work is to sustain commitment to the marriage. With one exception, the third parties in Oliker's study helped women resolve "marital conflicts by capitulation or adaptation" (p. 129) rather than conflict engagement. Oliker mentions two reasons for this emphasis on unilateral accommodation. The first concerns the implications of wives' contentiousness on the level of marital interaction, "Taking combative stances after confirmatory discussions with friends, Nancy and others found they provoked husbands' rage and triggered a level of conflict they had not anticipated" (p. 132). The second concerns the implications of wives' contentiousness on the level of losing the economic support associated with marriage, "A majority of women stated flatly that their biggest problem if their marriage ended would be economic survival" (p. 139). Aware of the implications of contentious conflict strategies, third parties helped to interpret the conflict in terms that made accommodative strategies seem more appropriate. This marriage work, supported by best friends, illustrates again how strategic choices can be constrained by power differences between partners arising from the arrangement of intimate relationships.

Support for Strategic Choices

Third parties can also influence strategic choices by approving of and encouraging certain strategies. This type of third party influence is well documented in the realm of bargaining and negotiation such as constituent pressure on negotiators to adopt a tough bargaining stance (Rubin & Brown, 1975). In a study of conflict strategies among young couples where partners were unmarried and the women, unlike those in Oliker's study, were not financially dependent on their partners, we found that those women who claimed support from their own network were less willing to compromise, and those women who claimed support from their partner's network were more willing to engage in contentious strategies (Klein & Milardo, 1995).

Another piece of evidence for the impact of approval by third parties comes from research on abusive peers (DeKeseredy, 1990a). Even if some forms of violence are detached from disagreements and are no longer conflict strategies in our definition (M. P. Johnson, 1995; Lloyd & Emery, 1994), we mention evidence on abusive peers because it is conceivable that aggressive and violent conflict strategies are shaped by third party support. DeKeseredy (1990a) reviewed evidence suggesting that men who have frequent contact with abusive male friends are more likely to abuse their female partners than men who are not exposed to this contact (DeKeseredy, 1990b). The positive correlation between having abusive friends and being abusive, of course, can have different reasons. First of all, it is possible that abusive men prefer to associate with other abusive men and thus actively seek out peer approval of their strategic choices. Secondly, it is not clear to what extent abusive peers are influential because they model aggression and violence, because they approve of violent strategies, or because they fail to disapprove of them.

Nonetheless, the evidence on abusive peers illustrates how third parties can be implicated in partners' strategic choices. More specifically, it illustrates how third parties may contribute to the creation of aggressors. A related question is to what extent third parties contribute to the creation of victims (i.e. easy targets of abuse) by depriving one partner of the resources needed to prevent, avoid, or retaliate against abuse.

Provision of Resources

Baumgartner (1993) cites several anthropological examples of how economic support (e.g., shelter) provided by a wife's family allows her to leave an abusive husband. The partisan support that grows out of strong ties between the wife and her family of origin in some cases includes retaliatory aggression against physical abuse by her husband (Baumgartner, 1993). Family also provide support through the provision of temporary housing. Kirkwood's (1993) study of women in the US and UK who left their abusers found that over one third of the group stayed with family or friends as one step in the process of escape (p. 93). Kirkwood and others have also argued for the central importance of the role of public agencies in providing information about available resources, temporary housing, and direct economic support during the transition from an abusive relationship to independence (Kirkwood, 1993, pp. 89–113; Dobash & Dobash, 1992).

TWO THEORETICAL PERSPECTIVES ON STRATEGIC CHOICE: SENSE-MAKING AND DIFFERENTIAL ADVANTAGE

This final section is guided by two questions about strategic choice: (1) does our understanding of conflict strategies improve if we treat them as evidence of partners' sense-making activity? (2) does our understanding of conflict strategies improve if we treat them as evidence of differential advantage? Sense-making suggests that partners' strategic choices reflect the meaning they impose on interaction sequences (Duck, 1994). Differential advantage suggests that partners' strategic choices reflect the specific constellation of interpersonal power that exists between partners at a given moment in their relationship (Gray-Little & Burks, 1983). In this section we weave the two questions together, as partners make sense of interaction within a context of power and utilize their resources in courses of action suggested by their interpretations (Noller, 1993).

Several authors across different disciplines have argued recently that the development of social relationships (Duck, 1994) and more specifically the management of controversies and disagreements (Morley, 1992) can be understood as a process of continuous interpretation through which the protagonists make sense of each other and their relationship. Examples of sense-making (Duck, 1994), or the construction of meaning, may be attributions of responsibility and blame (Fincham et al., 1990), relationship beliefs (Eidelson & Epstein, 1982), and account-making in relationships (Harvey, Weber & Orbuch, 1990).

A sense-making perspective can increase our understanding of conflict strategies in several ways. First, it draws attention to the processes through which partners interpret each other's behavior, such as attributions and accounts. Second, sense-making suggests that two partners can arrive at different interpretations, and thus draws attention to issues of perspective-taking and understanding (Acitelli, Douvan & Veroff, 1993). Finally, the notion of sense-making suggests that the course of conflict is contingent on any number of factors that influence the construction of meaning, such as cognitive factors in the processing of social relationships (see L. C. Miller & Read, 1991) or exposure to messages that influence the construction of meaning (see Fletcher & Kininmonth, 1991).

We think that a sense-making perspective can increase our understanding of strategic choice if we do not view the construction of meaning as an arbitrary, personal activity of equals who can construct and reconstruct meaning at will. We believe that we need to take into consideration that most strategic choices occur under conditions where one partner has some advantage over the other, whether it is temporary and minimal (e.g., asymmetrical conflict) or ongoing and profound (e.g., based upon differences in structural commitment to the relationship, or the threat and use of physical violence; Klein, 1998).

We use the term differential advantage rather than power in order to emphasize that the specific constellation of one's own interests, partner's behavior, age, third party support, and additional resources, can change over time and benefit one partner today and the other tomorrow (Millar & Rogers, 1988). Although resources (Blood & Wolfe, 1960) and physical force (Frieze & McHugh, 1992) can freeze differential advantage into long-term, unequal power differences, this does not always happen. For instance, higher income does not always translate into more influence on decision-making (see Blumstein & Schwartz, 1991) nor does body strength always translate into getting one's way in a controversy. We use the term differential advantage to convey the idea that it is the specific constellation of self, partner, and third parties at a given point in time that shapes strategic choice, such as the structure of the conflict, the commitment to the relationship, third party support, and other resources.

Sense-making itself may be shaped by the particular constellation among partners and third parties because when we talk about sense-making we can ask to whom things need to make sense and who is the audience for which we create meaning. If strategic choices need to make sense only to the self, then a partner has more freedom in constructing meaning than when strategic choices need to make sense to the partner or third parties. For example, if Melissa tries to make her partner take out the garbage every week, she can explain this to herself in whatever way pleases her most ("I enjoy making other people take out the garbage"). She probably has different explanations for her partner ("I always do the dishes, so you could take care of the garbage"), and maybe even for different third parties (for her mother: "You have to be tight with men, otherwise they dump all chores on you, like Daddy used to"; and for her female friends: "Jack and I really believe in equality in relationships, and we try to split household chores equally").

These scenarios could be considered "rhetorical situations" (Hauser, 1986). Hauser defines rhetorical situations as problems that "discourse can partially or completely resolve" (p. 33), in other words, "problems that can be meaningfully resolved through the uses of speech and writing" (p. 34). The immediate problem that Melissa's sense-making addresses is not garbage removal *per se* but how she, with her respective audience, defines and manages the symbolism of garbage removal for her relationship with her partner.

We need to consider the audience to which sense-making is directed. We need also to keep in mind that audiences are often more than passive recipients of sense-making. One's personal realities are socially constructed, in collaboration with a network of contemporaries, although both the individual and the network draw upon their personal and cultural stock of knowledge for the frameworks that help them to make sense of relationship events (Berger & Luckman, 1966; Schutz & Luckman, 1973). This network of friends, relatives, acquaintances, and professionals with whom one consults regarding one's relationship can be quite active participants in the sense-making process (M. P. Johnson, 1982, pp. 64–73). Thus, while a batterer may insist that he hits his partner only because she asks for it, the counselor and support group at the local women's shelter may offer quite a different interpretive structure (Pence & Paymar, 1993). Kirkwood (1993, pp. 76–78) provides the following example: "one woman explained how, despite the loss of most friends and the accompanying sense of intense isolation, one friend in particular continued to maintain close contact. She planned meetings with this woman nearly every day, away from the apartment she shared with her abuser. Most of their meetings were spent with the friend simply listening to the woman, although at times, she would make pertinent comments on how an event might be related to specific feelings voiced by the woman. Over time, the woman began to trust this friend and, together, they explored her relationship and its impact."

Although the self as the audience of sense-making may allow considerable freedom, it can impose limits such as when strategic choices are made in the service of saving face (Ting-Toomey, Gao, Trubisky, Yang, Kim, Lin & Nishida, 1991) or preserving the integrity of the self (Bartky, 1990). The partner as the audience can impose other limits on sense-making. For example, partners can be unable to understand what we mean (Kelley, 1979; Noller & Ruzzene, 1991; Sillars, Folwell, Hill, Maki, Hurst & Casano, 1994) or unwilling to share in our experience (Harber & Pennebaker, 1992). Partners and third parties as audiences can try to prescribe what they consider acceptable sense-making, for example by defining what are "rational" and "irrational" accounts for relationship problems. Partners and third parties can confront us with the limits of culturally acceptable accounts for strategic choices. A violent husband will find it easier to explain his wife-battering to his abusive peers than to the staff of the local women's shelter. More generally, it is easier to justify aggressive strategic choice to an audience who believe that escalation of conflict into physical violence is "normal" (Harris, Gergen & Lannamann, 1986), or that anger "triggers" violent outbursts (Averill, 1993; Tavris, 1982) than to an audience who objects to these beliefs.

Future research needs to examine to what extent sense-making and differential advantage explanations are useful in understanding either retrospective accounts of strategic choice or on-going strategic choices. A sense-making perspective may be particularly sensitive to the development of retrospective accounts of couple conflict (e.g., Buehlman, Gottman & Katz, 1992), whereas a differential advantage perspective may be sensitive to the development of ongoing choices in relationships. Of course, both aspects, sense-making and differential advantage may work together so that partners make some choices based on differential advantage and then look back and interpret their choices in light of a comprehensive organizing scheme. Kirkwood (1993, p. 114), for example, speaks of the "long-term reconstruction of their identity and self-

esteem . . . [and] continued recognition and rejection of the damaging messages about themselves instilled by their abusers" that is an important part of
the process of healing that follows the end of an abusive relationship. This
process is one example of the continued interpretation of one's biography that
has long been a theme of phenomenological sociology (Travisano, 1970).

Hopper (1993) concluded from his study of divorce rhetoric that "divorce
may be a more disorganized and more random unfolding of events" than we
presume (p. 811). Prior to the divorce both spouses reported "similar feelings
of indecision and ambivalence. They described pain, dissatisfaction, and feelings of being trapped; at the same time, they described good things that they
did not want to forgo." (Hopper, 1993, p. 806). As soon as one spouse had
announced the decision to divorce (which we might add could have been
made on the basis of differential advantage), spouses were cast into the roles
of initiator and non-initiator and from that point on their accounts differed
systematically, with initiators' rhetoric drawing from the vocabulary of change
and non-initiators' rhetoric drawing from the vocabulary of commitment. It is
as if the declaration of initiator had flipped an ambivalent and disturbing—
chaotic—experience into a coherent and meaningful one. Of course, these
chaotic experiences are not interpreted in isolation. Such dramatic experiences cry out for interpretation (P. L. Berger, 1963, pp. 147–163) that is
constructed in concert with others (Brown, Feldberg, Fox & Kohen, 1976).

Future research needs to address under what conditions sense-making improves or impedes conflict management. For instance, from a sense-making
perspective we would argue that distressed couples get caught in negative
exchanges because they interpret each other's behaviors in consistently negative terms, whereas non-distressed couples are able to exit negative exchanges
because they interpret each other's behaviors in positive terms (Fincham et
al., 1990). Both negative–negative and negative–positive exchanges could be
"reactive contingencies" (Jones & Gerard, 1967, pp. 505–513), in which the
behavior of one partner can be predicted from the behavior of the other
partner. However, the available evidence suggests that in non-distressed couples, one partner's behavior is not as contingent on the other's as in distressed
couples (Gottman, 1994, pp. 63–64). We wonder whether these "unpredictable" couples move from a reactive to a "pseudocontingency" (in which
partners' actions are not contingent on the other's behavior; Jones & Gerard,
1967, pp. 505–513) because they temporarily stop making sense of each other.
The question is whether sense-making can backfire if partners impose meanings on each other's behaviors that lead them into deadlock, when they would
be better off assuming occasional "senselessness" in their exchanges.

SUMMARY AND CONCLUSION

Many couple conflicts arise from incompatible goals and interests. To achieve
their goals, partners engage in a variety of conflict-management strategies
ranging from problem-solving and compromise to unilateral accommodation,

and the use of insults, threats, and physical force. In this chapter we discussed factors that shape partners choices among different strategies. Starting with the dual-concern model we explored how egoistic and altruistic motivations affect strategic choice. Using evidence on the demand/withdraw pattern we tried to show how strategic choices may result from interactions between individual motivations and features of partners' social contexts such as the structure of conflict.

We used evidence on negative reciprocity and physical violence among spouses to further illustrate how seemingly personal choices are made within the context of social constraints such as women's economic dependence on marriage. A different aspect of the social context of partners' strategic choices are third parties such as family, friends, and professionals who can influence couple conflict by interpreting the controversial issues, supporting strategic choices, and providing or withholding necessary resources. From a theoretical perspective the evidence on strategic choice in couple conflict speaks to the importance of partners' sense-making in the context of differential power and unequal resources.

We believe that the concept of strategic choice provides a fruitful starting point for our understanding of couples' conflict management. However, we believe that strategic choices cannot be understood as individual phenomena. Rather, it is necessary to pay attention to the features of partners' social contexts that shape and constrain their options. In a similar vein, Rubin et al. (1994) have argued that although concern motivates strategic choice, in order for strategies to be adopted, they need to be seen as feasible. We conclude from our review that the feasibility of conflict-management options in couple conflict depends on several aspects of each partner's social context: the other partner, culturally available interpretation schemes, third parties, and the precise configuration of interpersonal, social, and economic power.

Chapter 6

Work and Family from a Dyadic Perspective: Variations in Inequality

Ann C. Crouter

and

Heather Helms-Erikson

Penn State University, PA, USA

Employed men and women spend a large portion of their adult lives on the job. On work days, they head off to factories, mines, offices, hospitals, schools, and stores where they become engaged in activities that often have profound effects on their own psychological development, as well as on their family roles and relationships (Crouter & McHale, 1993).

For dual-earner families, the work–family interface is particularly complex because there are two sets of workplace influences to consider: his and hers (Hoffman, 1984). Husbands and wives in dual-earner families each bring to the family their own work-related histories and current work experiences that must be understood *in combination* with those of their partner. Understanding the impact of work on family relationships in dual-earner families requires attention both to the separate, work-related experiences of each spouse and to the relative experiences of a wife and her husband (Brayfield, 1992). It requires conceptualizing the work–family interface from the perspective of the dyad.

Families as Relationships.
Edited by Robert M. Milardo and Steve Duck. © 2000 John Wiley & Sons Ltd.

A dyadic perspective on the impact of work on family relationships underscores differences in the circumstances of paid employment for men and women. The work world is highly stratified by gender. Men and women generally work in different occupations, with women clustered in a narrow range of jobs that are relatively poorly paid and offer few chances for advancement (England & McCreary, 1987). Even when men and women are found in the same occupation, they tend to be clustered in different lines of work, or different types of firms, within that occupation (Bielby & Baron, 1984).

England and McCreary (1987) present four major factors underlying occupational segregation: gender role socialization in childhood and adolescence leading to differential educational choices and career aspirations on the part of men and women; differences in the extent to which men and women invest in their own "human capital" such as education and job training; discrimination against women in hiring, placement, and promotion; and differences in the structured mobility ladders within occupations. One clear correlate of gender segregation in the workplace is income inequality; in 1998, on average, employed women earned 76 cents for every dollar earned by men (Another real raise, 1999; White & Rogers, in press).

There are other important differences in the work-related experiences of wives and husbands, some of which stem from the fact that wives generally garner fewer resources from their jobs than do their husbands and hence may have less bargaining power in the context of family decision-making. Women are more likely than men to leave a job and to move to a new location in response to a job opportunity for their spouse (Shihadeh, 1991). Women are more likely to take time off at the birth of a child (Ferber, O'Farrell, & Allen, 1991) and to be absent from work when children are sick than are men (Fernandez, 1986). Even in Sweden, a country that has sought to promote equality between men and women, men are much less likely than women to take advantage of the generous parental leave benefits offered to new parents (Haas, 1992).

What does the fact that men and women have quite divergent occupational worlds mean for dual-earner couples? On average, husbands and wives have unequal access to work-related resources such as income and prestige. Other work conditions that are important influences on adults' psychosocial functioning—such as occupational self-direction, authority, and job complexity—are also likely to be unequal, on average, for a given husband and wife in a dual-earner family. But the term, "on average", masks considerable variability across families in the extent to which husbands and wives experience similar versus different work worlds. In many families, the occupational conditions of husbands and wives are so different that Perry-Jenkins and Folk (1994) have argued that "social class" is more accurately conceptualized and measured as an individual-level variable than as a family-level condition; in other families, spouses' experiences on the job are quite similar.

The circumstances that give rise to systematic differences in husbands' and wives' work experiences—and the implications of these "variations in inequality" for family roles and relationships—deserve to be a focus of study for research on work and family. This area of study can be examined from several theoretical perspectives. A focus on within-couple variability in the experience of work is consistent with a feminist perspective on the family because it emphasizes that the family is not "a unitary whole . . . (with) a single class position, standard of living, and set of interests" (Ferree, 1990, p. 867). It is also consistent with the notion of the family as "a non-shared environment". This construct has emerged from research in behavioral genetics to help to explain why siblings growing up "in the same family" are so different from one another (Dunn & Plomin, 1990), but it also nicely captures the dramatic differences in the work and family lives of many wives and husbands.

In this chapter, we consider three dimensions of work experience and their implications for relationships in dual-earner families. In reviewing the literature in each area, we take a dyadic perspective which recognizes that, in dual-earner families, the implications of one spouse's experiences at work can be understood only in relation to the partner's work experiences. The first dimension that we examine is spouses' access to work-related resources such as income and occupational prestige. In social exchange terms, a wife's resources, relative to those contributed by her husband, are one determinant of her power in the marriage. Most research in this area has focused on domestic work and has asked whether husbands are likely to perform a greater share of household work when their wives bring in a larger share of resources from work. Work status, income, and prestige tell only part of the story, however; it is also important to understand how husbands and wives think and feel about work and family roles. The second occupational condition we consider is job complexity and the extent to which work encourages adults to value self-direction for themselves and others. There is a rich body of sociological literature that has demonstrated that adults are socialized by the work that they do (Kohn, 1977; Kohn & Schooler, 1983; Mortimer, Lorence, & Kumka, 1986; Parcel & Menaghan, 1994). Men and women in jobs that offer opportunities to be self-directed and provide complex, challenging activities become intellectually better able to deal with complexity and more apt to create complex, stimulating environments for themselves and their children (Kohn & Schooler, 1983; Parcel & Menaghan, 1994). A dyadic perspective addresses the question: What implications does this process of work socialization have for families when husbands and wives have similar—or different—levels of access to complex, self-directed work? The third work condition of interest has to do with short-term work stressors and overloads, the daily work-related tensions and pressures that may spill over into family life. Here, a dyadic perspective draws attention to what we know about these processes for men and for women, and whether husbands and wives respond in the same way to their spouse's experience of day-to-day stress on the job.

HUSBAND–WIFE DIFFERENCES IN WORK-RELATED RESOURCES

We begin by considering the connections between husbands' and wives' access to work-related resources and their family roles and relationships. Most of the research in this area has focused on the division of housework, specifically the conditions under which men assume more responsibility for performing the household tasks that have been traditionally handled by women, such as cooking, cleaning, and laundry. The other role that has received attention is that of provider or breadwinner. As we will show, this field has evolved in interesting directions, as studies have gradually taken more complex and differentiated approaches to the study of family roles.

Before considering how family roles may be affected by spouses' access to work-related resources, it is important to understand what we mean by the term, "role." Peplau (1983) defines a role as a consistent pattern of individual activity composed of behavior, cognition, and affect. This pattern of activity develops in the context of a relationship with one or more other people and is influenced not only by expectations of the individuals involved but also by cultural norms and partners' shared relationship goals.

All three components of roles—behavior, cognition, and affect—must be considered in order to understand how the differential resources of wives and husbands are linked to how couples structure the homemaker and provider roles. Behavioral patterns refer to events and activities. Part of the provider role, for example, involves working at a paid job. Role behavior also refers to the distribution of activities between partners in a relationship, as in the way a husband and wife divide household tasks. The cognitive domain involves how spouses think about and ascribe meaning to their family roles. Wives and husbands, for example, develop notions of "fairness" that influence their level of involvement in family work (Thompson, 1991). Finally, affect accompanies roles. Emotional experiences are an important part of roles in close relationships, emerging not only as a response to behavior but also prompting behavior. These three components of roles (i.e., behavior, cognition, and affect) provide a useful way to organize the literature on how husbands' and wives' differential work-related resources influence family roles.

Until recently, far more attention was given to the behavioral than to the cognitive and emotional components of family roles. For many years, researchers assumed that as women entered the paid labor force in greater numbers, men would respond by increasing their level of behavioral involvement in unpaid family work. This logic was consistent with the principles of social exchange theory; the assumption was that women would gain new resources through paid employment with which to bargain for greater assistance with family work. However, time diary studies conducted in the 1970s revealed that husbands did *not* participate in more housework and child care when their wives worked outside the home (Meissner, Humphries, Meis, & Scheu, 1975; Robinson, 1977; Walker & Woods, 1976); men in dual-earner families performed proportionally more housework than their single-earner counterparts only because their wives decreased their level of involvement in housework when employed outside the home. More recent studies confirm this pattern; however, they also stress the *variability* across dual-earner families in the way wives and husbands divide family work (Ferree, 1991). Understanding the conditions under which wives and husbands divide housework more or less equally requires attention not only to spouses' work status, but to the absolute and relative levels of resources that each partner acquires on the job, as well as to partners' attitudes, cognitions, and feelings about work and family roles.

Research addressing the effects of absolute earnings and occupational prestige on husbands' and wives' family work has yielded mixed findings. Results from several studies indicate that husbands' and wives' incomes are important determinants of the division of family work (Berk & Berk, 1978; Kamo, 1988; Maret & Finlay, 1984); yet other findings reveal weak or no effects for income on how family work is allocated between spouses (Berardo, Shehan, Leslie, 1987; Coverman & Sheley, 1986). Likewise, several researchers have found that spouses' job prestige is not related to spouses' division of labor (Coverman, 1985; Berardo et al, 1987), while others have found husbands' relative share of housework to be related to their job prestige (Berk & Berk, 1978).

A dyadic perspective on work-related resources draws attention to the "gap" in work-related resources of wives relative to their husbands and how these measures may interact with gender (Ericksen, Yancey, & Ericksen, 1979; Ferree, 1988; Ross, 1987). For example, Ross (1987) demonstrated that the more husbands earn relative to their wives, the less husbands proportionally contribute to family work. Similarly, McHale and Crouter (1992) found that greater income and prestige discrepancies favoring husbands were associated with a more traditional division of housework.

Brayfield's (1992) study of Canadian couples reveals the importance of considering both absolute *and* relative work-related resources. In her study, wives at all income levels were found to "benefit" from a relative income advantage over their husbands, meaning that the more income wives earned relative to their husbands, the fewer female-type household tasks wives performed. Similarly, husbands performed fewer female-type tasks when they earned more than their wives. For husbands, however, the effect of the relative income advantage depended on husbands' absolute income. At the lower end of the income distribution, the relative income advantage was strongly connected to husbands' performing fewer tasks. At the upper end, however, the association was attentuated. Brayfield speculates that the relative advantage in income did not "benefit" high income men as much as low income men because men at the upper end of the income distribution tend to be better educated and to favor a more egalitarian division of labor. Brayfield's interpretation of her results illustrates the importance of examining role-related attitudes and cognitions in conjunction with behavior, data that were not available in her data set.

In recent years, there has been a "very substantial and continuing transformation of sex role attitudes in the United States" (Thornton, 1989, p. 875); men and women have generally become more egalitarian in their attitudes and expectations about family roles (Thornton, 1989). Underlying this demographic shift is considerable variability in attitudes across individuals, as well as differences between families in husbands' and wives' level of consensus on sex role attitudes. The way wives and husbands think about and define their work and family roles plays an important part in whether and how wives utilize power obtained from job earnings and prestige. Furthermore, the convergence of behavior and attitudes around work and family roles is linked to partners' subjective evaluations of their marital relationships.

The distinction between role enactment (i.e., behavior) and cognitions or attitudes is apparent in research on the role of provider or breadwinner. As Hood (1986) explained: "Provider roles are determined not only by incomes but also by each spouse's expectations of the other as a provider as well as each spouse's role attachments—that is, the investment one has in one's present role." (p.354). Although partners in dual-earner families both have incomes and thus can provide financial resources for the family, paid work often holds different meanings for husbands and wives. For example, even though most married women work outside the home and their earnings account for at least 30% of the family income on average, most wives are not assuming the provider role nor are husbands relinquishing breadwinning or the psychological responsibility to provide (Haas, 1986; Hood, 1986).

Hood (1986) used qualitative interviews with husbands and wives in dual-earner families to identify three types of providers. Main/secondary providers view the husband as responsible for providing for the family and the wife as primarily responsible for homemaking; the wife's income is seen as helpful, rather than necessary. In contrast, coproviders acknowledge the importance of both spouses' incomes to the family's financial stability and see both partners as responsible for providing. Finally, ambivalent coproviders are dependent on both partners' incomes but are unwilling to acknowledge the importance of the wife's role as a provider. Hood (1986) offered a revealing quote from an ambivalent coprovider husband:

> Like now, we just use her paycheck to pay the house payments. So that's about all we do with hers . . . just pay the house payments. So that's a whole lot of money I don't have to worry about (p. 355).

Provider-role attitudes are linked to husbands' and wives' behavior in the home. Examining couples in which both husbands and wives worked full-time, Perry-Jenkins and Crouter (1990) found that husbands' provider-role attitudes were associated with their involvement in family work; husbands ascribing to a main/secondary provider orientation were less involved in traditionally feminine household tasks than either ambivalent coproviders or coproviders. Furthermore, involvement in household tasks had different implications for men's marital satisfaction depending upon their provider role attitudes. Husbands who reported the greatest marital satisfaction were main/secondary providers who performed relatively few household tasks and coproviders who shared household task more equally with their wives. The combination of being highly involved in housework—yet holding ambivalent coprovider attitudes—was linked to lower levels of marital satisfaction for husbands.

Ferree (1987) provides converging evidence for the importance of providing or breadwinning from the perspective of wives. She found that women who defined themselves as breadwinners thought their husbands should con- tribute more to family work. This finding was particularly true for working- class wives for whom earning money and assuming the breadwinner role led to a willingness to insist on more help with housework from husbands. Ferree suggests that it is not the amount of paid work done by a wife, but rather what a wife's work means to the family that empowers wives to make greater demands on their husbands.

Thompson (1991) argues that the connections between spouses' paid work and family work cannot be understood without reference to their ideas about "fairness". Surprisingly, although most wives perform a greater proportion of household tasks than their husbands, only a small number of wives in dual- earner families view the division of family work as unfair (Thompson & Walker, 1989). Thompson suggests that husbands and wives assess fairness in their relationship based on how much each spouse values particular family chores, how well and how often they perform tasks as compared to other husbands and wives, and how well they can justify not performing certain tasks. Blair and Johnson (1992) note that the symbolic meaning of household tasks as an act of caring is an important correlate of fairness; women who feel that their contribution to housework is appreciated see the division of labor as more fair.

Concerns about lack of fairness can lead to low marital satisfaction and higher levels of conflict between spouses (Blair, 1993; Perry-Jenkins & Folk, 1994; Wilkie, Ratcliff & Ferree, 1992). For example, Wilkie et al. (1992) found that it was not partners' differences in the amount of domestic or paid work that determined marital satisfaction; rather, it was their different expectations about and the meanings they ascribed to the division of paid and unpaid work that predicted marital satisfaction. Blair (1993) found that wives' assessment of inequity in their marriages was the strongest predictor of both husbands' and wives' perceptions of marital conflict, a theme echoed by Perry-Jenkins and Folk's (1994) analyses of middle-class wives' perceptions of fairness and their reports of marital conflict. Finally, McHale and Crouter (1992) found that wives with relatively nontraditional sex-role attitudes—who nonetheless were experiencing a more traditional division of family work—reported lower marital quality, less marital satisfaction and greater marital conflict, in com- parison both to their own husbands and to other women. The same pattern held true for husbands who espoused traditional sex-role attitudes but were sharing family work more equally with their wives.

In sum, the relative and absolute resources that husbands and wives each bring from work to the family help to determine the way in which they divide family work. Earning similar or greater income than their husbands and achieving similar or greater occupational status helps wives to bargain for more involvement in housework on the part of their partners. But work- related resources reveal only a limited part of the picture. The division of labor also depends upon husbands' and wives' attitudes and cognitions about roles, including whether or not they have assumed the responsibility to be a provider or breadwinner. Finally, partners' feelings of dissatisfaction with the relationship are evoked when role behavior and attitudes are at odds and partners feel that their current arrangement is not fair.

SPOUSAL INEQUALITY IN WORK COMPLEXITY

We began our review by focusing on income and prestige because there is ample evidence that the extent of resources contributed to the family by wives versus their husbands is linked to the division of family work and to relationship dynamics. A less obvious occupational "resource" has to do with the *nature* of the work that men and women perform, specifically the complexity of the work and the extent to which it offers the worker opportunities to be independent and self-directed. While considerable research has been conducted in this area, attention to the occupational complexity experienced by husbands and wives in the same family is rare (see Parcel & Menaghan, 1994).

The focus on occupational complexity and self-direction grew out of Kohn's classic study on social class in relation to parental values and child-rearing strategies (Kohn 1969, 1977; Kohn & Schooler, 1983). Basing his conclusions on a national survey of over 3000 employed men, Kohn argued that men in working-class jobs come to value conformity and obedience in their children because they recognize that these are the qualities needed to be successful in a working-class world, while their counterparts in middle-class occupations come to value self-direction and independence for the same reason. As Kohn explained in *Class and Conformity* (1977):

> Members of different social classes, by virtue of enjoying (or suffering) different conditions of life, come to see the world differently—to develop different conceptions of social reality, different aspirations and hopes and fears, different "conceptions of the desirable" (p. 7).

In later work, Kohn and his colleagues focused on three occupational conditions that determine how self-directed one can be in one's work and thus lie at the heart of what has come to be understood as social class: freedom from close supervision, a nonroutinized flow of work, and substantively complex work. The substantive complexity of work has received the most attention and is most germane to the focus of this chapter.

Using ten-year longitudinal follow-up data on their national sample of employed men, Kohn and his colleagues demonstrated that having a job characterized by substantive complexity influences men's views of the world. That is, over time, men come to value self-direction for themselves and for others, and they become more "intellectually flexible", meaning that they are better able to manipulate ideas and to see multiple sides of an issue (Kohn & Schooler, 1983). Moreover, the substantive complexity of work, over time, promotes a more intellectual choice of leisure activities, "evidence that people generalize directly from job experience to the activities they perform in their leisure time" (Miller & Kohn, 1983, p. 240). Kohn and his colleagues were able to use their longitudinal data to explore whether the causal arrow also runs the other way, that is from intellectual flexibility and the intellectuality of leisure to substantive complexity on the job. Indeed, these processes exist, but they are generally lagged rather than contemporaneous, meaning that, over time, men modify their jobs or leave them for other jobs that are more consistent with their intellectual functioning. Despite these selection effects, strong processes are apparent that indicate that jobs socialize people in ways that have implications for personality and behavior off the job.

Kohn and his colleagues did not take their line of reasoning in the direction of considering the implications of occupational self-direction for family relationships, but others have. Pioneers in this area are Parcel and Menaghan (1994) who have utilized the National Longitudinal Survey of Youth to explore, with longitudinal data, the implications of parental work conditions for the kinds of home environments that parents establish for their young children and, in turn, for children's psychological functioning. Parcel and Menaghan document that, controlling for education, age, intelligence, income, and other potential confounding variables, mothers employed in jobs characterized by greater substantive complexity create more stimulating home environments for their children. Most interesting, from a dyadic perspective, although father's job complexity in and of itself is not related to the home environment, the positive effects of high maternal occupational complexity are most apparent when the father in the family is employed in a job that is low on complexity . A theme in Parcel and Menaghan's research is that the effects of one parent's working conditions depend upon those of the other parent.

Parcel and Menaghan's work is rife with interesting interaction effects that illustrate the complexity of work–family linkages from a dyadic perspective. For example, in an examination of the correlates of problem behavior in young children, they report that the effect of a mother quitting work and becoming a homemaker depends to a large extent on the nature of the paid work that she was performing. Quitting work has the positive effect of reducing subsequent behavior problems in the child *only if the mother's job had been characterized by low occupational complexity or very long hours.* Similarly, mothers with higher levels of intellectual ability tended to have children with greater verbal facility, but this association was enhanced when mothers worked in jobs characterized by complexity. Parcel and Menaghan argue that complex jobs reinforce and strengthen mothers' intellectual skills in ways that pay off for their children's learning.

Occupational complexity is not always uniformly positive in its effects, however. Parcel and Menaghan, again demonstrating sensitivity to the importance of considering husband–wife combinations of work conditions, report that jobs high in complexity tend to absorb time and energy and that this can be problematic for children's psychosocial functioning under certain conditions: when parents have large numbers of children, when they are adjusting to a recent birth, or when both parents in the family face the demands of highly complex jobs.

Parcel and Menaghan's research indicates that, "having a parent in a complex job can be a resource for children in that it sets a high level of expectation regarding self-direction and intellectual flexibility, qualities that should increase children's socioeconomic well-being as they mature" (1994, p. 14). The day-to-day experience of work socializes parents to have certain values regarding self-direction and either provides opportunities to practice intellectual and social skills that in turn can be applied to childrearing or impedes such opportunities and skills. But what of the marital relationship? Does the extent to which husbands and wives have access to complex and self-directed jobs have any implications for their marital relations?

Although few studies have explored the links between spouses' access to occupational self-direction and the marital relationship, there is ample evidence that this is an area well worth greater attention. Brayfield's (1992) analysis of Canadian data tested the idea, based on social exchange theory, that "husbands' and wives' employment characteristics influence the balance of power over the distribution of feminine-typed (household) tasks" (p. 20). Brayfield examined not only husbands' and wives' relative and absolute incomes, but also their levels of workplace authority, reasoning that, "Power on the job may influence power in the family" (p. 21). She found that women with greater workplace authority performed fewer household chores, especially if they had greater authority on their job than their husband had on his job. This effect was most pronounced for women at higher levels of authority.

The effects of relative access on the part of husbands and wives to jobs that encourage self-direction and provide complex, interesting work may be most apparent in situations in which the workplace—or the job—is undergoing a fundamental change in the way that it is organized. Crouter (1984a) conducted qualitative research in a manufacturing plant that was experimenting with "participative approaches to management". Blue collar workers on the factory floor were organized into work teams that were given an unusual level of responsibility for hiring and firing, quality control, and inventory management. The manufacturing and assembly work was also reorganized so that teams were responsible for large, complex tasks such as assembling an entire engine. Workers were paid on the basis of skill level, rather than seniority, and were encouraged to rotate through new tasks and to take training courses in order to master new skills quickly. The result of all of these changes was a push for self-directed, complex work at the blue collar level.

Open-ended interviews were conducted with men and women in a variety of types of work teams. The most striking comments relating to the marital relationship came from women in blue collar manufacturing and assembly teams. They described a complex process in which the challenges of participative work had pushed them to develop new skills and abilities, a process they described as both stimulating and stressful. As a result of these experiences, they reported feeling a new sense of self-confidence and self-efficacy, as well as a strong feeling of loyalty and commitment to fellow team members. Several women noted, however, that their husbands resented their new skills and felt threatened by their new levels of self-confidence. These men worked in traditionally managed factories in the same community and were denied the same opportunities for personal growth. As one female worker explained:

> My husband got to the point where he didn't want to hear about my work. He's a little threatened by my learning new things . . . He felt like he was stupid and I was smart, and he wanted to keep up with me (Crouter, 1984a, p. 80).

Differences in husbands' and wives' feelings of self-esteem and competence may underlie power dynamics in the marriage. Kompter (1989) argued that gender differences in perceptions of self and spouse "may be regarded as invisible power mechanisms because they confirm and justify power inequality ideologically, unintentionally, and often unconsciously" (p. 207). In Kompter's semi-structured interviews with Dutch, dual-earner, working and middle class couples, wives expressed less self-esteem than did men and saw themselves as less competent than their husbands. Husbands saw themselves as more competent than their wives, particularly when their wives were homemakers. As Kompter explains:

> The husbands' greater self-esteem gave them greater marital bargaining power . . . The power effect is invisible because the apparent naturalness of the assumed differences in personality traits prevents wives and husbands from acknowledging it. (Kompter, 1989, p. 208)

Kompter's argument reveals why the husbands of blue collar women who were engaged in highly demanding participative work felt threatened. It also illuminates why male employees in the same factory never described their wives as feeling threatened by their access to complex, self-directed work; those wives probably saw their husbands' growing sense of competence and self-esteem as expected and natural. These findings underscore themes that emerged earlier in our review of the literature on husbands' and wives' differential access to work-related resources. Again we see that differences in spouses' access to complex, self-directed work must be examined in light of their cognitive interpretations of these differences. Moreover, these cognitive schemata are gendered. For many couples, it may be "natural" for husbands to have jobs that provide more opportunities to exercise self-direction than their wife's job provides; when the situation is reversed, however, and the wife is given an opportunity to develop on the job that exceeds that of her husband, the situation is seen as unusual and, sometimes, as a source of resentment.

THE IMPACT OF DAILY WORK STRESS ON HUSBANDS AND WIVES

Thus far, we have written about husbands' and wives' employment as if it were an emotionally neutral experience. We have emphasized the importance of the differential resources garnered by husbands and wives through their jobs, and we have explored the psychological impact of substantively complex, self-directed work. Regardless of the kinds of jobs that men and women hold—and the resources they receive for performing that work—there is an emotional tone underlying the work experience that has implications for relationships in the family. Over the last decade, a small body of carefully conducted, methodologically sophisticated research has emerged that examines, on a day-to-day basis, whether—and how—fluctuations in stress and strain on the job affect interactions at home (see Larson & Almeida, 1999). Several studies have focused on how one partner's daily work stress is linked to the other partner's affect or behavior in the family, and the literature has consistently compared men's and women's emotional lives at work and at home, as well as the reactivity of men versus women to short-term stressors.

With an interest in the contextual conditions surrounding family members' experience of emotions, Larson and Richards (1994) collected data on mothers, fathers, and their adolescent offspring using the "experience sampling method", an approach in which family members carried electronic beepers throughout the day and were paged at random moments. When paged, they completed brief questionnaires about their activities, companions, and emotional states. Larson and Richards' data on the contrasting moods of mothers and fathers at work and at home underscore how differently men and women perceive and experience these contexts. Employed wives recorded their most positive moods while at work; indeed, wives' emotions were generally more positive than were husbands' when they were paged on the job. Wives, however, experienced an emotional decline at home during the evening hours which were filled with housework and child care (see also Wells, 1988). Husbands, on the other hand, recorded their most negative emotions in the workplace; at home, their moods lightened, in part because non-work time provided a source of leisure for them. Even when men performed housework or child care, however, their moods during these tasks were more positive than was the case for their wives when they performed the same activities. Larson and Richards (1994) propose that housework and child care elicit a more positive reaction from husbands than wives because it is seen as *voluntary* work by husbands. Men get involved when they are "in the mood," and their efforts are noted and appreciated by wives (see also Thompson, 1991).

What are the kinds of events at work or at home that elicit emotional reactions? Bolger, DeLongis, Kessler and Wethington (1989) asked 166 married couples to complete a daily diary for 42 consecutive days. The diary consisted of a short questionnaire about a variety of daily stressors , including the experience of "overloads" and "tensions or arguments" both at work and at home. In the analyses of these data, "day" was treated as the unit of analysis, and controls were entered to hold constant individual differences that were stable across days; thus, the analyses focused on intra-individual variability in the experience of stressors across days. Analyses of work-to-home spillover of stress revealed that, on days when husbands experienced an argument at work with a co-worker or supervisor, they came home and engaged in more arguments with their wives. The pattern was similar—though not statistically significant—when wives experienced arguments at work. On days when husbands experienced "overloads" at work (meaning having to do a lot of work), they performed less work at home; on those stressful days, their wives stepped in and performed more work at home. The parallel pattern did not occur, however; when wives experienced overloads at work they too performed less work at home, but their husbands did not step in and perform more. Bolger et al. (1989) summarize these data as follows:

> Thus, in terms of coping with a contagion of role overload from the workplace into the home, the most appropriate unit of analysis is clearly the marital dyad, with wives, in particular, acting as buffers for their husbands, protecting them from excessive accumulation of role demands. (p. 181)

Bolger and his colleagues offer this finding as one possible explanation for the fact that marriage has been found to benefit the emotional health of men more than that of women (Kessler & McRae, 1982). Building on the argument we have developed in this chapter, we would argue that this "asymmetry in the buffering effect" (Bolger et al., 1989, p. 182) mirrors the power dynamic in the marriage. Future research should explore the hypothesis that wives are more likely to take on the buffering role—and husbands less likely to do so—when wives are disadvantaged, relative to their husbands, in the extent to which their work provides income and prestige, as well as substantive complexity, encouragement of self-direction, and authority.

How are children influenced by daily fluctuations in their parents' experiences of stress and work? Bolger et al.'s study examined arguments with spouse and arguments with children separately and found no significant associations between work overload or work arguments and subsequent arguments with children, suggesting that parents may generally be able to buffer their children from these effects. Findings from a study of the implications of more global levels of work stress suggest otherwise, however. Crouter, Bumpus, Maguire, and McHale (1999) used structural equation modeling to examine the links between husbands' and wives' global reports of work pressure, feelings of role overload, conflict with adolescent offspring, and adolescent psychological well-being. Consistent with the Bolger et al. (1989) findings, Crouter et al. (1999) found that husbands' work pressure was related not only to their own feelings of role overload, but to their wives' role overload as well. In contrast, wives' reports of work pressure were linked only to their own feelings of role overload, not to their husbands'. Feelings of being overloaded were important because they were related in turn to heightened parent–adolescent conflict, which in turn predicted lower adolescent psychological well-being (as indexed by measures of general self-worth and depressive affect).

One of the mechanisms through which children may be buffered from the spillover of negative work experiences is emotional and behavioral withdrawal. Repetti and Wood (1994) examined this issue using an ingenious sampling strategy. To ensure that mothers' moods at the end of the work day were elicited by work experiences, and not by a long commute, errands, or other intervening experiences, Repetti and Wood (1994) identified their sample through a worksite child care center; all mothers picked their children up immediately at the end of their work shift. Using mood data collected at the end of the work shift and self-report and observational data collected in the first minutes of the mother–child reunion at the day care center, Repetti and Wood found that mothers of preschoolers were much more likely to withdraw from their children, both emotionally and behaviorally, on days during which they had experienced either overloads or negative interpersonal interactions at work. Stress on the job generally was not followed by aversive mother–child interaction. Indeed, Repetti and Wood found some evidence in the observational component of their study that mothers were actually somewhat more patient with their children after high stress work days, a pattern they interpret as part of emotional and behavioral withdrawal. The extent to which mothers were able to refrain from engaging in negative interaction depended, however, on the mother's own general level of psychosocial functioning. Mothers characterized as high on Type A behavior were less able to refrain from interacting negatively with their children than were mothers with low scores on that measure.

The finding that an inclination toward Type A behavior moderates the relationship between work stress and maternal negativity echoes an earlier study by Repetti (1994) of fathers who were employed as air traffic controllers, an occupation that is characterized by high day-to-day variability in stress. On high-stress days, traffic controllers were less engaged emotionally and behaviorally with their school-age children. Despite this pattern of withdrawal, however, the air traffic controllers also reported that they reacted more angrily and used more discipline on high-stress days. Repetti and Wood (1994) offer the hypothesis that "negative spillover responses occur primarily under background conditions of chronically high stress, such as among mothers whose children are difficult to manage . . . or mothers who are high in Type A or depression . . . or fathers in very demanding occupations . . ." (p. 32).

In comparison to studies on spouses' access to work-related resources or to research on occupational complexity, the literature on short-term stress in relation to family interaction is notable for its focus on day-to-day variability. These labor-intensive studies generally involve small samples but precise temporal sequencing of the experience of a stressor at work and subsequent interaction in the home. Studies focused on work stress could benefit from including more information about spouses' attitudes and cognitions about work and family in their designs. Exploring the extent to which husbands and wives monitor their partner's level of strain at the end of the work day, how each responds behaviorally to the other's psychological state, and how each partner interprets the chain of events in terms of "fairness" (Thompson, 1991) would begin to integrate this domain of research with other relevant studies in the area of work and family.

CONCLUSIONS, CAVEATS, AND NEW DIRECTIONS

The studies we have reviewed in this chapter focus on how spouses' work situations influence roles, relationships and daily activities in the family. Several themes cut across the three domains of literature we have reviewed. First, it is clear that family life in dual-earner families is linked in important ways not just to the husband's work situation, or to the wife's, but to the work pattern of both partners in combination.

Second, the gendered nature of the work–family interface is a theme that runs through all of this literature. Gender is not only an important determinant of occupation, and thus of income, prestige, and access to self-directed, complex work, but it also underlies how men and women think and feel about work and family roles. Having similar or greater access to work-related resources in comparison to one's husband may give a woman the objective circumstances from which to argue for more equal roles in the home, but she is unlikely to do so unless she perceives her current situation as unfair (Thompson, 1991). Perceptual filters tend to operate in such a way as to advantage men (Kompter, 1989) who are seen as more competent and therefore perhaps as more deserving of special consideration at home after a stressful day at work (Bolger et al., 1989) or of appreciation when they make a contribution to housework or child care.

In this chapter, we have focused on three ways in which adults' work experiences influence their roles and relationships off the job. We would be remiss, however, if we did not underscore several caveats. First, the relationship between work and family is far more complex than our seemingly unidirectional focus implies. While there has been less research on the effects of family experiences on workers' lives on the job, such processes clearly exist (Barnett, 1994; Bolger et al., 1989; Crouter, 1984b); indeed, the connections between work and family are probably bidirectional in nature.

Secondly, conceptualizing this set of issues under the heading of "work and family" puts the emphasis on context and downplays the active role that the individual plays in making choices in such areas as education, career, workplace, marital partner, children, and child care arrangements. These choices are based in part on psychological predispositions: values, attitudes, preferences, and skills (Vondracek, Lerner, & Schulenberg, 1986). No sophisticated statistical model can completely remove the presence of these naturally occurring selection effects; nor is it necessarily desirable to do so because these variables are intertwined in the real world. Understanding the complexities of selection processes into—and out of—work and family roles is an important, but often overlooked, research area in its own right (see, for example, Zaslow, McGroder, Cave & Mariner, 1999).

Not all selection effects occur at the level of the individual and his or her psychological predispositions. Structural inequalities in our society result in considerable variability across individuals—as a function of gender, social class, race, ethnicity, and historical cohort—in the range of choices available; options are often constrained by discrimination and lack of access to opportunity. The review of the literature must be interpreted in light of these caveats.

In which directions should the field move over the next decade? First, researchers need to continue to broaden the populations they study in terms of gender, race, class, and culture. In the research areas reviewed in this chapter, gender has been a central focus. Social class has received some attention, especially from researchers interested in occupational complexity and self-direction, as well as from scholars who are interested in whether men and women in working-class and middle-class families view breadwinning (Ferree, 1987) and men's and women's contributions to housework (Perry-Jenkins & Folk, 1994) differently. There is still a dearth of good empirical research that examines work and family issues for low-income populations (Lambert, 1999). Race has received somewhat less explicit attention in the work–family literature than social class. This is somewhat surprising given that, historically, African–American women have maintained a greater, and more continuous, level of participation in the paid labor force than have White women (Bose, 1987). There may be important differences as a function of race in how men and women conceptualize the provider role, the connections between providing and the division of household work, and perhaps in conceptions of fairness, making this an important area of future study.

Our selection of the husband–wife dyad as the lens through which to examine the work–family literature meant that we excluded research on single-parent families in this chapter. However, work and family issues may be at least as important to workers heading single-parent households as to employees in two-parent, dual-earner families (Perry-Jenkins & Gilman-Hanz, 1992). In addition, the transition from single-parent and household head to a first or second marriage offers researchers interested in the husband–wife dyad an opportunity to explore how the experience of heading a household and being a single parent influences men's and women's subsequent negotiation of work and family roles.

Another important direction involves integrating the work and family literature with the study of families and their socialization of children and adolescents. Much of the literature on child development has focused on the impact of maternal employment status (conceptualized all too often as maternal absence) on children's psychosocial adjustment rather than on the connections between mothers' and fathers' ongoing daily experiences at work and their children's ongoing daily experiences at home (Crouter & McHale, 1993). Parcel and Menaghan's research (1994) is an exemplar of what can be done in this area. Their work, however, has focused mostly on early childhood. The middle childhood and adolescent years are also deserving of attention because this is the developmental period during which children develop ideas and expectations about their own future work and family lives.

A final area that is deserving of attention is the role of workplace friendships in the work–family interface. It is curious how little research has been done on relationships at work, given that they are a common and valued feature of many people's work experience (Marks, 1994). Currently, Helms-

Erikson (in preparation) is focusing on the roles played by husbands' and wives' friends in the marital relationship. Using a sample of almost 200 dual-earner families raising adolescent offspring, she found that, of the partners who reported having a close friend, 21 percent of the husbands and 21 percent of the wives reported that their close friend was currently or had been a co-worker. How might relationships at work make a difference in terms of family relationships? Riley's (1990) research on fathers' social networks provides one example. He argues that the geographic mobility associated with contemporary white collar work uproots men from kin-based social networks with the result that "non-kin allies"—friends, co-workers, and neighbors—come to exert more influence on their behavior as fathers. The higher the proportion of non-kin allies in a father's social network, Riley reports, the more likely he is to be highly involved in child care; conversely, the higher the proportion of kin, particularly female kin, in his network, the less likely he is to become involved in parenting. Work plays two roles. First, it creates geographic mobility which affects the composition of the social network; secondly, it makes possible certain work-based friendships that in turn exert an effect on attitudes and behavior in the family domain. Additional work is needed that examines the separate and combined effects of husbands' and wives' work-based friendships on family roles, relationships, and activities.

Work and family, as the two central arenas of adult life, are interconnected in complex and interesting ways. As researchers in the field of personal relationships become increasingly attuned to the importance of contextual influences on relationships, this area of research will receive even more attention. Given the increasing predominance of two-parent, dual-earner families as a context for contemporary marital and parent–child relationships, we urge the next generation of researchers to pay equal attention to the work and family experiences of both employed partners, singly and in combination, and to chart, with greater precision and across a broader array of relationship phenomena, the antecedents and consequences of variations in spousal inequality.

ACKNOWLEDGEMENTS

This is a revised version of a chapter which appeared in the *Handbook of Personal Relationships* (1997; Steve Duck, editor; Robert Milardo, section editor) published by John Wiley. We are most appreciative of the advice and suggestions offered by Susan McHale and Maureen Perry-Jenkins throughout the preparation of the chapter, as well as the helpful feedback provided by Bob Milardo and Steve Duck. Correspondence should be addressed to Ann Crouter, Department of Human Development and Family Studies, Penn State University, S-110 Henderson Bldg., University Park, PA 16802.

Chapter 7

Social Networks and Marital Relationships

Robert M. Milardo

University of Maine, Orono, ME, USA

and

Graham Allan

University of Southampton, Hampshire, UK

> The individual is not a separate unit, but a link, a meeting place of relationships
> of every kind. (Levi, 1947, p. 259)

This chapter critically examines network theory, methodology and research as it relates to understanding the internal character of a marriage, or marriage-like relationship. We are concerned with questions about the influence of the personal associates of spouses or adult partners on the conduct of their relationship. Kin, friends, co-workers and the like may directly influence partners and their relationship through the provision of support, companionship, or criticism. Network members may also collectively influence partners through their coordinated efforts, yielding a structural effect, as we term it.

In the following pages we critically review the theory and corresponding research linking a network's structure with the internal character of a relationship, a tradition of research that began with the publication of Elizabeth Bott's curious study of twenty London families in 1955. We continue with a

Families as Relationships.
Edited by Robert M. Milardo and Steve Duck. © 2000 John Wiley & Sons Ltd.

critique of the structural perspective followed by a summary of advances in both the precise conceptualization of networks and their enumeration.

STRUCTURAL INFLUENCE: THEORY AND FINDINGS

Introduction

Elizabeth Bott (1955; 1971) was among the first to hypothesize a link between the structure of spouses' social networks and the internal character of their marriage. In Bott's case, the interest was in explaining conjugal roles. Through an extensive examination of the division of labor and leisure time amongst the couples included in her study and of the social relationships they were involved in outside the household, Bott postulated that there was a link between the structure of their social networks and the conjugal role relationships they developed. In particular, she suggested "the degree of segregation in the role-relationship of husband and wife varies directly with the connectedness of the family's social network" (1971, p. 60). Bott took "connectedness" to be "the extent to which the people known by a family know and meet one another independently of the family" (1971, p. 59). Since then the term "density" has replaced that of "connectedness" in the social network literature, but it essentially refers to the same structural property: the degree of linkage among the people in the network. Density is just one of many measures of a network's structural properties, though undoubtedly it is the most frequently used (and arguably over-used) in the social analysis of networks (Milardo, 1986; Parks, 1997; Scott, 1991; Surra, 1988).

In evaluating the adequacy of Bott's approach, it is useful to return to the concerns that initially led to the development of her hypotheses. Essentially Bott's "problem" was to uncover the features of a couple's social location that patterned and shaped the character of their marital relationship. Dissatisfied with the then standard attempts at doing this, for example through crude measurements of class position or geographical location, Bott interpreted the issue through a concern for what she termed the couple's "immediate social environment". In essence her argument was that an appropriate conceptualization and measurement of the immediate social environment would help explain the form that different marital relationships took. However, the concept of immediate social environment, theoretically suggestive as it was, was not readily operationalized. It needed further refining if it was to prove useful for empirical investigation. It was here that the leap to network analysis was made. By interpreting immediate social environment into the language of social networks, and consequently defining structural or configurational properties of networks as crucial variables, Bott was able to formulate her ideas in a testable format.

Undoubtedly this was an enormous advance on previous work. The use of the network conceptualization not only allowed a precision in the measurement of a couple's immediate social environment, but was also analytically persuasive in that intuitively network configuration did appear linked with patterns of informal social control, which in turn represented a mechanism for understanding why marital relationships might be differentially organized. What is important for the present purposes are the theoretical connections that this formulation entails between the concepts of "social location", "immediate social environment", "network configuration" and "informal social control".

At its root, the link Bott drew between marital relationships and network configurations is premised on the idea that the character of informal control that shapes the organization of marital (and by implication, other types of) relationships is influenced by network properties. As came to be recognized clearly in the decade following the publication of Bott's research, network approaches allowed these patterns of informal control to be mapped in a more convincing fashion than the then dominant functionalist role theories managed (Wellman, 1988). Bott, like other network analysts, showed how behavior was influenced by its relational context, rather than simply being norm-based.

Reframing the Bott Hypothesis

Although research in this area generally refers to a uniform or singular "Bott hypothesis" (e.g., Hill, 1988; Morris, 1985), in fact two models linking network structure and conjugal roles are implicit in Bott's work and much of the research that followed. The two models differ in the specific mechanisms linking structure and conjugal roles and in terms of the mediating variables they call into question. In the first model, Bott hypothesized that highly interconnected networks would be more apt to share similar values and beliefs regarding conjugal roles relative to loosely connected networks. Bott hypothesized a direct path, with network structure determining the strength of normative influence. The specific norm of interest concerned the segregation of conjugal roles. Highly interconnected networks should adopt a consistent gender-based ideology with husbands and wives having very separate responsibilities for decision making, household labor, and child care, as well as separate personal associates and leisure interests. Loosely connected networks would be less predictable. Without the co-ordinated influence of network members, pairs of spouses should be freer to adopt their own arrangement of roles and responsibilities and accordingly they might adopt separate or joint conjugal roles.

The strength of this first model rests on the recognition that marital outcomes (e.g., interactions between spouses and the outcomes of those interactions) could be affected by the ties linking network members (i.e., conditions existing apart from spouses' relationship to one another), with the vehicle of influence being a system of normative beliefs. This is an extraordinary contribution because it represents the first concrete attempt to define social structure in terms of the patterned interconnection of people, and subsequently to quantify the degree of structure (Mitchell, 1969). It contrasts sharply with traditional conceptualizations of social structure based on categorical memberships like sex, race or class, conceptualizations from which structure can be only inferred (Wellman, 1988). On the other hand, a sharp limitation of the model is a failure to explain why a network would ascribe to one belief, such as role segregation or patriarchal norms, rather than any other.

A second model that is inherent in Bott's work links structure and marital roles through a slightly different pathway. In this model the key norm is one concerning the exchange of mutual support, both instrumental and symbolic, presumably based upon a sense of felt obligation (Stein, 1993; Uehara, 1995). Members of interdependent networks will provide considerable aid to one another, a system of mutual exchange that is possible only to the extent that members know and interact with one another. In interdependent networks mutual assistance among members is high and as a consequence spouses will have less need for one another's practical aid and companionship, and segregated marital roles emerge. In contrast, in more loosely structured networks, members are less likely to know one another and less likely to provide mutual aid so spouses must rely more fully on one another, creating the conditions for joint conjugal roles to emerge. Joint conjugal roles were defined in terms of joint responsibility for household labor, child care, and the joint use of leisure time.

The Bott hypotheses have engendered considerable research interest, particularly because they offered non-intuitive explanations of marital action. However, as new research has been produced, Bott's hypotheses have not been widely supported. Of the fourteen empirical tests of the Bott hypotheses we have identified, five were generally supportive and two provided mixed results (see Tables 7.1 and 7.2). Several studies reported modest positive associations between network connectedness and segregated marital roles (Blood, 1969; M. D. Hill, 1988; Morris, 1985; Nelson, 1966; Turner, 1967). For example in M. D. Hill (1988) although high network density, as indicated by the proportion of kin living nearby, is associated with segregated roles (R^2 = 2%), spouses' beliefs and parental status are far more robust predictors: those who believe in sharing roles do so (R^2 = 16%), and those with young children do not (R^2 = 15%). This finding is similar to Turner (1967) and Gordon and Downing (1978) in that couples that originate and reside in the same locality are more likely to report close-knit networks and segregated roles relative to couples that reside in areas far from their families of origin. Similarly, Richards (1980) reports that segregated roles increase with the degree of contact with kin.

What is unclear in these findings is whether kin have a distinctly different collective impact relative to spouses' friends and whether this impact is purely a function of a network's structure. That is, rather than being a consequence of network structure, perhaps segregated roles are simply the result of the fact that some spouses have a life-long commitment to (or enmeshment with) kin and this precludes their developing a close marital bond with one another (Blood, 1969; Lee, 1979). Although this argument is conceivable, there is rather little evidence to support it.

Table 7.1 Research supporting the Bott hypotheses

Citation	Sample	Network	Measure of interconnectedness	Role segregation	Findings
Nelson, 1966	N = 131 wives, urban CT	Four kin or friends visited most often	Cliques who interact minimum once per week, with three or more partners	Attitudes toward marital roles	Clique members report less companionate marriage
Turner, 1967	N = 115 rural couples, GB	Kin and friends contacted minimum one per two weeks	Density of connections between households	Performance of domestic tasks, child-care, leisure	Density increases with role segregation
Blood, 1969	N = 781 Detroit wives	Kin	Percentage of kin in neighborhood	Mean number of household tasks by husband or wife	Role segregation increases with number of kin in neighborhood, but also with lower support from kin
Morris, 1985	N = 40 working-class couples, Wales	Kin and friends	Pattern of interaction, group oriented or dyadic	Performance of domestic tasks, child-care	Role segregation associated with same-sex, high-density networks
Hill, 1988	N = 150 working-class wives, Altoona, PA	Kin	Percentage of kin living in area (Altoona)	Performance of domestic tasks, child-care	Role segregation increases with percentage of kin in area

Table 7.2 Research failing to support the Bott hypotheses or showing mixed support

Citation	Sample	Network	Measure of interconnectedness	Role segregation	Findings
Udy & Hall, 1965	N = 43 middle-class couples, CA, plus interview with four best friends of each spouse	Four best friends with most contact in last year	Density	Performance of household tasks	No relationship of role segregation with density
Aldous & Straus, 1966	N = 391 wives, rural MN	Eight women visited most often	Density	Performance of household tasks	Greater density in farm vs. town families
Wimberly, 1973	N = 40 middle-class Japanese couples	Largely friends	Degree of interaction among friends	Performance of domestic tasks, child-care, use of leisure time	No support, but little variation in connectedness. No couple had a joint conjugal marriage
Hannan & Katsiaouna, 1977	N = 408 Irish farm couples	Confidants of spouses	Network homogeneity; overlap	Performance of household tasks, child-care, decision making	Greater overlap = less role segregation, shared household labor and decision making. Homogenous networks modestly correlated with shared household labor
Gordon & Downing, 1978	N = 686 wives, urban Ireland (Cork)	Six individuals or couples most frequently visited by wife	Density; overlap	Performance of domestic tasks, child-care, decision making, leisure	Greater overlap—less role segregation. Role segregation increases with number of husband's kin in area (marginal significance)
Richards, 1980	N = 331 working-class wives, Boston 1958	Network involvement, combines nine questions on contact with kin and non-kin	Degree of interaction	Performance of household tasks, decision making, leisure	Greater "network involvement"—less role segregation and greater joint leisure. Role segregation increases with kin contact
Rogler & Procidano, 1986	N = 200 Puerto Rican couples in New York City	Eight closest companions of same sex	Density; composition	Performance of household tasks, decision making, leisure	No association between network connected with sharing household tasks, decision making, or leisure
Chatterjee, 1977	N = 33 Indian couples	Kin, co-workers, neighbors	Density, overlap	Household and child-care tasks	Greater overlap and density, less role segregation
Goldenberg, 1984-5	N = 1170 societies	None identified	Residence patterns used as proxy. Patrilocal residence viewed as "connected," matrilocal as "dispersed"	Normative views of division of household labor	No difference in gender segregation of roles by residence patterns

Timmer, Veroff and Hatchett (1996), using single-item, global measures of closeness with kin, found among black wives closeness with in-laws corresponds with greater marital happiness for both spouses, while similar associations for white couples were non-significant. Timmer et al. suggest these findings indicate that integration of spouses with their in-laws balances over-identification with families of origin. This explanation could explain the connection of closeness to in-laws and marital quality for black wives, but it does not explain why such an association fails to appear for white couples nor is there any direct evidence for either race of the negative effects of over-identification with families of origin, so-called enmeshment. In fact, wives' closeness to families of origin is unrelated to either spouses' reports of marital quality. Indeed some research suggests a far more interesting pattern of interconnections based around gender and network composition, with higher levels of kinship solidarity having very different effects for wives and husbands.

Blood (1969), for example, reported that wives in kin-centered networks were less likely to discuss personal problems with their husbands and experienced lower levels of marital satisfaction. This intriguing finding could suggest the ill effects of over-identification with kin, but it may as well suggest the effects of a non-responsive partner and troubled marriage. In more recent work, Burger and Milardo (1995) found the association of marital qualities and kinship ties varied by gender, type of kin, and whether integration with kin was evidenced by simple enumeration of kin in a network, or by the frequency of interaction. Generally, global measures of the size of a kinship sector, or the perceived frequency of interaction with classes of kin (e.g., all in-laws) are inadequate because these measures obscure the profound effects of some kin relations, the apparent non-effects of others, and the completely contrasting effects of still others for wives and husbands. For instance, the presence of brothers-in-law in the networks of wives successfully predicts 52% of the variance in her own reports of marital conflict and 32% for her husband's (Burger, & Milardo, 1995). For husbands, contact with fathers is critical, being associated with husband's greater love of his partner, as well as lower levels of marital conflict reported by wives. The importance of husband's integration with kin is also evidenced in Cotton's studies of white Australian couples (Cotton, Autill & Cunningham, 1993; Cotton, 1995) and the Timmer et al. (1996) longitudinal study of early marriage, at least among Afro-American men. Neither study, however, differentiated between types of kin relationships.

Relations with friends, on the other hand, have distinctly different associations with marital outcomes. Whereas kin tend to provide a variety of supportive functions (Wellman & Wellman, 1992) and to be sources of criticism (Rook, 1992), friends are unique sources of companionship (Harrison, 1998; Larson & Bradney, 1988; Wellman & Wellman, 1992), resource acquisition (Uehara, 1994), and social comparison (O,Connor, 1992; Oliker, 1989; Surra & Milardo, 1991), and they are rarely linked directly to spouses' kin (Wellman, & Wellman, 1992). Not surprisingly, relations with friends show a different pattern of association with marital outcomes compared to relations with kin. Cotton (1995) reported husbands whose wives were embedded in dense friendship networks experienced lower marital satisfaction. Similarly, in a sample of US couples when wives report high frequencies of social contact with close friends, their husbands report high levels of conflict as well as ambivalence regarding their marriage, and lower love of their spouses (Burger & Milardo, 1995). It remains for future work to elucidate these potential sex differences and the causal pathways that produce them.

Few have directly questioned the relative influence of structure and composition, although Nelson (1966) examined whether segregated roles were the result of network structure or more simply a function of being integrated into traditional extended families. In this study, even wives with highly interconnected networks composed entirely of friends were more apt to favor traditional values (80%) than those with networks composed entirely of kin (56%), suggesting that network structure takes precedence over network composition. The measure of network structure he used is also unique. Rather than being based on proxy measures like the geographic dispersion of network members (e.g., Blood, 1969; Gordon & Downing, 1978; Hill, 1988), or the interconnectedness of households (Turner, 1967), Nelson used an index of clique structure, defined as a pool of network members who jointly and routinely interacted with one another. In many ways, clique structure is preferable to measures of density or geographic dispersion, because it is less influenced by overall network size (Kapferer, 1973; Milardo, 1986). Of less interest are studies testing the Bott hypotheses that lack even remotely adequate measures of key variables like network connectedness or conjugal roles, or adequate variability in these key variables (Goldenburg, 1984–85; Wimberly, 1973).

With respect to the dynamics underlying the link between network attributes and marital roles, no study has yet examined whether network structure (e.g., density) is linked to the consistency of members' beliefs or sanctioning of members' actions as Bott proposed, although several have examined the link between network support and conjugal roles with mixed results. In Hill's (1988) study, there was a modest association between wives receiving support from parents and segregated roles ($r = 0.16$), whereas Blood (1969) reported that greater support for wives from kin paralleled shared conjugal roles: "Helpful (non-segregated) spouses tend to have helpful relatives" (p. 181).

In addition several investigators have explored the connection of network structure to global measures of marital satisfaction and individual well-being. Generally spouses with denser networks report greater well-being (Acock & Hurlbert, 1993; Cotton et al., 1993) and those with overlapping or shared networks report greater marital satisfaction (Milardo & Helms-Erikson, 2000). Shared networks are thought to act as a stabilizing force by reinforcing a consistent set of group norms, underscoring the identity of partners as a couple and providing sources of social support and comparison (Healey, & Bell, 1990; Milardo, 1982; Parks, 1997; Stein, Bush, Ross & Ward, 1992). In an intriguing study that compared couples in terms of their relative configurations of shared and separate networks of kin and friends, Stein et al. (1992)

found spouses with the highest reported marital satisfaction were those who maintained relatively balanced proportions of joint and separate networks of family and friends. Given the cross-sectional nature of this work causal directions are not discernible and in fact Yi (1986) has argued persuasively that patterns of marital interaction, rather than resulting from network configuration, direct patterns of extrafamilial associations (cf. Wellman, & Wellman, 1992).

Nonhuman Primates

Curiously some of the finest work on the close relationship-network connection comes not from work on humans but on nonhuman primates. Maryanski and Ishii-Kuntz (1991) reviewed approximately 90 studies of 17 species of Old World primates, including three species of apes. Many primate species are well studied with observational data on entire communities, which contain both identifiable networks and mating pairs. Sentiments, of course, are difficult to determine. Nonetheless the strength of relational ties between individuals can be defined in terms of observable features such as interaction frequency, physical contact and proximity, including mutual grooming, food sharing, cooperative alliances, mutual aid, and protection, and for adults, relationship stability. Network density is defined in terms of the relative proportion of strong ties, as is occasionally the case in studies of humans (Marsden, 1990). For mating pairs, role segregation can be defined in terms of the amount of leisure time pairs spend with one another, the degree of father's participation in child care, the degree of shared family maintenance (e.g., defense against marauding intruders), and the relative dominance or status of partners. Pairs who share in three of the four domains are viewed as having joint conjugal roles.

Maryanski and Ishii-Kuntz argue the findings are generally supportive of Bott. Primates with highly segregated roles show close- or medium-knit networks, and two species with moderately segregated (gorillas) or joint roles (gibbons) show loose-knit networks. Among all species, close-knit networks are associated with greater support from network members—perhaps, as Bott suggested, accounting for the greater likelihood of segregated roles in conditions of high density. In addition, for monkeys and apes, dispersal from families of origin (natal units) is related to the prevalence of loose-knit networks, as is the case in much of the work on humans (Hannan & Katsiaouni, 1977; Hill, 1988; Turner, 1967).

In explaining the connection between the roles adopted by cohabiting partners and the structure of their networks, Maryanski and Ishii-Kuntz deviate from Bott's reliance on *normative influence* and instead focus on the particular *character of relationships* with network members, especially kin. They argue that most material and symbolic support flows through strong ties (Wellman & Wortley, 1990) and consequently such ties are highly valued and very costly to terminate. Strong ties require maintenance in that the potential receipt of support is balanced with an obligation to be supportive (Uehara, 1995), ensuring the stability of the tie. Thus, time spent in maintaining strong ties is not available for initiating new ties and indeed research on humans supports this argument (Salzinger, 1982).

Segregation of roles among cohabiting partners is possible because of the support available from network members and may be required to the extent that network members require reciprocal support, leaving partners with little time or need for one another. On the other hand, without the responsibility of maintaining strong ties or the availability of support derivative from them, joint roles among cohabiting pairs can flourish. Among gibbons, for example, "male and female roles almost fuse, seemingly because each partner has no enduring outside relationships . . . For gibbons, a co-partnership in domestic activities may serve to reinforce bonds that endure for almost a lifetime. It would appear that the modern, mobile, middle-class family is but a less ex-treme variant of the gibbon nuclear family" [without the patriarchy] (Mar-yanski & Ishii-Kuntz, 1991, p. 418). Among human and nonhuman primates there appear to be inherent and fundamental properties of social networks and the relationships that compose them, properties that operate similarly across intelligent species.

Problems of Comparison

Examining the impact of different network configurations on the involvement of pairs of nonhuman primates is highly innovative, though in a number of respects methodologically less problematic than studying human couples. To begin with, the possibility of observation is made simpler because issues of access and privacy are of little consequence. Equally the exchange basis of the various relationships involved, and how these change over time, can be measured through observation more straightforwardly than when intention and human agency are involved. In contrast, the different attempts there have been to test Bott's ideas on human relationships have been fraught with conceptual and methodological problems. Making sound comparisons between the research reported in the literature is extremely difficult because of the different ways in which the elements in Bott's hypotheses have been operationalized. Few studies provide more than basic descriptive information about the networks generated. Information on average size, composition, or density, is often omitted, so that reliable comparison and theorizing is se-verely hampered (see Tables 7.1 and 7.2).

Equally few of the studies report on the precise wording of the network-eliciting questions. This is important because different methods yield different constituencies, i.e. different types of questions generate different networks which may well have different structural characteristics and distinct influences (Bass & Stein, 1997; Campbell & Lee, 1991; Milardo, 1992; Neyer, 1997; Surra & Milardo, 1991; van der Poel, 1993). Moreover some research, like Bott's, focuses on the couple's collective network, whereas other work relies on data from only one of the spouses, usually the wife. So too, in their identification of network members, many studies limited the size of a network to the six or fewer close associates. Yet a variety of research demonstrates that approximately 30% of North Americans have more that six intimates in their networks (Milardo, 1992), even if it is accepted that it is appropriate to focus only on intimates. Severe limitations in the size of a network limit the variation in other structural features, and most likely produce overestimates of other network properties like density.

This in turn raises the issue of which structural properties of networks are most suitable for examining the impact of informal control on couples' norms and behavior. As we have seen, the measure Bott used was network density— the ratio of actual linkages in the network to all possible linkages—and it is this feature that has dominated most analyses of personal networks. However, it is only one of a number of possible ways of characterizing the structural properties of networks, and there is little debate in the literature about why theoretically it is the best for capturing the effective exercise of informal social control over the organization of marital relationships. It could well be that other measures, in unison or collectively, offer better possibilities for explaining the various empirical patterns which occur. As we have suggested, clique structure, as used by Nelson (1966) and Salzinger (1982), may be a more suitable measure than overall density. (For a discussion of different measures of network structure, see Milardo (1986), Scott (1991), Surra (1988), and Wellman (1988).)

Recasting the Bott Hypotheses

In considering the collective work on the network structure–conjugal role link, with human and nonhuman primates alike, the overall empirical support is less than clear-cut. We suspect this is the case for two reasons: (1) because of an inadequate specification of the underlying theoretical model; and (2) because conceptual definitions of networks have lagged behind advances in methodology.

We argue that Bott's model was misspecified in two important ways. The first misspecification concerns the confusion of network structure with the content of members' beliefs. Bott's work, as well as nearly all the work that was to follow, assumed that all dense networks would subscribe to traditional norms. This may have been the case in the working class environs of mid-1950 London where her study was conducted, but it is an unnecessary limitation to the model. Bott's basic argument that network structure determines degree of influence works regardless of the particular beliefs of members. Their impact should be evidenced equally in cases where they hold radical feminist views or traditional patriarchal views. The point is that if a network is structurally interdependent, the possibility of more concerted informal control operating among its members is greater than if it is not so. In short, the precise beliefs of network members is a variable and can not sensibly be assumed to take any particular form. In reframing the original model, we believe it will be useful to allow for variation by treating consensus of normative beliefs as a variable, as well as allowing for variation in content whereby network members may subscribe to a range of beliefs, including those that promote patriarchal norms and those that do not.

Second, while recognizing the greater informal social control likely to be exercised in highly interconnected networks (or clusters), it does not automatically follow that the higher the network density the greater the consensus over values is, as assumed in Bott's arguments. We suspect many people's networks are much like contemporary legislators with a variety of interest groups holding different sets of values. This fracturing of networks into distinct subsets is dramatically illustrated in work on lesbian relationships. Among lesbian couples, networks are often fractured into those that know of and approve of the couple's sexual orientation and those that do not, sectors that are apt to share very different sets of values (Ulin & Milardo, 1992).

So too network members may differ in their beliefs across generations, or social contexts (e.g., kin vs. non-kin, co-workers vs. close friends) and as a consequence form distinct sectors. To express this slightly differently, given the social and economic conditions of late modernity, individuals have a degree of freedom in the construction of their social identity (Allan, 1993). Writers like Goffman (1959) and Giddens (1991) have emphasized that the way we present ourselves depends on situational and contextual factors, as well as on more inherent personality or character traits. Thus we highlight certain aspects of self in one setting, but other aspects elsewhere. The extent to which we can do this successfully is likely to depend on how well "insulated" from each other the different settings are, and, as Goffman (1959) argued, on the willingness of those permitted into the "back region" to sustain and give credence to the performance.

While it can be argued that behaviorally different presentations of self are unlikely in the specific context of marital and domestic organization, such considerations nonetheless highlight the possibility that individuals have variant social identities within different segments of their overall network (Klein & Milardo, 1993). In such cases, as with the lesbian couples mentioned above, the informal control exercised by the network overall is unlikely to be acting uniformly or in concert. This in turn suggests that the structural influence of a network is only crudely assessed by measures of composition or overall density, and can be more sensitively assessed with measures of clique structure or the clustering of members into highly interconnected subsectors of the overall network (cf. Nelson, 1966; Salzinger, 1982). Clustering is far less sensitive to changes in the overall size of a network, relative to measures of density, and it may well be a keener index of other structural features such as sex composition or proportional measures of kin and non-kin (Kapferer, 1973; Milardo, 1986).

This discussion leads us to several related hypotheses. Where networks are highly interdependent structurally, or where there are highly interdependent cliques, optimal conditions exist for the development, maintenance and enforcement of a consistent set of normative beliefs and expectations, and any deviations from those beliefs are most visible. Structure is thereby closely tied to the development of norms, the flow of information between members, and the sanctioning of individual behavior. Where networks are highly structured, spouses, like all other structurally equivalent members, will experience considerable influence to act in accord with those norms. In contrast, among members of networks low in structural interdependence, the development, maintenance, and sanctioning of common norms is inhibited and personal discretion over marital behavior is substantial. As Bott herself suggested, the development of industrial society fosters this within marriage, except possibly amongst those with the fewest resources whose poverty is likely to result in more restricted and more localized networks.

Defining and Enumerating Networks

What is not entirely clear is which types of network members are most likely to be influential or even how networks are best defined. How are the networks used in attempting to explain marital organization to be constructed? It is now widely recognized that the configurational properties of personal (or couple) networks are not immutable, given and ready to be recorded by the analyst, but depend entirely on what he or she takes to constitute a link. As Mitchell (1974, p.292) indicated, "any statement we may wish to make about the morphological features of a social network must be premised upon what links constituting the framework of the network are assumed to be" (see also Barnes, 1979; Scott, 1991). Whether researchers attempt to plot all those "known" or "known well" to the individuals concerned, whether they rely on their three (or six, or whatever) "closest", "most intimate" or "most significant" personal ties, or whether they attempt to specify different exchange bases of relationships, the resultant network is clearly a construction resulting from these decisions (cf. Campbell & Lee, 1991; Laireiter, Baumann, Reisenzein, & Untner, 1997; Milardo, 1992; van der Poel, 1993). Consequently, in examining how network configuration impinges upon marital relationships, it is important to determine theoretically the appropriate criteria for the inclusion or exclusion of particular relationships within the analyzed network. In our view this issue has not been resolved at a theoretical level. Little heed has been paid to the definition of theoretically significant tie within the context of the informal social controls exercised over marriages.

A second issue here is the question of equivalence of relationships that have been constructed within the network. Aside from the theoretical void surrounding configurational decisions, there is the question of whether all ties within the network exert equivalent influence, depending only upon their configurational location. The argument of the original Bott approach is that configuration rules. What matters is the overall constellation of ties in the network irrespective of the strength or character of individual relationships within it. On *a priori* grounds, this might be questioned, because some relationships are likely to have a greater or lesser influence in term of the informal control they can exert, independently of their structural location within the network.

More recent approaches have clearly recognized that relationships are not all the same (Burger & Milardo, 1995; Milardo & Wellman, 1992) and that the constructed network needs to incorporate in more detail the exchange basis, or other differential characteristics of relationships. As indicated earlier, different schemes of categorizing relationships have been developed in recent years. However, what remains underdeveloped is the theoretical rationale for adducing the relative influence of different categories of relationships, and different constellations of relationships within the constructed networks, in terms of their impact on marital (or other relational) conditions. The issue here is not whether we possess appropriate mathematical network tools and techniques for analyzing networks containing variable ties (and arguably we do), but rather whether from a sociological standpoint we have sufficient knowledge of theoretical principles and practices for analyzing the relative impact of these ties on behavior. As various commentators have indicated, there is quite a discrepancy between the complexity of mathematical and sociological theories invoked in network analyses (Emirbayer & Goodwin, 1994; Grannoveter, 1979; Scott, 1991; Wellman, 1988).

Expressed most simply, it is not clear how "additive" different types of relationships are within a constructed network. From the standpoint of sociological theorizing about informal social control, the relative pull or force of different types of relationships is, as yet, under-theorized. As a result there is little basis for determining which measures of structure and which corresponding mathematical principles are the most appropriate for assessing the collective impact of the detailed network configuration. It is worth adding here that this point remains true regardless of what form of relationship typology is drawn upon. Whether it be premised on exchange characteristics, measures of emotional closeness or social distance, or simply social categorizations such as kinship or friendship, the difficulty of calculating the cumulative impact of a given network configuration remains.

In attempting to address these issues we can usefully speak of two distinct networks: those with whom we interact routinely but may or may not consider close, and those we consider significant or especially close but may or may not interact with frequently. Earlier work suggests the two types of ties represent very different ways of conceptualizing networks that are distinct both theoretically and empirically (Milardo, 1992; Surra & Milardo, 1991).

Psychological networks are composed of people considered important or significant to respondents. These are "people to whom P is committed emotionally and psychologically, who provide P with a concept of self, and who can sustain or alter one's self definition through communication" (Surra & Milardo, 1991, p. 12). People become members through a history of direct interaction or indirectly through their association with others considered important (e.g., a parent of a fiance), but once established such a relationship need *not* require frequent, recent or long interaction. In contrast, *interactive networks* are composed of the people with whom interactions occur routinely.

Unlike the largely sentimental ties that comprise the psychological network, these are the kin, friends, co-workers and other personal associates with whom we routinely exchange aid, information, advice, and occasionally criticism (Milardo, 1992).

In a direct comparison of the composition of psychological and interactive networks, Milardo (1989) required spouses to identify members of their psychological networks in face-to-face interviews, i.e., people who were believed to be providers of material or symbolic aid, important confidants, or social companions. Members of the interactive network were identified via seven phone interviews of non-consecutive days. During each interview, a spouse was asked to identify the people with whom interactions occurred over the previous 24 hours.

We might expect the two types of networks to be reasonably similar; they are not. In a direct comparison the network types overlapped minimally. Spouses each identified an average of 39 network members. Seventy-five percent of these individuals were identified by one procedure but not the other. Moreover, there is no appreciable covariation in the size of each network, or in the size of the psychological network and the frequency of interaction with members of the interactive network. Spouses with relatively large psychological networks are not necessarily socially active and those with modest psychological networks are not necessarily socially isolated (Milardo, 1989).

We examine interactive networks because we are interested in the potential for the contemporary exchange of normative influence. On the other hand, the significant others who compose psychological networks shape beliefs merely by the imagination and subsequent anticipation of their reactions (e.g., "If my father could only see me know. He'd . . ."). Their influence is not necessarily tied directly to contemporary interaction but it is nonetheless current, and potentially significant. It remains for future research to compare these two distinct types of networks in terms of their structural properties, and to delineate models for predicting their relative importance in predicting relational outcomes. In what domains are the interior furnishings of one's mind apt to be of consequence, compared to the daily enterprise of social conduct?

Issues for Future Research

As we have said, while there have been a good number of studies that have set out to test Bott's hypotheses, the empirical evidence generated has not been noticeably supportive. One response to this might be to reject her ideas and stop searching for correlations between network configuration and marital organization. We do not consider this to be appropriate. Bott's work remains one of the most insightful and suggestive studies conducted on any aspect of family life. Recently Gordon Marshall, writing from a British perspective, has gone even further in declaring: "Her purposes may have been purely exploratory, but to my mind at least, her achievement constitutes probably the most original piece of sociological research to have emerged during the postwar era" (1990, p. 237). Many of the empirical tests of Bott's ideas have used methods so different from her's that their adequacy as tests is called into question. Bott's fieldwork was both qualitative and intensive—between eight and nineteen lengthy interviews were conducted with each couple. Restudies that rely on brief interviews with only one spouse and focus exclusively on a small number of network members may not be capable of capturing the holistic perspective that was central in Bott's analysis.

Yet questions clearly remain. In particular, there must be doubts about the extent to which purely configurational properties of a couple's network are of themselves capable of explaining conjugal role relationships, or indeed other social actions. In other areas of social inquiry that draw on network analysis there does seem to have been a move away from claiming singular explanatory power for network analysis towards using it more descriptively as one element within a broader explanation of behavior. For example, in studies of community ties, network analysis tends to be used as a tool for mapping out and contrasting the different structure of people's social universes, with these differences then being explained by other aspects of their economic and social location (e.g., see Allan, 1993; Wellman, 1985; Wellman, Carrington & Hall, 1988). Similarly studies of the impact of marital separation and divorce (or other changes in personal circumstances) on patterns of social participation may be informed by a network perspective but still draw on extraneous factors to help account for these changes (see, for example, Rands, 1988).

So it can be argued that Bott's approach gave too high a priority to network configuration. In effect what such an approach misses is any way of integrating wider contextual issues into the analysis. The effectiveness of informal control is likely to be influenced by aspects of network structure, but other features of the contexts shaping social action also need considering. Bott's notion of "immediate social environment" is particularly relevant here as this incorporates a broader field of relevance into the perspective. Translating this into network configuration made it more easily operationable, but arguably in the process rendered it too specific. In a sense it is this broader context that is missing from the central Bott equation of "configuration leads to content". Without some contextualizing, it is hard to see how action (i.e. content) can be properly understood or theorized. "Network analysis gains its purchase upon social structure only at the considerable cost of losing its conceptual grasp upon agency and process" (Emirbayer & Goodwin, 1994, p. 1446–7).

The difficulty with this of course is that it renders Bott's initial hypotheses somewhat less powerful than they otherwise are. In saying network structure can be important but it is only one of a number of factors that may influence people's role relationships, the taut elegance of Bott's approach is undermined. In the absence of clear confirmatory support for her argument though, and in the light of the types of conceptual and methodological matters we have expressed in this chapter, this perhaps should not be of too much concern. It would be curious indeed if the social and economic contexts in which marriages are constructed, for example whether or not wives were employed or the presence of children in the household, did not influence the role expectations spouses hold about one another, irrespective of network formation. This can be accepted without thereby saying that couples' immediate social environments are of no consequence, that different patterns of informal social control do not operate, or that network configuration is not an important influence. The task for the future is to develop more fully the theorization of the impact on conjugal role relationships of different network configurations in specific contexts and then assess such theorizing using appropriate, rather than simply convenient, empirical measures.

Chapter 8

Divorce: Societal Ill or Normative Transition?

Mark A. Fine

Department of Human Development and Family Studies, University of Missouri Columbia, Columbia, MO, USA

and

David H. Demo

Department of Human Development and Family Studies, University of North Carolina at Greensboro, Greensboro, NC, USA

> Divorce is a wrenching experience for many adults and almost all children. It is almost always more devastating for children than for their parents. (Wallerstein & Blakeslee, 1989, p. 297)

> . . . I believe that the consequences of divorce are not as strong as people once thought, that most children of divorce adjust well, and that divorce is not as problematic as are other stressors, such as abuse or poverty. (Amato, 1993a, p. 52)

> Contrary to the view of some social scientists in recent years, who believed that the effects of family fragmentation on children were both modest and ephemeral, there is now substantial evidence to indicate that the child outcomes of these alternative family forms are significantly inferior to those of families consisting of two biological parents . . . Moreover, some of these negative effects have been shown to persist into adult life. (Popenoe, 1994, p. 5)

> Most of the studies upon which alarmist views (of divorce) rely conflate the negative economic, geographic, and social consequences that children now

Families as Relationships.
Edited by Robert M. Milardo and Steve Duck. © 2000 John Wiley & Sons Ltd.

unjustly suffer after many divorces with the psychological effects of marital
rupture. Yet the most careful studies suggest that it is not the loss of a parent, but
a hostile emotional environment preceding this loss that causes most of the
emotional damage to children. (Stacey, 1993, p. 547)

As illustrated in these quotes from prominent family scholars, divorce and its
sequelae have generated considerable controversy and wide differences in
opinion. In fact, few issues related to families have generated as much scholarly and public interest as has divorce and its effects on children, parents, and
society. In this chapter, we depart somewhat from standard academic pro-
tocol. Instead of reviewing the literature on divorce and presenting our conclusions, we take a step back and look at the issues that underlie this wide
disparity of scholarly views and impressions. Our primary aim is to highlight
the variability in conclusions that have been drawn in the scientific literature
and to examine the reasons for and implications of this variability. In doing so,
we hope to provide readers with both the necessary context and some tools to
make better sense out of the sometimes confusing literature(s) on divorce.

To achieve these goals, we review the wide variability in scholarly conclusions pertaining to several aspects of the divorce process; examine why these
conclusions are so discrepant; discuss a number of key values that influence
scholarly conclusions; and draw implications designed to help readers navi-
gate through this complex and multifaceted literature.

Why is it important to examine the process of how inferences and conclusions
are drawn from the divorce literature? Important social policies depend on
societal views of divorce and the extent to which it negatively impacts children.
Laws pertaining to marriage and divorce are formed based on prevailing social
views of these institutions, and social views, to some unknown extent, are
informed by how social scientific evidence is portrayed to the public. For example, recent efforts to make it more difficult for couples to divorce (e.g.,
longer waiting periods, return to "fault"-based laws) have been fueled by growing social concern about the deterioration of the family and the role of divorce
in this decline (Popenoe, 1993). Social views of divorce are also reflected in the
private sector, such as in employee benefit packages. For these reasons, the
discourse on the effects of divorce is more than just an "academic" exercise.

THE WIDE LANDSCAPE OF VIEWS REGARDING THE RELATIONS BETWEEN DIVORCE AND WELL-BEING

In this section, we illustrate the diverging findings and inferences drawn by
researchers in five divorce-related areas: parent–child relationships, interparental relationships, psychological outcomes for children, psychological
outcomes for adults, and socioeconomic outcomes. Because our purpose is to
highlight variability in researchers' conclusions and the diversity of individuals' responses to divorce, we have not attempted to be exhaustive in our
coverage.

Parent–Child Relationships

Most research on intergenerational relationships following divorce has been concerned with the degree to which dependent-aged children are able to maintain close and supportive relations with their parents, particularly non-residential fathers. Research illustrates a multitude of postdivorce living arrangements for children and considerable variability and fluidity in the quality of parent–child relationships following divorce. For example, Maccoby and Mnookin (1992), in their 3-year study beginning when the parents filed for divorce, documented substantial shifts over time in the degree to which each parent was involved in the children's lives. Further, more than one-fourth of the children changed residences during that time frame.

Studies report that 30% of children who live with single mothers never saw their nonresidential father in the past year; one-fourth saw their father at least weekly; fathers were uninvolved in childrearing decisions; and less than half of nonresidential fathers paid any child support (King, 1994a; Seltzer, 1991). Other studies, however, have suggested that frequent interaction and close relationships between nonresidential fathers and children are more common in African–American families and among fathers who enjoyed close relationships with their children prior to the divorce, those who live near their children, and those who have joint custody (Arditti & Keith, 1993; Mott, 1990). Further, children who live with their fathers postdivorce tend to report very close and satisfying relationships with their fathers (Arditti, 1999) and frequent contact with nonresidential mothers (Maccoby & Mnookin, 1992). King (1994a, 1994b) documents that a number of factors influence the relationship between nonresidential father involvement and child well-being.

There are also discrepant findings and interpretations regarding parents' ability to maintain effective and consistent discipline following marital dissolution. Many studies report postdivorce increases in parents' stress, hostility, and punitiveness, and deteriorations in parental supervision, monitoring, and control (Hetherington & Stanley-Hagan, 2000; McLanahan & Sandefur, 1994; Simons & associates, 1996). Some scholars argue that it is harder for single parents to maintain control and that many relinquish control, blurring generational boundaries (Dornbusch, Carlsmith, Bushwall, Ritter, Liederman, Hastrof, & Gross, 1985; Nock, 1988; Weiss, 1979). On the other hand, other studies have found that most parents are competent and exercise appropriate control and consistent support, regardless of family structure (Acock & Demo, 1994; Amato, 1987; Simons & associates, 1996). Further, there is evidence that the altered authority structure in single-parent families facilitates closeness, autonomy, and mutual support in parent–child relationships (Arditti, 1999).

Interparental Relationships

There is also considerable variability in the quality of interparental relationships following divorce. Maccoby and Mnookin (1992) characterize one-fourth of divorced couples as being cooperative in coparenting, one-third as conflicted, one-fourth as disengaged, and one in ten as combining high communication with high conflict. One reason that researchers are interested in ex-spouse relationships is that it is widely believed that lingering interparental conflict is detrimental to children's well-being. Ample empirical evidence supports this claim and suggests further that recurring tensions and hostilities between former spouses inhibit effective parenting (Amato, 1993b; Buchanan, Maccoby, & Dornbusch, 1996; Demo & Acock, 1996a). However, King and Heard (1999) report that interparental conflict over visitation occurred in less than one-fourth of single-mother families.

An extensive analysis by Kitson (1992) illustrates diversity both in the frequency of contact between former spouses and in their feelings about each other. One year after the divorce, 52% had spoken with their ex-spouses by telephone; this declined to 42% by 2–3 years postdivorce. At both observation points, only 1 in 3 had spoken to their former spouses in person within the past few weeks. At the extremes of the distribution, 1 in 6 did not see their ex-partners at all in the first year postdivorce, but 1 in 10 former spouses had gone out on dates with each other. Emotionally, one-third still loved or liked their former spouse 2 years postdivorce, while one-fifth simply felt sorry for their ex-spouses. Kitson reports that 23% of the divorced felt strong anger at their former spouses, while 64% exhibited low anger.

Psychological Outcomes for Children

A common assumption is that parental divorce has adverse consequences for children's socioemotional development and well-being. Yet a substantial body of research over the past two decades documents wide variation in children's and adolescents' adjustment to divorce, and widely differing interpretations regarding the proximate causes and magnitude of the effects. Some scholars argue that children's experience of parental divorce and subsequent arrangements in single-parent (usually single-mother) households have severe and longlasting effects, significantly undermining social development, emotional well-being, and academic performance (McLanahan & Sandefur, 1994; Popenoe, 1996; Simons and associates, 1996). Wallerstein and Blakeslee (1989) suggest that deleterious effects persist for over a decade following divorce, and that, for some children, the damage is permanent.

On the other hand, considerable evidence indicates that most children are resilient, adapt well to parental divorce, and function in the normal range of adjustment (Hetherington & Stanley-Hagan, 2000). Group comparisons reveal modest and sometimes statistically nonsignificant differences between the adjustment of children in first marriage families and those who have experienced parental divorce (Amato, 2000; Demo & Acock, 1996a). Further, many researchers emphasize that, for most children, emotional difficulties are most salient during the period immediately preceding and following parental separation and divorce, and that these difficulties subside within one to two years.

Psychological Outcomes for Adults

Research suggests that the process of marital dissolution is stressful for both women and men. Consensus is lacking, however, regarding sex differences and the duration and severity of effects. Some studies indicate declines in the emotional well-being of women, and improvements for men, in the first two years postdivorce (Coysh, Johnston, Tschann, Wallerstein, & Kline, 1989; Doherty, Su, & Needle, 1989). Demo and Acock (1996b) found that divorced and continuously single mothers had lower self-esteem and more depression than married mothers, but emphasized that group differences are small and that marital status, *per se*, explains little variation in mothers' well-being.

Findings from longitudinal studies yield additional insights, but also lead to inconsistent findings and, sometimes, contrasting conclusions. Booth and Amato (1991) observed that unhappiness and psychological stress intensify as predivorce events unfold, but that, by 2 years postdivorce, married and divorced individuals exhibit comparable mental health. Kitson (1992) observed that 30–40% of divorced women and men experienced moderate or high emotional distress at the time of filing for divorce, but that, at 4 years postseparation, there was little difference in the psychological functioning of married and divorced individuals, and no significant differences by sex. In contrast, Hetherington (1987) found that, 6 years after divorce, men reported higher general life satisfaction than women, and Wallerstein and Blakeslee (1989) reported high levels of distress persisting 10 years after the divorce.

Socioeconomic Outcomes

Much has been written about postdivorce economic decline, especially for women and children, and the failure of many nonresidential fathers to pay child support. Again, however, there is considerable variation in standards of living within and among postdivorce family forms (Duncan & Hoffman, 1985; Seltzer & Brandreth, 1994), and widely differing interpretations of women's and men's economic plight (or recovery) following marital dissolution. One-fourth of divorced women and their families live in poverty for a period of time shortly after divorce (L. A. Morgan, 1989), 40% lose more than half their predivorce family income (Arendell, 1995), and the sharpest drops in family income are suffered by African–American women and women who had higher incomes during marriage (Holden & Smock, 1991).

Sparking scholarly and public attention, Weitzman (1985) argued, on the basis of analyses that have since been found to be flawed (Peterson, 1996), that, after divorce, women experienced a 73% decline in their standard of living, while men experienced a 42% increase. Peterson (1996) reanalyzed the same data Weitzman used and reported that the correct figures indicated a 27% decline for women and a 10% increase for men. Peterson notes that Weitzman's (incorrect) figures were enormously influential and widely cited throughout the social sciences, in the popular press, and even in the US

Supreme Court. And Braver (1998) contends that Weitzman's finding of such a dramatic disparity was accepted so widely because it "fit too well the image our society had adopted for us to question it. It 'proved' what we wanted to believe: Divorced moms suffer, while bad divorced dads profit" (p. 62).

Other studies suggest modest or no differences in women's and men's postdivorce standard of living. Duncan and Hoffman (1985) estimated that men's family income one year after divorce is 90% of their predivorce income, and by two years postdivorce their family income is slightly higher than before divorce. But Braver (1998) argued that researchers have consistently made a number of errors in calculating postdivorce family incomes (e.g., failing to consider differential tax consequences for women and men), and he concluded that there is no difference in women's and men's after-tax incomes following divorce.

WHY ARE VIEWS OF DIVORCE APPARENTLY SO DISCREPANT AMONG SOCIAL SCIENTISTS?

Having shown the wide variability in inferences pertaining to the effects of divorce, we now turn to an examination of *why* there is such divergence in researchers' conclusions.

Differences in Theoretical Orientation

One factor contributing to the variability in conclusions is that many investigators in this area have conducted studies without the benefit of an explicit theoretical orientation. We emphasize again the lack of an *explicit* orientation, because we believe that all research is driven by some sort of conceptual perspective (cf. Duck & Montgomery, 1991), even if outside the conscious awareness of the investigator. The atheoretical nature of some of the work on divorce adds to the variability in inferences because there is a greater likelihood that scholars will have misunderstandings stemming from different meanings attached to various terms, constructs, measures, and findings. In other words, among the many benefits of explicating the conceptual underpinnings of studies is the achievement of greater precision in communicating what one did, what one found, and what the findings mean.

Another obvious explanation for why scholars might reach differing conclusions regarding the effects of divorce is that researchers who conceptually ground their work employ a wide range of perspectives. Such theoretical perspectives as evolutionary/sociobiology, exchange, systems, psychoanalytic, social learning, and many others have been used in this area of research. Not surprisingly, these theoretical orientations lead their proponents in somewhat different directions as they frame their research questions, conduct their research, and draw conclusions. For example, psychoanalytic followers might look for disruptions in the socialization and identity development of children, mostly boys, who live primarily with their cross-sex parent, whereas exchange theorists might examine the relative weights of the benefits and costs, relative to possible alternatives, of divorce.

In addition to the observation that different researchers are guided by varying theoretical perspectives, individual investigators themselves often use more than one theoretical perspective. When investigators pick and choose from a number of different theories, this is often referred to as *eclecticism*. At its best, eclecticism can lead to a productive merging of different theoretical perspectives (Allport, 1968). However, eclecticism does not come without risk. Some researchers refer to their approach as an eclectic one, when, in fact, they are either actually not systematically using any theoretical perspectives or they are using so many perspectives that they fail to achieve a coherent, integrated theoretical package. An effective use of an eclectic approach requires that there be a high degree of consistency in how various terms and assumptions are used across theories. If what appears to be the same assumption actually means something quite different in two different theoretical perspectives (e.g., "identification" has a different meaning in psychoanalytic theories than it has in social learning theory), our ability to understand the phenomenon of interest is compromised (Henle, 1961).

However, differences in theoretical orientations alone cannot explain the diverging conclusions found in this literature. Scholars do not adopt theoretical orientations in a vacuum, but rather these theoretical preferences themselves emerge from the scholar's values, assumptions, and experiences. Thus, we argue that it is helpful to examine differences in theoretical perspectives, but it is also important to probe more deeply into the values, beliefs, assumptions, and preferences that lead scholars to choose particular theoretical orientations.

Basing Conclusions on Different Literatures

Fine and Kurdek (1994) defined a *literature* as a "body of theory and knowledge on a given topic" (p. 374). There is no single (or even clear) way of demarcating where one literature stops and another begins. In the divorce area, one could identify distinct (although overlapping) literatures in communication, psychology, child development, sociology, demography, anthropology, counseling, social work, and others. To what extent are researchers who draw differing conclusions related to divorce examining the same literature? To what extent are researchers drawing different conclusions about divorce because they read in and contribute to different literatures? Certainly, if researchers draw varying conclusions from the same body of work, this may be cause for considerable consternation. However, even if different conclusions are a product of separate literatures, this is still a concern because researchers may gravitate toward literatures that are most consistent with their values and interpretations of the literature.

The divorce literature is so voluminous that the divergent conclusions tend to be generated from different studies and literatures. Thus, in our view, divergent conclusions often have their origin in a process in which scholars examine different bodies of work and form differing conclusions based on reasonable interpretations of the research reviewed. In fewer cases, opposing conclusions are drawn from the very same literature. For example, a number of scholars have suggested that family structure effect sizes are quite small (Acock & Demo, 1994; Amato, 2000), whereas others (Simons, 1996) note that the rates at which children who have experienced divorce exhibit behavior problems are two or three times the rate for children in first-marriage families. Both conclusions are reasonable inferences from the available data, but they lead to quite different implications. In the former case, one might infer that divorce has a reliable, although small, effect on children's behavior problems, whereas, in the latter, one might infer that divorce substantially increases the risk of behavior problems.

A Positivist Perspective Dominates the Literature

The key features of a positivist perspective are that one assumes that there is a "truth" in any particular research area, that there is probably a single truth, and that the challenge for researchers is to discover the truth through the most scientific approaches available. Despite growing criticism of the positivist approach (for an early critique, see O'Keefe, 1975), our sense is that most scholars still adopt a positivist perspective, which is not surprising given that it is the most commonly accepted view of the nature of knowledge, that it is the predominant way that social scientists are trained in their graduate programs, and that it has generated considerable knowledge and advances in the "natural" sciences and, to a lesser extent, in the social sciences.

However, positivism has important limitations. Among these are that, in its pursuit of a singular truth, it contributes to a failure to recognize that many events are experienced quite differently by those affected and that context (e.g., historical era, situational circumstances, cultural values) contributes to this diversity in experience and reactions (Duck, West, & Acitelli, 1997). In terms of drawing conclusions from the literature, a positivist perspective leads scholars to attempt to draw inferences that generalize to all children, parents, and families. Further, such a perspective leads to "either–or" or dichotomous conclusions (e.g., divorce does or does not negatively affect children) rather than "both–and" (e.g., divorce negatively affects some children and not others) and continuous conclusions (e.g., identifying circumstances or contexts in which divorce has positive and negative effects for some children and the magnitudes of these effects). Duck et al. (1997) have made a similar point in noting that research tends to assume that relationships are either good or bad, but not both simultaneously; researchers also have not tended to explore the dynamic aspects of how individuals and relational partners manage the tensions between the ever-changing good and bad aspects of relationships.

The Price of Scientific Precision

In an attempt to isolate the effects of the independent variable (e.g., divorce status or family structure) on the dependent variable (e.g., outcomes such as personal well-being), researchers often institute methodological or statistical controls. In a sense, some of the complexity of people's experience is artificially stripped away in the hope of providing a "purer" or "cleaner" comparison from which to draw inferences. For example, we may choose to compare the adjustment of a group of white, middle-class, early adolescents who have experienced parental divorce with a comparison group of adolescents who have not experienced parental divorce. To isolate the extent to which divorce is "responsible" for any observed differences between the groups, researchers are trained to try to match as closely as possible the characteristics of the comparison group with those of the divorce group, *with the sole exception* of the key variable in the study—divorce status. While such comparisons may be helpful in adding to our understanding of divorce effects, they create a somewhat artificial and simplistic comparison that neglects differences between and within groups in terms of a whole host of complexity-generating factors, such as geographical region, ethnicity, historical era, and so forth.

Another way that researchers attempt to maximize the information gained from their studies is to isolate only a very few phenomena in any particular study. For example, a researcher may study one particular parenting practice, such as nurturing behaviors, to determine factors that are related to how frequently divorced parents engage in that particular practice. While reductionistic methodological practices like this have a host of advantages (and our aim is *not* to disparage such practices), they have the important disadvantage of stripping away the context and meaning in which the behavior of interest naturally occurs. As noted by Duck et al. (1997), "Having, for good reason, focused on a single process or the interaction of just two processes by momentarily removing them from their active sites and contexts of operation, any explainer of those processes has to remember to reinsert the previously removed parts of the picture" (p. 5). Of course, the big challenge is how to "reinsert" the "removed parts" and we return to this in the final section of this chapter.

A final example of the costs of methodological precision is the search for group similarities, regularities, and commonalities at the expense of describing variability within groups. Many researchers attempt to simplify the "state of affairs" by examining measures of central tendency, determining how these averages differ in various structural arrangements, and/ or exploring how certain variables relate to other variables *on average* across individuals. While useful, these practices come with the cost of losing sight of the important intra-individual and/or intrafamily differences in many socioemotional processes and outcomes. Diversity in reactions to particular experiences may be as meaningful as indices of central tendency.

The Challenge of Studying Sensitive Topics

The study of the effects of divorce is very sensitive in multiple ways. It is sensitive because it addresses issues that can be emotionally upsetting to those affected, it deals with what is often considered a private aspect of individuals' personal lives, it focuses on a continually evolving process, it involves the sharing of information that has the potential to be used against the discloser (e.g., information related to a child support decision), and it involves an experience that some consider to be nonnormative or socially unacceptable. These considerations make divorce an especially difficult phenomenon to study and understand.

This sensitivity makes researchers' tasks more challenging than is typically the case in social science research, because they have to be more concerned with such issues as a social desirability response set; whether to seek information only from family members or from others outside of the immediate family (e.g., the "insider vs. outsider" dilemma); the fact that people are not static, but ever-changing as they progress over their life course; and the typically discrepant views of individuals within the same family. For example, Seltzer and Brandreth (1994), based on analyses from the National Survey of Families and Households, showed that nonresidential fathers reported being more involved with their children than mothers reported them to be (also see Braver, 1998). Divergent perspectives within the same family compound a common challenge in family research—the unit of analysis problem. The unit of analysis challenge addresses whether data should be analyzed at the individual level, the dyadic level (e.g., difference scores between reports by fathers and mothers, mean marital satisfaction score), or at the level of the entire family (e.g., observational ratings of family interaction, mean cohesiveness scores of family members).

KEY VALUES THAT INFLUENCE THE RESEARCH PROCESS

Values have been defined as the set of cultural, social, and individual beliefs concerning preferential or healthier life styles (Fine, Schwebel, & Myers, 1987). These values influence all stages of the research process. However, it is important to draw a distinction between "values" and "bias". Kaplan defined bias as ". . . adherence to values of such a kind or in such a way as to interfere with scientific objectivity" (p. 373), suggesting that bias involves allowing one's values not only to influence the research process (which is inevitable), but also to cloud one's scientific judgement (which is not inevitable). From this point of view, bias should be avoided to whatever extent possible, whereas values cannot be eliminated from the process. It is not uncommon in the divorce arena for scholars to suggest that others have allowed their values to bias their research. For example, Popenoe (1996) stated that ". . . a little

ideology crept into the research. Divorcing academics and antifamily feminists of the time were perhaps overeager to turn up the minimal effects of
divorce so that their own emotional lives would be spared or their negative
views of the traditional nuclear family upheld" (p. 61).

Below, we discuss several values that we consider to be of critical importance. Because our goal is to identify the differing positions that scholars can
and have taken on these value dimensions, we do not discuss our position on
some of these value dimensions until the Implications section at the end of the
chapter.

Which Outcomes Should be Examined?

A researcher's values influence the choice of which outcomes he or she
chooses to study. Two illustrations are provided. First, researchers' views on
the effects of divorce influence their choice of outcome variables. For example, an investigator who suspects that divorce has negative consequences
on children might examine children's behavior problems (perhaps comparing
a group of children who have experienced divorce with a group of children
from traditional, nuclear families), whereas a researcher who predicts that
there are positive outcomes related to divorce might examine such issues as
whether experiencing a divorce leads to children growing up "faster" (Dornbusch et al., 1985; Weiss, 1979) or whether children who have experienced
parental divorce have more realistic expectations regarding marriage than
those children whose parents have not divorced. It is important to note that a
scholars's views of the effects of divorce may not be born out in their findings;
a researcher could examine outcomes that he or she suspects, at some level of
consciousness, will demonstrate negative divorce effects and yet still generate
findings that have positive implications (e.g., divorce does not lead to an
increase in child behavior problems) and examine outcomes that one suspects
will yield positive divorce effects and find negative consequences (e.g., children from divorced families do not have particularly realistic expectations
about marriage). However, the important point is that there are limitations
imposed by the type of outcomes that are examined; these limitations to some
extent predetermine, or at least constrain, the range of possible findings and
the manner in which new knowledge will be generated.

Second, what general types of outcomes should be considered? Fine et al.
(1987) argued that a critical reason why there were such divergent views of
African–American families was that some researchers focused primarily on
socioeconomic outcomes (e.g., educational attainment, employment history,
income achieved), while others focused on socioemotional outcomes (e.g.,
emotional well-being, life satisfaction, absence of psychological problems). At
the risk of oversimplifying matters and recognizing that a minimal level of
resources is necessary for survival, because socioeconomic status is based
upon the extent to which individuals have "succeeded" in acquiring socially
valued resources, scholars who emphasize socioeconomic standing place

emphasis on the importance of individuals conforming to the societal status quo. By contrast, because socioemotional well-being is not necessarily rooted in conforming to the status quo (e.g., one can have high self-esteem regardless of one's level of annual income), scholars who emphasize socioemotional outcomes are emphasizing conformity less so than are those who focus on socioeconomic outcomes. Similarly, we argue that this issue underlies some of the discrepancies in conclusions drawn in the divorce area. Researchers who value socioeconomic indicators of well-being are more likely to draw negative inferences regarding the effects of divorce than are those who advocate socioemotional indicators, because, although there is considerable variability in findings, divorce effects tend to be stronger in the former range of outcomes than the latter.

Are Divorce Effects Primarily Environmental or Intrapersonal?

Some researchers derive their results based on the assumption that the sequelae of divorce are solely due to the environmental and situational stressors stemming from the process of divorce. Other investigators seem to assume that some individuals are more vulnerable to negative divorce effects because of factors intrinsic to the individual, such as genetic make-up, undesirable personality characteristics (e.g., "neuroticism"), being "poor marriage material," or other factors that lead to some individuals being more likely to divorce than others (Hetherington, Bridges, & Insabella, 1998). Where a scholar falls on this intrapersonal to environmental continuum will influence how studies are designed and how results are interpreted. For example, researchers who believe that divorce effects are primarily due to personal factors may be more likely to conduct longitudinal studies to determine if conditions that are observed following divorce also preceded divorce.

How Influential are Children in Affecting Parenting Behaviors and Other Family Processes?

Another value that affects multiple aspects of the investigative process is the extent to which children are conceptualized as passive recipients of environmental influences, in general, and of parental divorce, in particular. The majority of studies in this area assume that children are both directly affected by certain aspects of divorce (e.g., decrease in family socioeconomic status) and indirectly affected through the effects of divorce on parents (e.g., changes in parenting practices). However, in both types of effects, the assumption is that children are affected by their environmental surroundings. On the other end of this continuum is the view that children and their behavior affect parental behaviors and family processes. This possibility of children affecting the manner in which they are treated has seldom been investigated, although a special issue of the *Journal of Social and Personal Relationships* (August, 1997) was devoted to bidirectional influences between children and parents (also see the companion volume in this series, which addresses this point from a developmental perspective; Mills & Duck, 1999).

At the Societal Level, Should Divorce be Considered as Inevitable or as a Practice that Should be Prevented?

Some scholars (e.g., Popenoe, 1994) have suggested that the prevalence of divorce, coupled with the consistency and severity of its negative consequences, justifies the conclusion that societal efforts should be directed towards preventing divorce. This view is reflected in societal and judicial efforts to make it more difficult to obtain a divorce (e.g., longer waiting periods, returning to grounds-based divorces) and/or to make marriage a more lasting commitment (e.g., efforts to have different types of marriage that vary in how difficult it is to obtain a divorce). On the other hand, other scholars suggest that divorce and marital breakup are inevitable aspects of social life in the western world and that, even in countries that either barred divorce or strongly discouraged it, couples whose marriages were "broken" found ways outside of legal divorce to end their relationship and/or decrease their amount of mutual interaction (Fine & Fine, 1994). These scholars argue that divorce (or marital dissolution) will occur despite efforts to prevent it and that research and practice are most effectively directed towards furthering our understanding of divorce and how to help those individuals who experience it.

To What Extent Should We Pursue Scientific Precision and Sacrifice Ecological Validity?

Researchers vary in the extent to which they advocate using scientific methods that retain the precision and control necessary to be able to make causal inferences. At the possible cost of being overly simplistic, it is reasonable to think of a tradeoff between scientific precision and ecological validity (i.e., the ability to draw conclusions about individuals in the context of their lived experiences). To the extent that one emphasizes scientific precision, one may enhance internal validity (i.e., the ability to draw causal inferences), but bear the cost of studying people in unnatural, unfamiliar, and artificial settings.

For example, a common practice when comparing individuals who have been through a divorce with those who have not is to statistically control for variables that distinguish between groups. For example, scholars often recommend that if children in a divorced group come from families with lower annual family incomes than those from first-marriage families, the researcher should control for annual family income when comparing the children's well-being across the two groups. However, this apparently benign statistical practice involves an important value. By controlling for naturally occurring group differences (such as income levels), one is creating an artificial comparison by attempting to isolate divorce effects from other possible differences between the groups. The result is an analysis that, in fact, may aid in determining the unique effects attributable to divorce, but that is based on an artificial comparison between groups that do not exist in the "real" world (i.e., the two groups are not equivalent in the population in terms of socioeconomic status, but are treated as if they are or could be).

One of the alternative strategies is to not statistically control for differences between groups that exist in the populations from which the samples were drawn. This choice reflects the value that the most useful comparison between groups is one that reflects naturally occurring differences between the groups. This practice, although having the virtue of more accurately reflecting the interrelated network of characteristics of the various groups, has the disadvantage of making it more difficult to isolate divorce effects (e.g., differences between groups could be due to divorce, but could also be due to uncontrolled socioeconomic or other differences between the groups). Obviously, the results can vary greatly depending on which way this issue is addressed. This example shows that a relatively common and often unquestioned statistical decision can have important implications for the inferences one draws about divorce effects.

What is the Relative Value of Examining Family Structure vs. Family Process Effects?

Researchers also differ in the extent to which they emphasize examining divorce effects due to family structure (first-marriage vs. single-parent family) as opposed to those related to processes within families (e.g., parenting practices, interparental conflict). Some scholars (e.g., Fine, 2000) have argued that simple family structure comparisons are of limited utility and that we have already gained about as much as we can from these studies. Others have suggested that family structure represents a meaningful and common distinction among families and that such comparisons, if carefully and sensitively conducted, can yield useful information (Amato, 1993b). With respect to family processes, some scholars argue that these processes should be the prime focus of our research efforts, because their effects are judged to be greater in magnitude than are family structure effects and because family processes, such as parenting practices, are more amenable to intervention than is family structure (Fine, 2000).

How Scientifically Stringent are the Criteria Used to Determine Whether Correlates of Divorce Can be Considered to be Causally Related to Divorce?

The issue of whether divorce *causes* negative consequences or if it is merely associated with particular outcomes is of obvious importance. As a result, the standards used to evaluate whether causality has been established are of the utmost significance. On one extreme, some scholars argue that only experimental designs, with random assignment to family structure groups, can yield results that speak to the issue of causality. Because random assignment is impossible in this area, such scholars would argue that no single study can yield evidence relevant to causality. On the other extreme, some scholars, although a relatively small number, might contend that even purely correlational research designs shed some light on the issue of causality. Lying in between these two extremes are a multitude of intermediate positions. For example, scholars differ in the extent to which they believe that causality is demonstrated in longitudinal studies beginning before divorce that show that divorce is predictive of changes over time in well-being. The more stringent the criteria endorsed by the scholar, the less likely it is that he or she will attribute causal effects to divorce. Clearly, then, the "burden of proof" established to be able to infer causality has a tremendous impact on conclusions drawn.

THE CRITICAL IMPORTANCE OF RESEARCHERS' VALUES AT ALL STAGES OF THE INVESTIGATIVE PROCESS

Now that we have provided an overview of some of the major values that influence researchers, we turn to an examination of how these values influence the investigative process. The discussion below is not intended to be exhaustive, but to describe many of the most important stages in the investigative process.

Choosing Research Questions

The questions that are addressed in a research project do not emerge out of a vacuum, nor is there an objective way to generate them. Rather, investigators identify research questions in a variety of ways, including personal experience, previous research, guidance from theoretical perspectives, and observations of social phenomena. The identified questions emerge from the subjective judgement of the researcher, at least part of which is based on values.

Which Literature is Read and Reviewed

One of the determinants of what researchers study and how they conduct their investigations is the literature (or literatures) that they choose to read. The literature in an area as broad as divorce is too vast for any one individual to completely digest. As a result, only a portion of the literature can be read and all scholars, to a greater or lesser extent, must rely on others' reviews. Thus, because what is read is obviously very influential in directing scholars' work, these choices have important implications. For a variety of reasons, some literatures suggest conclusions that are qualitatively different from those of other literatures. For example, perhaps partly because the participants they observe and study are typically those seeking help for psychological problems, publications written by clinicians in applied outlets (e.g., journals created for clinicians) tend to provide a more negative view of divorce effects than do those written by nonapplied scholars in nonclinical outlets. While there are many factors (e.g., disciplinary training, current work setting) that determine which sources a scholar will choose to read and review, her or his values certainly play an important role.

Which Methods are Chosen

The research designs used to study divorce-related phenomena influence the range of possible results that can be obtained and the conclusions that can be drawn. For example, research designs that involve comparisons of children's well-being in single-parent and first-marriage families have yielded valuable broad generalizations about how children fare in different family structures. Of course, as a field develops, such group comparisons often become increasingly refined; instead of comparing the adjustment of children who have experienced divorce with those whose parents are continuously married, one might compare children who have experienced divorce with children whose parents are still married, but have highly conflictual marriages. Indeed, more fine-grained comparisons have become increasingly common in the divorce literature, a trend that we support. By contrast, "within-group" designs, involving only individuals from divorced families, obviously cannot be used to draw inferences regarding how children from divorced families compare to children in other family arrangements, but are more likely to generate information pertinent to the issue of which factors predict how well children will cope following divorce.

As another example, large-scale surveys of thousands of individuals can yield valuable insights into some general aspects of divorce, but are less likely than small-scale interview studies to yield rich information describing how divorce is experienced, interpreted, and coped with by those affected by it. No single method is inherently superior to all others, because, in well-constructed studies, the designs chosen will closely follow the identified research questions.

How Data are Analyzed and Interpreted

Data analysis strategies, at least in the realm of "quantitative" data, are often considered to be objectively chosen based on specific features of the research design. Indeed, there is a relatively narrow range of "appropriate" data analytic techniques for any given set of data; however, even within this narrow band, most scholars now believe that there are still some subjective aspects to this decision-making process. Some of these decisions include whether one uses the hypothetico-deductive method (involving testing the null hypothesis with prespecified criteria for statistical significance [e.g., $p < 0.05$]), the stringency of criteria used to judge whether causality has been established (discussed earlier), the relative weight placed on the cost of making a Type I error vs. a Type II error (e.g., will a finding significant at the $p < 0.10$ level be considered a trend deserving of interpretation or just another nonsignificant finding?), how closely one's analysis decisions are governed by the assumptions underlying particular statistical procedures, and how meaningful the relevant effect sizes are. Decisions on each of these issues affects the range of possible results and the consequent conclusions.

With qualitative research, there are a host of equally subjective decisions that need to be made, such as which data analytic strategy to use, the number of research team members used to code and interpret the results, the extent to which the researchers seek input on interpretations from the participants and revises results based on this feedback, and the extent to which the results are couched in a way that makes them amenable to facilitate social change.

Where One Chooses to Disseminate Results

A rarely discussed part of the investigative process is the determination of how to disseminate one's findings. There are numerous options, such as newsletters/publications generated by "think tanks," peer-reviewed scholarly journals, book chapters, books, and others. These outlets differ along a number of dimensions, including target audience, level of methodological sophistication, academic prestige, and the relative emphasis placed on providing a balanced view of research findings. For example, articles published in peer-reviewed journals are typically targeted to academicians and some practitioners, usually are written in a methodologically detailed and sophisticated way, are likely to have high levels of academic prestige, and highly value the presentation of balanced views. By contrast, articles published in a "think tank" outlet are intended for audiences supportive of the positions endorsed by the think tank, are written in a less technical manner, have relatively little academic prestige, and are more concerned with making a compelling argument for a particular position than with balance. In the divorce area, for example, there have been numerous pieces written for publications generated by "conservative" organizations that have emphasized the negative effects of divorce on children, parents, and families. Clearly, one's values with respect to academic prestige, balanced presentation, and intended audience(s) influence where one attempts to publish one's work and these decisions impact how scholars and society at large evaluate the literature.

IMPLICATIONS

In this section, we make recommendations to researchers who wish to take on the challenge of contributing to this body of knowledge and, in doing so, we also hope to help scholars who are trying to make sense out of the disparate conclusions that are found in this literature. In doing so, of course, we reveal our own values regarding scholarship in general and this area of study in particular.

Researchers Should Make Their Values Explicit

Consistent with the arguments we have made in this chapter, we suggest that researchers make as explicit as possible their values pertaining to research methodology and divorce. Given that this is very rarely done in the mainstream literature in the social sciences, it is probably unrealistic (and unnecessary) to expect that each and every value judgement be included in researchers' written work; rather, we advocate for a gradual shift toward making explicit more and more of scholars' values. Researchers might begin by explicating their most important values (e.g., value placed on socioemotional rather than socioeconomic functioning) and, if the field is accepting, to gradually provide more of this information. The explicit statement of the researcher's values should help readers place the research endeavor into its appropriate context.

As a corollary to making one's values more explicit, it is also important, to whatever extent possible, for the researcher to illustrate how his or her values, and their resulting assumptions, influence the research process. Researchers can and should do a better job of providing compelling arguments, stemming from the attendant values and assumptions, concerning the various choices that were made throughout the process, such as deciding which research questions to study, which variables to examine, which measures to use, and so forth.

Researchers Should Consider Knowledge on Divorce to be Contextualized

As discussed earlier, we adopt the value that all knowledge is contextualized and that there are few, if any, "facts" (i.e., universal truths that apply across situations and time periods) that characterize the literature on divorce. Does this mean that we believe that it is not possible to advance our knowledge about the effects of divorce? No, to the contrary, we believe that research can contribute to our understanding of how divorce affects family members. The key distinction is that we do not believe that there is a single "truth" that accurately depicts how divorce affects family members regardless of differences in contexts, historical eras, and cultures. In other words, we believe that there are multiple views and perspectives that can justifiably compete for a place in our knowledge reservoir. In some instances, the various perspectives may be quite consistent over time, in different historical periods, and across family members, such as the conclusion that divorce leads to changes that can be stressful. In other instances, the conclusions may be much more context-specific and defy wide generalization, such as the inference that children fare better when their parents have joint custody. Thus, conclusions drawn regarding divorce and its effects vary on a continuum ranging from extremely context-dependent to quite reliable or patterned (i.e., the conclusions apply to a large proportion of those who have experienced divorce, across cultures, time, and families).

In addition, we suspect that scholarly views regarding the effects of divorce will covary with the prevailing beliefs in a particular culture and/or in a particular historical era. For example, in eras in which divorce is viewed particularly negatively, we would expect that the scholarly interpretation of divorce effects would be less positive than they would be in a cultural climate that was more supportive of divorce.

Researchers Should Draw Inferences Cautiously and With Appropriate Generalizations

Along with most social scientists, one of our values is that we should draw inferences from scientific research only with caution, believing that it is preferable to err on the side of making Type II errors (concluding that there is no evidence supporting the presence of divorce effects when there actually are such effects in the population) rather than Type I errors (concluding that there are divorce effects when there actually are not). This does not mean that we wish to bias conclusions in the direction of proclaiming that there are no divorce effects; rather, before we are willing to infer that we have discovered some important phenomena (e.g., divorce effects), we prefer to have a number of studies that have replicated the observed effect before declaring that the phenomenon is "real."

In addition, we also advocate making generalizations to various populations only with extreme caution. Given our view that research results are contextual and time-bound, we advise scholars to restrict their generalizations to populations that closely match the characteristics of their samples. For example, while this may seem obvious, a study conducted on middle-class white families living in the midwest in the 1970s should not be used to draw generalizations about families in general, about African–American families, or about families in the 1990s. Again, caution and scholarly patience are the operative recommendations.

Researchers Should Present a More Accurate View of How their Research Unfolded

Researchers in the social sciences, and in the divorce area specifically, tend to present their results in a polished and mechanical way, as if the investigation progressed in a linear and objective manner. Of course, few studies are conducted in the "recommended" sequence of stages (i.e., development of research hypotheses, followed by choice of methods, analysis of data to test the already-formed hypotheses, and, finally, interpretation of the results). Scholars have been trained to write in a single authoritative "voice" that does not give credence to the multitude of difficult decisions that are made throughout the research process, the decisions that one would change if the study could be conducted over again, and gray areas of how to interpret the meaningfulness of the findings (Acitelli, 1997). Kaplan (1964) drew a similar distinction between "logic-in-use" (p. 8), which consists of the logic actually used by the investigator, and "reconstructed logic" (p. 8), which involves the investigator's account of the logic used during the research process. What a scholar actually believes or does may be quite different from the constructed account of what he or she believes or does; further, the investigator may not be aware of the reconstructed nature of the account, believing that the two are equivalent.

We suggest that researchers be at least a bit more open to sharing their foibles, concerns, and uncertainties in their journal articles and book chapters. To do so would provide a more accurate sense of how the research process naturally unfolds and may give the reader greater insights into how findings contribute to an area as complex and nuanced as divorce. We hope that researchers and scholars will be more sensitive to the tensions, contradictions, and changes that people experience in a long-term process such as relationship dissolution and divorce.

Researchers Should Consider Several Methodological Approaches

No single research design has a privileged place as the ideal approach to further our understanding of divorce and how it affects family members. On the other hand, given the points that have been made throughout this chapter, we offer a few reflections on the usefulness of various methodological approaches.

In terms of designs that we do not think will be fruitful, simple group comparisons between those who have experienced divorce and any number of other groups containing individuals who have some different experiences are unlikely to provide substantially new information. We have learned a great deal from the vast number of such comparisons that have been conducted over the years and might learn more from the more sophisticated kinds of group comparison designs that were mentioned earlier. However, we feel that our research resources will be better spent on other approaches.

Nevertheless, this recommendation does not mean that we believe that family structure has no value as a construct. We agree with Amato (1993a) that we need to study family structure in combination with other relevant variables, such as family processes. Designs that examine how family processes are related to various outcomes in a number of different family structures (i.e., family process–family structure interactions) have considerable potential. Such designs could answer such key questions as "Is the relationship between family conflict and poor child outcomes stronger in divorced, single-parent families than it is in first-marriage families?" Studies examining such questions would be particularly useful if the grouping variable (e.g., family structure) were operationally defined in specific and targeted ways (e.g., children who experienced divorce and witnessed high levels of marital conflict vs. children who experienced divorce, but whose parents did not engage in high levels of overt conflict).

Consistent with our views that divorce involves an extended process with ongoing changes and adaptations to new circumstances, we find considerable value in longitudinal research designs, whether implemented in the context of a quantitative or qualitative approach. We will be better able to capture the nuances and complexity of the divorce process when we attempt to understand people's experience in more than one time period.

We also see value in the emerging area of "genetically informed" designs that attempt to tease apart genetic and environmental contributions to various outcomes. Partly because our theories tend to assume environmental contributions and partly because we have lacked the technology to study genetic effects, the divorce literature contains very little data that speak to the issue of how much of what we consider to be divorce effects actually may be attributable to genetic similarities between parents and children, siblings, and so forth. Such designs have the potential to advance our understanding of the extent to which divorce itself, apart from other factors such as genetic similarity, is the causal agent responsible for various levels of adjustment.

Finally, we also see the need for qualitative data to complement and supplement insights gleaned from quantitative findings. We agree with Duck et al. (1997), who stated, ". . . we recommend that relationship researchers ask individuals about their relationships while taking into account their social context; ask those partners *in depth* about their relationship in a search for narrative themes and take across time assessments of what people are actually *doing* in relationships" (p. 19). Such questioning and probing would help flesh out the meaning of various findings and would provide a richness and depth to the field that is currently lacking.

Researchers Should do a Better Job of Becoming Familiar with Other Scholars' Work

Researchers need to make greater efforts to become familiar with the work of those outside their primary discipline (Duck et al., 1997). Reading only within one's own discipline and, even within a particular discipline, reading those who tend to share similar views contributes to the variability in inferences drawn in this vast area.

Given the breadth of these various literatures and of the divorce literature as a whole, it may seem like a daunting task to be conversant in all or even a majority of these various literatures. Indeed, it is a challenging task, but there are some steps that can be taken to increase the chances that a scholar is adequately exposed to the diverse research in this area; all of these steps require that one maintain an open mind to the possible usefulness of other points of view. First, with the proliferation of computer-based search services available, one can search for literature on divorce from the journals and books of an ever-growing number of disciplines. Second, scholars need to make a more concerted effort to read each other's work. For example, it is essential for psychologists to deliberately seek out research published in sociology, communication, and other disciplines. Finally, it is important for scholars to attend and participate in professional conferences outside of one's home discipline. The interchanges that can occur at such conferences, both within and outside of formal presentations, can be invaluable in extending one's scholarly range of vision.

Chapter 9

Personal Relationships in Later Life Families

Victoria Hilkevitch Bedford

University of Indianapolis

and

Rosemary Blieszner

Virginia Polytechnic Institute and State University

OVERVIEW

The field of family and aging now spans a broad array of issues, theories, and applications from many disciplines (cf. Blieszner & Bedford, 1995). Focusing on dominant western societies, we examine *relationships* among family members where at least one member is old. Because references to family in the personal relationship literature often do not apply to old members or else relegate them to the family periphery, the first aim of this chapter is to arrive at a definition of family that includes old people, even the very old (85 years of age and more). To do this we review some demographic data that reveal the kinds of family relationships available to old people.

Next, we identify features of family relationships that are not typical of the kinds of relationships usually targeted in personal relations research, such as their ascribed (nonvoluntary) status and their longevity. In a review of the available literature, we consider how such features affect the nature of family relationships.

Families as Relationships.
Edited by Robert M. Milardo and Steve Duck. © 2000 John Wiley & Sons Ltd.

TOWARD AN INCLUSIVE DEFINITION OF FAMILY

Among dominant western societies, most old people are widows (i.e., single women) and most old people live alone. *Family* typically refers to the nuclear family, a household consisting of two adults engaged in an intimate heterosexual relationship and their biological or adopted children (Aerts, 1993; Broderick, 1993). By this definition, the expression "family and aging" is a contradiction in terms. At best, the older family members are among the "incidental linkages of nuclear families to their kin" (Riley, 1983, p. 447). We suggest, instead, that *family* is more accurately and inclusively represented as a class of relationships that are determined by biology, adoption, marriage, and in some societies, social designation. Note that in this chapter, the term marriage includes intimate relationships between gay or lesbian couples and between common-law heterosexual couples.

Below we describe current and projected structures of families that include older adults, based on recent demographic data. Our purpose is to identify which family relationships are available to people generally, and to old people in particular.

Demographics of Family and Aging

Consideration of the age structure of Western society reveals that the modal relationship involves an adult child and an adult parent, not an immature child and a parent. In other words, people spend more time as adult children than as parents of young offspring. In further support of the relative infrequency of parent-dependent child relationships, evidence suggests that adults are having fewer children (Dwyer, 1995). Gerontologists have predicted, therefore, that kinship structure is tending towards "verticalization" wherein few members occupy any one generation, but many of these sparsely populated generations will survive into old and very old age (Hagestad, 1984; Bengtson, Rosenthal, & Burton, 1990). This vertical family structure conjures up images of several generations of adults doting on one small child rather than a flock of children vying for the attention of one or two surviving grandparents.

Not everyone agrees with the verticalization of family prediction. Investigators of the families of very old persons have not found many generations living concurrently yet; many very old people have few family relationships available. Often they have survived even their own children besides their spouse and siblings. In a study of the very old, 32% of white and 45% of black Americans either had no surviving children or never had children (Johnson & Barer, 1995); demographic studies forecasting to 2020 project even fewer children in future cohorts (Dwyer, 1995). Not surprisingly, few of the very old childless adults have grandchildren or great grandchildren (6% of whites and 18% of blacks) (Johnson & Barer, 1995). Nonetheless, most old people (75%) have grandchildren and about 50% have great grandchildren (Robertson, 1995).

Others have also challenged the notion that few family members will be found within any one generation. Today the members of the baby boom generation (born 1946 to 1964) are known for their large siblingships. Many of these siblings should be available to them when they begin to reach old age in 15 years. By 2020, baby boom elders will be more likely to have surviving children than previous elders were (Dwyer, 1995). Despite these inconsistencies in number of members within families, relationships between members of adult generations rather than between adults and dependent children are the modal family relationships. A comprehensive definition of family needs to account for these ties.

Another demographic trend that affects the definition of family is seen in the structure of the marital bond and its equivalent. People are living in marriages much longer now than in the past. Whereas long-term marriages endured for an average of 35 years in 1900, in the 1980s long-term marriages lasted an average of 47 years (C. L. Johnson, 1988). Still, this increase is not as great as gains in longevity would predict (Riley, 1983) due to the gender mortality gap (women lived two to three years longer than men in 1900 and nine years longer in 1990) and the rising divorce rate (about 12% of marriages contracted in 1900 ended in divorce compared to a projected divorce rate of approximately 50% of the marriages begun in 1990) (Dwyer, 1995). Thus, an older man's family often includes a spouse (nearly half of men older than 85 years live with a spouse), whereas an older woman's family is frequently without a spouse (7% to 10% of women over age 85 live with a spouse) (Dwyer, 1995; Huyck, 1995). At the same time, a trend in developed countries reveals a tendency to avoid marriage altogether. The highest rate of never married adults is in Sweden where, in 1985, 39% of men and 30% of women had never married at all (Kinsella, 1995).

Finally, a definition of family inclusive of older adults, who are often spouseless, demands that coresidence with family members cannot continue to be a criterion. Whereas in developing countries old people tend to live with others, the tendency is toward living alone in developed countries. Considerable evidence shows that old people prefer the latter living arrangement if they can afford it. This preference is not a rejection of family, but rather, a relational style of "intimacy at a distance" (Gratton & Haber, 1993). The implication is that family relationships are enhanced rather than curtailed by separate household arrangements. In support of this position, a recent finding on a national probability sample of adults aged 18–80 years demonstrated that having an uncongenial household member takes a greater toll on one's well-being than living alone (Ross, 1995). No doubt, independent households in later life serve to manage potential family conflict.

An Inclusive Definition of Family

Having reviewed some trends and projections in family vital statistics, we can move on to consider other dimensions of a more suitable definition of family. Most attempts at including old people in a such definition rely on the anthropological practice of segregating them within the kinship system (Baum & Page, 1991; Johnson, 1993; Johnson & Barer, 1995; Riley, 1983). In other words, *family* refers to nuclear family, whereas *kin* refers to all other relatives. Although relationships with and by old people are taken into account using the dual family terminology, it contains the assumption of nonmutuality in the designation of one another: adult children belong to their parents' family, but their parents belong to the adult children's kinship system, not to their family. The "modified extended family" concept (Litwak, 1960) includes the notion of linked households, but excluded intergenerational coresidential households, which constitute 18% of all American households of elders with a living child (Lawton, 1994).

In contrast, Riley's definition of family, "a continuing interplay among inter-twined lives within the entire changing kinship structure," does not incorporate a household-related restriction (1983, p. 447). This definition improves on the one based on the kinship concept by not overtly segregating old people, but it excludes many family ties of aged persons that are activated only when needed or are based on the expectation that they could be activated although they may rarely or never be so activated (Bedford, 1995; Johnson, 1993). These pos-sibilities are included, however, in another description of family by Riley as "a matrix of latent relationships . . . relationships that are latent because they might or might not become close and significant during a lifetime . . . a latent web of continually shifting linkages that provide the *potential* for activating and intensifying close family relationships" (1983, p. 441).

Although Riley's conception of family encompasses potential family rela-tionships, it still neglects two important aspects of old people's families. That is, 40–45% of the very old depict their family relationships as either devoid of contact while personally significant (15% to 20%) or virtually nonexistent (attenuated) (25%) (Johnson, 1993). These relationships, too, must be ac-counted for within any definition of family.

Taking all of the above issues into consideration, we offer the following addi-tion to our initial definition of family. A *family* is a set of relationships determined by biology, adoption, marriage, and in some societies, social designation, and existing even in the absence of contact or affective involvement, and, in some cases, even after the death of certain members. This implies that the boundaries of a family cannot be described by an observer; one must ask the respondent because family, according to this definition, is subjective (see Duck, 1994 for a discussion of subjective experience as the location of relationships). Having ar-rived at a definition of family that does not exclude elders, we next turn attention to special features of families that count old people among their members.

PERSONAL RELATIONSHIPS WITH FAMILY MEMBERS

Our proposed definition of family brings into focus a number of issues concern-ing the scope of personal relations scholarship. Most personal relations research examines active, on-going, voluntary relationships, such as romantic and friendship affiliations. Further, these relationships have a course of development marked by periods of formation, maintenance, and dissolution. The qualities of voluntary affiliations, high activity level, and distinct stages of development are not nearly as salient to nonspousal family relationships, especially in old age. Yet, family relationships meet Hinde's (1979) criteria of personal relationships: ties between two or more people who are personally known to each other and who have had a period of intense interaction at some point in their history.

The study of family relationships, then, provides an opportunity to scrutinize a fuller range of the kinds of interactions that come under the rubric of personal relationships. Specifically, studying family relationships of old people gives attention to bonds that are (a) ascribed, or nonvoluntary; (b) persistent, bounded only by birth and death (Riley, 1983); (c) primarily sentimental or symbolic, often in the absence of much face-to-face contact; (d) unstable, as the pool of potential resources diminishes during the course of old age (Johnson, 1993); (e) embedded within and influenced by a kinship system of relationships that span generations of members both living and dead; and (f) subsume a variety of role types (e.g., sibling, spouse, child), each with some unique norms and expectations. In the following sections we analyze each of these characteristics in turn.

Ascribed Status

Because family relations are usually assigned by birth, adoption, or marriage (with the exception of spouses in nonarranged marriages, who are not included in this discussion of ascribed relationships), the objects of these relationships are a matter of choice; they are "givens". As mentioned previously, one focus of personal relations research has been the formation of close ties, such as the role that attraction plays in the initiation process. The principles learned from such research might be applied usefully to voluntary aspects of family ties, but do not illuminate the meaning that ascribed status has for the nature and development of relationships.

It appears that the ascribed status of family ties provides a sense of security, allowing those in need of help to take it for granted that family members may be asked and are likely to respond with the desired assistance. Thus, family relationships need not be earned or won. This confidence explains a pattern rarely found in voluntary relationships, whereby intimacy is found when the need arises, even in the absence of seeking out or enjoying the person's company generally. The sense of security engendered by ascribed status also permits a greater ability to maintain active long-distance relationships with family members than with voluntary ties (Wellman & Wortley, 1989).

Persistence

The longevity of family relationships is remarkable. In Wellman and Wortley's (1989) study of 40-year-old Canadians living in East York, for instance, kin had known each other an average of 35 years, which was three times as long as for nonkin ties. Siblings usually share the longest lived relationship of all. The significance of relationship persistence to the nature of the bond might be due to any of three influences: (a) simply the passage of time, (b) the formative nature of early experiences which largely occur with family members, and (c) the storehouse of joint experiences and knowledge of one another that accumulates over the years and that few others know.

Effects of the Passage of Time

Few relationship scholars consider the effect of the passage of time. One exception is the study of long-term friendship (e.g., Shea, Thompson & Blieszner, 1988. Also see Duck, 1994). An example of research on the effects of time is found in marriage, where persistence seems to predict marital stability. In other words, the longer a marriage has lasted, the more likely it will continue; most marriage break-ups occur during the first few years and the number of break-ups decreases as the length of marriage increases (Troll, 1985). Nonetheless, vulnerable periods occur throughout the course of marriage, such as when a couple's children reach adolescence (Huyck, 1995).

A potential source of knowledge about the influence of persistence on relationships is to study old people's marriages. Based upon reports from volunteers, old people (but husbands more than wives) rate their long-term marriages as happy or very happy, and they report high marital satisfaction (Huyck, 1995). Further, compared to younger people, old people are less likely to admit to experiencing negative feelings in their marriages, but they are also less likely to report as many positive interactions (Gilford & Bengtson, 1979). Also, in a study based on observational coding of a conflict resolution episode, older couples were less emotionally negative and more affectionate than middle-aged couples were (Carstensen, Gottman & Levenson, 1995). Of course, in all these cross-sectional investigations, age of partners covaries with length of marriage, and age marks other potential relational influences such as personality development (Gutmann, 1987; Helson & Moane, 1987; Helson & Wink, 1992). Further, greater satisfaction in late life marriage may be influenced by the attrition of unhappy marriages due to divorce. By controlling for both divorce and age, Glenn (1998) found that cohort effects mostly accounted for late life marital satisfaction.

Longitudinal retrospective and prospective studies both support and refute cross-sectional findings. Using long-married Harvard graduates, Vaillant and Vaillant's (1993) analysis of marital satisfaction showed a weak curvilinear trend when they used retrospective analytic methods, but when they reanalyzed the data using a prospective approach, they found a pattern of stability in marital satisfaction. In a prospective study of very long-lived marriages (50–69 years in length), satisfaction and feelings of closeness increased over time for 47% of the women and 37% of the men. However, this result was linked to more contact with children and less club and church activity, not to relationship longevity *per se*. Also, period effects and cohort specificity could not be ruled out. Finally, although the most common pattern of marital satisfaction was curvilinear (highest in early and late adulthood, lower in middle adulthood), diversity of reactions to marriage was the rule (Weishaus & Field, 1988).

Thus, it appears that long-term marriage research gives contradictory findings on the effects of persistence on close relationships. Findings on the passage of time in intergenerational relationships may be more consistent. Rossi and Rossi (1990) found that the older the adult children, the greater their feelings of closeness toward their old parents and the greater their intimacy with them. Clearly, additional research is warranted. Specifically, investigations designed expressly to focus on relationship duration effects and studies of other long-enduring relationships such as sibling ties are needed to understand fully the unique importance of persistence in personal relationships.

Effects of Early Experiences

Both attachment and psychodynamic theories could explain the effects of early experiences in family relationships on their later nature. According to attachment theory, internal working models of relationships with primary caregivers, formed during infancy, are subject to modification but tend to be quite stable (Levitt, Coffman, Guacci-Franco & Loveless, 1994). The theory, however, postulates a shift in the attachment object in adolescence and young adulthood, so that the patterns of intimacy learned with the early attachment figures apply in adulthood to new relationships, usually with a romantic partner (Weiss, 1982). Because of this theoretically expected shift, adult attachment styles typically are not studied in connection with the family relationships in which they originally formed. One exception is the case of siblings, who sometimes function as attachment figures for infants (e.g., Stewart & Marvin, 1984). Results of a recent study indicated that attachment style in general contributed considerably to attachment feelings toward siblings in middle and old age (Bedford, 1993), signifying the utility of studying nonromantic attachment in adulthood.

The focus of psychodynamic theories on early experience has informed some family theories. Although usually employed in the context of clinical interventions, they can also be applied to study of the nature of later life family relationships. Qualls (1995) explained that the way in which children's needs are met in the original family context has much to say about adult children's response to dependent parents' needs in adulthood. For example, when adult children use geographical or emotional withdrawal to regulate conflict resulting from unmet childhood needs, resumption of an active relationship for the sake of parent care might reactivate early feelings of distress and result in overt interpersonal conflict.

A few systematic studies of early experience effects in adult family relationships have appeared recently. For instance, one study indicated that for three within-family generations of Swedish adults, the memory of parental preference toward a sibling compromised the level of warmth and affection between parent and child in each generation, although the association weakened in the oldest generations. It could not be determined whether the effect of early experiences weakened due to the distance (in time) from the event, or whether the early experience was never so intense for the older generation in the first place (Bedford, 1992). Of course, these correlational findings do not preclude the possibility that adults' feelings distort their childhood memories or that a covariate of both the memory and the contemporary feelings explains the finding, such as a positive or negative response style.

Several studies have demonstrated that adults' behaviors as well as feelings toward family members appear to be related to early experiences within the family. For instance, Whitbeck, Simons and Conger (1992) and Whitbeck, Hoyt and Huck, (1994) found that adults' memories of negative parental characteristics were related to low levels of intergenerational exchange. Similarly, positive memories of parental characteristics were related to a higher likelihood of helping parents. Using prospective rather than retrospective accounts of early experiences in the family, Parott and Bengtson (1999) found similar patterns with respect to positive early affection toward parents. In this case, intergenerational exchanges of help and support were more likely to be reciprocal than in the absence of early affection. Early conflict with parents, however, did not interfere with intergenerational exchanges involving adult offspring. Apparently parents and adult children have a sense of obligation toward one another, which overrides early antagonisms.

Effects of Shared Experiences

Relationship persistence is often accompanied by an accumulation of shared experiences. This shared history has been invoked to help understand the frequent finding that sibling relationships seem to mellow in later life (Bedford, 1989; Gold, 1989). Accordingly, siblings might increasingly value their relationship over time, at least in part because siblings become a repository of shared family experiences. With age, therefore, siblings become unique as persons with whom to reminisce. Through co-reminiscing, siblings are a source of affirmations that one's sense of self has continuity, just as other forces, such as physical change and role loss, threaten to disrupt it. For those adults whose parents are deceased, siblings are the only witnesses of early experiences in the immediate family. Intergenerational reciprocity in help and support, as described in the preceding section, may also be accounted for in part by a history of shared experiences (Parrott & Bengtson, 1999).

Sentimental and Symbolic Ties

Sentimental Ties

Many family relationships of old people are emotionally important despite little or no contact with individual members. These personal relationships are sustained by memories of intense interaction that occurred earlier in life.

Adult siblings who are geographically distant often fall within this category (Bedford, 1989; Cicirelli, 1985). Johnson legitimized this kind of relationship in her study of the oldest old with her notion of "the family as a vessel of sentiment" (Johnson, 1993). Characterizing family rather than individual relationships, Johnson explained that in these families "no instrumental functions are performed, roles have become inactive, and reciprocity is absent. Even when feelings of attachment persist, contacts are usually confined to intermittent letters and telephone calls. Thus, most of the time, the family persists in the memories of surviving members." (p. 326).

Recognizing purely sentimental family relationships is a significant change from the decades-old pattern of using frequency of contact with family members as a handy measure of the psychosocial importance of ties with relatives. Today much evidence supports the fact that rate of interaction among family members is not directly associated with the quality of the relationships, their meaning to the partners, or the level of satisfaction derived from them (e.g., Field & Minkler, 1993; Thompson & Walker, 1984). Johnson's (1993) findings illustrate that quite a few very old people derive considerable satisfaction from relationships that include very little contact or are devoid of it altogether. The question arises, then, under what circumstances does contact (or its lack) either enhance or interfere with satisfying family relationships in later life?

Lack of contact with a relative who is geographically distant, has limited financial resources, or suffers poor health might be easier to excuse than with one whose neglect appears to be volitional. Interestingly, deprivation of contact due to death is not always excused by the surviving relative. An initial grief response is frequently anger, sometimes directed at the deceased person (Kübler-Ross, 1969), even though death is not usually considered to be purposeful unless it was caused by suicide or an extremely unhealthy life style. Perhaps the underlying quality of the relationship plays a mediating role in the association between contact frequency and relationship satisfaction. For instance, limited contact would relate to positive feelings in a basically conflicted relationships when physical distance is used to manage tension (Weisner, 1982). As mentioned earlier however, when frequent contact is again resumed, any problematic aspects of the relationship are often reactivated (Allan, 1977; Laverty, 1962).

Also, attributing negative motivation to a family member's contact is likely to interfere with deriving pleasure from visits. When there is no contact, this is not an issue; an old person does not have to worry, for instance, that the family member is in touch purely out of obligation, which is often assumed by old persons when they are ill (Field & Minkler, 1993). Lack of contact, thus, can potentiate the idealization of family relationships and the containment of difficult relationships within a manageable context.

Symbolic and Attenuated Ties

Relationships with deceased family members have not been studied, but Moss and Moss (1995) recommended this as a topic of future research. In support of this recommendation, Troll (1994) found that 59% of her sample of adults in their 80s named a deceased person as an attachment figure. It appears, then, that such relationships might be central to the lives of quite a few older adults. An important question is how such ties are sustained; possible means are through diary entries addressed to a deceased relative, plans to meet in a later life, and regular communications at the grave site of a relative. Also, nothing in known about the location of such ties within personal networks, nor the network characteristics that support such ties. For instance, are continued ties with deceased family members most likely to be found among individuals whose active social needs are met? Or do they substitute for impoverished relationships or depleted social networks? Do they answer a need for immortality, providing hope that the survivor's memory will be sustained similarly?

Some old people have nonactive ties with relatives that do not even engage the emotional life of the elders, namely, the "attenuated ties" identified by Johnson (1993). Typically, at least for very old persons, these relationships were broken off due to severe conflict or they resulted from the death of relatives who were subsequently forgotten. Sibling ties attenuated earlier in adulthood often prove to be latent and resume activity later when life circumstances permit (Bank & Kahn, 1982).

Such a change is not likely to occur in late life when few years of existence remain, but nothing is known about the meaning of a lack of family ties in old age. Does such an absence serve some adaptive function for old people who must cope with multiple losses or neglect from family members? Does it reflect unresolved conflicts with family members? Do elders with no family ties have substitutions for family relations via fictive kin or friends? Nor is much known about the effect of an attenuated family on the well-being of old persons, except that they are likely to lack informal caregivers, should the need for care arise (Johnson & Troll, 1996).

One special case of attenuated ties with family members occurs among some Holocaust survivors who avoid conversation and thoughts about relatives who perished in the ordeal. Perhaps refraining from emotional engagement with the memories of these relatives is unconsciously motivated by a wish to keep them alive. Specifically, the lack of engagement actually helps to maintain ties with the dead. By avoiding overt references to the murdered relatives, the survivors avoid mourning their loss, which, in turn, maintains the illusion that the relatives are still alive. The price of the illusion, however, is buried memories and an incomplete family history to share with future generations (Shoshan, 1989). Whether this formulation has application to other attenuated ties in old age awaits further study.

Instability

The loss of family members, particularly through death, creates a situation of social instability in the lives of old people. Geographic mobility and death are the chief sources of family losses. Geographic distance can be bridged through technological means (telephone calls, electronic mail, travel) when financial and temporal resources are available, when health permits, and when distal communication alone becomes unacceptable to those who formerly communicated face-to-face. Loss through death, of course, eliminates the possibility of any kind of interaction other than the symbolic form described earlier. Other losses result from functional causes, as when the family partner is no longer coherent or able to maintain one side of the partnership. Whatever the cause, these losses alter the interpersonal life of old individuals.

Whether relationship instability affects the quality of family ties in later life is another area deprived of direct research results. Nevertheless, a large literature on widowhood offers some insight into this question where one central loss has been experienced. Also, an interesting conception of the interpersonal process that ensues from multiple losses was developed in the friendship literature by Sarah Matthews (1986).

Widowhood as an Example of Instability

Relationship instability manifested in widowhood gives a fairly concrete picture of how loss affects other family relationships in old age. Widowhood is a common experience of older adults, especially women. Among adults aged 65 years and older, 70% of women but only 22% of men are widowed. Further, women are widowed for a longer period on average (15 years) than are men (6 years) (O'Bryant & Hansson, 1995).

Despite a vast literature on widowhood, the consequences of its anticipation for other relationships have not been investigated. Perhaps its near universality for women at least helps to account for women's greater involvement in friendship networks than men's (Blieszner & Adams, 1992) and the fact that married women, unlike their husbands, share confidences outside their marital relationship (Oliker, 1989). Although other reasons are usually given for such gender differences in social networks, anticipated widowhood would seem to be a sensible motive as well.

Research on adaptation after widowhood with respect to other relationships indicates that widows tend to preserve their independence from other family members, but to move geographically nearer to them. Sometimes, an adult child moves in with a widowed parent (O'Bryant & Hansson, 1995). After controlling for family size in longitudinal analyses of family interaction among widows, findings indicated that the number of family contacts increased for older widows, but did not change for widowers (Morgan, 1984). This pattern suggests that widowed persons are not seeking substitutes but are attempting to compensate for the spousal loss in some way with more access to other family members than they had prior to their widowhood. Other analyses indicate that over time, widows also shifted their networks to include more widowed than married friends (Morgan, Carder, & Neal, 1997).

Studies of remarried widowed persons compared with non-remarried widowed persons demonstrate many social and emotional advantages of remarriage. Apparently, for many bereaved elders the best adjustment to the loss of a marital partner is to remarry. These findings are consistent with Weiss's (1982) observation that one type of relationship cannot substitute effectively for another. Despite increased contact with other family members, intimacy needs specifically met by a marital partner cannot be met by others, except perhaps in relationships between sisters. In fact, loneliness is the major affective problem of widowed persons. Children tend to provide financial aid when needed and to help more with household tasks than before their parent was widowed, but these services do not address their parent's loneliness. Nevertheless, widowed persons' typical stated reasons for wanting to remarry do not address alleviation of loneliness. Rather, widowers express the desire for a friend and confidant, whereas widows desire the prestige and status afforded them by their social circle when they are courted (O'Bryant & Hansson, 1995). It is important to note, however, that not all widowed persons desire to remarry, although they may remain interested in conversation and companionship with members of the opposite sex (Talbott, 1998).

Adaptation to Instability

Matthews (1986) developed a typology of relational responses to friendship loss that might apply to family relationships as well. According to the typology, the effect of a friendship loss on people's lives depends on how they defined the relationship. For example, people who define a loss in terms of friendship generally, rather than in terms of a particular individual, are able to substitute a new friend for the old one, thereby replenishing the pool of associates. At first glance, applying this friendship style to family ties reveals that many lost family relationships, such as those with a child, spouse (particularly for women given the dearth of available men in later life), or sibling, have no literal replacement. Studies of childless older adults indicate, however, that a broader definition of family can open the possibilities for substitutions. Whereas attempts at vertical substitutions (up and down generational lines) limit the pool of eligible relatives, collateral substitutions, typical of those practiced by blacks and Italians, provide more possibilities (Johnson & Barer, 1995, 1997). Cousins, nephews, and nieces, for instance, can substitute for absent siblings and children in old age.

Another adaptation to friendship loss is to let circumstances dictate their substitution (Matthews, 1986). Thus, friends are where one finds them; when friends depart, those who inhabit one's life circumstances take their place. This coping style can be applied to family loss in terms of the adoption of fictive kin. In Johnson's sample, an aunt explained that her niece, whom she reared, is thus her daughter. Fictive kin are not necessarily relatives of a different degree; they need not be related at all. Particularly in black communities, fictive kin can take the place of relatives who died, were never present, or were rarely needed earlier, as in the case of old people who never had children (Johnson & Barer, 1995, 1997).

Family Systems

Just as at other stages of the life course, family relationships in the later years take place within a family system. In late life families, the family system typically refers to the totality of kinship relationships, synonymous to a social network of relatives. The implication, however, is that this network follows the principles of an organic or cybernetic system. The basic principle of such systems is that the part (any individual or subgroup within the family) "cannot be identified except with reference to the whole" (La Gaipa, 1981, p. 67). In other words, each member of the family and particular relationships between members cannot be regarded as independent units that function in isolation from one another. One person's behavior is influenced, whether knowingly or unknowingly, by behaviors of others, within and across generations and households. In turn, each member's behaviors are responded to by others, resulting in complex feedback loops (Hendricks, 1997).

Applications of Systems Theory

Clinicians have applied such principles to understanding problematic relationships between family members and psychological disorders of individuals. Geropsychologists such as Hanson (1997), Knight and McCallum (1998), and Qualls (1995) have expanded this application to understanding issues involving old members of families. According to the systems formulation, presenting problems are symptoms of basic dysfunctional processes within the family. Typical symptoms in later life families are cut-off relationships, in which one family member breaks off all contact with another; excessive disability in one member, usually an older one; and excessive conflict surrounding care of aged parents, whether between child and parent, or among siblings. Such symptoms are believed to channel attention away from more fundamental problems. Symptoms are difficult to alleviate, because doing so would enable the underlying problems involving other family members to erupt (Qualls, 1995). For example, in a sibling caregiver support group, some primary caregivers who felt they received no cooperation from their siblings learned that they (the caregivers) were actually pushing their siblings away in a last ditch effort to finally win favored status from their parent which they had coveted since childhood (Altschuler, Jacobs & Shiode, 1985). Thus, an unrecognized parent–child conflict, which might have had roots in the parent's original family, is manifested in sibling conflict over parent care.

The systems framework is usually used to understand the behaviors of whole families rather than personal relationships within the family (Sprey, 1991), in part because general systems are much simpler than highly complex, constantly changing, less organized family processes (Broderick, 1993). Recent examples include research on normative family processes such as the division of parent care tasks among siblings (Matthews & Sprey, 1989) and assignment of the family kin-keepers (Troll, 1996).

The systems model is also useful for identifying many family-level variables that might contribute to personal family relationships (La Gaipa, 1981). Properties of systems that might be applied to understanding older families are (a) their openness, referring to input to the family system from the environment and output from the family system to the environment; (b) their ongoing nature, suggesting that they are constantly in flux, responding to environmental pressures (e.g., income loss) and changes in family members (e.g., onset of illness or developmental transitions); (c) their goal seeking, indicating the selection, rank ordering, and pursuit of aims; and (d) their self-regulating nature, or responding appropriately with change (adaptation) or maintenance of stability (homeostasis) in order to preserve the integrity of the system when threatened (Broderick, 1993).

Effects of Systems Properties on Family Relationships

How do these general systems properties influence family relationships with and by old members? Openness and stability are two systemic properties that have particular relevance to relationships in later life families. The openness of the system can be translated into the dimension of cohesiveness [see Olsen, Russell & Sprenkle's (1979) presentation of the circumplex model for a thorough discussion of this dimension]. Cohesive or highly integrated families provide a sense of belonging and of integration with the family group, responding to the need for connection. An opposing need is the individual's desire to differentiate from the family unit and to forge a separate identity which requires distancing from others while engaging in independent interests, ideas, and relationships. The needs for connection and separateness do not present problems in family relationships when the relative strength of these opposing needs is similar for an interacting set of partners, because the shifting "relational distance" between them in response to one or the other need is mutually satisfying (Broderick, 1993). When relational distance needs conflict and a compromise cannot be negotiated, however, problems can emerge, such as the disenchantment evident in long-term marriages and the loneliness expressed by Swedish wives (Josselson, 1992). The concept of *intimacy at a distance*, referring to a pattern of living in a separate household but staying closely connected to family members, is an example of a satisfactory resolution of these opposing needs for "bonding and buffering" in relation to family members (Josselson, 1992). By maintaining separate households, old people protect their privacy and independence, meeting such personal needs as self-reflection (see Gratton & Haber, 1993).

Stability, or degree of adaptiveness to change by the family system, is another helpful concept for understanding relationships in later life families. As the focus moves from the level of whole systems to subsystems to individuals, stability decreases. In other words, individuals and dyads change more easily than the family as a whole does. For instance, even if a family member dies or a couple divorces, family celebrations of holidays are not likely to be affected too much. The system is usually maintained by one or more kin-keepers who host and organize such functions. As a testimony to the stability of the system, kin-keepers who die or are no longer able to carry out their functions are invariably replaced by other family members, even in very loosely bonded families. In such families, though, the succession process is less smooth and the number of kin-keepers participating is smaller than in more tightly bonded families (Troll, 1996).

Making decisions about goals and their relative priorities and executing them is a complex process that involves the relative power of family members, pragmatic needs, resources, and other concerns. Family gerontologists have been criticized for ignoring the systems level when investigating the processes involved in caregiving (see Matthews & Sprey, 1989; Sprey, 1991). A recent attempt to analyze the decision to institutionalize a parent demonstrated rather dramatically the degree to which systemic- as opposed to individual-level factors accounted for the decision. Change in the health status of the frail family member was not a significant factor in the decision. Instead, a wide array of family variables contributed to the determination to use an institution: placement was more likely when there were more, not fewer caregivers, when no spouse was present, and when the caregiver's subjective distress increased (Lieberman & Kramer, 1991). Fingerman and Berman (in press) provided many other examples of the theoretical and empirical usefulness of applying principles of family systems theory to the study of kin relationships in adulthood and old age. For example, the principle of maintaining equilibrium helps to explain some adults' difficulty in accepting changes in aged parents' needs and abilities. Fingerman and Berman (in press) also pointed out the limitations to understanding that are engendered by ignoring the systemic properties of late life families. In particular, these limitations include overlooking within-family differences, such as variations among siblings in the research on parent–adult child relationships, and minimizing between-family differences in favor of cultural and generational similarities.

Role Type

Effects of Role Types

Family role type appears to contribute some unique information about the ensuing relationship. Family role types include consanguineous kin (mother, father, child, sister, brother, aunt, uncle) and affinal kin (spouse, in-laws). In the social support literature, relationship category is considered to be a property of a personal relationship (e.g., Pierce, Sarason & Sarason, 1990; Sarason, Sarason & Pierce, 1994). No doubt this property subsumes many expectations of the role, expectations derived from personal experiences with someone in that role, the norms peculiar to one's own family system, and the social norms of broader reference groups. Of interest here is whether a family role type has shared meaning (within or across cultures), what the nature of that shared meaning might be, and how that meaning affects the nature of family relationships in later life in addition to the other influences already discussed. Recent reviews of research on old age parent–child, sibling, marital, and marital-like relationships appear in Blieszner and Bedford (1995). Little is available on in-law relationships (but see Kivett, 1989, for a review of mother- and daughter-in-law relationships and Globerman, 1996 and Merrill, 1993 for information on care provision by daughters- and sons-in-law).

Of particular concern to gerontologists are the functions various family role types provide old people. Empirical studies converge on the finding that, in general, some social support provisions cluster around certain role types. In other words, in most categories of network members, people provide a few specialized functions (Fehr & Perlman, 1985; Wellman & Wortley, 1989). Similarly, using a very large sample, Dykstra (1993) found among the Dutch that overlap among relationship categories occurs, but people in every category also provide some unique forms of social support. An important exception is parents and adult children who engage in exchanges of multiple provisions (Wellman & Wortley, 1989). Other inter- and intragenerational distinctions are discussed further in the next sections.

In a study by van Tilburg (1990), type of role relationship was not a good proxy for social support functions of relationships. This finding did not rule out the possibility that role type conveys other important information about social support, however. Those occupying various relationship categories might behave similarly, such as providing the same services, but the effect of these functions might be experienced quite differently, depending on who (in terms of role type) is carrying out the task (Pierce et al., 1990; Sarason et al., 1994). In fact, this expectation has been demonstrated in several studies. The same specific behaviors, for example, are differentially helpful to cancer patients, depending upon the source of the support given (Dakof & Taylor, 1990; Felton & Berry, 1992). Also, contact with family members of different role types appears to be differentially associated with marital satisfaction. Further, the direction of the association might be different for husbands and wives. Wives' kin contacts, particularly with their brothers-in-law, are associated with negative marital qualities, whereas husbands' contacts with kin, particularly with their father, are associated with positive marital qualities (Burger & Milardo, 1995).

Effects of Generational Categories

These investigations indicate, then, that role type differentiates relationships both according to some functions and according to the shared meanings individuals attribute to their actions. Role types fall into two broader categories, however, that also differentially affect family relationships. These categories are intergenerational (vertical) and intragenerational (horizontal) relationships. They are distinguished by generational membership within the family, and, it is assumed, by cohort difference. The latter distinction, that familial generations occupy different generations in time, or cohorts, should not be taken for granted, however. One's sibling might be comparable in age to one's child and one's step parent, aunt, or uncle might be near one's own age. In the typical case, however, when cohort differences are much greater between generations than within generations, one important difference between inter- and intragenerational relationships is that the former involve individuals who have different historical backgrounds. Historical events experienced by different generations are likely to shape their expectations and outlooks differently (Hagestad, 1984). Thus, intergenerational partners are faced with divergent value systems, technological advances, interests, and experiences. Apparently outright conflict is avoided in families by steering clear of sensitive topics and by reciprocal socialization, or educating each about the other. Hagestad suggested that those who occupy both parent and child roles simultaneously in multigenerational families might play a special role in bridging intergenerational differences because of their personal insight into both positions. As such, they function as "brokers" of stability and change across generations (p. 141).

Intragenerational relationships also have unique properties. Most noticeable is the status equivalence between these relatives compared to that of inter- generational relatives (Johnson & Barer, 1995). In western societies, intra- generational ties are more voluntary than intergenerational ones. Therefore, when intragenerational ties are active, they are more likely than intergenera- tional ones to be based on affection (Leigh, 1982). A comparison of black and white siblings in old age indicates important differences, however. For instance, value consensus is a key predictor of sibling association among whites, whereas blacks are more likely to associate with a sibling who is different—specifically younger in age or less educated (Suggs, 1989). Another characteristic that differentiates collateral from intergenerational bonds is that collateral ties usu- ally recruit more relatives. Strong sibling relationships lead to more ties with cousins, nieces, and nephews who also occupy collateral family positions, whereas a vertical emphasis results in peripheral relations with collateral rela- tives. The result of having the wider pool of relatives that accompanies an emphasis on collateral ties is that old people in such families are likely to have their social support needs fully met, as seen in the black community (Dilworth- Anderson, 1992). Nowhere is the difference between the emphasis on collateral and vertical ties more noticeable than in the family support systems of very old childless blacks, who are relatively unaffected by the absence of children of their own, and very old childless whites, whose family resources are greatly impoverished by having no children (Johnson & Barer, 1995).

SUMMARY AND CONCLUSION

In the first section of the chapter, we used demographic trends and projections to illustrate characteristics of families that include old people. We also evalu- ated various definitions of family, developing them to arrive eventually at one that incorporates elderly members and accounts for the structure and pro- cesses found when families have elderly members.

In the second section, we examined family relationships of old people in terms of a selection of features that tend to be invisible in the more commonly studied relationships of the personal relations field, namely, marriage and friendship. Thus, we identified six themes that typify family bonds generally, some of which are brought into sharper focus when older adults are involved. The literature on these themes was mined for their known effects on relationships, the effects, in sum, of ascribed rather than voluntary relationships, persistent interactions, sentimental or symbolic ties, unstable relationship resources, systemic functioning, and varying role types.

The literature associated with these dimensions of family bonds is vast and we could provide only a few examples and brief summaries in this review. Readers should realize, nevertheless, that the family gerontology literature reveals a rich array of interaction patterns and outcomes that hold much promise for extending the findings from research on romantic and friendship relationships, and, for a much fuller understanding of interpersonal life in general.

Not only does study of the family relationships with and by old people expand and sharpen the vision of personal relations study, this category of relationship experience is becoming increasingly normative in the lives of adults and it is enduring through ever longer periods of their lives. Demographic data suggest that most people's lives will be touched by increased involvements with older family members of the same or different generations. It makes no sense, therefore, to continue segregating the study of relationships with and by older adults in a separate research specialty; such relationships should be integrated within mainstream research on personal relationships.

It is also important to keep in mind that personal relations research has much to contribute to the understanding of older families which are, of course, composed of personal relationships, albeit highly interconnected ones. A constructive dialogue between the two sets of scholars holds much promise in unraveling many unsolved riddles about human relationships. One highly intriguing one, with significant practical implications, is how social support buffers stress. For instance, in research comparing spouses and siblings providing care for a frail old person, why was it found that only siblings suffered when the relationship was of poor quality, and why did siblings suffer more than spouses from lack of respite and from perceived conflict in their lives (Mui & Morrow-Howell, 1993)? Perhaps this example shows that family and aging scholars have contributed to the personal relationships literature in general by highlighting a previously hidden dimension of marriage, that is, the marital relationship *per se* can have a powerful buffering effect on stressful experiences, even when the marital partner himself or herself is a source of stress. In turn, perhaps personal relations scholars can glean new insights about the affective consequences to a relationship of having accumulated a vast store of social debt within it. Thus, reciprocal interplay between family gerontology and personal relations research has potential for greatly enhanced understanding of the functions and processes of personal relationships across the life course.

Chapter 10

Family Life as an Experiential Quilt

Steve Duck
University of Iowa, Iowa City, IA, USA

Linda K. Acitelli
University of Houston, TX, USA

and

John H. Nicholson
San Angelo State University, San Angelo, TX, USA

The question "What is a personal relationship?" was offered several years ago as a central issue facing researchers of personal relationships (Kelley, 1979; Duck, 1990), but the importance of the question is not limited to local issues within the field of personal relationships. Relational studies, and the issues surrounding them, are significant for the larger field of family studies as the nature of the family is questioned, debated, and extended by an increasing number of scholars (for some selected examples, see Chapters 1, 8 and 9, and Fisher, 1996). The question can be restated as the issue of whether relationships are best represented as attitudes (Berscheid & Walster, 1978), communicated emotions (Teti & Teti, 1996), patterns of organization (Chapter 1), reciprocity in behaviors (A. Russell & Searcy, 1997), patterns and qualities of interaction (Hinde, 1981), forms and processes of communication (Duck & Pond, 1989), patterns of mutual under-standing (Kluwer, this volume), the product of tensions between opposing dialectical forces (Baxter & Montgomery, 1996), or all or some blend of (some of) the above and much else besides (see, for example, Fincham, 1995).

Families as Relationships.
Edited by Robert M. Milardo and Steve Duck. © 2000 John Wiley & Sons Ltd.

This chapter claims that such high level and abstract issues can be made more concrete by reference to the psychological and communication practices that occur in family life, as defined by a given researcher, and that the natures of relationships are partly to be found at the level of daily communication (the ways in which people talk in and about the relationship). Such talk, and other talk within the family context, creates daily experiences for people and transmits it to other people whether by way of direct discussion of attitudes, open expressions of love, implicit exercise of power structures in talk, demonstrations of mutual (mis)understanding, gossip with third parties, network talk, or the representation of both cultural and individual psychological experience to other people.

In short, we encourage family researchers to focus more on relating rather than on relationships. In order to address this theme in the chapter, five main issues particularly salient to the study of families will be considered. The five issues are:

(1) *Adopting an* **approach** *to studying families.* This entails articulating as well as implementing one's theoretical and measurement tools of choice. These choices have implications for what one sees (and thus ignores), and how one interprets data (Chapter 8). A related issue in many respects is:

(2) *Choosing a* **topic** *of interest: substance and focus.* This process includes recognizing that in choosing a topic, some family scholars now appear to be moving from a structural to a functional perspective (i.e., moving from categories and static variables towards focusing on dynamic processes). Also, the bulk of research has examined a limited range of substantive constructs, most of which fall into such categories as understanding, conflict, power, equity, marital satisfaction, and stability.

(3) *Choosing the (best?) informant* (i.e., insider versus outsider perspective).

(4) *Recognizing the importance of context.*

(5) *Family members' experiences of multiple relationships* in the course of the routine happenings of their everyday lives.

These themes are, of course, interrelated and frequently overlap both conceptually and practically, and some are not easily partitioned quite so exactly in the chapter.

WHAT IS A RELATIONSHIP?

Given the interconnection of the above themes, family members themselves as well as researchers can be unclear whether (and what sort of) a relationship really exists between any two people in the family. The opening questions thus take on a particular significance in terms of various ontological, epistemological, and methodological research orientations, practices, and operationalizations. If relationships are attitudes, then we need only ask the attitude holder some questions in order to establish the type and quality of the relationship. On this model, we would learn by assessing attitudes about intimacy or attitudes towards other family members and using them as the basis for assessing intimacy or satisfaction between people, and for appraisal of beliefs about social experience and family life. Such an approach presumes that explicit statements of individuals' attitudes on such things are (a) reliable sources of information; (b) unambiguous; (c) all the information that is needed. If relationships are primarily the product of a mixture of an individual's emotional experience, internal working models, styles of attachment, and communication of feelings (see Chapter 4), then one would do research focused on the discovery of individual internal states relevant to relating. If relationships are patterns of interaction, from which an observer might deduce a pattern of emotions, etc., then one might focus somewhere else, for example on the establishment and modification of relational bonds (Cooney, 1997; this volume). If relationships are in existence only when both partners agree that they are, then one must tap both partners as part of the research process, and not rely only on one-sided perspectives (Bigelow, Tesson & Lewko, 1996; Ickes & Duck, 2000), and would attend to the *theoretical* significance of the differences in perceptions (Olson, 1977; Duck & Sants, 1983). If relationships are characterized by dialectical tensions and their management (Baxter & Montgomery, 1996), then one should not necessarily expect general consistency of behavior by a given relational partner or by given individuals across relationships with different family members. Particularly if given relationships are interdependent with other relationships (Klein & Johnson, 1997; Klein & Milardo, 1993; Chapter 7), such that even the personal is truly the social (Milardo & Wellman, 1992), then we face the positively Clintonian problem of defining whether in fact relationships can ever *be* anything—or can be measured—in isolation from the influence of the other relationships with which they co-exist (Dunn, 1988; Milardo & Wellman, 1992). Finally, if relationships are essentially bidirectional in their influences (Pettit & Lollis, 1997), then one must stop seeing them as the possessions of individual participants or of the family as a whole and instead focus on the ways in which they are enacted moment by moment between particular partners at specific times.

These considerations might prompt the recognition that the use of the term "family relationship" is actually a summary label or claim that freezes processes at a particular moment and also masks a variety of activities, motivations, experiences, and directions of influence—a convenient summary term but a summary term all the same. As such, use of the term confronts researchers with important choices about the summarized aspects on which to focus attention. As Manke and Plomin (1997) advise, for example, one choice for relationship researchers is the level of analysis at which to explain relationship activity, whether the level be the individual, the dyad, or the larger family system (or, one might also add, the cultural environment that defines the acceptable natures of relationships, Chapter 1; Duck, 1998; Milardo & Allan, 1997, and Chapter 7). This choice is a prerequisite for researchers even identifying or differentiating relationships and their gradations.

There is a second choice facing researchers also, and identified by Duck and Sants (1983), that even once the unit of analysis is decided, one is then faced with the choice of the perspective to take upon it: any two individuals in the same family may have different views of it. When one of the observers is a relational partner and one is a researcher, what is one to do if the two perspectives are different and irreconcilable? Who is right? The matter is more than vacuous, especially when some researchers rate children's friendships by asking peers and teachers to identify a target's friends and then compare those ratings with the target's self-ratings not of the friendship but of something else (social behavior) and then use them an independent variable relative to some other (dependent) variable such as "likelihood of producing pro-social behavior", as Menesini (1997) did. Another example is when researchers themselves argue about the ways to count family members (who is? who isn't?), especially in light of cultural and ethnic differences in the boundaries of a family (Allen & Walker, this volume; Fisher, 1996). The implicit depiction here is that researchers *know*, and hence that families are objectifiable and determinable from the observations made by scholars. (Obviously those who accept such definitions could not count as relationships any form of secret extra-marital affair.)

In the case of families including children, the choices are further complicated by the fact that children and adults have different cognitive abilities and so also a different grasp of social concepts. Thus even once one identifies a relationship within a family and classifies it (as a parent–child relationship, for example), one needs to recognize that the two partners are, in a subtle psychological sense, *not* (cognitively) in the same relationship, since one person has deeper understanding of some psychological processes of the other person than is true vice versa (Duck, 1994a). However, the same point applies also if we look at practice in addition to or instead of cognition and the point is not exclusive or unique to parent–child relationships. The two-cultures gender perspective would speak to this, as would many intercultural perspectives. In addition to having different cognitive resources, family members also (as we argue later) have different contexts for their relating. There are layers of contexts, some shared, some not, that also are affected by and influence the resources that are available, and those that are deemed proper or appropriate in a given situation, in addition to those of which a relational partner will be cognizant.

Nor are the relative influences of their bidirectional effects equivalent (Dunn, 1997) whether or not one compounds the observation by consideration of power issues in relationships (Chapter 1). Also, to a lesser extent, the same is true of sibling pairs in the family, where one partner might, by reason of more advanced cognitive development, understand the relationship in ways different from the other or seek to enter secret alliances with one another to defeat various aspects of parental control without the parents' awareness (Nicholson, 1998). In such cases the strength of bidirectional effects could differ between partners in the same relationship, as well as in different relationships of the same target person (Lollis & Kuczynski, 1997). Hence the matters of deciding what is a relationship, how one recognizes it, how it may be measured, what happens in it, and who should legitimately tell us about it become relevant sites of reflection. But not necessarily in that order or that separately.

CHOICES OF TOPIC AND STYLE OF RESEARCH AS IMPLICIT THEORIES OF RELATING

Following several previous commentators (Dunn, 1997; Montgomery & Duck, 1991), we note that an investigator's attempts to remove context in order to focus on a notionally key variable, like the intention to reach for a particular methodological tool or to exclude certain phenomena from the study, is itself a decision about the *nature* of the problem to be researched. Built into our methods of inquiry and our strategies of empirical study are outlooks, presumptions, and perspectives that mold the way we pursue the investigation of a problem. This is as true in the study of family relationships as elsewhere: to look for a stable, reliable measure of a family's emotional life or of marital satisfaction, for example, is to presume that the relevant emotions are stable (Duck, West & Acitelli, 1997; Fisher, 1996; Chapter 8); to assume that relationships have bidirectional influences is to make an assumption about the nature, distribution, and operators of power in a relationship (Duck, Acitelli, Manke & West, 2000); to treat families as enduring beyond the observable patterns of interaction is to locate a mechanism of endurance within the persons involved (Manke & Plomin, 1997), and within the social structures in which they are embedded (Chapter 1).

Such issues are important when researchers set out to focus on particular aspects of families and specific pairs of relationships within them. Defining a family relationship as, for instance, "two adults living as committed partners in the same household with expectations of futurity to the relationship" is a simple structural or categorical definition rather than a functional psychological one or one defined in terms of qualities of experience or by reference to the daily communication that occurs between people in the family. We also know that any family member's network of relationships involves a set of other people, sociometrically interconnected in some way (Chapter 7), and we can deduce from that pattern of connection whether or not a person is well integrated into other networks (Milardo & Allan, 1997) and whether a family's child is popular, rejected, or neglected (Asher & Coie, 1990). But again that is primarily a structural concept, and a network cannot be said meaningfully to exist at all without interaction and communication or, indeed, choices of how to spend time within the structure (Bronfenbrenner, 1979). Can a network truly exist without some communication actually taking place between members or choices being not only expressed but also *enacted*?

As soon as one focuses on these issues, then one is forced to recognize that the nature of the relationship is itself strongly influenced by the nature of communication and interaction as well as by the presumed existence of structure. It is a given in most communication analysis that a speaker reports not objective facts but circumstances seen by that speaker in the context of his or her psychological experience, the circumstances of speaking, and the audiences to whom the remarks are made, among other things. In the circumstances of daily life, such rhetorical frameworks (VanderVoort & Duck, in press) involve the relational circumstances in which the speakers operate, such that there are relational messages contained in every utterance (Watzlawick, Beavin & Jackson, 1967). The implications of this are that relationships between family members are partly avowed, partly transformed, and partly re-enacted during every conversation between family members. Therefore, one must consider the role of actual communication in the family processes that we readily assume to underlie the structural and behavioral interactive aspects of family life (Duck et al., 1997).

Any reliance on structure rather than on process also conceals the fact that, from the point of view of the subjects of our studies living their complex lives, those lives are characteristically uncertain and dynamic. Part of the reason why human beings (both research participants and research conductors) prefer prediction and control is to reduce the sensation of complexity that is otherwise ubiquitous—and holding on to a sense of enduring structure is one way to reduce the complexity to manageable form. One pervasive human characteristic is to develop categories and labels that imply stasis and fixity (Bowlby, 1980; Bruner, 1990; Duck, 1994a). The fluid and uncertain quality of relationships is absent from much theory and research that seeks reliability as a criterion of successful measurement. However, the creation of such order is a psychological process of construction, not simply the uncovering of an existing state of affairs (Bruner, 1990). All the same, family members are surely aware that relationships can break up or become stormy as well as endure in tranquillity. At that point of disturbance, structure is nothing and process is everything.

This is particularly important when one acknowledges that relationships are depicted in research and in subjective reports at the moment of observation, even where researchers develop techniques to assess such things as synchronicity with others (Pettit & Mize, 1993). Such summary measurement risks depicting relationship processes themselves in a form generalized from that moment, or all synchronicities as typified by the one observed, so that families (and relationships more broadly) are then discussed as entities characterized totally by that one measurement or report. Yet in treating relationships as cross-sections, unities, states, plateaux, or turning points on a graph, researchers or speakers may overlook the *simultaneous* presence and intersection of a number of features and options or the pressures of real alternative options to the path actually taken. For example, behavioral choices are always made between real alternative options (Kelly, 1955): to understand the choice, one has also to understand the psychological and social context of alternatives in which it was made (Dixson & Duck, 1993). Any description of events represents the observer's choices about what to notice and how to describe it to a given or presumed audience, whether that audience be another family member, a network contact, or a researcher. It is also necessary to portray the rhetorical context by which the choice was circumscribed and the audience to whom it was reported, and to depict not only the outcome but the processes and dynamics surrounding it. Our point here is that everyday family life itself normally provides many such instances.

Many scholars have pointed to the importance of the commonplace circumstances and activities of daily life that actually serve *as* the conduct of relationships (e.g., Fitch, 1998). Such scholars remind us that *everyday* communication is the means by which emotions are conveyed, cognitions are represented, behaviors performed and explained, power is exercised and negotiated, norms are established, and thus relationships are conducted—indeed, it is how they manifest their existence. Yet, what is everyday communication? In one sense, it is contrasted with exceptional and extraordinary relational and communicative events such as instances of intimate self-disclosure, or sharp conflictive arguments, or turning points, which, by their very nature are not typical or representative of that relationship's ordinary daily conduct. Significant, dramatic, and, as it turns out, rare, behaviors are well researched, as for example is intimate self-disclosure, something that happens only 2% of the time in daily life (Dindia, 1994). Everyday conversation is more likely to be trivial, task focused, gossipy, jocular, playful or light than it is to be heavy with significant intimacy, conflict, or deep connection of minds—and yet it does important relational work (Duck, Rutt, Hurst, & Strejc, 1991).

In another sense, the term "everyday communication" points to the range of positive and negative relational and communicative experiences that people have every day, all the time. These experiences include not only the positive side of relationships (Andersen, 1993; Berger, 1988, 1993; Berscheid, 1994; Fehr, 1993; Fincham & Bradbury, 1987; Fletcher & Fitness, 1993; Honeycutt, 1993; Kelley, Berscheid, Christensen, Harvey, Huston, Levinger, McClintock, Peplau & Peterson, 1983) but also the negative or difficult, such as embarrassment (R. S. Miller, 1996), shame and anger (Retzinger, 1995), daily hassles, (Bolger & Kelleher, 1993), or the dark side of relationships (Cupach & Spitzberg, 1994; Duck, 1994b), right up to and including violence and abuse. Thus a focus on the everyday experiences of family communication entails attention not only to routine and trivial activities on the one hand, but also to the complex mixture of good and bad experiences that are matched and managed and, indeed, composed into the summary description of the relationship as it is offered by some particular person on a given occasion to a particular audience.

We believe that the problems of implied uniformity of experience are exemplified in many literatures, including the attachment, parent–child, and family studies literatures (and in the other companion volumes in this series). A particularly good example of the problems associated with the use of categories can be seen in the use of Baumrind's (1972) typology of parenting in a family. Although one parent in a family may be characterized as authoritative (high on demandingness and warmth) another parent in the same family may not be authoritative. Likewise, parents may use one type of parenting style (e.g., authoritative) with one child in a family, but an entirely different parenting style (e.g., permissive) with another child—and such differences may be systematic (e.g., related to gender, age and so on). Furthermore, the disadvantages of using typologies to categorize families as a whole are to be found in the exclusion of the variability that occurs not just within a parent or across (and within) children but throughout daily life. A parent could vary in parenting style with the same child depending on the issue in question (e.g., homework versus recreational issues), or the kind of day the parent had at work, or as a function of human changes in mood and circumstance. These three types of within-family variability are typically ignored when researchers employ this parenting typology, thereby masking the complex dynamic nature of the family experience. Of course, readers will readily appreciate that we use this one example when other examples of such typologies likewise exist in family studies and are subject to the same critique.

In keeping with developing trends in several disciplines (Acitelli, Duck & West, 2000; Barrett, 2000; Berscheid & Reis, 1998), we thus urge focus on personal relationships not as abstract constructs or attitudinal products of various precipitating factors, but as lived experiences of social life. Such everyday social and personal experiences pose special dilemmas for individuals that are not fully captured when one taps only into social cognitive processes—particularly if one focuses on the cognitions of just one relational participant (Ickes & Dugosh, in press; Ickes & Duck, 2000). The truly social aspects of social experience are only partially reflected in one person's thoughts about social objects. Increasingly, researchers are recognizing that social interactions may be perceived differently by the partners, and appreciate the importance of assessing the degree and type of congruence or incongruence between the perceptions of dyad or family members (Acitelli, Douvan & Veroff, 1993; Kenny, 1994; Ickes & Gonzalez, 1996). A *social* point is that in real life conduct of family relationships, those differences of perspective are understood, or tacitly accepted in varying degrees, by the participants. These cognitive differences can have significant behavioral consequences that can manifest themselves in several interactions.

Moreover, social experiences are deeply rooted in such selective perception. When researchers select particular parts for attention according to their own preferences, they may therefore do incomplete justice to the subjective experience of partners. Accordingly, Berscheid and Reis (1998) note that relationship scholars themselves still do not agree about which aspects (frequency, type, nature, etc., or combination thereof) of interaction actually define a relationship. In essence, then, researchers must attend to all behavioral enactments and contingent interdependencies that we recognize as relationships, even if those interactions are, at some level, routine and trivial.

Furthermore, in real life, particular parts of family life are variably foregrounded from time to time, and the relationship is not one consistent experience all the time, as measures defining *the* closeness or stability of a family or marital relationship imply. Thus people in life and in research studies are made to choose particular roles or aspects of the relationship as foci on different occasions. For example, central to the understanding of personal relationships and social support is the issue of how particular circumstances *warrant* different psychological reconstructions of the relationship between people. A sudden disaster warrants and evokes different facets of relational obligations and duties (Kaniasty & Norris, 2000) from those regarded as normal at other times. Thus, whereas friends are normally valorized for doing such paradigmatically friendly things as confiding in one another, disclosing, talking, having fun together, and showing intimacy (Davis & Todd, 1985), the occurrence of a disaster may warrant switches from confiding to physical support, from playfulness to emotional assistance, and from intimate disclosure to self-sacrifice and perhaps physical effort. (The event may also transform a supportive relationship into a decidedly non-supportive one.) In the mundane exigencies of everyday life, choices about emphasis or switching of appropriateness are clearly a common experience: families do not sit and express satisfaction with one another intensely all day long, day after day. Rather, they play (Baxter, 1992), chat (Duck, et al., 1991), have small talks (Spencer, 1994), argue (Wood, 1995), go shopping or play sports or have coffee or go on vacation (Wood, 1993), and so on.

In parallel with the selectivity of perception by family members that is composed into one total summary experience (or data point), all of the substantive choices made by researchers in conceptualizing relationships involve similar stripping away of some of the normal variabilities, accompaniments, and contexts so that researchers can choose to focus their study more effectively. The literature in family studies shows us that researchers usually focus on marital satisfaction, conflict, power, stability and marital adjustment, and less often explore respect, expectations, guilt, humor, daily conversation, or leisure. A supplementary list would include such common aspects of everyday life as inconsistency, unpredictability, fear, anxiety, worry, impatience, sense of progress and achievement, and a host of other things that might be relevant to the way a family, particularly a child or adolescent, might experience life in the family, especially as age changes all family members' senses of personal goals and needs in life.

Family research also tends to focus on particular relationships, such as parent–child relationships or relationships between committed partners, but has until recently had less to say about such relationships as siblings (Dunn, 1996) or, within that, greater subtleties such as the way in which siblings gang up against parents (Nicholson, 1998). Although there is a growing awareness of the experiential significance of the fact that every dyadic relationship occurs in a nexus of other relationships (Burkes & Parke, 1996; Milardo & Wellman, 1992; Chapter 7), the interactions of those relationships are a rich ground for continued diligence if researchers wish to understand fully the family's experience of relational life. As part of our argument, we propose, then, that whatever messy parts of real life and social context are stripped away by a researcher's need to provide realism in studies or conceptual clarity in theory they must later be consciously and explicitly reconnected to the explanation of the stripped down processes (Acitelli, 1995).

We do not deny the value of focused research certainties or styles of explanation, but instead we see many of them as preferences of explanatory style chosen by scholars from the range of possible explanations. From the phenomenal pool of uncertainty, observations are retrospectively made into predictable patterns from the many different sequences possible from a given starting point—whether by relaters or by researchers (Duck, 1994a). The kinds of predictabilities and certainties chosen by everyday relaters on the one hand and researchers on the other are partly determined by the different projects, needs, and audiences for whom each set of persons creates those explanations at a given moment. In the case of social scientists, our methods encourage researchers to isolate particular aspects of family relationships from others in order that we may study them more effectively. The consequence is that certain occurrences in those relationships are given priority by such methods. The nature of family relationships—despite all their tedium, repetitious boredom or occasional unpredictable flourishes—tends to be represented by *interesting phenomena* that evince researchers' local and focused enthusiasms for theoretical topics, like conflict or power, rather than the mundane conduct and experience of everyday life beyond such things. Researchers' enthusiasms essentially lead to the endorsement of the proposition that relationships are composed of all (and only) those notable things to which researchers have so far given their attention—as if everyday family life were experienced as the news headlines.

We believe, therefore, that the chapter's opening questions come most sharply into focus if one attends to communication and contexts in modifying and influencing the ways in which relat*ing* is carried out in a family (Duck, 1993; 1994a). Scholars such as Hinde and Stevenson-Hinde (1988) and Crouter and Helms-Erickson (1997 and Chapter 6) have taken a bottom-up approach and looked for patterns across such contexts as school, work, and home. Others such as Hartup (1989) and Veroff et al. (Chapter 2) take a top-down approach and explore the ways in which different contexts ultimately constitute resources for the person in different relationships. It is important to note that context is differently theorized in these cases. A weak view of context is that it is the momentary backdrop against which otherwise consistent actions are carried out (such as place, environment, or situation; Argyle, Furnham, & Graham, 1981)—rather like a scenic backdrop in a stage play. A stronger view is that place, time, school environment, ritual, family life, ceremony, celebration, and other temporal contexts such as life-developmental stage, render different the experiences of relaters on those occasions or in those places (Werner, Altman, Brown & Ginat, 1993; Pettit & Mize, 1993). The strongest view is that context is like the water in which fishes swim, and is inextricably part of everything that is done there, such that relationships are steeped in societal, cultural, educational, attitudinal, societal, normative, conversational, and dialectical or pedagogical contexts (Allan, 1993; French & Underwood, 1996; Putallaz, Costanzo & Klein, 1993).

Certainly those who note the effects of culture on relationships and vice versa (Fitch, 1998) are making a different version of the same point as those who argue that relational partners exert influence on each other. Just as a family is a context, so too are specific parental beliefs (Mills & Rubin, 1993), and siblings, family styles, school, and friendships. Each and all of these exert influences on the individual, as do cultural milieu and cultural or historical differences (Chapter 1). The upshot of this view is essentially that one focuses on the occasions and practices that are meaningfully described as relational. These practices and behaviors of particular relationships may well differ from those observable in other relationships and thus it is not in any *simple* sense that persons replicate in other relationships the things they learn from interaction within family households. Such things as power are perhaps enacted in family relationships differently from the way they are with peers or at work, for instance. Such differences arise because of the complexity of the family power dynamics over time (as when children become adolescents for example), the complex and extensive relational history, interdependence, and changes in family relationships over time that rely on practices of power rather than structures alone.

THE EXPERIENCE OF MEMBERSHIP IN MULTIPLE RELATIONSHIPS

In discussing families we should not overlook the fact that both adults' (or parents') and children's lives are played out primarily through time spent in relationships with others who are not family members, whether at work, at school, or in friendships. In the context of our other remarks, we note a hidden and, so far as we know, unrecognized implication of this fact which follows on from the above observations. The children in a family face a number of challenges and types of relational stress that appear to extend beyond those experienced by the adults, where subtle differences of age and grade are less relevant forms of complexity. Where researchers have recognized the varieties of relationships that children experience, such as siblings, family, parents, peers, and teachers, there is less attention to the fact that these are all kinds of relationships that children must handle and handle differently, in context. Especially for children, resolution of contradictions of demands by different powerful adults may be a source of both learning and tension (for example, where teachers and parents set different standards for behavior). Moving between these psychological, behavioral, and relational contexts and managing their tensions and contradictions are features of childhood, and hence of family life, that merit at least as much attention as that presently given to the carry-over between home and work in the adults in the family (Crouter & Helms-Erickson, 1997).

Equally, the everyday conduct of family life can involve momentary choices between relationships in the family, between different distributions of time with different partners, and even strains on loyalties to different persons who may make simultaneous, competing demands on one's relational resources or provisions (Baxter, Mazanec, Nicholson, Pittman, Smith & West, 1997). Often people must choose to give time to one equally deserving and important relationship over another or to devote time to work instead of family (Chapter 6). A person may also be faced with conflicts between or among different relationships—to spend time with spouse or with kids alone, with family or with co-workers, with partner alone or with the family as a whole, staying longer at a work social event or going home to play with the kids, in fulfilling obligations to elderly parents or to neighbors and so on. In real life everyday relationships, a person's commitments to a particular relationship within the family can be assessed as much by the relative distribution of time *between* relationships as by the balance between internal reward and cost systems *within* each relationship.

Not only do particular circumstances *warrant* different psychological reconstructions of the relationship between family members as noted above, but adults experience tensions of competing loyalties between relationships, needing occasionally to make a choice to give time to one equally deserving relationship over another (Baxter et al., 1997). For example, work and home are not the only competing pressures on adult family members but choices must be made between play and work, responsibilities to ascendant and descendant generations of an adult's family, efforts directed at couple maintenance or towards children, or family group and individual issues. Even the everyday conduct of the family's relationships probably involves momentary choices between particular pairings within the family, between different distributions of time with different partners, and even strains on loyalties to different persons who may make simultaneous, competing demands on their relational resources or provisions. There could be requirements to balance out the demands of friends and family (Chapter 6) or needs to negotiate amounts of time spent with extended kin (Chapter 9). Equally, a child or adolescent may be faced with conflicts between or among different relationships—to spend time with playmates or alone, with siblings or school pals, to stay longer at an enjoyable school social event or return home at an hour appointed by parents, fulfilling obligations to parents or to other adolescents, or, in the particular case of adolescent girls, spending time with self-preferred partners or with those approved by the peer group (Senchea, 1998). In real life everyday relationships, a person's commitments to a particular relationship can be assessed as much by the relative distribution of time *between* relationships as by the balance between internal reward and cost systems *within* relationships. This problem is not duly assessed for children in research that explores relationships as if a relationship were a decontextualized entity *in* which the person simply exists (Baxter & Montgomery, 1996).

All family members must negotiate membership in multiple relationships simultaneously and much recent scholarship focuses on the ways in which experience in one relationship may be translated to other relationships. Little of this research, however, focuses on the ways in which persons combine competing and complementary relationships to form a psychologically coherent social network (or even an incoherent one). Just as this is a very important point for developmental psychologists, who have only recently begun to look at the discrepancies among children's relationships (e.g., how children's sibling relationships differ from peer relations), so too it is important for other family researchers. We need to go even one step further to examine how people combine all of these relationships, despite the discrepancies, into a functional social network.

THE PARADOXES OF SCIENTIFIC OBSERVATION

Whereas some researchers have noted that there are insider and outsider ways to look at relationships (Olson, 1977; Duck & Sants, 1983; Surra & Ridley, 1991; Wood & Cox, 1993), less often is it noted that the outsider position is not simply outside the experience of the insiders, but that it typically imports other consequential elements into its depiction of those inside phenomena. This is the case whether the outsider is a network member, an elder parent, a child watching parents argue, a relative, a school-teacher thinking about the family dynamics, a family therapist, a researcher—you name it! In the case when a researcher is the outsider, his or her reports and descriptions present only one cross section in time, whereas the insider position is enriched by many cross sections in time because partners can rely on memory as well as any present observations (Dixson & Duck, 1993). The researcher's outsider position necessarily stabilizes the interior dynamics of the participants by recording their momentary position rather than their fluctuations.

While the limits of the outsider perspective are clear, though underreported in scientific articles, the insider's view is also imperfect. For example, insiders can become enmeshed in their experience and thus do not see a full picture of what is happening in their relating. Outsiders, particularly researchers with complex understandings of particular stratified processes, may have theoretical and critical lenses that allow them to notice and comprehend things that insiders do not even see. A position that claims outsiders are objective and detached can go too far, but one can also go too far in honoring the insider's perspective. Insiders have information to give, insights to offer, experiences to report in depth, but they may also experience a reality that is partial, flawed, complex, overbearing or incomplete in ways that are different from *but no less than* the realities experienced by researchers.

The issue of reliability now resurfaces as the issue of how to get inside (as well as outside) a relationship and to reassemble the model of the interior as we describe the exterior. The cross-sectional outsider position adopted by most social scientific research on relationships will necessarily represent relationships processes as monochromatic objects, and our goal in the future must be to color them in. The main way to do this is for researchers to look within individual families on several occasions in order to depict the variety of patterns, rather than presume a fixed pattern of experience in the family on the basis of one point of measurement. Present research designs often allow only for one-shot data collection, with research findings then used to generalize beyond that moment, and represent the relationship (e.g., its intimacy) *in toto*. Where Hinde (1981) called for more description of relationships (using an ethological analogy), we call for more work on the variabilities perceived by relationship partners such as the contradictions and uncertainties with which partners must cope (Duck, 1994b; Duck & Wood, 1995), variations in expectations about the relationship (Miell, 1987), and the changing or varied patterns of talk in and about relationships (Acitelli, 1988, 1993; Duck, et al., 1991). Here we place less emphasis (but still place some emphasis) on external, behaviorally based description alone. By analogy, if a researcher adopts metaphors that focus on monolithic stasis, it is like assuming that the real point about boiling water is the particular mark it reaches on the thermometer, not the interior ebullience and structural change that takes place in the fluid mechanics of its constitution, or that good sex is a check mark in a diary rather than something energetic, diachronic, and composed of complex actions.

The more complex overlay of the preceding point is that even if data collection occurred more than once, force-fit answers to questionnaires could still limit participants' ability to explain the nuances of giving the same answer at two different points of data collection (for example a "2" on a Likert scale of intimacy may not mean exactly the same to all family members on all occasions with the constancy that the number 2 implies) or from the simultaneous perspective of the insider and outsider measured separately. What occurs is a glossing of difference: participants summarize the variety of their experience and so speak to their general feeling of the relationship rather than describing only the specific moment (yet in real life break up of relationships, for example, individuals may be guided by the fear that to give voice to specific dissatisfaction can make it real, Duck 1982). Researchers must compare not only the variegated range of experiences of the insider and outsider perspectives but must go further and connect the insider and outsider perspectives: gathering of questionnaire data should be supplemented by dialogue between researcher and participants about those data.

We suggest, therefore, in keeping with our arguments about representations that have integrity, that external observation must in the future be more consistently combined with internal observations gathered over a long enough time period to display internal variabilities. Researchers must also replace the simple emphasis on reliability (which deliberately seeks to strip out variability) and instead recall what it is that reliability leaves out of our understanding of the fluctuations of relationships.

CONCLUSIONS

To recognize continuous tensions and variability in relational emphases is to require a representation of family relationships that sees them as complex, variable, subject to re-characterization, describable in many ways simultaneously, open-ended, to some extent contentious, and certainly the kind of conceptual entity that can be the subject of legitimate disputes about their true nature on occasion. Such tensions and choices may be viewed as descriptive or rhetorical (as may their management). One observation in the study of communication and personal relationships is that partners make choices about the language in which to characterize a relational act at a given point in time (Duck & Pond, 1989). These choices carry rhetorical, moral, and social behavioral implications (Shotter, 1992). A person obviously also has a choice to describe a particular relational act in a way that decontextualises it from the processes that swarmed around it at the time. Any person's selection of a description of features of a relationship at a particular time is a rhetorical act, not a simple descriptive one; that is to say, people in families (including children) describe their experiences—or anything else—in a way that is consistent with a particular world-view and purpose, on a particular occasion, for a particular audience, or in a particular context (Duck, Pond & Leatham, 1994).

Equally, researchers have similar kinds of descriptive and rhetorical choices available to them and the choice of "mechanisms to emphasize will depend on the theoretical perspective and methods chosen by a particular investigator" (Dunn, 1997, p. 569). The selection of items to describe or explain within the mix of available phenomena is itself not dictated only by the phenomena but also partly by the conventions of research, partly by the preferences of the researcher, and partly by the impulse of a theory to direct attention towards particular things. It is therefore important if we are to describe relationships usefully—let alone explain them—that researchers keep reminding themselves to return (to the Discussion section) reference to that which they analytically stripped away in the Methods section in order to create a better experiment or a more focused study for a particular purpose on a particular occasion. Having, for good reasons, focused on a single process or the interaction of just two processes by momentarily removing them from their active sites and contexts of operation, any explanation of those processes has to remember to reinsert the previously removed parts of the picture. Dunn (1997, p. 569) warns that researchers must be aware of the extent to which "choices of level of description and analysis constrain the kinds of conclusions we can draw".

We believe that in making such claims relationship researchers should ask what research designs would look like if we were to investigate *relating* rather than *relationships*? A shift from focusing on the noun to the verb could be profitable in our quest to see how behaviors construct (over and over again) the loose definition of partners, friends, and family.

REFERENCES

Acitelli, L. K. (1988). When spouses talk to each other about their relationship. *Journal of Social and Personal Relationships*, **5**, 185–199.

Acitelli, L. K. (1993). You, me, and us: Perspectives on relationship awareness. In S. W. Duck (Ed.) *Individuals in relationships [Understanding relationship processes 1]*. (pp. 144–174). Newbury Park, Sage.

Acitelli, L. K. (1995). Disciplines at parallel play. *Journal of Social and Personal Relationships*, **12**, 589–596.

Acitelli, L. K. (1996). The neglected links between marital support and marital satisfaction. In G. R. Pierce, B. R. Sarason & I. G. Sarason (Eds), *Handbook of social support and the family* (pp. 83–103). New York: Plenum Press.

Acitelli, L. K. (1997). Sampling couples to understand them: Mixing the theoretical with the practical. *Journal of Social and Personal Relationships*, **14**, 243–261.

Acitelli, L. K., Douvan, E. & Veroff, J. (1993). Perceptions of conflict in the first year of marriage: How important are similarity and understanding? *Journal of Social and Personal Relationships*, **10**, 5–19.

Acitelli, L. K., Duck, S. W. & West, L. (2000). Embracing the social in personal relationships and research. In W. Ickes & S. W. Duck (Eds), *Social psychology and personal relationships* (pp. 215–227). Chichester: Wiley.

Acock, A. C. & Demo, D. H. (1994). *Family diversity and well-being*. Thousand Oaks, CA: Sage.

Acock, A. C. & Hurlbert, J. S. (1993). Social networks, marital status, and well-being, *Social Networks*, **15**, 309–334.

Aerts, E. (1993). Bringing the institution back in. In P. A. Cowan, D. Field, D. A. Hansen, A. Skolnick & G. E. Swanson (Eds), *Family, self, and society: Toward a new agenda for family research* (pp. 3–41). Hillsdale, NJ: Erlbaum.

Agger, B. (1998). *Critical social theories*. Boulder, CO: Westview Press.

Aldous, J. & Straus, M. A. (1966). Social networks and conjugal roles: A test of Bott's hypothesis, *Social Forces*, **44**, 576–580.

Allan, G. (1977). Sibling solidarity. *Journal of Marriage and the Family*, **39**, 177–184.

Allan, G. (1993). Social structure and relationships. In S. W. Duck (Ed.), *Social Context and Relationships [Understanding Personal Relationships 3]* (pp. 1–25). Newbury Park, CA: Sage.

Allen, K. R. & Demo, D. H. (1995). The families of lesbians and gay men: A new frontier in family research. *Journal of Marriage and the Family*, **57**, 111–127.

Allport, G. (1968). Fruits of eclecticism: Bitter or sweet. In G. Allport (Ed.), *The person psychology: Selected essays* (pp. 3–27). Boston, MA: Beacon Press.

Altschuler, J., Jacobs, S. & Shiode, D. (1985). Psychodynamic time-limited groups for adult children of aging parents. *American Journal of Orthopsychiatry*, **53**, 397–403.

Amato, P. R. (1987). Family processes in one parent, stepparent, and intact families: The child's point of view. *Journal of Marriage and the Family*, **49**, 327–337.

Amato, P. R. (1993a). Family structure, family process, and family ideology. *Journal of Marriage and the Family*, **55**, 50–54.

Amato, P. R. (1993b). Children's adjustment to divorce: Theories, hypotheses, and empirical support. *Journal of Marriage and the Family*, **55**, 23–38.

Amato, P. R. (2000). Diversity within single-parent families. In D. H. Demo, K. R. Allen & M. A. Fine (Eds), *The handbook of family diversity*. New York: Oxford University Press.

Andersen, P. A. (1993). Cognitive schemata in personal relationships. In S. W. Duck (Ed.), *Individuals in relationships [Understanding relationship processes 1]* (pp. 1–29). Newbury Park, Sage.

Another real raise in 1998 (1999). Monthly Labor Review Online, published January 20. http://www.bls.gov.opub/ted/tedhome.html>

Antonucci, T. C. (1994). A lifespan view of women's social relations. In B. F. Turner & L. Troll (Eds) *Women Growing Older* (pp. 239–269). Thousand Oaks, CA: Sage.

Aquilino, W. S. & Supple, K. R. (1991). Parent–child relations and parent's satisfaction with living arrangements when adult children live at home. *Journal of Marriage and the Family*, **53**, 13–27.

Arditti, J. A. (1999). Rethinking relationships between divorced mothers and their children: Capitalizing on family strengths. *Family Relations*, **48**, 109–119.

Arditti, J. A. & Keith, T. Z. (1993). Visitation frequency, child support payment, and the father–child relationship postdivorce. *Journal of Marriage and the Family*, **55**, 699–712.

Arendell, T. (1995). *Fathers and divorce*. Thousand Oaks, CA: Sage.

Arendell, T. (1997). A social constructionist approach to parenting. In T. Arendell (Ed.), *Contemporary parenting* (pp. 1–44). Thousand Oaks, CA: Sage.

Argyle, M & Furnham, A. (1983). Sources of satisfaction and conflict in long-term relationships. *Journal of Marriage and the Family*, **48**, 849–855.

Argyle, M., Furnham, A. & Graham, J. (1981). *Social Situations*. Cambridge: Cambridge University Press.

Aron, A., Aron, E. N. & Smollan D. (1992). Inclusion of Other in the Self Scale and the structure of interpersonal closeness. *Journal of Personality and Social Psychology*, **63**, 596–612.

Asher, S. R., & Coie, J. D. (1990). *Peer rejection in childhood*. Cambridge, UK: Cambridge University Press.

Askham, J. (1984). *Identity and stability in marriage*. New York: Cambridge University Press.

Atkinson, M. P. (1989). Conceptualizations of the parent-child relationship: Solidarity, attachment, crescive bonds, and identity salience. In J. A. Mancini (Ed.), *Aging parents and adult children* (pp. 81–97). Lexington, MA.: Lexington Books.

Averill, J. R. (1993). Illusions of anger. In R.B. Felson & J.T. Tedeschi (Eds), *Aggression and violence* (pp. 171–192). Washington, DC: APA.

Babcock, J. C., Waltz, J., Jacobson, N. S. & Gottman, J. M. (1991). Power and violence: The relationship between communication patterns, power discrepancies, and domestic violence. *Journal of Consulting and Clinical Psychology*, **61**, 40–50.

Babcock, J. C., Waltz, J., Jacobson, N. S. & Gottman, J. M. (1993). Power and violence: The relation between communication patterns, power discrepancies, and domestic violence. *Journal of Consulting and Clinical Psychology*, **61**, 40–50.

Baber, K. M. & Allen, K. R. (1992). *Women and families: Feminist reconstructions*. New York: Guilford.

Bakan, D. (1966). *The duality of human existence: isolation and commitment in western man*. Boston, MA: Beacon Press.

Bank, S. P. & Kahn, M. D. (1982). *The sibling bond*. New York: Basic Books.

Barling, J. (1990). Employment and marital functioning. In F. D. Fincham & T. N. Bradbury (Eds), *Psychology of marriage* (pp. 201–225). New York: Guilford.

Barnes, J. (1979). Network analysis: orienting notion, rigorous technique or substantive field of study? In P. W. Holland & S. Leinhardt (Eds), *Perspectives on social network research*. New York: Academic Press.

Barnett, R. (1994). Home-to-work spillover revisited, *Journal of Marriage and the Family*, **56**, 647–656.

Barnett, R. C., Kibria, N., Baruch, G. K. & Pleck, J. H. (1991). Adult daughter–parent relationships and their associations with daughters' subjective well-being and psychological distress. *Journal of Marriage and the Family*, **53**, 29–42.

Barnett, R. C., Marshall, N. L. & Pleck, J. H. (1992). Adult son–parent relationships and their associations with sons' psychological distress. *Journal of Family Issues*, **13**, 505–525.

Barrett, K. C. (2000). The development of the self-in-relationships. In R. S. L. Mills & S. W. Duck (Eds), *Developmental psychology and personal relationships* (pp. 91–108). Chichester: Wiley.

Bartky, S. L. (1990). *Femininity and domination*. New York: Routledge.

Baruch, G. & Barnett, R. C. (1983). Adult daughters' relationships with their mothers. *Journal of Marriage and the Family*, **45**, 601–612.

Bass, L. A. & Stein, C. H. (1997). Comparing the structure and stability of network ties using the social support questionnaire and the social network list. *Journal of Social and Personal Relationships*, **14**, 123–132.

Baucom, D. H., Epstein, N., Burnett, C. K. & Rankin, L. (1993). Conflict in marriage: A cognitive/behavioral formulation. In S. Worchel & J. A. Simpson (Eds), *Conflict between people and groups: Causes, processes, and resolutions* (pp.7–29). Chicago, IL: Nelson Hall.

Baum, M. & Page, M. (1991). Caregiving and multigenerational families. *The Gerontologist*, 31, 762–769.

Baumgartner, M. P. (1993). Violent networks: The origins and management of domestic conflict. In R.B. Felson & J.T. Tedeschi (Eds), *Aggression and violence* (pp. 209–231). Washington, DC: APA.

Baumrind, D. (1972). "Socialization and instrumental competence in young children". In W. W. Hartup (Ed.), *The young child: Reviews of research*, (Vol. 2). Washington, DC: National Association for the Education of Young Children.

Baxter, L. A. (1992). Forms and functions of intimate play in personal relationships. *Human Communication Research*, **18**, 336–363.

Baxter, L. A. & Dindia, K. (1990). Marital partners' perceptions of marital maintenance strategies. *Journal of Social and Personal Relationships*, **7**, 187–208.

Baxter, L. A. & Montgomery, B. M. (1996). *Relating: dialogs and dialectics*. New York: Guilford Press.

Baxter, L. A., Mazanec, M., Nicholson, L., Pittman, G., Smith, K. & West, L. (1997). Everyday loyalties and betrayals in personal relationships: A dialectical perspective. *Journal of Social and Personal Relationhips*, **14**, 655–678.

Baxter, L. A., Wilmot, W.W., Simmons, C.A. & Swartz, A. (1993). Ways of doing conflict: A folk taxonomy of conflict events in personal relationships. In P.J. Kalbfleisch (Ed.), *Interpersonal communication: Evolving interpersonal relationships* (pp. 89–107). Hillsdale, NJ: Erlbaum.

Becker, G. (1981). *A treatise on the family*. Cambridge, MA: Harvard University Press.

Bedford, V. H. (1989). Ambivalence in adult sibling relationships. *Journal of Family Issues*, **10**, 211–224.

Bedford, V. H. (1992). Memories of parental favoritism and the quality of parent–child ties in adulthood. *Journal of Gerontology: Social Sciences*, **47**, S149-S155.

Bedford, V. H. (1993, June). Attachment to a sibling in adulthood: Predisposing conditions. Paper presented at the Fourth Conference of the International Network on Personal Relationships, Milwaukee.

Bedford, V. H. (1995). Sibling relationships in middle and old age. In R. Blieszner, & V. H. Bedford (Eds), *Handbook of aging and the family* (pp. 201–222). Westport, CT: Greenwood Press.

Bell, D. C. & Bell, L. G. (1983). Parental validation and support in the development of adolescent daughters. In H. D. Grotevant & C. R. Cooper (Eds), *Adolescent development in the family* (pp. 27–42). San Francisco, CA: Jossey-Bass.

Belsky, J. (1984). The determinants of parenting: A process model. *Child Development*, **55**, 83–96.

Belsky, J. & Kelly, J. (1994). *The transition to parenthood*. New York: Delacorte Press.

Belsky, J. & Pensky, E. (1988). Marital change across the transition to parenthood. *Marriage and Family Review*, **12**, 133–156.

Belsky, J., Ward, H. & Rovine, M. (1986). Prenatal expectations, postnatal experiences and the transition to parenthood. In R. Ashmore & D. Brodzinsky (Eds) *Perspectives on the Family*. Hillsdale, NJ: Erlbaum.

Bem, S. L. (1983). Gender schema theory and its implications for child development: Raising gender-aschematic children in a gender-schematic society. *Signs*, **8**, 598–616.

Ben-Yoav, O. & Pruitt, D. G. (1984a). Accountability to constituents: A two-edged sword. *Organizational Behavior and Human Performance*, **34**, 283–295.

Ben-Yoav, O. & Pruitt, D. G. (1984b). Resistance to yielding and the expectation of cooperative future interaction in negotiation. *Journal of Experimental Social Psychology*, **34**, 323–335.

Bengtson, V. L. & Kuypers, J. A. (1971). Generational differences and the developmental stake. *International Journal of Aging and Human Development*, **2**, 249–260.

Bengtson, V. L. & Mangen, D. J. (1988). Family intergenerational solidarity revisited: Suggestions for future management. In D. J. Mangen, V. L. Bengtson & P. H. Landry, Jr. (Eds), *Measurement of intergenerational relations* (pp. 222–238). Newbury Park, CA: Sage.

Bengtson, V. L. & Roberts, R. E. L. (1991). Parent–child relations. In D. Mangen & W. A. Peterson (Eds), *Research instruments in social gerontology* (Vol. 2., pp. 115–186). Minneapolis: University of Minnesota Press.

Bengtson, V. L. & Schrader, S. (1982). Parent–child relations. In D. Mangen & W. A. Peterson (Eds), *Research instruments in social gerontology* (Vol. 2., pp. 115–186). Minneapolis: University of Minnesota Press.

Bengtson, V. L., Olander, E. B. & Haddad, A. A. (1976). The "generation gap" and aging family members: Toward a conceptual model. In J. E. Gubrium (Ed.), *Time, roles and self in old age* (pp. 237–263). New York: Human Sciences Press.

Bengtson, V., Rosenthal, C. & Burton, L. (1990). Families and aging: diversity and heterogeneity. In R. H. Binstock & L. K. George (Eds) *Handbook of aging and the social sciences* (3rd edn., pp. 263–287). New York: Academic.

Berardo, D. H., Shehan, C. L. & Leslie, G. R. (1987). A residue of tradition: Jobs, careers, and spouses' time in housework. *Journal of Marriage and the Family*, **49**, 381–390.

Berger, C. R. (1988). Uncertainty and information exchange in developing relationships. In S. W. Duck (Ed.), *Handbook of Personal Relationships* (pp. 239–256). Chichester: Wiley.

Berger, C. R. (1993). Goals, plans and mutual understanding in personal relationships. In S. W. Duck (Ed), *Individuals in relationships [Understanding relationship processes 1]* (pp. 30–59). Newbury Park, CA: Sage.

Berger, P. L. (1963). *Invitation to sociology*. New York: Doubleday.

Berger, P. L. & Kellner, H. (1964). Marriage and the construction of reality: An exercise in the microsociology of knowledge. *Diogenes*, **46**, 1–23.

Berger, P. L. & Luckman, T. (1966). *The social construction of reality*. Garden City, NY: Doubleday.

Berk, R. A. & Berk, S. F. (1978). A simultaneous equation model for the division of household labor. *Sociological Methods & Research*, **6**, 431–468.

Berk, S. F. (1985). *The gender factory: The apportionment of work in American households*. New York: Plenum.

Bernard, J. S. (1933). An instrument for the measurement of success in marriage. *American Sociological Society*, **27**, 94–106.

Bernard, J. S. (1981). The rise and fall of the good provider role. *American Psychologist*, **36**, 1–12.

Bernard, J. S. (1982). *The future of marriage* (2nd edn). New Haven, CT: Yale University Press.

Berscheid, E. (1994). Interpersonal relationships. *Annual Review of Psychology*, **45**, 79–129.

Berscheid, E., & Lopes, J. (1997). A temporal model of relationship satisfaction and stability. In R. J. Sternberg & M. Hojjat (Eds), *Satisfaction in close relationships* (pp. 129–159). New York: Guilford.

Berscheid, E. & Reis, H. T. (1998). Attraction and close relationships. In D. T. Gilbert, S. F. Fiske & G. Lindzey (Eds), *The Handbook of Social Psychology* (4th edn) (Vol. 2, pp. 193–281). Boston, MA: McGraw-Hill.

Berscheid, E. & Walster, E. H. (1978). *Interpersonal attraction, second edition*. Reading, MA: Addison Wesley.

Beutler, I. V., Burr, W.R., Barr, K.S. & Herrin, D.A. (1989a). The family realm: Theoretical contributions for understanding its uniqueness. *Journal of Marriage and the Family*, **51**, 805–815.

Beutler, I. V., Burr, W.R., Barr, K.S. & Herrin, D.A. (1989b). A seventh group has visited the elephant. *Journal of Marriage and the Family*, **51**, 826–830.

Bielby, W. & Baron, J. (1984). A woman's place is with other women: Sex segregation within organizations. In B.Reskin (Ed.), *Sex segregation in the workplace* (pp. 27–55). Washington, DC.: National Academy Press.

Bigelow, B., Tesson, G. & Lewko, J. (1996). *Children's rules of friendship*. New York: Guilford.

Black, D. (1993). *The social structure of right and wrong*. San Diego, CA: Academic Press.

Blades, J. (1985). *Family mediation*. Eglewood Cliffs, NJ: Prentice-Hall.

Blair, S. L. (1993). Employment, family, and perceptions of marital quality among husbands and wives. *Journal of Family Issues*, **14**, 189–212.

Blair, S. L. & Johnson, M. P. (1992). Wives' perceptions of the fairness of the division of household labor: The intersection of housework and ideology. *Journal of Marriage and the Family*, **54**, 570–581.

Blake, R. R. & Mouton, J. S. (1964). *The managerial grid*. Houston: Gulf Publishing.

Blieszner, R. & Adams, R. G. (1992). Adult friendship. Newbury Park, CA: Sage.

Blieszner, R. & Bedford, V. H. (Eds). (1995). *Handbook of aging and the family*. Westport, CT: Greenwood Press.

Blood, R. O. (1969). Kinship interaction and marital solidarity. *Merrill Palmer Quarterly*, **15**, 171–184.

Blood, R. O. & Wolfe, D.M. (1960). *Husbands and wives*. Glencoe, IL: The Free Press.

Blos, P. (1967). The second individuation process of adolescence. *Psychoanalytic Study of the Child*, **22**, 162–186.

Blos, P. (1979). *The adolescent passage*. New York: International Universities Press.

Blumstein, P. & Schwartz, P. (1991). Money and ideology. In R.L. Blumberg (ed.), *Gender, family, and economy: The triple overlap* (pp. 261–288). Newbury Park, CA: Sage.

Bolger, N. & Kelleher, S. (1993). Daily life in relationships. In S. W. Duck (Ed.), *Social Contexts of Relationships [Understanding Relationship Processes 3]* (p. 100–109). Newbury Park, CA: Sage.

Bolger, N., DeLongis, A., Kessler, R. C. & Wethington, E. (1989). The contagion of stress across multiple roles. *Journal of Marriage and the Family*, **51**, 175–183.

Booth, A. & Amato, P. R. (1991). Divorce and psychological stress. *Journal of Health and Social Behavior*, **32**, 396–407.

Booth, A. & Johnson, D. R. (1994). Declining health and marital quality. *Journal of Marriage and the Family*, **56**, 218–223.

Bose, C. E. (1987). Devaluing women's work: The undercount of women's employment in 1900 and 1980. In C. Bose, R. Feldberg, & N. Sokoloff (Eds), *Hidden aspects of women's work* (pp. 95–115). New York: Praeger.

Bott, E. (1955). Urban families: Conjugal roles and social networks, *Human Relations*, **8**, 345–384.

Bott, E. (1971). *Family and social network* (2nd edn). New York: Basic Books.

Botwin, M. D., Buss, D. M. Shackelford, T. K. (1997). Personality and mate preferences: Five factors in mate selection and marital satisfaction. *Journal of Personality*, **65**, 107–136.

Bouchard, G., Sabourin, S., Lussier, Y., Wright, J. & Richer, C. (1998). Predictive validity of coping strategies on marital satisfaction: Cross-sectional and longitudinal evidence. *Journal of Family Psychology*, **12**, 112–131.

Bowlby, J. (1969). *Attachment and loss:* Vol. I. *Attachment*. New York: Basic Books.

Bowlby, J. (1980). *Attachment and loss:* Vol. III. *Loss: sadness and depression.* New York: Basic Books.

Bowman, M. L. (1990). Coping efforts and marital satisfaction: Measuring marital coping and its correlates. *Journal of Marriage and the Family*, **52**, 463–474.

Boxer, A. M., Cook, J. A. & Cohler, B. J. (1986). Grandfathers, fathers, and sons: Intergenerational relations among men. In K. A. Pillemer & R. S. Wolf (Eds), *Elder abuse: Conflict in the family* (pp. 9–121). Dover, MA: Auburn House.

Bradbury, T. N. & Fincham, F. D. (1990). Attributions in marriage: Review and critique. *Psychological Bulletin*, **107**, 3–33.

Bradbury, T. N. & Fincham, F. D. (1992). Attributions and behavior in marital interaction. *Journal of Personality and Social Psychology*, **63**, 613–628.

Bradbury, T. N. & Karney, B.R. (1993). Longitudinal study of marital interaction and dysfunction: Review and analysis. *Clinical Psychology Review*, **13**, 15–27.

Bradbury, T. N., Cohan, C. L. & Karney, B. R. (1998). Optimizing longitudinal research for understanding and preventing marital dysfunction. In T. N. Bradbury (Ed.), *The developmental course of marital dysfunction* (pp. 279–311). New York: Cambridge University Press.

Braver, S. L. (1998). *Divorced dads: Shattering the myths*. New York: Tarcher Putnam.

Brayfield, A. A. (1992). Employment resources and housework in Canada. *Journal of Marriage and the Family*, **54**, 19–30.

Brennan, K. A. & Shaver, P. R. (1993). Attachment styles and parental divorce. *Journal of Divorce & Remarriage*, **21**, 161–175.

Brennan, P. L., Moos, R. H. & Kelly, K. M. (1994). Spouses of late-life problem drinkers: Functioning, coping responses, and family context. *Journal of Family Psychology*, **8**, 447–457.

Broderick, C. B. (1993). *Understanding family process*. Newbury Park, CA: Sage.

Bronfenbrenner, U. (1979). *The ecology of human development*. New York: Harvard University Press.

Brown, C., Feldberg, R., Fox, E. & Kohen, J. (1976). Divorce: Chance of a new lifetime. *Journal of Social Issues*, **32**, 119–134.

Bruner, J. (1990). *Acts of meaning*. Cambridge, MA: Harvard University Press.

Buchanan, C. M., Maccoby, E. & Dornbusch, S. M. (1996). *Adolescents after divorce*. Cambridge, MA: Harvard University Press.

Buehlman, K., Gottman, J.M. & Katz, L. (1992). How a couple views their past predicts their future: Predicting divorce from an oral history interview. *Journal of Family Psychology*, **5**, 295–318.

Bui, K. T., Peplau, L. A. & Hill, C. T. (1996). Testing the Rusbult model of relationship commitment and stability in a 15-year study of heterosexual couples. *Personality & Social Psychology Bulletin*, **22**, 1244–1257.

Bulcroft, K. & Bulcroft, R. (1991). The timing of divorce: Effects on parent-child relationships in later life. *Research on Aging*, **13**, 226–243.

Bumpass, L. L., Sweet, J. A. & Cherlin, A. (1991). The role of cohabitation in declining rates of marriage. *Journal of Marriage and the Family*, **53**, 913–927.

Burger, E. & Milardo, R. M. (1995). Marital interdependence and social networks. *Journal of Social and Personal Relationships*, **12**, 403–415.

Burgess, E. W. & Cottrell, L. S. (1939). *Predicting success or failure in marriage*. NY: Prentice-Hall.

Burkes, V. S. & Parke, R. D. (1996). Parent and child representations of social relationships: Linkages between families and pees. *Merrill–Palmer Quarterly*, **42**, 358–378.

Burman, B. & Margolin, G. (1992). Analysis of the association between marital relationships and health problems: An interactional perspective. *Psychological Bulletin*, **112**, 39–63.

Burman, B. Margolin, G. & John, R.S. (1993). America's angriest home videos: Behavioral contingencies observed in home reenactments of marital conflict. *Journal of Consulting and Clinical Psychology*, **61**, 28–39.

Burr, W. R., Herrin, D. A., Day, R. D. Beutler, I. F. & Leigh, G. K. (1987). An epistemological basis for primary explanations in family science. Paper presented at the Theory and Methods Workshop at the annual meetings of the National Council on Family Relations. Atlanta, GA.

Burton, L. (1992). Black grandparents rearing children of drug-addicted parents: Stressors, outcomes and the social service needs. *The Gerontologist*, **32**, 744–751.

Burton, L. (1996). Age norms, the timing of family role transitions, and intergenerational caregiving among aging African American women. *The Gerontologist*, **36**, 199–208.

Buunk, A. P. & Van der Eijnden, R. J. J. M. (1997). Perceived prevalence, perceived superiority, and relationship satisfaction: Most relationships are good, but ours in the best. *Personality & Social Psychology Bulletin*, **23**, 219–228.

Buunk, A. P., Collins, R. L., Taylor, S. E., VanYperen, N.W. & Dakof, G. A. (1990). The affective consequences of social comparison: Either direction has its ups and downs. *Journal of Personality and Social Psychology*, **59**, 1238–1249.

Byrne, C. A. & Arias, I. (1997). Marital satisfaction and marital violence: Moderating effects of attributional processes. *Journal of Family Psychology*, **11**, 188–195.

Campbell, K. E. & Lee, B .A. (1991). Name generators in surveys of personal networks, *Social Networks*, **13**, 203–221.

Canary, D. J., Cupach, W. R. & Messman, S. J. (1995). *Relationship conflict*. Thousand Oaks: Sage.

Carnelley, K. B., Pietromonaco, P. R. & Jaffe, K. (1994). Depression, working models of others, and relationship functioning. *Journal of Personality and Social Psychology*, **66**, 127–140.

Carnevale, P. J. & Pruitt, D. G. (1992). Negotiation and mediation. *Annual Review of Psychology*, **43**, 531–582.

Carstensen, L. L., Gottman, J. M. & Levenson, R. W. (1995). Emotional behavior in long-term marriage. *Psychology and Aging*, **10**, 140–149.

Chatterjee, M. (1977). Conjugal roles and social networks in an Indian urban sweeper locality. *Journal of Marriage and the Family*, **39**, 193–202.

Cheal, D. (1991). *Family and the state of theory*. Toronto: University of Toronto Press.

Christensen, A. (1988). Dysfunctional interaction patterns in couples. In P. Noller & M.A. Fitzpatrick (Eds), *Perspectives on marital interaction* (pp. 31–52). Clevedon, England: Multilingual Matters.

Christensen, A., & Heavey, C. L. (1990). Gender and social structure in the demand/withdraw pattern of marital conflict. *Journal of Personality and Social Psychology*, **59**, 73–82.

Christensen, A. & Schenk, J. L. (1991). Communication, conflict, and psychological distance in non-distressed, clinic, and divorcing couples. *Journal of Consulting and Clinical Psychology*, **59**, 458–463.

Christensen, H. T. (1964). Development of the family field of study. In H. T. Christensen (Ed.), *Handbook of marriage and the family* (p. 3–32). Chicago: Rand McNally.

Christopher, F. S. & Frandsen, M.M. (1990). Strategies of influence in sex and dating. *Journal of Social and Personal Relationships*, **7**, 89–105.

Cicirelli, V. G. (1985). Sibling relationships throughout the life cycle. In L. L'Abate (Ed.), *Handbook of family psychology and therapy* (Vol. 1, pp. 177–214). Homewood, IL: Dorsey Press.

Clark, M. S., & Reis, H. T. (1988). Interpersonal processes in close relationships. *Annual Review of Psychology*, **39**, 609–672.

Cohan, C. L. & Bradbury, T. N. (1994). Assessing responses to recurring problems in marriage: Evaluation of the Marital Coping Inventory. *Psychological Assessment*, **6**, 191–200.

Colarusso, C. A. & Nemiroff, R. A. (1982). The father in midlife: Crisis and the growth of paternal identity. In S. H. Cath, A. R. Gurwitt & J. M. Ross (Eds), *Father and child: Developmental and clinical perspectives* (pp. 315–327). Boston, MA: Little, Brown.

Coleman, M. & Ganong, L. H. (1994). *Remarried Families*. Newbury Park, CA: Sage.

Collins, N. L. & Read, S. J . (1990). Adult attachment, working models, and relationship quality in dating couples. *Journal of Personality and Social Psychology*, **58**, 644–663.

Collins, P. H. (1990). *Black feminist thought: Knowledge, consciousness, and the politics of empowerment*. Cambridge, MA: Unwin Hyman.

Coltrane, S. (1998). *Gender and families*. Thousand Oaks, CA: Pine Forge Press.

Condran, J. G. & Bode, J. G. (1982). Rashomon, working wives, and family division of labor: Middletown, 1980. *Journal of Marriage and the Family*, **44**, 421–425.

Conger, R. & Elder, G. (1994). *Families in troubled times: adapting to change in rural America*. New York: Aldine deGruyter.

Contreras, R., Hendrick, S. S. & Hendrick, C. (1996). Perspectives on marital love and satisfaction in Mexican-American and Anglo-American couples. *Journal of Counseling & Development*, **74**, 408–415.

Cooney, T. M. (1989). Coresidence with adult children: A comparison of divorced and widowed women. *The Gerontologist*, **29**, 779–784.

Cooney, T. M. (1994). Young adults' relations with parents: The influence of recent parental divorce. *Journal of Marriage and the Family*, **56**, 45–56.

Cooney, T. M. (1997). Parent child relations across adulthood. In S. W. Duck (Ed.), *Handbook of Personal Relationships, Second Edition* (pp. 451–468). Chichester UK.: Wiley.

Cooney, T. M. & Uhlenberg, P. (1992). Support from parents over the life course: The adult child's perspective. *Social Forces*, **71**, 63–84.

Cooney, T. M., Smyer, M. A., Hagestad, G. O. & Klock, R. C. (1986). Parental divorce in young adulthood: Some preliminary findings. *American Journal of Orthopsychiatry*, **56**, 470–477.

Coontz, S. (1992). *The way we never were: American families and the nostalgia trap*. New York: Basic.

Cooper, C. R., Grotevant, H. D. & Condon, S. M. (1983). Individuality and connectedness in the family as a context for adolescent identity formation and role-taking skill. In H. D. Grotevant & C. R. Cooper (Eds), *Adolescent development in the family* (pp. 43–59). San Francisco: Jossey-Bass.

Cotton, S. (1995). Support networks and marital satisfaction, Unpublished manuscript, Macquarie University, Sidney, Australia.

Cotton, S., Cunningham, J. & Antill, J. (1993). Network structure, network support, and the marital satisfaction of husbands and wives. *Australian Journal of Psychology*, **45**, 176–181.

Coverman, S. (1985). Explaining husbands' participation in domestic labor. *The Sociology Quarterly*, **26**, 81–97.

Coverman, S. & Sheley, J. F. (1986) Change in men's housework and child care time. *Journal of Marriage and the Family*, **48**, 413–422.

Cowan, C. P. & Cowan, P. A. (1988). Who does what when partners become parents: Implications for men, women, and marriage. *Marriage and Family Review*, **12**, 105–31.

Cowan, C. P. & Cowan, P. A. (1992). *When partners become parents*. New York: Basic Books.

Cowan, P. A. & Cowan, C. P. (1994). Where's the romance? What happens to marriage when partners become parents. Paper presented at conference on Intimate Relationships at Iowa State University, Ames, IA, September 29, 1994.

Cowan, C. P. & Cowan, P. A. (1997). Working with couples during stressful transitions. In S. Dreman (Ed.), *The family on the threshold of the 21st century: Trends and implications* (pp. 17–47). Mahwah, NJ: Lawrence Erlbaum.

Cowan, C. P., Cowan, P. A., Heming, G. & Miller, N. B. (1991) Becoming a family: Marriage, parenting, and child development. In P. A. Cowan & M. Hetherington (Eds), *Family transitions*. Hillsdale, NJ: Erlbaum.

Coyne, J. C. & Smith, D. A. (1991). Couples coping with a myocardial infarction: A contextual perspective on wives' distress. *Journal of Personality and Social Psychology*, **61**, 404–412.

Coysh, W. S., Johnston, J. R., Tschann, J. M., Wallerstein, J. S. & Kline, M. (1989). Parental postdivorce adjustment in joint and sole physical custody families. *Journal of Family Issues*, **10**, 52–71.

Crawford, D. W. & Huston, T. L. (1993). The impact of the transition to parenthood on marital leisure. *Personality and Social Psychology Bulletin*, **19**, 39–46.

Creamer, M. & Campbell, I. M. (1988). The role of interpersonal perception in dyadic adjustment. *Journal of Clinical Psychology*, **44**, 424–30.

Crohan, S. E. (1988). The relationship between conflict behavior and marital happiness: Conflict beliefs as moderators. Unpublished dissertation. Ann Arbor, Michigan: University of Michigan.

Crohan, S. E. (1992). Marital happiness and spousal consensus and beliefs about marital conflict: A longitudinal investigation. *Journal of Personal and Social Relationships*, **9**, 89–102.

Crohan, S. E. (1996). Marital quality and conflict across the transition to parenthood in African–American and white couples. *Journal of Marriage and the Family*, **58**, 933–944.

Crouter, A. C. (1984a). Participative work as an influence on human development. *Journal of Applied Developmental Psychology*, **5**, 71–90.

Crouter, A. C. (1984b). Spillover from family to work: The neglected side of the work-family interface. *Human Relations*, **37**, 425–442.

Crouter, A. C. & Helms-Erikson, H. (1997). Work and family from a dyadic perspective: Variations in inequality. In S. W. Duck, K. Dindia, W. Ickes, R. Milardo, R. Mills & B. Sarason (Eds), *Handbook of Personal Relationships* (2nd edn, pp. 487–504). Chichester UK.: Wiley.

Crouter, A. C. & McHale, S. M. (1993). The long arm of the job: Influences of parental work on childrearing. In T. Luster & L. Okagaki (Eds), *Parenting: An ecological perspective* (pp. 179–202). Hillsdale, NJ: Erlbaum.

Crouter, A. C., Bumpus, M. F., Maguire, M.C. & McHale, S.M. (1999). Linking parents' work pressure and adolescents' well-being: Insights into dynamics in dual-earner families. *Developmental Psychology*, **35**, 1453–1461.

Crouter, A. C., Maguire, M. C., Helms-Erikson, H. & McHale, S. M. (1999). Parental work in middle childhood: Links between employment and the division of housework, parent-child activities, and parental monitoring. In T. L. Parcel (Ed.), *Work and Family: Research in the Sociology of Work* (Vol. 7, pp. 31–54). Stamford, CT: JAI Press.

Cupach, W. R. & Spitzberg, B. H. (Eds). (1994). *The dark side of interpersonal communication*. Hillsdale NJ: LEA.

Cutrona, C. E. (1996). *Social support in couples*. London: Sage.

Cutrona, C. E. & Suhr, J. A. (1994). Social support communication in the context of marriage: An analysis of couples' supportive interactions. In B. Burleson, T. Albrecht & I. Sarason (Eds) *The Communication of Social Support: Message, Interaction, and Community* (pp. 113–135). Thousand Oaks, CA: Sage.

Dakof, G. A. & Taylor, S. E. (1990). Victims' perceptions of social support: What is helpful from whom? *Journal of Personality and Social Psychology*, **58**, 80–89.

Daly, K. (1997). *Families and time*. Thousand Oaks, CA: Sage.

Davis, K. E. & Todd, M. J. (1985). Assessing Friendship: Prototypes, Paradigm Cases and Relationship Description. In S. W. Duck & D. Perlman (Eds), *Understanding Personal Relationships* (pp. 17–38). London: Sage.

De Dreu, C. K. W., Nauta, A. & Van de Vliert, E. (1995). Self-serving evaluations of conflict behavior and escalation of the dispute. *Journal of Applied Social Psychology*, **25**, 2049–2066.

DeKeseredy, W. S. (1990a). Male peer support and woman abuse: The current state of knowledge. *Sociological Focus*, **23**, 129–139.

DeKeseredy, W. S. (1990b). Woman abuse in dating relationships: The contribution of male peer support. *Sociological Inquiry*, **60**, 236–243.

Delphy, C. & Leonard, D. (1992). *Familiar exploitation: A new analysis of marriage in contemporary western societies*. Cambridge, MA: Polity.

D'Emilio, J. & Freedman, E. B. (1997). *Intimate matters* (2nd edn). Chicago, IL: University of Chicago Press.

Demo, D. H. & Acock A. C. (1993). Family diversity and the division of domestic labor: How much have things changed? *Family Relations*, **42**, 323–31.

Demo, D. H. & Acock, A. C. (1996a). Family structure, family process, and adolescent well-being. *Journal of Research on Adolescence* **6**, 457–488.

Demo, D. H. & Acock, A. C. (1996b). Singlehood, marriage, and remarriage: The effects of family structure and family relationships on mothers' well-being. *Journal of Family Issues*, **17**, 388–407.

Depner, C. (1978). Adult roles and subjective evaluation of marital quality. Unpublished doctoral dissertation. Ann Arbor, MI: University of Michigan.

Dill, B. T. (1988). Our mothers' grief: Racial-ethnic women and the maintenance of families. *Journal of Family History*, **13**, 415–431.

Dilworth-Anderson, P. (1992). Extended kin networks in Black families. *Generations*, **XVI**, 29–32.

Dindia, K. (1994). The intrapersonal–interpersonal dialectical process of self-disclosure. In S. W. Duck (Ed.), *Understanding relationship processes 4: Dynamics of relationships* (pp. 27–57). Newbury Park, CA: Sage.

Dindia, K. & Canary, D.J. (1993). Special issue on relational maintenance. *Journal of Social and Personal Relationships*, **10**(2).

Dixson, M. D. & Duck, S. W. (1993). Understanding relationship processes: Uncovering the human search for meaning. In S. W. Duck (Ed.), *Individuals in relationships [Understanding relationship processes 1]* (pp. 175–206). Newbury Park: Sage.

Dobash, R. E. & Dobash, R.P. (1992). *Women, violence, and social change*. New York: Routledge.

Doherty, W. J., Su, S. & Needle, R. (1989). Marital disruption and psychological well-being: A panel study. *Journal of Family Issues*, **10**, 72–85.

Donohue, W. A., Lyles, J. & Rogan, R. (1989). Issue development in divorce mediation. *Mediation Quarterly*, **24**, 19–28.

Dornbusch, S. M., Carlsmith, J. M., Bushwall, S. J., Ritter, P. L., Liederman, H., Hastrof, A. H. & Gross, R. T. (1985). Single parents, extended households, and the control of adolescents. *Child Development*, **56**, 326–341.

Dressel, P. L. & Clark, A. (1990). A critical look at family care. *Journal of Marriage and the Family*, **52**, 769–782.

Duck, S. W. (1982). A topography of relationship disengagement and dissolution. In S. W. Duck (Ed.), *Personal relationships 4: Dissolving personal relationships* (pp. 1–30). London: Academic Press.

Duck, S. W. (1990). Relationships as unfinished business: Out of the frying pan and into the 1990s. *Journal of Social and Personal Relationships*, **7**, 5–28.

Duck, S. W. (1993). Preface on social contexts. In S. W. Duck (Ed.), *Understanding relationship processes 3: Social contexts of relationships*. Newbury Park, CA: Sage.

Duck, S. W. (1994a). *Meaningful relationships: Talking, sense, and relating.* Thousand Oaks, CA: Sage.

Duck, S. W. (1994b). Stratagems, spoils and a serpent's tooth: On the delights and dilemmas of personal relationships. In W. R. Cupach & B. H. Spitzberg (Eds), *The dark side of interpersonal communication* (pp. 3–24). Hillsdale, NJ: Erlbaum.

Duck, S. W. (1998). *Human relationships* (3rd edn) London: Sage.

Duck, S. W. & Montgomery, B. M. (1991). The interdependence among interaction substance, theory, and methods. In B. M. Montgomery & S. Duck (Eds), *Studying interpersonal interaction* (pp. 3–15). New York: Guilford Press.

Duck, S. W. & Pond, K. (1989). Friends, Romans, Countrymen; lend me your retrospective data: Rhetoric and reality in personal relationships. In C. Hendrick (Ed.), *Close relationships* (Vol. 10, pp. 17–38). Newbury Park, CA: Sage Publications.

Duck, S. W. & Sants, H. (1983). On the origins of the specious: Are personal relationships really interpersonal states? *Journal of Social and Clinical Psychology*, **1**, 27–41.

Duck, S. W. & Wood, J. T. (1995). For better for worse, for richer for poorer: The rough and the smooth of relationships. In S. W. Duck & J. T. Wood (Eds), *Confronting relationship challenges [Understanding relationship processes 5]* (pp. 1–21). Thousand Oaks, CA: Sage.

Duck, S. W., Acitelli, L. K., Manke, B. & West, L. (2000). Sewing relational seeds: Contexts for relating in childhood. In R. S. L. Mills & S. W. Duck (Eds), *Developmental psychology and personal relationships* (pp. 1–14). Chichester: Wiley.

Duck, S. W., Dindia, K., Ickes, B., Milardo, R., Mills, R., & Sarason, B. (Eds) (1997). *Handbook of personal relationships* (2nd edn). New York: John Wiley.

Duck, S. W., Pond. K. & Leatham, G. B. (1994). Loneliness and the evaluation of relational events. *Journal of Social and Personal Relationships*, **11**, 235–260.

Duck, S. W., Rutt, D. J., Hurst, M. & Strejc, H. (1991). Some evident truths about conversations in everyday relationships: All communication is not created equal. *Human Communication Research*, **18**, 228–267.

Duck, S. W., West, L. & Acitelli, L. K. (1997). Sewing the field: The tapestry of relationships in life and research. In S. Duck (Ed.), *Handbook of personal relationships: Theory, research and interventions* (2nd edn, pp. 1–23). Chichester, UK: Wiley.

Duncan, G. J. & Hoffman, S. D. (1985). Economic consequences of marital instability. In M. David & T. Smeeding (Eds), *Horizontal equity, uncertainty, and economic well-being* (pp. 427–467). Chicago, IL: University of Chicago Press.

Dunn, J. (1988). Relations among relationships. In S. W. Duck, D. F. Hay, S. E. Hobfoll, W. Ickes & B. Montgomery (Eds), *Handbook of Personal Relationships*. Chichester: Wiley.

Dunn, J. (1996). Siblings: The first society. In N. Vanzetti & S. W. Duck (Eds), *A lifetime of relationships*, **12**, 103–120.

Dunn, J. (1997). Lessons from the study of bi-directional effects. *Journal of Social and Personal Relationships*, **14**, 565–573.

Dunn, J. & Plomin, R. (1990). *Separate lives: Why siblings are so different.* New York: Basic Books.

Durkheim, E. (1893). *The division of labor in a society.* Translated by G. Simpson. New York: Free Press.

Duvall, E. (1971). *Family development.* Philadelphia, PA: J. B. Lippincott.

Dwyer, J. W. (1995). The effects of illness on the family. In R. Blieszner & V. H. Bedford (Eds), *Handbook of aging and the family* (pp. 401–421). Westport, CT: Greenwood Press.

Dykstra, P. A. (1993). The differential availability of relationships and the provision and effectiveness of support to older adults. *Journal of Social and Personal Relationships*, **10**, 355–570.

Edgerton, R. (1997, September). *Higher education white paper.* Philadelphia, PA: Pew Charitable Trusts.

Eggebeen, D. (1992). Family structure and intergenerational exchanges. *Research on Aging*, **14**, 427–447.

Eggebeen, D. J. & Hogan, D. P. (1990). Giving between generations in American families. *Human Nature*, **1**, 211–232.

Eidelson, R. J. & Epstein, N. (1982). Cognition and relationship maladjustment: Development of a measure of relationship beliefs. *Journal of Consulting and Clinical Psychology*, **50**, 715–720.

Elder, G. H., Jr. (1981). History and the family: The discovery of complexity. *Journal of Marriage and the Family*, **43**, 489–519.

Emirbayer, M. & Goodwin, J. (1994). Network analysis and the problem of agency. *American Journal of Sociology*, **99**, 1411–1454.

Endler, N. S. & Parker, J. D. A . (1994). Assessment of multidimensional coping: Task, emotion, and avoidance strategies. *Psychological Assessment*, **6**, 50–60.

England, P. & McCreary, L. (1987). Gender inequality in paid employment. In B. Hess and M. Ferree (Eds), *Analyzing gender: A handbook of social science research* (pp. 286–320). Newbury Park, CA: Sage.

Epstein, N., Baucom, D.H. & Rankin, L.A. (1993). Treatment of marital conflict: A cognitive-behavioral approach. *Clinical Psychology Review*, **13**, 45–57.

Erbert, L. A. & Duck, S. W. (1997). Rethinking satisfaction in personal relationships from a dialectical perspective. In R. J. Sternberg & M. Hojjat (Eds), *Satisfaction in close relationships* (pp. 190–216). New York: Guilford.

Erel, O. & Burman, B. (1995). Interrelatedness of marital relations and parent-child relations: A meta-analytic review. *Psychological Bulletin*, **118**, 108–132.

Ericksen, J. A., Yancey, W. L. & Ericksen, E. P. (1979). The division of family roles. *Journal of Marriage and the Family*, **41**, 301–313.

Erikson, E. (1968). *Identity, youth and crisis*. New York: Norton.

Espiritu, Y. L. (1997). *Asian American women and men*. Thousand Oaks, CA: Sage.

Eysenck, H. J. & Eysenck, M. W. (1985). *Personality and individual differences: A natural sciences approach*. New York, NY: Plenum.

Falbo, T. & Peplau, L.A. (1980). Power strategies in intimate relationships. *Journal of Personality and Social Psychology*, **38**, 618–628.

Falk, P. (1989). Lesbian mothers: Psychosocial assumptions in family law. *American Psychologist*, **44**, 941–947.

Farrell, M. P. & Rosenberg, S. D. (1981). Parent–child relations at middle age. In C. Getty & W. Humphreys (Eds), *Understanding the family: Stress and change in American family life* (pp. 57–76). New York: Appleton-Century-Crofts.

Feeney, J. A. (1994). Attachment style, communication patterns and satisfaction across the life cycle of marriage. *Personal Relationships*, **1**, 333–348.

Feeney, J. A. & Noller, P. (1990). Attachment style as a predictor of adult romantic relationships. *Journal of Personality and Social Psychology*, **58**, 281–291.

Fehr, B. (1993). How do I love thee? . . . Let me consult my prototype. In S. W. Duck (Ed.), *Individuals in relationships [Understanding relationship processes 1]* (pp. 87–120). Newbury Park, CA: Sage.

Fehr, B. & Perlman, D. (1985). The family as a social network and support system. In L. L'Abate (Ed.), *Handbook of family psychology and therapy* (Vol. 1, pp. 323–356). Homewood, IL: Dorsey Press.

Felton, B. J. & Berry, C. A. (1992). Do the sources of the urban elderly's social support determine its psychological consequences? *Psychology of Aging*, **7**, 89–97.

Ferber, M. A., O'Farrell, B. & Allen, L. (Eds) (1991). *Work and family: Policies for a changing work force*. Washington, D.C.: National Academy Press.

Fernandez, J. P. (1986) *Child care and corporate productivity: Resolving family/work conflicts*. Lexington, MA: Lexington Books.

Ferree, M. M. (1987). The struggles of superwoman. In C. Bose, R. Feldberg & N. Sokoloff (Eds), *Hidden aspects of women's work* (pp. 161–180). New York: Praeger.

Ferree, M. M. (1988, November). Negotiating household roles and responsibilities: Resistance, conflict, and change. Paper presented at the annual meeting of the National Council on Family Relations, Philadelphia, PA.

Ferree, M. M. (1990). Beyond separate spheres: Feminism and family research. *Journal of Marriage and the Family*, **52**, 866–884.

Ferree, M. M. (1991). The gender division of labor in two-earner marriages: Dimensions of variability and change. *Journal of Family Issues*, **12**, 158–180.

Field, D. & Minkler, M. (1993). The importance of family in advanced old age: The family is "forever." In P. A. Cowan, D. Field, D. A. Hansen, A. Skolnick & G. E. Swanson (Eds), *Family, self, and society: Toward a new agenda for family research* (pp. 331–351). Hillsdale, NJ: Erlbaum.

Fincham, F. D. (1995). From the orthogenic principle to the fish scale model of omniscience: advancing understanding of personal relationships. *Journal of Social and Personal Relationships*, **12**, 523–527.

Fincham, F. D. & Beach, S. R. H. (1999). Conflict in marriage: Implications for working with couples. *Annual Review of Psychology*, **20**, 47–77.

Fincham, F. D. & Bradbury, T. N. (1987). The assessment of marital quality: A re-evaluation. *Journal of Marriage and the Family*, **49**, 797–809.

Fincham, F. D., & Bradbury, T. N. (1993). Marital satisfaction, depression, and attributions: A longitudinal study. *Journal of Personality and Social Psychology*, **64**, 442–52.

Fincham, F. D. & Linfield, K. J. (1997). A new look at marital quality: Can spouses feel positive and negative about their marriage? *Journal of Family Psychology*, **11**, 489–502.

Fincham, F. D. & Osborne, L. N. (1993). Marital conflict and children: Retrospect and prospect. *Clinical Psychology Review*, **13**, 75–88.

Fincham, F. D., Beach, S. R. H. & Kemp-Fincham, S. I. (1997). Marital quality: A new theoretical perspective. In R. J. Sternberg & M. Hojjat (Eds), *Satisfaction in close relationships* (pp. 275–304). New York: Guilford.

Fincham, F. D., Bradbury, T. N. & Scott, C. K. (1990). Cognition in marriage. In F.D. Fincham & T.N. Bradbury (Eds), *The psychology of marriage* (pp. 118–149). New York: Guilford.

Fincham, F. D., Bradbury, T. N., Arias, I., Byrne, C. A. & Karney, B. R. (1997). Marital violence, marital distress, and attributions. *Journal of Family Psychology*, **11**, 367–372.

Fine, M. A. (2000). Divorce and single parenting. In C. Hendrick & S. S. Hendrick (Eds), *Sourcebook of close relationships* (pp. 139–152). Newbury Park, CA: Sage.

Fine, M. A. & Fine, D. R (1994). An examination and evaluation of recent changes in divorce laws in five Western countries: The critical role of values. *Journal of Marriage and the Family*, **56**, 249–263.

Fine, M. A. & Kurdek, L. A. (1994). Publishing multiple journal articles from a single data set: Issues and recommendations. *Journal of Family Psychology*, **8**, 371–379.

Fine, M. A. Schwebel, A. I., & Myers, L. J. (1987). Family stability in black families: Values underlying three different perspectives. *Journal of Comparative Family Studies*, **18**, 1–23.

Fingerman, K., L. & Berman, E. (in press). Applications of family systems theory to the study of adulthood. *International Journal of Aging and Human Development*, **50**(4).

Finkelstein, M. (1999, Spring). Academic careers in 2000 and beyond. *AAC&U Peer Review*, **1**(3), 4–8.

Finley, N. J. (1989). Theories of family labor as applied to gender differences in caregiving for elderly parents. *Journal of Marriage and the Family*, **51**, 79–86.

Fischer, L. R. (1981). Transitions in the mother-daughter relationship. *Journal of Marriage and the Family*, **43**, 613–622.

Fischer, L. R. (1986). *Linked lives: Adult daughters and their mothers.* New York: Harper and Row.

Fisher, S. W. (1996). *The family and the individual: reciprocal influences.* In N. Vanzetti & S. W. Duck (Eds), *A lifetime of relationships* (pp. 311–335). Pacific Grove, CA.: Brooks/Cole.

Fitch, K. L. (1998). *Speaking Relationally: Culture, communication, and interpersonal connection.* New York: Guilford.

Fletcher, G. J. O. & Fitness, J. (1993). Knowledge structures and explanations in intimate relationships. In S. W. Duck (Ed.), *Understanding relationship processes 1: Individuals in relationships* (pp. 121–143). Newbury Park CA: Sage.

Fletcher, G. J. O. & Kininmonth, L. (1991). Interaction in close relationships and social cognition. In G.J.O. Fletcher & F.D. Fincham (Eds) *Cognition in close relationships* (pp. 235–255). Hillsdale, NJ: Erlbaum.

Folkman, S. & Lazarus, R. S. (1988). Coping as a mediator of emotion. *Journal of Personality and Social Psychology*, **54**, 466–475.

Fowers, B. J. (1991). His and her marriage: A multivariate study of general and marital satisfaction. *Sex Roles*, **24**, 209–21.

Fowers, B. J. & Applegate, B. (1995). Do marital conventionalization scales measure a social desirability response bias? A confirmatory factor analysis. *Journal of Marriage & the Family*, **57**, 237–241.

Fowers, B. J. & Olson, D. H. (1993). ENRICH Marital Satisfaction Scale: A brief research and clinical tool. *Journal of Family Psychology*, **7**, 176–185.

Fowers, B. J., Lyons, E. M. Montel, K. H. (1996). Positive marital illusions: Self-enhancement or relationship enhancement? *Journal of Family Psychology*, **10**, 192–208.

Frank, S. J., Avery, C. B. & Laman, M. S. (1988). Young adults' perceptions of their relationships with their parents: Individual differences in connectedness, competence, and emotional autonomy. *Developmental Psychology*, **24**, 729–737.

French, D. C. & Underwood, M. K. (1996). Peer relations during middle childhood. In N. Vanzetti & S. W. Duck (Eds), *A lifetime of relationships* (pp. 155–180). Pacific Grove, CA.: Brooks/Cole.

Freud, A. (1969). Adolescence as a developmental disturbance. In G. Kaplan & S. Lebovici (Eds), *Adolescence: Psychological perspectives* (pp. 5–10). New York: Basic Books.

Friedan, B. (1963). *The feminine mystique.* New York: Norton.

Frieze, I. H. & McHugh, M. C. (1992). Power and influence strategies in violent and nonviolent marriages. *Psychology of Women Quarterly*, **16**, 449–465.

Fromm, E. (1956). *The Art of Loving.* New York: Harper & Row.

Fry, W. R., Firestone, I. J. & Williams, D. L. (1983). Negotiation process and outcome of stranger dyads and dating couples: Do lovers lose? *Basic and Applied Social Psychology*, **4**, 1–16.

Fullinwider-Bush, N., & Jacobvitz, D. B. (1993). The transition to young adulthood: Generational boundary dissolution and female identity development. *Family Process*, **32**, 87–103.

Gaelick, L., Bodenhausen, G.V. & Wyer, R.S. (1985). Emotional communication in close relationships. *Journal of Personality and Social Psychology*, **49**, 1246–1265.

Galvin, K. M. & Brommel, B.J. (1986). *Family communication.* Glenview, IL: Scott, Foreman.

Gergen, K. J. (1991). *The saturated self: Dilemmas of identity in contemporary life.* New York: Basic.

Giddens, A. (1991). *Modernity and self-identity.* Cambridge: Polity.

Gilford, R. & Bengtson, V. (1979). Measuring marital satisfaction in three generations: Positive and negative dimensions. *Journal of Marriage and the Family*, **41**, 387–398.

Gilligan, C. (1982). *In a different voice: Psychological theory and women's development.* Cambridge, MA: Harvard University Press.

Gittins, D. (1993). *The family in question* (2nd edn). London: Macmillan.

Glass, J., Bengtson, V. L. & Dunham, C. C. (1986). Attitude similarity in three-generation families: Socialization, status inheritance, or reciprocal influence. *American Sociological Review*, **51**, 685–698.

Glenn, E. N. (1987). Gender and the family. In B. B. Hess & M. M. Ferree (Eds), *Analyzing gender* (pp. 348–380). Newbury Park, CA: Sage.

Glenn, N. D. (1990). Quantitative research on marital quality in the 1980s: A critical review. *Journal of Marriage and the Family*, **52**, 818–831.

Glenn, N. D. (1998). The course of marital success & failure in five American 10-year marriage cohorts. *Journal of Marriage and the Family*, **60**, 569–576.

Globerman, J. (1996). Daughters- and sons-in-law caring for relatives with Alzheimer's disease. *Family Relations*, **45**, 37–45.

Goffman, E. (1959). *The presentation of self in everyday life*, Garden City. N.Y.: Doubleday Anchor.

Gold, D. T. (1989). Sibling relationships in old age: A typology. *International Journal of Aging and Human Development*, **28**, 37–51.

Goldenburg, S. (1984–85). An empirical test of Bott's hypotheses, based on analysis of ethnographic atlas data. *Behavioral Science Research*, **19**, 127–158.

Gonzalez, R. & Griffin, D. (1997). On the statistics of interdependence: Treating dyadic data with respect. In S. W. Duck (Ed.), *Handbook of Personal Relationships* (pp. 271–302). New York: Wiley.

Gordon, M. & Downing, H. (1978). A multivariate test of the Bott hypothesis in an urban Irish setting. *Journal of Marriage and the Family*, **40**, 585–593.

Gottman, J. M. (1979). *Marital Interaction: Experimental Investigations*. New York: Academic Press.

Gottman, J. M. (1994). *What predicts divorce? The relationships between marital processes and marital outcomes*. Hillsdale, NJ: Lawrence Erlbaum.

Gottman, J. M. & Krokoff, L. J. (1989). Marital interaction and satisfaction: a longitudinal view. *Journal of Consulting and Clinical Psychology*, **57**, 37–52.

Gottman, J. M. & Levenson, R. W. (1986). Assessing the role of emotion in marriage. *Behavioral Assessment*, **8**, 31–48.

Gottman, J. M. & Levenson, R. W. (1988). The social psychophysiology of marriage. In P. Noller & M. A. Fitzpatrick (Eds), *Perspectives on marital interaction* (pp. 182–202). Clevedon, Avon, England: Multilingual Matters.

Gottman, J. M. & Levenson, R. W. (1992). Marital processes predictive of later dissolution: Behavior, physiology, and health. *Journal of Personality and Social Psychology*, **63**, 221–233.

Gottman, J. M., Coan, J., Carrere, S. & Swanson, C. (1998). Predicting marital happiness and stability from newlywed interactions. *Journal of Marriage and the Family*, **60**, 5–22.

Gottman, J., Markman, H., & Notarius, C. (1977). The topography of marital conflict: A study of verbal and nonverbal behavior. *Journal of Marriage and the Family*, **39**, 461–477.

Gove, W. R., Hughes, M. & Style, C. (1983). Does marriage have a positive effect on the psychological well-being of the individual? *Journal of Health and Social Behaviors*, **24**, 122–131.

Granovetter, M. (1979). The theory-gap in social network analysis. In P. W. Holland and S. Leinhardt (Eds), *Perspectives on Social Network Research*. New York: Academic Press.

Gratton, B. & Haber, C. (1993). In search of "intimacy at a distance": Family history from the perspective of elderly women. *Journal of Aging Studies*, **7**, 183–194.

Gray-Little, B. & Burks, N. (1983). Power and satisfaction in marriage: A review and critique. *Psychological Bulletin*, **93**, 513–538.

Greene, A. L. & Boxer, A. M. (1986). Daughters and sons as young adults: Restructuring the ties that bind. In N. Datan, A. L. Greene & H. W. Reese (Eds), *Life-span developmental psychology: Intergenerational relations* (pp. 125–149). Hillsdale, NJ: Erlbaum.

Greven, P. (1992). *Spare the child: The religious roots of punishment and the psychological impact of physical abuse*. New York: Vintage.

Grotevant, H. D. & Cooper, C. R. (1982). Identity formation and role-taking skill in adolescence: An Investigation of family structure and family process antecedents. Final report prepared for the National Institute of Child Health and Human Development, University of Texas at Austin.

Grych, J. H. & Fincham, F. D. (1990). Marital conflict and children's adjustment: A cognitive-contextual framework. *Psychological Bulletin*, **108**, 267–290.

Gutmann, D. L. (1987). *Reclaimed powers: Toward a new psychology of men and women in later life*. New York: Basic Books.

Gwanfogbe, P. N., Schumm, W. R., Smith, M. & Furrow, J. L. (1997). Polygyny and marital/life satisfaction: An exploratory study from rural Cameroon. *Journal of Comparative Family Studies*, **28**, 55–71.

Haas, L. (1986). Wives' orientation toward breadwinning: Sweden and the United States. *Journal of Family Issues*, **7**, 358–381.

Haas, L. (1992). *Equal parenthood and social policy*. Albany, NY: SUNY Press.

Hackel, L. & Ruble, D. N. (1992). Changes in the marital relationship after the first baby is born: Predicting the impact of expectancy disconfirmation. *Journal of Personality and Social Psychology*, **62**, 944–957.

Hagestad, G. O. (1979). Patterns of communication and influence between grandparents and grandchildren in a changing society. Paper presented at the World Congress of Sociology, Uppsala, Sweden.

Hagestad, G. O. (1981). Problems and promises in the social psychology of intergenerational relations. In R. W. Fogel, E. Hatfield, S. B. Kiesler & E. Shanas (Eds), *Aging: Stability and change in the family* (pp. 11–46). New York: Academic Press.

Hagestad, G. O. (1982). Parent and child: Generations in the family. In T. M. Field, A. Huston, H.C. Quay, L. Troll, & G.E. Finley (Eds), *Review of human development* (pp. 485–499). New York: Wiley.

Hagestad, G. O. (1984). The continuous bond: A dynamic, multigenerational perspective on parent-child relations between adults. In M. Perlmutter (Ed.), *Parent–child interactions and parent–child relations in child development. The Minnesota Symposium on Child Psychology* (Vol. 17, pp. 129–158). Hillsdale, NJ: Erlbaum.

Hahlweg, K., Reisner, L., Kohli, G., Vollmer, M., Schindler, L. & Revenstorf, D. (1984). Development and validity of a new system to analyse interpersonal communication (KPI). In K. Hahlweg & N.S. Jacobson (Eds), *Marital interaction: Analysis and modification* (pp. 182–198). New York: Guilford.

Halpern, J. (1994). The sandwich generation: Conflicts between adult children and their aging parents. In D.D. Cahn (ed.), *Conflict in personal relationships* (pp. 143–160). Hillsdale, NJ: Erlbaum.

Hammock, G. S. & Richardson, D. R. (1992). Aggression as one response to conflict. *Journal of Applied Social Psychology*, **22**, 298–311.

Hannan, D. F. & Katsiaouni, L. A. (1977). *Traditional Families? From Culturally Prescribed to Negotiated Roles in Farm Families*. Dublin: Economic and Social Research Institute.

Hanson, B. (1997). Who's seeing whom? General systems theory and constructivist implications for senile dementia intervention. *Journal of Aging Studies*, **11**, 15–25.

Harber, K. D. & Pennebaker, J.W. (1992). Overcoming traumatic memories. In S. A. Christianson (ed.), *The handbook of emotion and memory* (pp. 359–387). Hillsdale, NJ: Erlbaum.

Hareven, T. K. (1991). The history of the family and the complexity of social change. *American Historical Review*, **96**, 95–124.

Harris, L. M., Gergen, K. J. & Lannamann, J. W. (1986). Aggression rituals. *Communication Monographs*, **53**, 252–265.

Harrison, K. (1998). Rich friendships, affluent friends: middle-class practices of friendship. In R. G. Adams & G. Allan (Eds), *Placing friendship in context* (pp. 92–116). Cambridge: Cambridge University Press.

Hartmann, H. (1981). The family as locus of gender, class, and political struggle: The example of housework. *Signs*, **6**, 336–94.

Hartup, W. (1989). Social relationships and their developmental significance. *Amercian Psychologist*, **44**, 120–126.

Harvey, J. H., Weber, A. L. & Orbuch, T. L. (1990). *Interpersonal accounts: A social psychological perspective*. Oxford: Blackwell.

Hauser, G. A. (1986). *Introduction to rhetorical theory*. New York: Harper & Row.

Hazan, C. & Shaver, P. (1987). Romantic love conceptualized as an attachment process. *Journal of Personality and Social Psychology*, **52**, 511–524.

Healey, J. G. and Bell, R. A. (1990). Effects of social networks on individuals' responses to conflicts in friendship. In D. D. Cahn (Ed.), *Intimates in Conflict: A Communication Perspective* (pp. 121–150). Lawrence Erlbaum: Hillsdale, NJ.

Heavey, C. L., Christensen, A. & Malamuth, N. M. (1995). The longitudinal impact of demand and withdraw during marital conflict. *Journal of Consulting and Clinical Psychology*, **63**, 797–801.

Helms-Erikson, H. (in preparation). Marriage and friendship: A contextual view of husbands' and wives' relationships with their close friends. Unpublished doctoral dissertation, The Pennsylvania State University, University Park, PA.

Helson, R. & Moane, G. (1987). Personality change in women from college to midlife. *Journal of Personality and Social Psychology*, **53**, 176–186.

Helson, R. & Wink, P. (1992). Personality change in women from the early 40s to the early 50s. *Psychology and Aging*, **7**, 46–55.

Hendricks, J. (1997). Bridging a contested terrain: Chaos or prelude to a theory. *Canadian Journal on Aging*, **16**, 197–217.

Henle, M. (1961). Some problems of eclecticism. In M. Henle (Ed.), *Documents of Gestalt psychology* (pp. 76–89). Berkeley, CA: University of California Press.

Hetherington, E. M. (1987). Family relations six years after divorce. In K. Pasley & M. Ihinger-Tallman (Eds), *Remarriage and stepparenting: Current research and theory* (pp. 185–205). New York: Guilford Press.

Hetherington, E. M. (1989). Coping with family transitions: Winners, losers, and survivors. *Child Development*, **60**, 1–14.

Hetherington, E. M. & Stanley-Hagan, M. (2000). In D. H. Demo, K. R. Allen., & M. A. Fine (Eds), *Handbook of Family Diversity*. New York: Oxford University Press.

Hetherington, E. M. Bridges, M., & Insabella, G. M. (1998). What matters? What does not? Five perspectives on the association between marital transitions and children's adjustment. *American Psychologist*, **53**, 167–184.

Hicks, M. & Platt, M. (1970). Marital happiness and stability: A review of the research in the sixties. *Journal of Marriage and the Family*, **32**, 553–574.

Hill, C. T. & Peplau, L. A. (1998). Premarital predictors of relationship outcomes: A 15-year follow-up of the Boston Couples Study. In T. N. Bradbury (Ed.), *The developmental course of marital dysfunction* (pp. 237–278). New York: Cambridge University Press.

Hill, M. D. (1988). Class, kinship density, and conjugal role segregation. *Journal of Marriage and the Family*, **50**, 731–741.

Hill, R. (1949). *Families under stress*. New York: Harper.

Hill, R. & Rodgers, R. H. (1964). The developmental approach. In H. T. Christensen (Ed.), *Handbook of marriage and the family* (pp. 171–211). Chicago: Rand McNally.

Hinde, R. A. (1979). *Toward understanding relationships*. New York: Academic Press.

Hinde, R. A. (1981). "The bases of a science of interpersonal relationships". In S. W. Duck & R. Gilmour (Eds), *Personal Relationships 1: Studying Personal Relationships* (pp. 1–22). London, New York, San Francisco: Academic Press.

Hinde, R. A. & Stevenson-Hinde, J. (Eds). (1988). *Relationships within families*. Oxford: Oxford University Press.

Hirschman, A. O. (1970). *Exit, voice, and loyalty: Responses to decline in firms, organizations, and states*. Cambridge, MA: Harvard University Press.

Hochschild, A. (1983). *The managed heart: Commercialization of human feeling*. Berkeley: University of California Press.

Hochschild, A. (1989). *The Second Shift: Working Parents and the Revolution at Home.* New York: Viking.

Hoffman, J. A. (1984). Psychological separation of late adolescents from their parents. *Journal of Counseling Psychology*, **31**, 170–178.

Hoffman, J. A. & Weiss, B. (1987). Family dynamics and presenting problems in college students. *Journal of Counseling Psychology*, **34**, 157–163.

Hoffman, L. W. (1984). Work, family, and the socialization of the child. In R. D. Parke (Ed.), *Review of Child Development Research*, **7** (pp.223–282). Chicago, IL: Chicago University Press.

Hogan, D. P. & Astone, N. M. (1986). The transition to adulthood. *Annual Review of Sociology*, **12**, 109–130.

Holden, K. C. & Smock, P. J. (1991). The economic costs of marital dissolution: Why do women bear a disproportionate cost? *Annual Review of Sociology*, **17**, 51–78.

Holmes, J. G. (1991). Trust and the appraisal process in close relationships. *Advances in Personal Relationships*, **2**, 57–104.

Holmes, J. G. & Boon, S. D. (1990). Developments in the field of close relationships: Creating foundations for intervention strategies. *Personality and Social Psychology Bulletin*, **16**, 23–41.

Holtzworth-Munroe, A., Smutzler, N. & Stuart, G. L. (1998). Demand and withdraw communication among couples experiencing husband violence. *Journal of Consulting and Clinical Psychology*, **66**, 731–743.

Homans, G. C. (1961). *Social behavior: Its elementary forms.* New York: Harcourt Brace & World.

Hondagneu-Sotelo, P. (1992). Overcoming patriarchal constraints: The reconstruction of gender relations among Mexican immigrant women and men. *Gender and Society*, **6**, 393–415.

Honeycutt, J. M. (1993). Memory structures for the rise and fall of personal relationships. In S. W. Duck (Ed.), *Individuals in relationships [Understanding relationship processes 1]* (pp. 60–86). Newbury Park, CA: Sage.

Hood, J. C. (1986). The provider role: Its meaning and measurement. *Journal of Marriage and the Family*, **48**, 349–359.

Hopper, J. (1993). The rhetoric of motives in divorce. *Journal of Marriage and the Family*, **55**, 801–813.

Howard, J. A., Blumstein, P., & Schwartz, P. (1986). Sex, power, and influence tactics in intimate relationships. *Journal of Personality and Social Psychology*, **51**, 102–109.

Hunsley, J., Vito, D., Pinsent, C., James, S. & Lefebvre, M (1996). Are self-report measures of dyadic relationships influenced by impression management biases? *Journal of Family Psychology*, **10**, 322–330.

Huston, T. L. & Chorost, A. F. (1994). Behavioral buffers on the effect of negativity on marital satisfaction: A longitudinal study. *Personal Relationships*, **1**, 223–39.

Huston, T. L. & Robins, E. (1982). Conceptual and methodological issues in studying close relationships. *Journal of Marriage and the Family*, **44**, 901–925.

Huston, T. L., McHale, S. & Crouter, A. (1986). When the honeymoon's over: Changes in the marriage relationship over the first year. In R. Gilmour & S. Duck (Eds) *The Emerging Field of Personal Relationships* (pp. 109–32). Hillsdale, NJ: Erlbaum.

Huyck, M. H. (1995). Marriage and close relationships of the marital kind. In R. Blieszner & V. H. Bedford (Eds), *Handbook of aging and the family* (pp. 181–200). Westport, CT: Greenwood Press.

Ickes, W. & Duck, S. W. (2000). Personal Relationships and Social Psychology. In W. Ickes & S. W. Duck (Eds), *Personal Relationships and Social Psychology* (pp. 1–8). Chichester: Wiley.

Ickes, W. & Dugosh, J. W. (in press). An intersubjective perspective on social cognition and aging. *Basic and Applied Social Psychology (special issue on Social Cognition and Aging)*.

Ickes, W., & Gonzales, R. (1996). "Social" cognition and social cognition: From the subjective to the intersubjective. In J. Nye & A. Brower (Eds), *What's So Social about Social Cognition? Social Cognition Research in Small Group*. Newbury Park, CA: Sage.

Jacobson, N. S. (1989). The politics of intimacy. *Behavior Therapist*, **12**, 29–32.

Jacobson, N. S. (1990). Commentary: Contributions from psychology to an understanding of marriage. In F.D. Fincham & T.N. Bradbury (Eds), *The psychology of marriage* (pp. 258–275). New York: Guilford.

Jacobson, N. S. & Addis, M.E. (1993). Research on couples and couple therapy: What do we know? Where are we going? *Journal of Consulting and Clinical Psychology*, **61**, 85–93.

Jacobson, N. S. & Holtzworth-Munroe, A. (1986). Marital therapy: A social learning-cognitive perspective. In N.S. Jacobson & A.S. Gurman (Eds), *Clinical handbook of marital therapy* (pp. 29–70). New York: Guilford.

Jacobson, N. S., Gottman, J. M., Waltz, J., Rushe, R., Babcock, J. & Holtzworth-Munroe, A. (1994). *Journal of Consulting and Clinical Psychology*, **62**, 982–988.

Johnson, C. L. (1988). *Ex familia*. New Brunswick: Rutgers University Press.

Johnson, C. L. (1993). The prolongation of life and the extension of family relationships: The families of the oldest old. In P. A. Cowan, D. Field, D. A. Hansen, A. Skolnick & G. E. Swanson (Eds), *Family, self, and society: Toward a new agenda for family research* (pp. 317–330). Hillsdale, NJ: Erlbaum.

Johnson, C. L. & Barer, B. M. (1995). Childlessness and kinship organization: Comparisons of very old Whites and Blacks. *Journal of Cross-cultural Gerontology*, **10**(4), 289–306.

Johnson, C. L. & Barer, B. M. (1997). Life beyond 85 years: The aura of survivorship. New York: Springer.

Johnson, C. L. & Troll, L. (1996). Family structure and the timing of transitions from 70 to 103 years of age. *Journal of Marriage and the Family*, **58**, 178–187.

Johnson, M. P. (1982). Social and cognitive features of the dissolution of commitment to relationships. In S. W. Duck (ed.), *Personal relationships 4: Dissolving personal relationships* (pp. 51–73). New York: Academic Press.

Johnson, M. P. (1991). Commitment to personal relationships. In W.H. Jones & D. Perlman (Eds), *Advances in personal relationships*, Vol. 3 (pp. 117–143). Jessica Kingsley Publishers.

Johnson, M. P. (1995). Patriarchal terrorism and common couple violence: Two forms of violence against women. *Journal of Marriage and the Family*, **57**, 283–294.

Johnson, M. P. & Kapinus, C.A. (1995). Gendered commitments: Gender and family life-course as factors in the strength of relationship ties. Unpublished manuscript.

Johnson, M. P. & Milardo, R. M. (1984). Network interference in pair relationships: A social psychological recasting of Slater's theory of social regression. *Journal of Marriage and the Family*, **46**, 893–9.

Johnson, M. P., Huston, T. L. & Milardo, R. M. (1983). Developing close relationships: changing patterns of interaction between pair members and social networks. *Journal of Personality and Social Psychology*, **44**, 964–76.

Jones, E. E. & Gerard, H.B. (1967). *Foundations of social psychology*. Wiley: New York.

Josselson, R. (1988). The embedded self: I and thou revisited. In D. K. Lapsley & F. C. Power (Eds), Self, ego, and identity: Integrative approaches (pp. 91–106). New York: Springer-Verlag.

Josselson, R. (1992). *The space between us: Exploring the dimensions of human relationships*. San Francisco: Jossey-Bass.

Kaiser, A., Hahlweg, K., Fehm-Wolfsdorf, G. & Groth, T. (1998). The efficacy of a compact psycho-educational group training program for married couples. *Journal of Consulting & Clinical Psychology*, **66**, 753–760.

Kalmuss, D., Davidson, A. & Cushman, L. (1992). Parenting expectations, experiences, and adjustment to parenthood: A test of the violated expectations framework. *Journal of Marriage and the Family*, **54**, 516–526.

Kamo, Y. (1988). Determinants of household division of labor: Resources, power, and ideology. *Journal of Family Issues*, **9**, 177–200.

Kaniasty, K. & Norris, F. H. (2000). Social suport dynamics in adjustment to disasters. In B. Sarason & S. W. Duck (Eds), *Clinical psychology and personal relationships*. Chichester: Wiley.

Kapferer, B. (1973). Social network and conjugal role in urban Zambia: Towards a reformulation of the Bott hypothesis. In J. Bossevain & J. Mitchell (Eds), *Network analysis: Studies in human interaction* (pp. 83–110). The Hague: Mouton.

Kaplan, A. (1964). *The conduct of inquiry: Methodology for behavioral science*. San Francisco: Chandler Publishing Company.

Karney, B. R. & Bradbury, T. N. (1995). The longitudinal course of marital quality and stability: A review of theory, method, and research. *Psychological Bulletin*, **118**, 3–34.

Karp, D. A., Holmstrom, L. L. & Gray, P. S. (1998). Leaving home for college: Expectations for selective reconstruction of self. *Symbolic Interaction*, **21**, 253–276.

Kaslow, F. W., Hansson, K. & Lundblad, A. (1994). Long term marriages in Sweden: And some comparisons with similar couples in the United States. *Contemporary Family Therapy*, **16**, 521–537.

Kaufman, G. & Uhlenberg, P. (1998). Effects of life course transitions on the quality of relationships between adult children and their parents. *Journal of Marriage and the Family*, **60**, 924–938.

Kayser, K. (1993). *When Love Dies*. New York: Guilford.

Kelley, H. H. (1979). *Personal relationships: Their structure and process*. Hillsdale, NJ: Erlbaum.

Kelley, H. H. & Thibaut, J. W. (1978). Interpersonal relations: A theory of interdependence. New York: Wiley.

Kelley, H. H., Berscheid, E., Christensen, A., Harvey, J., Huston, T. L., Levinger, G., McClintock, D., Peplau, L. A. & Peterson, D. (1983). *Close Relationships*. San Francisco: Freeman.

Kelly, G. A. (1955). *The psychology of personal constructs*. New York: Norton.

Kenny, D. A. (1994). *Interpersonal perception: A social relations analysis*. New York: Guilford Press.

Kenny, D. A. (1996). Models of non-independence in dyadic research. *Journal of Social and Personal Relationships*, **13**, 279–294.

Kenny, D. A. & LaVoie, L. (1985). Separating individual and group effects. *Journal of Personality and Social Psychology*, **48**, 339–348.

Kenny, M. E. & Donaldson, G. A. (1992). The relationship of parental attachment and psychological separation to the adjustment of first-year college women. *Journal of College Student Development*, **33**, 431–438.

Kessler, R. C. & McRae, J. A., Jr. (1982). The effects of wives' employment on the mental health of married men and women. *American Sociological Review*, **47**, 216–217.

Kidwell, J., Fischer, J. L., Dunham, R. M. & Baranowski, M. (1983). Parents and adolescents: Push and pull of change. In H. I. McCubbin & C. R. Figley (Eds), *Stress in the family*, Volume I: *Coping with normative transitions* (pp. 74–89).

King, V. (1994a). Nonresident father involvement and child well-being: Can dads make a difference? *Journal of Family Issues*, **15**, 78–96.

King, V. (1994b). Variation in the consequences of nonresident father involvement for children's well-being. *Journal of Marriage and the Family*, **56**, 963–972.

King, V. & Heard, H. E. (1999). Nonresident father visitation, parental conflict, and mothers' satisfaction: What's best for child well-being? *Journal of Marriage and the Family*, **61**, 385–396.

Kinsella, K. (1995). Aging and the family: Present and future demographic issues. In R. Blieszner & V. H. Bedford (Eds), *Handbook of aging and the family* (pp. 32–56). Westport, CT: Greenwood Press.

Kinsella, K. (1996). Aging and the family: Present and future demographic issues. In R. Blieszner & V. H. Bedford (Eds), *Aging and the family: Theory and research* (pp. 32–56). Westport, CT: Praeger.

Kirkpatrick, L. A. & Davis, K. E. (1994). Attachment style, gender, and relationship stability: A longitudinal analysis. *Journal of Personality and Social Psychology*, **66**, 502–512.

Kirkwood, C. (1993). *Leaving abusive partners*. Newbury Park: Sage.

Kitson, G. C. (1992). *Portrait of divorce: Adjustment to marital breakdown*. New York: Guilford Press.

Kivett, V. R. (1989). Mother-in-law and daughter-in-law relations. In J. A. Mancini (Ed.), *Aging parents and adult children* (pp. 17–32). Lexington, MA: Lexington Books.

Klein, R. C. A. (1995). Conflict-resolution in close relationships. Report to the German Science Foundation.

Klein, R. C. A. (1998). Conflict and violence in the family: Cross-disciplinary issues. In R.C.A. Klein (Ed.), *Multidisciplinary perspectives on family violence* (pp. 1–13). London: Routledge.

Klein, R. C. A. & Johnson, M. P (1997). Strategies of couple conflict. In S. Duck (Ed.), *Handbook of Personal Relationships*, (2nd Edn). (pp. 469–86). Chichester: Wiley.

Klein, R. C. A. & Lamm, H. (1996). Legitimate interest in couple conflict. *Journal of Social and Personal Relationships*, **13**, 619–626.

Klein, R. C. A. & Milardo, R. M. (1993). Third-party influences on the development and maintenance of personal relationships. In S. W. Duck (Ed.), *Social contexts of relationships [Understanding relationship processes: Vol. 3:]* (pp. 55–77). Newbury Park, CA: Sage.

Klein, R. C. A. & Milardo, R. M. (1995). The social context of pair conflict: Paper presented at the International Network of Personal Relationships 1995 Conference, Williamsburg, Virginia.

Klohnen, E. C. & Bera, S. (1998). Behavioral and experiential patterns of avoidantly and securely attached women across adulthood: A 31-year longitudinal perspective. *Journal of Personality and Social Psychology*, **74**, 211–223.

Kluwer, E. S. (1998). Responses to gender inequality in the division of family work: The status quo effect. *Social Justice Research*, **11**, 337–357.

Kluwer, E. S., De Dreu, C. K. W. & Buunk, B. P. (1998). Conflict in intimate versus non-intimate relationships: When gender role stereotyping overrides biased self-other judgment. *Journal of Social and Personal Relationships*, **15**, 637–650.

Kluwer, E. S., Heesink, J. A. M. & Van de Vliert, E. (1996). Marital conflict about the division of household labor and paid work. *Journal of Marriage and the Family*, **58**, 958–969.

Kluwer, E. S., Heesink, J. A. M. & Van De Vliert, E. (1997). The marital dynamics of conflict over the division of labor. *Journal of Marriage and the Family*, **59**, 635–653.

Kluwer, E. S., Heesink, J. A. M. & Van de Vliert, E. (1999). The division of family work across the transition to parenthood: A (longitudinal) test of the distributive justice framework.

Kluwer, E. S., Heesink, J. A. M. & Van de Vliert, E. (in press). The division of labor in close relationships: An asymmetrical conflict issue. *Personal Relationships*.

Knight, B. G. & McCallum, T. J. (1998). Psychotherapy with older adult families: The contextual, cohort-based maturity/specific challenge model. In I. E. Nordhus & G. R. VandenBos (Eds), *Clinical geropsychology* (pp. 313–328). Washington, DC: American Psychological Association.

Kobak, R. R. & Hazan, C. (1991). Attachment in marriage: Effects of security and accuracy of working models. *Journal of Personality and Social Psychology*, **60**, 861–869.

Kohn, M. L. (1969). *Class and conformity: A study in values*. Homewood, IL: Dorsey Press.

Kohn, M. L. (1977). *Reassessment: A preface to the second edition of class and conformity.* Chicago: University of Chicago Press.

Kohn, M. L. & Schooler, C. (1983). *Work and personality: An inquiry into the impact of social stratification.* Norwood, NJ: Ablex.

Kompter, A. (1989). Hidden power in marriage. *Gender & Society,* **3,** 187–216.

Krokoff, L. J., Gottman, J. M. & Roy, A.K. (1988). Blue-collar and white-collar marital interaction and communication orientation. *Journal of Social and Personal Relationships,* **5,** 201–221.

Kübler-Ross, E. (1969). *On death and dying.* New York: Macmillan.

Kuijer, R. G., Ybema, J. F., Buunk, B. P., De Jong, M., Thijs-Boer, F. & Sanderman, R. (in press). Active engagement, protective buffering, and overprotection: Three ways of giving support by intimate partners of patients with cancer. *Journal of Social and Clinical Psychology.*

Kurdek, L. A. (1989). Relationship quality for newly married husbands and wives: Marital history, stepchildren, and individual-difference predictors. *Journal of Marriage and the Family,* **51,** 1053–64.

Kurdek, L. A. (1991). Marital stability and changes in marital quality in newly wed couples: A test of the contextual model. *Journal of Social and Personal Relationships,* **8,** 27–48.

Kurdek, L. A. (1993a). Predicting marital dissolution: A 5-year prospective study of newlywed couples. *Journal of Personality and Social Psychology,* **64,** 221–42.

Kurdek, L. A. (1993b). The allocation of household labor in gay, lesbian, and heterosexual married couples. *Journal of Social Issues,* **49,** 127–139.

Kurdek, L. A. (1994). Conflict resolution styles in gay, lesbian, heterosexual nonparent, and heterosexual parent couples. *Journal of Marriage and the Family,* **56,** 705–722.

Kurdek, L. A. (1998). Developmental changes in marital satisfaction: A 6-year prospective longitudinal study of newlywed couples. In T. Bradbury (ed.) *The Developmental Course of Marital Dysfunction* (pp. 180–204) New York: Cambridge University Press.

La Gaipa, J. L. (1981). A systems approach to personal relationships. In S. W. Duck & R. Gilmour (Eds), *Personal relationships. 1: Studying personal relationships.* New York: Academic Press.

Laireiter, A., Baumann, U., Riesenzein, E., & Untner, A. (1997). A diary method for assessment of interactive social networks: The interval-contingent diary SONET-T. *Swiss Journal of Psychology,* **56,** 217–238.

Lambert, S. J. (1999). Lower-wage workers and the new realities of work and family. *The Annals of the American Academy of Political and Social Science,* **562,** 174–190.

Landry, P. H., Jr. & Martin, M. E. (1988). Measuring intergenerational consensus. In D. J. Mangen, V. L. Bengtson & P. H. Landry, Jr. (Eds), *Measurement of intergenerational relations* (pp. 126–155). Newbury Park, CA: Sage.

Lane, C., Christensen, A. and Heavey, C. L. (1993). Gender and conflict structure in marital interaction: A replication and extension. *Journal of Consulting and Clinical Psychology,* **61,** 16–27.

Lang, M. E., Rovine, M. & Belsky, J. (1985). Stability and change in marriage across the transition to parenthood: a second study. *Journal of Marriage and the Family,* **47,** 855–865.

Lapsley, D. K., Rice, K. G. & Shadid, G. E. (1989). Psychological separation and adjustment to college. *Journal of Counseling Psychology,* **36,** 286–294.

Larson, R. & Almeida, D. (1999). Emotional transmission in the daily lives of families: A new paradigm for studying family process. *Journal of Marriage and the Family,* **61,** 5–20.

Larson, R. W. & Bradney, N. (1988). Precious moments with family members and friends. In R. M. Milardo (Ed.), *Families and Social Networks* (pp. 107–126). Newbury Park, CA: Sage.

Larson, R. & Richards, M. H. (1994). *Divergent realities: The emotional lives of mothers, fathers, and adolescents.* New York: Basic Books.

Lasch, C. (1977). *Haven in a heartless world: The family besieged.* New York: Basic.

Laslett, B. & Brenner, J. (1989). Gender and social reproduction: Historical perspectives. *Annual Review of Sociology*, **15**, 381–404.

Laverty, R. (1962). Reactivation of sibling rivalry in older people. *Social Work*, **7**, 23–30.

Lawton, M. P. (1994, August). The aging family in multigenerational perspective. Paper presented at the Annual Convention of the American Psychological Association, Los Angeles.

Lee, G. (1979). Effects of social networks on the family. In W. Burr, R. Hill, F. I. Nye & I. Reiss (Eds), *Contemporary Theories about the Family*, Vol. 1 (pp. 27–56). New York: Free Press.

Leigh, G. K. (1982). Kinship interaction over the family life span. *Journal of Marriage and the Family*, **44**, 197–208.

Lennon, M. C. & Rosenfield, S. (1994). Relative fairness and the division of housework: The importance of options. *American Journal of Sociology*, **100**, 506–531.

Leonard, K. E. & Roberts, L. J. (1998). Marital aggression, quality, and stability in the first year of marriage: Findings from the Buffalo Newlywed Study. In T. N. Bradbury (Ed.). *The developmental course of marital dysfunction* (pp. 44–73). New York: Cambridge University Press.

Levenson, R. W., Carstensen, L. L. & Gottman, J. M. (1993). Long-term marriage: Age, gender, and satisfaction. *Psychology & Aging*, **8**, 301–313.

Levi, C. (1947). *Christ stopped at Eboli.* New York: Times Books.

Levinger, G. (1976). A social psychological perspective on marital dissolution. *Journal of Social Issues*, **32**, 21–47.

Levinger, G. & Pietromonaco, P. (1989). A measure of perceived conflict resolution styles in relationships. Unpublished manuscript. University of Massachusetts.

Levitt, M. J., Coffman, S. Guacci-Franco, N. & Loveless, S. C. (1994). Attachment relationships and life transitions: An expectancy model. In M. B. Sperling & W. H. Berman (Eds), *Attachment in adults: Clinical and developmental perspectives* (pp. 232–255). New York: Guilford.

Lewis, R. A. & Spanier, G. B. (1979). Theorizing about the quality and stability of marriage. In W. R. Burr, R. Hill, F. I. Nye & I. L. Reiss (Eds), *Contemporary theories about the family* (Vol. 1, pp. 268–294). New York: Free Press.

Lieberman, M. A. & Kramer, J. H. (1991). Factors affecting decisions to institutionalize demented elderly. *The Gerontologist*, **31**, 371–374.

Litwak, E. (1960). Geographic mobility and extended family cohesion. *American Sociological Review*, **25**, 9–21.

Lloyd, S. A. (1987). Conflict in premarital relationships: Differential perceptions of males and females. *Family Relations*, **36**, 290–294.

Lloyd, S. A. & Cate, R.M. (1985). The developmental course of conflict in dissolution of premarital relationships. *Journal of Social and Personal Relationships*, **2**, 179–194.

Lloyd, S. A. & Emery, B.C. (1994). Physically aggressive conflict in romantic relationships. In D.D. Cahn (Ed.), *Conflict in personal relationships* (pp. 27–46). Hillsdale, NJ: Erlbaum.

Locke, H. J. & Wallace, K. M. (1959). Short marital adjustment prediction tests: Their reliability and validity. *Marriage and Family Living*, **21**, 251–255.

Lollis, S. & Kuczynski, L. (1997). Beyond one hand clapping? Seeing bi-directionality in parent–child relationships. *Journal of Social and Personal Relationships*, **14**, 441–461.

Lopata, H. & Thorne, B. (1978). On the term "sex roles." *Signs*, **3**, 638–651.

Lopez, F. G., Campbell, V. L. & Watkins, C. E., Jr. (1986). Depression, psychological separation, and college adjustment: An investigation of sex differences. *Journal of Counseling Psychology*, **33**, 52–56.

Lopez, F. G., Campbell, V. L. & Watkins, C. E., Jr. (1989). Effects of marital conflict and family coalition patterns on college student adjustment. *Journal of College Student Development*, **30**, 46–52.

Lorde, A. (1984). *Sister outsider*. Freedom, CA: Crossing Press.

Luescher, K. & Pillemer, K. (1998). Intergenerational ambivalence: A new approach to the study of parent–child relations in later life. *Journal of Marriage and the Family*, **60**, 413–425.

Lussier, Y., Sabourin, S. & Turgeon, C. (1997). Coping strategies as moderators of the relationship between attachment and marital adjustment. *Journal of Social and Personal Relationships*, **14**, 777–791.

Lye, D. N. (1996). Adult child–parent relationships. *Annual Review of Sociology*, **22**, 79–102.

Lykes, M. B. (1985). Gender and individualistic vs. Collectivist bases for notions about the self. *Journal of Personality*, **53**, 356–83.

Maccoby, E. E. (1990). Gender and relationships. *American Psychologist*, **45**, 513–520.

Maccoby, E. E. & Mnookin, R. H. (1992). *Dividing the child: Social and legal dilemmas of custody*. Cambridge, MA: Harvard University Press.

MacDermid, S. M., Huston, T. L. & McHale, S. M. (1990). Changes in marriage associated with the transition to parenthood: Individual differences as a function of sex-role attitudes and changes in the division of household labor. *Journal of Marriage and the Family*, **52**, 475–486.

Maguire, M. C. (1999). Treating the dyad as the unit of analysis: A primer on three analytic approaches. *Journal of Marriage and the Family*, **61**, 213–223.

Mahler, M. S. (1968). *On human symbiosis and the vicissitudes of individuation*. New York: International Universities Press.

Malley, J. (1989). The balance of agency and commmunion: Adjustment and adaptation. *Dissertation Abstracts International*, **50**, 2-B.

Mancini, J. A. & Blieszner, R. (1989). Aging parents and aging children: Research themes in intergenerational relations. *Journal of Marriage and the Family*, **51**, 275–290.

Manke, B. & Plomin, R. (1997). Adolescent familial interactions: A genetic extension of the social relations model. *Journal of Social and Personal Relationships*, **14**, 505–522.

Maret, E. & Finlay, B. (1984). The distribution of household labor among women in dual-earner families. *Journal of Marriage and the Family*, **46**, 357–364.

Margolin, G. (1988). Marital conflict is not marital conflict is not marital conflict. In R. De V. Peters et al. (Eds), *Social learning and systems approaches to marriage and the family* (pp. 193–216). New York: Brunner/Mazel.

Margolin, G., & Wampold, B.E. (1981). Sequential analysis of conflict and accord in distressed and nondistressed marital partners. *Journal of Consulting and Clinical Psychology*, **49**, 554–567.

Margolin, G., Burman, B. & John, R.S. (1989). Home observations of married couples reenacting naturalistic conflicts. *Behavioral Assessment*, **11**, 101–118.

Margolin, G., John, R. S. & Gleberman, L. (1988). Affective responses to conflictual discussions in violent and nonviolent couples. *Journal of Consulting and Clinical Psychology*, **56**, 24–33.

Markman, H. J. (1991). Constructive conflict is NOT an oxymoron. *Behavioral Assessment*, **13**, 83–96.

Markman, H. J. & Hahlweg, K. (1993). The prediction and prevention of marital distress: An international perspective. *Clinical Psychology Review*, **13**, 29–43.

Markman, H. J. & Kraft, S. A. (1989). Men and women in marriage: Dealing with gender differences in marital therapy. *The Behavior Therapist*, **12**, 51–6.

Markman, H. J., Renick, M. J., Floyd, F. J., Stanley, S.M. & Clements, M. (1993). Preventing marital distress through communication and conflict management training: A 4- and 5-year follow-up. *Journal of Consulting and Clinical Psychology*, **61**, 70–77.

Marks, S. R. (1987). Critique of Burr et al.: An epistemological basis for primary explanations in family science. Paper presented at the Theory and Methods Workshop at the annual meetings of the National Council on Family Relations. Atlanta, GA.

Marks, S. R. (1994). Studying workplace intimacy: Havens at work. In D.L. Sollie & L. A. Leslie (Eds), *Gender, families, and close relationships: Feminist research journeys* (pp.145–167). Thousand Oaks: Sage.

Marsden, P. (1990). Network data and measurement, *Annual Review of Sociology*, **16**, 435–463.

Marshall, G. (1990). *In Praise of Sociology*. London: Unwin-Hyman.

Marshall, V. W., Matthews, S. H. & Rosenthal, C. J. (1993). Elusiveness of family life: A challenge for the sociology of aging. In G. L. Maddox & M. P. Lawton (Eds), *Annual Review of Gerontology and Geriatrics*, **13**, (pp. 39–72). New York: Springer.

Maryanski, A. & Ishii-Kuntz, M. (1991). A cross-species application of Bott's hypothesis on role segregation and social networks, *Sociological Perspectives*, **34**, 403–425.

Mather, L. & Yngvesson, B. (1981). Language, audience, and the transformation of disputes. *Law & Society Review*, **15**, 775–821.

Matthews, L. S., Conger, R. D., & Wickrama, K. A. S. (1996). Work-family conflict and marital quality: Mediating processes. *Social Psychology Quarterly*, **59**, 62–79.

Matthews, S. H. (1986). *Friendships through the life course*. Beverly Hills, CA: Sage.

Matthews, S. H., & Sprey, J. (1989). Older family systems: Intra-and intergenerational relations. In J. A. Mancini (Ed.), *Aging parents and adult children* (pp. 63–78). Lexington, MA: Lexington Books.

May, R. (1973). *Love and Will*. New York: Delta.

McDonald, G. W. (1981). Structural exchange and marital interaction. *Journal of Marriage and the Family*, **43**, 825–839.

McGoldrick, M. (1980). The joining of families through marriage: The new couple. In E. A. Carter & M. McGoldrick (Eds) *The Family Life Cycle* (pp. 93–120). New York: Gardner.

McGonagle, K. A., Kessler, R. C. & Gotlib, I. H. (1993). The effects of marital disagreement style, frequency, and outcome on marital disruption. *Journal of Social and Personal Relationships*, **10**, 385–404.

McHale, S. M. & Crouter, A. C. (1992). You can't always get what you want: Incongruence between sex-role attitudes and family work roles and it implications for marriage. *Journal of Marriage and the Family*, **54**, 537–47.

McHale, S. M. & Huston, T. L. (1985). The effect of the transition to parenthood on the marriage relationship. *Journal of Family Issues*, **6**, 409–33.

McLanahan, S. S. & Sandefur, G. (1994). *Growing up with a single parent*. Cambridge, MA: Harvard University Press.

Mead, M. (1967). The life cycle and its variations: The division of roles. *Daedalus*, **96**, 871–875.

Meissner, M., Humphreys, E. W., Meis, S. M. & Scheu, W. J. (1975). No exit for wives: Sexual division of labour and the cumulation of household demands. *Canadian Review of Sociology and Anthropology* **12**, 424–439.

Menesini, E. (1997). Behavioral correlates of friendship status among Italian schoolchildren. *Journal of Social and Personal Relationships*, **14**, 109–121.

Merrill, D. M. (1993). Daughters-in-law as caregivers to the elderly. *Research on Aging*, **15**, 70–91.

Miell, D. E. (1987). Remembering relationship development: Constructing a context for interactions. In R. Burnett, McPhee, J. & Clarke, D. D. (Ed.), *Accounting for Relationships* (pp. 60–73). London: Methuen.

Mikula, G., Athenstaedt, U., Heschgl, S. & Heimgartner, A. (1998). Does it only depend on the point of view? Perspective-related differences in justice evaluations of negative incidents in personal relationships. *European Journal of Social Psychology*, **28**, 931–962.

Milardo, R. M. (1982). Friendship networks in developing relations: Converging and diverging enviroments. *Social Psychology Quarterly*, **45**, 162–72.

Milardo, R. M. (1986). Personal choice and social constraint in close relationships: Applications of network analysis. In V.J. Derlega & B. Winstead (Eds), *Friendship and social interaction* (pp. 145–165). New York: Springer.

Milardo, R. M. (1989). Theoretical and methodological issues in identifying the social networks of spouses. *Journal of Marriage and the Family*, **51**, 165–174.

Milardo, R. M. (1992). Comparative methods for delineating social networks. *Journal of Social and Personal Relationships*, **9**, 447–461.

Milardo, R. M. (1998). Gender asymmetry in common couple violence. *Personal Relationships*, **5**, 423–438.

Milardo, R. M. & Allan, G. A. (1997). Social Networks and marital relationships. In S. W. Duck (Ed.), *Handbook of personal relationships, second edition* (pp. 505–522). Chichester, UK: Wiley.

Milardo, R. M. & Helms-Erikson, H. (2000). Network overlap and third-party influence in close relationships. In S. S. Hendrick & C. Hendrick (Eds), *Close relationships: A sourcebook* (pp. 33–45). Newbury Park, CA: Sage.

Milardo, R. M. & Klein, R. C. A. (1992). Dominance norms and domestic violence: The justification of aggression in close relationships. Paper presented at the NCFR Theory Construction and Research Methodology Workshop, Orlando.

Milardo, R. M. & Wellman, B. (1992). The personal is social, *Journal of Social and Personal Relationships*, **9**, 339–342.

Millar, F. E., & Rogers, L. E. (1988). Power dynamics in marital relationships. In P. Noller & M.A. Fitzpatrick (Eds), *Perspectives on marital interaction* (pp. 78–97). Clevedon: Multilingual Matters.

Miller, J. B. (1976). *Toward a new psychology of women*. Boston: Beacon Press.

Miller, K. A., & Kohn, M. L. (1983). The reciprocal effects of job conditions and the intellectuality of leisure-time activities. In M. L. Kohn & C. Schooler (Eds), *Work and personality: An inquiry into the impact of social stratification*. Norwood, NJ: Ablex.

Miller, L. C. & Read, S. J. (1991). On the coherence of mental models of persons and relationships: A knowledge structure approach. In G. J. O. Fletcher & F. D. Fincham (Ed.), *Cognition in close relationships* (pp. 69–99). Hillsdale, NJ: Erlbaum.

Miller, P. C., Lefcourt, H. M., Holmes, J. G., Ware, E. E. & Saleh, W. E. (1986). Marriage locus of control and marital problem solving. *Journal of Personality and Social Psychology*, **51**, 161–9.

Miller, R. S. (1996). *Embarrassment: Poise and peril in everyday life*. New York: Guilford.

Mills, C. W. (1959). *The sociological imagination*. London: Oxford University Press.

Mills, R. S. L. & Duck, S. W. (Eds) (1999). *The developmental psychology of personal relationships*. Chichester, UK: Wiley.

Mills, R. S. L. & Rubin, K. H. (1993). Parental ideas as influences on children's social competence. In S. W. Duck (Ed.), *Learning about relationships [Understanding Relationship Processes 2]* (pp. 98–117). Thousand Oaks: Sage.

Mintz, S. & Kellogg, S. (1988). *Domestic revolutions*. New York: Free Press.

Mitchell, J. C. (1969). The concept and use of social networks. In J. C. Mitchell (Ed.), *Social Networks* in Urban Situations (pp. 1–50). Manchester University Press.

Mitchell, J. C. (1974). Social networks. *Annual Review of Anthropology*, **3**, 279–99.

Montgomery, B. M. (1988). Quality communication in personal relationships. In S. W. Duck (Ed.), *Handbook of Personal Relationships* (pp. 343–359). New York: Wiley.

Montgomery, B. M. & Duck, S. W. (Eds). (1991). *Studying Interpersonal Interaction*. New York: Guilford.

Morgan, D. L., Carder, P. & Neal, M. (1997). Are some relationships more useful than others? The value of similar others in the networks of recent widows. *Journal of Social and Personal Relationships*, **14**, 745–759.

Morgan, L. A. (1984). Changes in family interaction following widowhood. *Journal of Marriage and the Family*, **46**, 323–333.

Morgan, L. A. (1989). Economic well-being following marital termination: A comparison of widowed and divorced women. *Journal of Family Issues*, **10**, 86–101.

Morley, I. E. (1992). Intra-organizational bargaining. In J. F. Hartley & G.M. Stephenson (Eds), *Employment*. Cambridge, MA: Blackwell.

Morris, L. (1985). Local social networks and domestic organizations: a study of redundant steel workers and their wives. *The Sociological Review*, **33**, 327–342.

Morrow, K. A., Thoreson, R. W. & Penney, L. L. (1995). Predictors of psychological distress among infertility clinic patients. *Journal of Consulting and Clinical Psychology*, **63**, 163–167.

Mortimer, J. T., Lorence, J. & Kumka, D. S. (1986). *Work, family, and personality*. Norwood, NJ: Ablex.

Moss, M. S. & Moss, S. Z. (1995). Death and bereavement. In R. Blieszner & V. H. Bedford (Eds), *Handbook of aging and the family* (pp. 422–439). Westport, CT: Greenwood Press.

Mott, F. L. (1990). When is a father really gone? Paternal-child contact in father-absent homes. *Demography*, **27**, 499–517.

Mui, A. C. & Morrow-Howell, N. (1993). Sources of emotional strain among the oldest caregivers: Differential experiences of siblings and spouses. *Research on Aging*, **15**, 50–69.

Murphey, E. B., Silber, E., Coelho, G. V., Hamburg, D. A. & Greenberg, I. (1963). Development of autonomy and parent–child interaction in late adolescence. *American Journal of Orthopsychiatry*, **33**, 643–652.

Murray, S. L., Holmes, J. G. & Griffin, D. W. (1996). The benefits of positive illusion: Idealization and the construction of satisfaction in close relationships. *Journal of Personality and Social Psychology*, **70**, 79–98.

Myers, S. M. & Booth, A. (1996). Men's retirement and martial quality. *Journal of Family Issues*, **17**, 336–357.

National Center for Health Statistics (1991). Advance report of final marriage statistics, 1988. *Monthly Vital Statistics Report*, **30**, Number 12, Suppl. 2. Hyattsville, MD: Public Health Service.

Nelson, J. (1966). Clique contacts and family orientations, *American Sociological Review*, **31**, 663–672.

Newman, B. M. & Newman, P. R. (1975). *Development through life: A psychosocial approach*. Homewood, IL: Dorsey.

Neyer, F. J. (1997). Free recall or recognition in collecting egocentered networks: The role of survey techniques. *Journal of Social and Personal Relationships*, **14**, 305–316.

Nicholson, J. H. (1998). Sibling alliances: Joining forces in the family. *Communication Studies*. Iowa City, University of Iowa.

Nock, S. L. (1988). The family and hierarchy. *Journal of Marriage and the Family*, **50**, 957–966.

Noller, P. (1993). Gender and emotional communication in marriage: Different cultures or differential social power. *Journal of Language and Social Psychology*, **12**, 132–152.

Noller, P. & Feeney, J. A. (1998). Communication in early marriage: responses to conflict, nonverbal accuracy, and conversational patterns. In T. Bradbury (Ed.) *The developmental course of marital dysfunction* (pp. 11–43). New York: Cambridge University Press.

Noller, P. & Ruzzene, M. (1991). Communication in marriage: The influence of affect and cognition. In G. J. O. Fletcher & F. D. Fincham (Eds), *Cognition in close relationships* (pp. 203–233). Hillsdale, NJ: Erlbaum.

Noller, P., Feeney, J. A., Bonnell, D. & Callan, V. J. (1994). A longitudinal study of conflict in early marriage. *Journal of Social and Personal Relationships*, **11**, 233–252.

Norton, R. (1983). Measuring marital quality: A critical look at the dependent variable. *Journal of Marriage and the Family*, **45**, 141–151.

Notarius, C. I., & Pellegrini, D. S. (1987). Differences between husbands and wives: implications for understanding marital discord. In K. Halweg & M. Goldstein (Eds) *Understanding Major Mental Disorder: The Contribution of Family Interaction Research*. New York: Family Process.

Notarius, C. I., Benson, P. R., Sloane, D., Vanzetti, N.A. & Hornyak, L.M. (1989). Exploring the interface between perception and behavior: An analysis of marital interactions in distressed and nondistressed couples. *Behavioral Assessment*, **11**, 39–64.

Nydegger, C. N. (1991). The development of paternal and filial maturity. In K. Pillemer & K. McCartney (Eds), Parent–child relations throughout life (pp. 93–112). Hillsdale, NJ: Lawrence Erlbaum.

Nydegger, C. N. & Mitteness, L. S. (1991). Fathers and their adult sons and daughters. In S. K. Pfeifer & M. B. Sussman (Eds), *Families: Intergenerational and generational connections* (pp. 249–266). New York: The Haworth Press.

O'Bryant, S. L. & Hansson, R. O. (1995). Widowhood. In R. Blieszner & V. H. Bedford (Eds), *Handbook of aging and the family* (pp. 440–458). Westport, CT: Greenwood Press.

O'Connor, P. (1992). *Friendships Between Women: A Critical Review*. Guilford: London.

O'Keefe, D. J. (1975). Logical empiricism and the study of human communication. *Speech Monographs*, **42**, 169–185.

O'Leary, K. D. & Vivian, D. (1990). Physical aggression in marriage. In F.D. Fincham & T.N. Bradbury (Eds), *The psychology of marriage* (pp. 323–348). New York: Guilford.

Oldersma, K. L., Buunk, B. P. & De Dreu, C. K. W. (1998). Cognitive downward comparison as a relationship-enhancing mechanism: The role of relational discontent and individual differences in social comparison orientation. Unpublished manuscript.

Oliker, S. J. (1989). *Best friends and marriage*. Berkeley: University of California Press.

Olson, D. H. (1977). "Insiders' and outsiders' views of relationships: Research studies". In G. Levinger & H. Raush (Eds), *Close relationships: Perspectives on the meaning of intimacy* (pp. 115–135). Amherst: UMass Press.

Olson, D. H., Russell, C. S. & Sprenkle, D. H. (1979). Circumplex model of marital and family systems: Cohesion and adaptability dimensions, family types, and clinical applications. *Family Process*, **8**, 3–28.

Orbuch, T. L. & Custer, L. (1995). The social context of married women's work and its impact on black husbands and white husbands. *Journal of Marriage and the Family*, **57**, 33–45.

Orbuch, T. L., House, J. S., Mero, R. P., & Webster, P. S. (1996). Marital quality over the life course. *Social Psychology Quarterly*, **59**, 162–171.

Oropesa, R. S. (1993). Using the service economy to relieve the double burden: Female labor force participation and service purchases. *Journal of Family Issues*, **14**, 438–473.

Osborne, L. N. & Fincham, F. D. (1994). Conflict between parents and their children. In D.D. Cahn (Ed.), *Conflict in personal relationships* (pp. 117–141). Hillsdale, NJ: Erlbaum.

Osmond, M. W. & Thorne, B. (1993). Feminist theories: The social construction of gender in families and society. In P. G. Boss, W. J. Doherty, R. LaRossa, W. R. Schumm & S. K. Steinmetz (Eds), *Sourcebook of family theories and methods: A contextual approach* (pp. 591–623). New York: Plenum.

Parcel, T. L. & Menaghan, E. G. (1994). *Parents' jobs and children's lives*. New York: Aldine de Gruyter.

Parks, M. R. (1997). Communication networks and relationship life-cycles. In S. W. Duck (Ed.), *Handbook of personal relationships*, (2nd edn) (pp. 35–372). Chichester: Wiley.

Parks, M. R. & Eggert, L (1991). The role of social context in the dynamics of personal relationships. In W. Jones & D. Perlman (Eds). *Advances in Personal Relationships*, Vol 2 (pp. 1–34). London: Jessica Kingsley.

Parrott, T. M. & Bengtson, V. L. (1999). The effects of earlier intergenerational affection, normative expectations, and family conflict on contemporary exchanges of help and support. *Research on Aging*, **21**, 73–105.

Parsons, T. (1964). *Social structure and personality*. London: Free Press.

Patterson, C. J. (1992). Children of lesbian and gay parents. *Child Development*, **63**, 1025–1042.

Patterson, D. G. & Schwartz, P. (1994). The social construction of conflict in intimate same-sex couples. In D.D. Cahn (ed.), *Conflict in personal relationships* (pp. 3–26). Hillsdale, NJ: Erlbaum.

Peirce, R. S., Pruitt, D.G. & Czaja, S.J. (1991). Complainant- respondent differences in procedural choice. Unpublished manuscript.

Pence, E. & Paymar, M. (1993). *Education groups for men who batter: The Duluth model*. New York: Spring.

Peplau, L. A. (1983). Roles and gender. In H. H. Kelley, E. Berscheid, A. Christensen, J. H. Harvey, T. L. Huston, G. Levinger, E. McClintock, L. A. Peplau & D. R. Petersen (Eds), *Close relationships* (pp.220–264). New York: Freeman.

Peplau, L. A. & Gordon, S. (1985). Women and men in love: Gender differences in close heterosexual relationships. In V. E. O'Leary, R. K. Unger & B. S. Wallston (Eds), *Women, gender, and social psychology* (pp. 257–291). Hillsdale, NJ: Erlbaum.

Perry-Jenkins, M. & Crouter, A. C. (1990). Men's provider-role attitudes: implications for household work and marital satisfaction. *Journal of Family Issues*, **11**, 171–88.

Perry-Jenkins, M. & Folk, K. (1994). Class, couples, and conflict: Effects of the division of labor on assessments of marriage in dual-earner families. *Journal of Marriage and the Family*, **56**, 165–180.

Perry-Jenkins, M. & Gilman-Hanz, S. (1992, November). *Processes linking work and the well-being of parents and children in single-parent and two-parent families*. Paper presented at the annual meeting of National Council on Family Relations, Orlando, Florida.

Peterson, D. R. (1983). Conflict. In H.H. Kelley, E. Berscheid, A. Christensen, J.H. Harvey, T.L. Huston, G. Levinger, E. McClintock, L.A. Peplau & D.R. Peterson (Eds), *Close relationships* (pp. 360–396). New York: Freeman.

Peterson, R. R. (1996). A re-evaluation of the economic consequences of divorce. *American Sociological Review*, **61**, 528–536.

Petronio, S. (1994). Privacy binds in family interactions: The case of parental privacy invasion. In W. R. Cupach & B. H. Spitzberg (Eds), *The dark side of interpersonal communication* (pp. 241–257). Hillsdale, NJ: Erlbaum.

Pettit, G. S. & Lollis, S. (1997). Reciprocity And Bidirectionality In Parent-Child Relationships: New Approaches To The Study Of Enduring Issues. *Journal of Social and Personal Relationships*, **14**, 435–440.

Pettit, G. S. & Mize, J. (1993). Substance and style: Understanding the ways in which parents teach children about social relationships. In S. W. Duck (Ed.), *Learning about relationships [Understanding Relationship Processes 2]* (pp. 118–151). Thousand Oaks, CA: Sage.

Pierce, G. F., Sarason, B. R. & Sarason, I. G. (1990). Integrating social support perspectives. In S. W. Duck with R. C. Silver (Eds), *Personal Relationships and Social Support*. (pp. 173–189). Newbury Park, CA: Sage.

Pina, D. L. & Bengston, V. L. (1993). The division of household labor and women's happiness: ideology, employment and perception of support. *Journal of Marriage and the Family*, **55**, 901–12.

Pittman, J. F. (1993). Functionalism may be down, but it surely is not out: Another point of view for family therapists and policy analysts. In P. G. Boss, W. J. Doherty, R. LaRossa, W. R. Schumm, & S. K. Steinmetz (Eds), *Sourcebook of family theories and methods: A contextual approach* (pp. 218–221). New York: Plenum.

Pleck, J. (1985). *Working Wives/Working Husbands*. Beverly Hills, CA: Sage.

Popenoe, D. (1993). American family decline, 1960–1990: A review and appraisal. *Journal of Marriage and the Family*, **55**, 527–555.

Popenoe, D. (1994). The evolution of marriage and the problem of stepfamilies: A biosocial perspective. In A. Booth & J. Dunn (Eds), *Stepfamilies: Who benefits? Who does not?* (pp. 3–27). Hillsdale, NJ: Erlbaum.

Popenoe, D. (1996). *Life without father*. New York: Free Press.

Poster, M. (1978). *Critical theory of the family*. New York: Seabury Press.

Prager, K. J. (1991). Intimacy status and conflict conflict resolution. *Journal of Social and Personal Relationships*, **8**, 505–526.

Pruitt, D. G. (1991). Complainant-respondent differences and procedural choice in asymmetrical social conflict. Paper presented at the Fifth Annual Conference of the International Association for Conflict Management, Minneapolis.

Pruitt, D. G. & Carnevale, P.J. (1993). *Negotiation in social conflict*. Pacific Grove, CA: Brooks/Cole.

Ptacek, J. T. & Dodge, K. L. (1995). Coping strategies and relationship satisfaction in couples. *Personality & Social Psychology Bulletin*, **21**, 76–84.

Putallaz, M., Costanzo, P. R. & Klein, T. P. (1993). Parental Childhood Social Experiences and Their Effects on Children's Relationships. In S. W. Duck (Ed.), *Learning about relationships [Understanding relationship processes 2]* (pp. 63–97). Newbury Park, CA: Sage.

Putnam, L. L. (1994). New developments in conflict styles and strategies. Paper presented at the annual conference of the International Association for Conflict Management. Eugene, Oregon.

Qualls, S. H. (1995). Clinical interventions with later-life families. In R. Blieszner & V. H. Bedford (Eds), *Handbook of aging and the family* (pp. 475–487). Westport, CT: Greenwood Press.

Rabin, C. & Shapira-Berman, O. (1997). Egalitarianism and marital happiness: Israeli wives and husbands on a collision course? *American Journal of Family Therapy*, **25**, 319–330.

Rahim, M. A. (1983). A measure of styles of handling interpersonal conflict. *Academy of Management Journal*, **26**, 368–376.

Rahim, M. A., Kaufman, S. & Magner, N. (1993). A structural equations model of wife's styles of handling conflict and husband's evaluation of marital satisfaction and instability. Paper presented at the 5th Annual Conference of the International Association for Conflict Management, Houthalen, Belgium.

Rands, M. (1988). Changes in social network following marital separation and divorce. In R. M. Milardo (Ed.), Families and *Social Networks* (pp. 127–146). Newbury Park: Sage.

Raush, H. L., Barry, W. A., Hertel, R. K. & Swain, M. A. (1974). *Communication and conflict in marriage*. San Francisco: Jossey-Bass.

Renick, M. J., Floyd, F. J. & Markman, H. J. (1993). Preventing marital distress through communication and conflict management training: a 4- and 5-year follow-up. *Journal of Consulting and Clinical Psychology*, **61**, 70–77.

Repetti, R. (1994). Short-term and long-term processes linking job stressors to father-child interaction, *Social Development*, **3**, 1–15.

Repetti, R. & Wood, J. (1994). The effects of daily stress at work on mothers' interactions with preschoolers. Unpublished manuscript, University of California at Los Angeles.

Retzinger, S. M. (1995). Shame and anger in personal relationships. In S. W. Duck & J. T. Wood (Eds), *Relationship challenges: Understanding relationship processes 5* (Vol. 5, pp. 22–42). Thousand Oaks, CA: Sage.

Revenstorf, D., Hahlweg, K., Schindler, L. & Vogel, B. (1984). Interaction analysis of marital conflict. In K. Hahlweg & N. S. Jacobson (Eds), *Marital interaction: Analysis and modification* (pp. 159–181). New York: Guilford.

Richards, E. F. (1980). Network ties, kin ties, and marital role organization: Bott's hypothesis reconsidered. *Journal of Comparative Family Studies*, **11**, 139–151.

Riley, D. (1990). Network influences on father involvement in child rearing. In M. Cochran, M. Larner, D. Riley, L. Gunnarsson & C.R. Henderson, Jr. (Eds), *Extending families: The social networks of parents and their children* (pp. 131–153). New York: Cambridge University Press.

Riley, M. W. (1983). The family in an aging society: A matrix of latent relationships. *Journal of Family Issues*, **4**, 439–454.

Rinehart, L. (1992). Coping with conflict: Implications for relationship satisfaction. Paper presented at the Sixth International Conference on Personal Relationships, Orono, Maine.

Risman, B. J. (1998). *Gender vertigo*. New Haven, CT: Yale University Press.

Roberts, R. E. L. & Bengtson, V. L. (1990). Is intergenerational solidarity a unidimensional construct? A second test of a formal model. *Journal of Gerontology: Social Sciences*, **45**, S12–20.

Robertson, J. F. (1995). Grandparenting in an era of rapid change. In R. Blieszner & V. H. Bedford (Eds), *Handbook of aging and the family* (pp. 243–260). Westport, CT: Greenwood Press.

Robinson, J. (1977). *How Americans use time: A social-psychological analysis*. New York: Praeger.

Rogers, S. J. (1999). Wives' income and marital quality: Are there reciprocal effects? *Journal of Marriage and the Family*, **61**, 123–132.

Rogler, L. & Procidano, M. (1986). The effects of social networks on marital roles. *Journal of Marriage and the Family*, **48**, 693–702.

Rollins, B. C. & Feldman, H. (1970). Marital satisfaction over the family life cycle. *Journal of Marriage and the Family*, **32**, 20–27.

Rollins, J. (1985). *Between women: Domestics and their employers*. Philadelphia, PA: Temple University Press.

Rook, K. S. (1992). Detrimental aspects of social relationships. In H. O. Veiel & U. Baumann (Eds), *The Meaning and Measurement of Social Support* (pp. 157–169). Hemisphere, New York.

Ross, C. E. (1987). The division of labor at home. *Social Forces*, **65**, 816–833.

Ross, C. E. (1995). Conceptualizing marital status as a continuum of social attachment. *Journal of Marriage and the Family*, **57**, 129–140.

Ross, L. (1977). The intuitive psychologist and his shortcomings: Distortions in the attribution process. In L. Berkowitz (Ed.), *Advances in experimental social psychology* (Vol. 10, pp. 173–220). New York: Academic Press.

Rossi, A. S. & Rossi, P. H. (1990). *Of human bonding: Parent–child relations across the life course*. New York: Aldine de Gruyter.

Rubin, C. M. & Rubin, J. Z. (1993). Dynamics of conflict escalation in families. In D. Perlman & W.H. Jones (Eds), *Advances in personal relationships* (Vol. 4, pp. 165–191). London: Kingsley.

Rubin, J. Z. & Brown, B. R. (1975). The social psychology of bargaining and negotiation. New York: Academic Press.

Rubin, J. Z., Pruitt, D. & Kim, H. K. (1994). *Social conflict* (2nd ed.). New York: McGraw-Hill.

Rubin, L. B. (1983). *Intimate strangers: Men and women together*. New York: Harper & Row.

Rubin, L. B. (1994). *Families on the fault line*. New York: Harper Perennial.

Ruble, D. N., Fleming, A. S., Hackel, L. S., & Stangor, C. (1988). Changes in the marital relationship during the transition to first time motherhood: Effects of violated expectations concerning division of household labor. *Journal of Personality and Social Psychology*, **55**, 78–87.

Rusbult, C. E. (1983). A longitudinal test of the Investment Model: The development (and deterioration) of satisfaction and commitment in heterosexual involvements. *Journal of Personality and Social Psychology*, **45**, 101–117.

Rusbult, C. E. (1987). Responses to dissatisfaction in close relationships: The exit-voice-loyalty-neglect model. In D. Perlman & S. W. Duck (Eds), Intimate relationships (pp. 209–237). Newbury Park, CA: Sage.

Rusbult, C. E. & Buunk, A. P. (1993). Commitment processes in close relationships: An interdependence analysis. *Journal of Social and Personal Relationships*, **10**, 175–203.

Rusbult, C. E. & Martz, J. M. (1995). Remaining in an abusive relationship: An investment model analysis of non-voluntary dependence. *Personality & Social Psychology Bulletin*, **21**, 558–571.

Rusbult, C. E., Bissonnette, V. L., Arriaga, X. B. & Cox, C. L (1998). Accommodation processes during the early years of marriage. In T. Bradbury (Ed.) *The Developmental Course of Marital Dysfunction* (pp. 74–113) New York: Cambridge University Press.

Rusbult, C. E., Johnson, D. J. & Morrow, G. D. (1986). Impact of couple patterns of problem solving on distress and non-distress in dating relationships. *Journal of Personality and Social Psychology*, **50**, 744–753.

Rusbult, C. E., Martz, J. M. & Agnew, C. R. (1998). The Investment Model Scale: Measuring commitment level, satisfaction level, quality of alternatives, and investment size. *Personal Relationship*, **5**, 357–392.

Rusbult, C. E., Verette, J., Whitney, G.A., Slovik, L.F. & Lipkus, I. (1991). Accommodation processes in close relationships: Theory and preliminary empirical evidence. *Journal of Personality and Social Psychology*, **60**, 53–78.

Russell, A. & Searcy, E. (1997). The contribution of affective reactions and relationship qualities to adolescents' reported responses to parents. *Journal of Social and Personal Relationships*, **14**, 539–548.

Russell, C. S. (1974). Transition to parenthood: problems and gratifications. *Journal of Marriage and the Family*, **36**, 294–302.

Russell, R. J. H. & Wells, P. A. (1992). Social desirability and quality of marriage. *Personality & Individual Differences*, **13**, 787–791.

Russell, R. J. H. & Wells, P. A. (1994). Personality and quality of marriage. *British Journal of Psychology*, **85**, 161–168.

Ruvolo, A. (1990). Interpersonal ideals and personal change in newlyweds: a longitudinal analysis. Unpublished doctoral dissertation, Ann Arbor, University of Michigan.

Ruvolo, A. P. & Veroff, J. (1997). For better or worse: Real-ideal discrepancies and the marital well-being of newlyweds. *Journal of Social and Personal Relationships*, **14**, 232–42.

Sabatelli, R. M. (1988). Measurement issues in marital research: A review and critique of contemporary survey instruments. *Journal of Marriage and the Family*, **50**, 891–915.

Sabatelli, R. M. & Shehan, C.L. (1993). Exchange and resource theories. In P.G. Boss, W.J. Doherty, R. LaRossa, W.R. Schumm & S.K. Steinmetz (Eds), *Sourcebook of family theories and methods: A contextual approach* (pp. 385–411). New York: Plenum.

Salzinger, L. (1982). The ties that bind: The effects of clustering on dyadic relationships, *Social Networks*, **4**, 117–145.

Sanchez, L. (1994). Material resources, family structure resources, and husbands' housework participation: A cross-national comparison. *Journal of Family Issues*, **15**, 379–402.

Sarason, I. G., Sarason, B. R. & Pierce, G. R. (1994). Social support: Global and relationship-based levels of analysis. *Journal of Social and Personal Relationships*, **11**, 295–312.

Sattell, J. (1976). The inexpressive male: Tragedy or sexual politics? *Social Problems*, **23**, 469–477.

Scanzoni, J. (2000). *Designing families: The search for self and community in the information age*. Thousand Oaks, CA: Pine Forge Press.

Scanzoni, J. & Marsiglio, W. (1993). New action theory and contemporary families. *Journal of Family Issues*, **14**, 105–132.

Scanzoni, J. Polonko, K., Teachman, J. & Thompson, L. (1989). "Framing the problem" and "A fresh construct" in Scanzoni (Ed.), *The sexual bond* (pp. 12–50). Newbury Park, CA: Sage.

Schaap, C., Buunk, A. P. & Kerkstra, A. (1988). Marital conflict resolution. In P. Noller & M.A. Fitzpatrick (Eds), *Perspectives on marital interaction* (pp. 202–244). Clevedon, England: Multilingual Matters.

Schumm, W. R., Paff-Bergen, L. A., Hatch, R. C., Obiorah, F. C., Copeland, J. M., Meens, L. D. & Bugaighis, M. A. (1986). Concurrent and discriminant validity of the Kansas Marital Satisfaction Scale. *Journal of Marriage & the Family*, 48, 381–387.

Schutz, A. & Luckman, T. (1973). *The structures of the life-world* (translated by R.M. Zaner & H.T. Englehardt). Evanston: Northwestern University Press.

Schwartz, P. (1994). *Peer marriage*. New York: Free Press.

Schwartz, P. & Rutter, V. (1998). *The gender of sexuality*. Thousand Oaks, CA: Pine Forge Press.

Scott, J. (1991). *Social network analysis: A handbook*. London: Sage.

Scott, J. W. & Tilly, L. A. (1975). Women's work and the family in nineteenth-century Europe. *Comparative Studies in Society and History*, **17**, 36–64.

Seltzer, J. A. (1991). Relationships between fathers and children who live apart: The father's role after separation. *Journal of Marriage and the Family*, **53**, 79–101

Seltzer, J. A. & Brandreth, Y. (1994). What fathers say about involvement with children after separation. *Journal of Family Issues*, **15**, 49–77.

Seltzer, J. A. & Kalmuss, D. (1988). Socialization and stress explanations for spouse abuse. *Social Forces*, **67**, 473–492.

Senchak, M. & Leonard, K. E. (1992). Attachment styles and marital adjustment among newlywed couples. *Journal of Social and Personal Relationships*, **9**, 51–64.

Senchea, J. A. (1998). Gendered constructions of sexuality in adolescent girls' talk. *Communication Studies*. Iowa City: University of Iowa.

Sexton, C. S. & Perlman, D. S. (1989). Couples' career orientation, gender role orientation, and perceived equity as determinants of marital power. *Journal of Marriage and the Family*. **51**, 933–41.

Shea, L., Thompson, L. & Blieszner, R. (1988). Resources in older adults' old and new friendships. *Journal of Social and Personal Relationships*, **5**, 93–96.

Shehan, C. L. & Dwyer, J. W. (1989). Parent–child exchanges in the middle years: Attachment and autonomy in the transition to adulthood. In J. A. Mancini (Ed.), *Aging parents and adult children*. Lexington, MA: Lexington Books.

Shek, D. T. L. (1995). Gender differences in marital quality and well-being in Chinese married adults. *Sex Roles*, **32**, 699–715.

Sheldon, A. (1992). Conflict talk: Sociolinguistic challenges to self-assertion and how young girls meet them. *Merrill-Palmer Quarterly*, **38**, 95–117.

Shihadeh, E. S. (1991). The prevalence of husband-centered migration: Employment consequences for married women. *Journal of Marriage and the Family*, **53**, 432–444.

Shoshan, T. (1989). Mourning and longing from generation to generation. *American Journal of Psychotherapy*, **43**, 193–207.

Shotter, J. (1992). What is a "personal" relationship? A rhetorical–responsive account of "unfinished business". In J. H. Harvey, T. L. Orbuch & A. Weber (Eds), *Attributions, accounts and close relationships* (pp. 19–39). New York: Springer-Verlag.

Sillars, A., Folwell, A. L., Hill, K. C., Maki, B. K., Hurst, A. P. & Casano, R. A. (1994). Marital communication and the persistence of misunderstanding. *Journal of Social and Personal Relationships*, **11**, 611–617.

Silverberg, S. B. (1996). Parents' well-being at their children's transition to adolescence. In C. Ryff & M. M. Seltzer (Eds), *The parental experience in midlife* (pp. 215–254). Chicago: University of Chicago Press.

Silverberg, S. B. & Steinberg, L. (1987). Adolescent autonomy, parent-adolescent conflict, and parental well-being. *Journal of Youth and Adolescence*, **16**, 293–312.

Silverberg, S. B., Jacobs, S. L. & Raymond, M. (1998). When mothers turn to their adolescent daughters: Predicting daughters' vulnerability to negative adjustment outcomes. Paper presented at the meetings of the Society for Research on Adolescence, San Diego, March.

Silverstein, M. & Bengtson, V. L. (1997). Intergenerational solidarity and the structure of adult child-parent relationships in American families. *American Journal of Sociology*, **103**, 429–460.

Simons, R. L. & associates. (1996). *Understanding differences between divorced and intact families: Stress, interaction, and child outcome*. Thousand Oaks, CA: Sage.

Simpson, J. A. (1990). Influence of attachment styles on romantic relationships. *Journal of Personality and Social Psychology*, **59**, 683–692.

Skolnick, A. (1991). *Embattled paradise: The American family in an age of uncertainty*. New York: Basic.

Slater, P. E. (1963). On social regression. *American Sociological Review*, **28**, 339–64.

Smith, D. E. (1993). The Standard North American Family: SNAF as an ideological code. *Journal of Family Issues*, **14**, 50–65.

Smith, M. D. (1990). Patriarchal ideology and wife beating: A test of a feminist hypothesis. *Violence and Victims*, **5**, 257–273.

Snyder, D. K. (1979). Multidimensional assessment of marital satisfaction. *Journal of Marriage & the Family*, **41**, 813–823.

Sobal, J., Rauschenbach, B. S. & Frongillo, E. A. (1995). Obesity and marital quality: Analysis of weight, marital unhappiness, and marital problems in a US national sample. *Journal of Family Issues*, **16**, 746–764.

Spanier, G. B. (1976). Measuring dyadic adjustment: New scales for assessing the quality of marriage and similar dyads. *Journal of Marriage and the Family*, **38**, 15–28.

Spanier, G. B. & Lewis, R. A. (1980). Marital quality: A review of the seventies. *Journal of Marriage and the Family*, **42**, 825–839.

Spanier, G. B., Rovine, M. & Belsky, J. (1983). Stability and change in marriage across the transition to parenthood. *Journal of Marriage and the Family*, **45**, 567–577.

Spencer, E. E. (1994). Transforming relationships through ordinary talk. In S. W. Duck (Ed.), *Understanding relationship processes 4: Dynamics of relationships*, (pp. 58–85). Newbury Park.: Sage.

Spitzberg, B. H., Canary, D. J. & Cupach, W. R. (1994). A competence based approach to the study of interpersonal conflict. In D.D. Cahn (ed.), *Conflict in personal relationships* (pp. 183–202). Hillsdale, NJ: Erlbaum.

Spitze, G. & Logan, J. R. (1992). Helping as a component of parent–adult child relations. *Research on Aging*, **14**, 291–312.

Sprey, J. (1991). Studying adult children and their parents. In S. K. Pfeifer & M. B. Sussman (Eds), Families: Intergenerational and generational connections (pp. 221–235). New York: The Haworth Press.

Stacey, J. (1990). *Brave new families: Stories of domestic upheaval in late twentieth century America*. New York: Basic.

Stacey, J. (1993). Good riddance to "The Family": A response to David Popenoe. *Journal of Marriage and the Family*, **55**, 545–547.

Stacey, J. (1996). *In the name of the family*. Boston: Beacon Press.

Stack, C. B. (1974). *All our kin: Strategies for survival in a Black community*. New York: Harper & Row.

Stafford, L. & Canary, D.J. (1991). Maintenance strategies and romantic relationship type, gender and relational characteristics. *Journal of Social and Personal Relationships*, **8**, 217–242.

Stanton, A. L., Tennen, H., Affleck, G. & Mendola, R. (1992). Coping and adjustment to infertility. *Journal of Social & Clinical Psychology*, **11**, 1–13.

Stein, C. H. (1993). Felt obligation in adult family relationships. In S. W. Duck (Ed.), *Social Context and Relationships [Understanding Personal Relationships 3]* (pp. 78–99). Newbury Park, CA: Sage.

Stein, C. H., Bush, E. G., Ross, R. R. & Ward, M. (1992). Mine, yours and ours: A configural analysis of the networks of married couples in relation to marital satifaction and individual well-being. *Journal of Social and Personal Relationships*, **9**, 365–383.

Steinberg, L. & Steinberg, W. (1994). *Crossing paths.* New York: Simon and Schuster.

Stets, J. E. & Pirog-Good, M.A. (1990). Interpersonal control and courtship aggression. *Journal of Social and Personal Relationships*, **7**, 371–394.

Stewart, R. B. & Marvin, R. S. (1984). Sibling relations: the role of conceptual perspective-taking in the ontogeny of sibling caregiving. *Child Development*, **55**, 1322–1332.

Straus, M. A. (1994). *Beating the devil out of them.* San Francisco: Jossey-Bass.

Straus, M. A. & Gelles, R.J. (1990). *Physical violence in American families.* New Brunswick, NJ: Transaction.

Suggs, P. K. (1989). Predictors of association among older siblings: A black/white comparison. *American Behavioral Scientist*, **33**, 70–80.

Sullaway, M. & Christensen, A. (1983). Assessment of dysfunctional interaction patterns in couples. *Journal of Marriage and the Family*, **45**, 653–660.

Surra, C. A. (1988). The influence of the interactive network on developing relationships. In R. M. Milardo (Ed.), *Families and Social Networks* (pp. 48–82). Newbury Park, CA: Sage.

Surra, C. A. & Milardo, R. (1991). The social psychological context of developing relationships: Psychological and interactive networks. In D. Perlman & W. Jones (Eds), *Advances in Personal Relationships* (Vol. 3, pp. 1–36). London: Jessica Kingsley.

Surra, C. A. & Ridley, C. (1991). Multiple perspectives on interaction: Participants, peers and observers. In B. M. Montgomery & S. W. Duck (Eds), *Studying Interpersonal Interaction* (pp. 35–55). New York: Guilford.

Sutherland, L. E. (1990). The effect of premarital pregnancy and birth on the marital well-being of black and white newlywed couples. Unpublished doctoral dissertation (Microfilm # 28189). Ann Arbor, MI: University of Michigan.

Syna, H. (1984). Couples in conflict: Conflict resolution strategies, perceptions about sources of conflict and relationship adjustment. Doctoral dissertation. State University of New York at Buffalo.

Talbott, M. M. (1998). Older widows' attitudes towards men and remarriage. *Journal of Aging Studies*, **12**, 429–449.

Tallman, I. & Riley, A. (1995). Gender role expectations and couple interactions in newly married couples. Unpublished manuscript, Washington State University.

Tallman, I., Burke, P. J. & Gecas, V. (1998). Socialization into marital roles: Testing a contextual, developmental model of marital functioning. In T. Bradbury (Ed.) *The Developmental Course of Marital Dysfunction* (pp. 312–342). New York: Cambridge University Press.

Tavris, C. (1982). *Anger: The misunderstood emotion.* New York: Simon & Schuster.

Taylor, R. L. (1998). Black American families. In R. L. Taylor (Ed.), *Minority families in the United States* (2nd edn, pp. 19–45). Upper Saddle River, NJ: Prentice Hall.

Taylor, S. E. (1991). Asymmetrical effects of positive and negative events: The mobilization–minimization hypothesis. *Psychological Bulletin*, **110**, 67–85.

Teachman, J. D. (2000). Diversity of family structure: Economic and social influences. In D. H. Demo, K. R. Allen & M. A. Fine (Eds), *Handbook of family diversity* (pp. 32–58). New York: Oxford University Press.

Teachman, J. D., Tedrow, L. M. & Crowder, K. D. (in press). The changing demography of America's families. *Journal of Marriage and the Family*, **63**.

Teti, D. M. & Teti, L. (1996). Infant–parent relationships. In N. Vanzetti & S. W. Duck (Eds), *A lifetime of relationships* (pp. 77–104). Pacific Grove, CA.: Brooks/Cole.

Thibaut, J. W. & Kelley, H. H. (1959). *The social psychology of groups.* New York: Wiley.

Thomas, J. B., Shankster, L. J. & Mathieu, J.E. (1994). Antecedents to organizational issue interpretation: The roles of single-level, cross-level, and content cues. *Academy of Management Journal*, **37**, 1252–1284.

Thompson, L. (1991). Family work: Women's sense of fairness. *Journal of Family Issues*, **12**(2), 181–196.

Thompson, L. (1992). Feminist methodology for family studies. *Journal of Marriage and the Family*, **54**, 3–18.

Thompson, L. & Walker, A. J. (1984). Mothers and daughters: Aid patterns and attachment. *Journal of Marriage and the Family*, **46**, 313–322.

Thompson, L. & Walker, A. J. (1989). Gender in families: Women and men in marriage, work, and parenthood. *Journal of Marriage and the Family*, **51**, 845–871.

Thompson, S. C. & Pitts, J. S. (1992). In sickness and in health: Chronic illness, marriage, and spousal caregiving. In: S. Spacapan & S. Oskamp. (Eds). *Helping and being helped* (pp. 115–151) Newbury Park: Sage.

Thomsen, D. G. & Gilbert, D. G. (1998). Factors characterizing marital conflict states and traits: Physiological, affective, behavioral and neurotic variable contributions to marital conflict and satisfaction. *Personality & Individual Differences*, **25**, 833–855.

Thorne, B. (1992). Feminism and the family: Two decades of thought. In B. Thorne, with M. Yalom (Eds), *Rethinking the family: Some feminist questions* (rev. edn; pp. 3–30). Boston: Northeastern University Press.

Thornton, A. (1989). Changing attitudes toward family issues in the United States. *Journal of Marriage and the Family*, **51**, 873–893.

Tichenor, V. J. (1999). Status and income as gendered resources: The case of marital power. *Journal of Marriage and the Family*, **61**, 638–650.

Timmer, S. G., Veroff, J. & Hatchett, S (1996). Family ties and marital happiness: The different marital experiences of black and white newlyweds. *Journal of Personal and Social Relationships*, **13**, 337–62.

Ting-Toomey, S., Gao, G., Trubisky, P., Yang, Z., Kim, H.S., Lin, S.-L. & Nishida, T. (1991). Culture, face maintenance, and styles of handling interpersonal conflict: A study in five cultures. *The International Journal of Conflict Management*, **2**, 275–296.

Travisano, R. (1970). Alternation and conversion as qualitatively different transformations. In G. Stone & H. Farberman (Eds), *Social psychology through symbolic interaction*. Waltham, MA: Xerox College Publishing.

Troll, L. E. (1985). *Early and middle adulthood* (2nd edn). Monterey, CA: Brooks/Cole.

Troll, L. E. (1994). Family connectedness of old women: Attachments in later life. In B. F. Turner & L. E. Troll (Eds), *Women growing older: Psychological perspectives* (pp. 169–201). Thousand Oaks, CA: Sage.

Troll, L. E. (1996). Modified-extended families over time: Discontinuity in parts, continuity in wholes. In V. L. Bengtson & M. Leiberman (Eds), *Continuities and discontinuities in adulthood and aging: Research contributions in honor of Bernice Neugarten*. New York: Springer Publishing Company.

Tronto, J. C. (1987). Beyond gender difference to a theory of care. *Signs, 12*, 644–663.

Tucker, J. S. & Anders, S. L. (1999). Attachment style, interpersonal perception accuracy, and relationship satisfaction in dating couples. *Personality & Social Psychology Bulletin*, **25**, 403–412.

Turner, C. (1967). Conjugal roles and social networks: A re-examination of an hypothesis, *Human Relations*, **20**, 121–130.

US Bureau of the Census (1992). *Money income of households, families, and persons in the United States: 1992.* (Current Population Reports, Series P60–184).

US Bureau of the Census. (1995). *Statistical abstract of the United States, 1995*. Washington, DC: Government Printing Office.

Udry, J. R. & Hall, M. (1965). Marital role segregation and social networks in middle-class, middle-aged couples. *Journal of Marriage and the Family*, **27**, 392–395.

Uehara, E. (1994). The influence of the social network's "second order zone" on social support mobilization: A case example, *Journal of Social and Personal Relationships*, **11**, 277–294.

Uehara, E. (1995). Reciprocity reconsidered: An application of Gouldner's concept of the moral norm of reciprocity to social support. *Journal of Social and Personal Relationships*, **12**, 483–490.

Ulin, M. & Milardo, R. M. (November, 1992). Network interdependence and lesbian relationships. Paper presented at the National Council on Family Relations, Orlando, Florida.

Unger, D. G., Jacobs, S. B. & Cannon, C. (1996). Social support and marital satisfaction among couples coping with chronic constructive airway disease. *Journal of Social and Personal Relationships*, **13**, 123–142.

Uttal, L. (1996). Custodial care, surrogate care, and coordinated care: Employed mothers and the meaning of child care. *Gender and Society*, **10**, 291–311.

Vaillant, C. O. & Vaillant, G. E. (1993). Is the u-curve of marital satisfaction an illusion? A 40-year study of marriage. *Journal of Marriage and the Family*, **55**, 230–239.

van de Vliert, E. (1990). Positive effects of conflict: A field assessment. *The International Journal of Conflict Management*, **1**, 69–80.

van der Poel, M. G. M. (1993). *Personal Networks: a Rational-choice Explanation of their Size and Composition*. Swets & Zeitlinger: Lisse.

Van Lange, P. A. M. & Rusbult, C. E. (1995). My relationship is better than—and not as bad as—yours is: The perception of superiority in close relationships. *Personality and Social Psychology Bulletin*, **21**, 32–44.

Van Lange, P. A. M., Rusbult, C. E., Drigotas, S. M., Arriaga, X. B., Witcher, B. S. & Cox, C. L. (1997). Willingness to sacrifice in close relationships. *Journal of Personality and Social Psychology*, **72**, 1373–1395.

van Tilburg, T. (1990). Support in close relationships: Is it better to assess the content or the type of relationship? In C. P. M. Knipscheer & T. C. Antonucci (Eds), *Social network research* (pp. 151–159). Amsterdam: Swets & Zeitliner.

VanderVoort, L. A. & Duck, S. W. (in press) Talking about "Relationships": Variations on a theme. In K. Dindia & S. W. Duck (Eds) *Communication and personal relationships*. Wiley: Chichester.

Vangelisti, A. L. & Huston, T. L. (1994). Maintaining marital satisfaction and love. In D. J. Canary & L. Stafford (Eds), *Communication and Relational Maintenance* (pp. 165–86). San Diego, CA: Academic Press.

Veroff, J. (1994). Balance in the early years of marriage. Paper presented at conference in intimate relationships at Iowa State. Ames, Iowa. September 29.

Veroff, J. & Veroff, J. B. (1980). *Social Incentives*. New York: Academic Press.

Veroff, J., Douvan, E. & Hatchett, S. (1995). *Marital Instability: A social and behavioral study of the early years*. Westport, CT: Praeger.

Veroff, J., Douvan, E., Orbuch, T. & Acitelli, L. (1998). Happiness in stable marriages: The early years. In T. Bradbury (Ed.) *The developmental course of marital dysfunction* (pp. 152–79) New York: Cambridge University Press.

Veroff, J., Sutherland, L., Chadiha, L. & Ortega, R. (1993). Newlyweds tell their stories. *Journal of Personal and Social Relationships*, **10**, 437–57.

Veroff, J., Douvan E. & Kulka, R. (1981). *The Inner American*. New York: Basic.

Vinokur, A. D. & Van Ryn, M. (1993). Social support and undermining in close relationships: Their independent effect on the mental health of the unemployed person. *Journal of Personality and Social Psychology*, **65**, 350–59.

Vondracek, F. W., Lerner, R. L. & Schulenberg, J. E. (1986). *Career development, a life-span developmental approach*. Hillsdale, NJ: Erlbaum.

Walker, A. J. (1999). Gender and family relationships. In M. B. Sussman, S. K. Steinmetz & G. W. Peterson (Eds), *Handbook of marriage and the family* (2nd edn, pp. 439–474). Hingham, MA: Kluwer Academic/Plenum.

Walker, K. & Woods, M. (1976). *Time use: A measure of household production of family goods and services.* Home Economics Association, Washington.

Wallerstein, J. S., & Blakeslee, S. (1989). *Second chances: Men, women and children a decade after divorce.* New York: Ticknor & Fields.

Watkins, S. C., Menken, J. A. & Bongaarts, J. (1987). Demographic foundations of family change. *American Sociological Review, 52,* 346–358.

Watzlawick, P., Beavin, J. & Jackson, D. (1967). *Pragmatics of human communication: a study of interactional patterns, pathologies and paradoxes.* New York: Norton.

Webster, P. S. & Herzog, A. R. (1995). Effects of parental divorce and memories of family problems on relationships between adult children and their parents. *Journal of Gerontology: Social Sciences,* **50B**, S24–S34.

Webster, P. S., Orbuch, T. L. & House, J. S. (1995). Effects of childhood family background on adult marital quality and perceived stability. *American Journal of Sociology,* **101**, 404–432.

Weishaus, S. & Field, D. (1988). A half century of marriage: Continuity or change? *Journal of Marriage and the Family, 50,* 763–774.

Weisner, T. S. (1982). Sibling interdependence and child caretaking: A cross-cultural view. In M. E. Lamb & B. Sutton-Smith (Eds), *Sibling relationships: Their nature and significance across the lifespan.* Hillsdale, NJ: Erlbaum.

Weiss, R. L. & Heyman, R.E. (1990). Observation of marital interaction. In F.D. Fincham & T.N. Bradbury (Eds), *The psychology of marriage* (pp. 87–117). New York: Guilford.

Weiss, R. S. (1979). Growing up a little faster: The experience of growing up in a single-parent household. *Journal of Social Issues, 35,* 97–111.

Weiss, R. S. (1982). Attachment in adult life. In C. M. Parkes, & J. Stevenson-Hinde (Eds), *The place of attachment in human behavior* (pp. 171–184). New York: Basic Books.

Weitzman, L. (1985). *The divorce revolution: The unexpected social and economic consequences for women and children in America.* New York: Free Press.

Wellman, B. (1985). Domestic work, paid work and net work. In S. W. Duck & D. Perlman (Eds), *Understanding Personal Relationships* (pp. 159–191). London: Sage.

Wellman, B. (1988). Structural analysis: From method and metaphor to theory and substance. In B. Wellman & S. Berkowitz (Eds), *Social structures: a network approach* (pp. 15–61). Cambridge: Cambridge University Press.

Wellman, B. & Wellman, B. (1992). Domestic affairs and network relations. *Journal of Social and Personal Relationships, 9,* 385–409.

Wellman, B. & Wortley, S. (1989). Brothers' keepers: Situating kinship relations in broader networks of social support. *Sociological Perspectives, 32,* 273–306.

Wellman, B. & Wortley, S. (1990). Different strokes from different folks: Which community ties provide what social support, *American Journal of Sociology, 96,* 558–88.

Wellman, B. Carrington, P., & Hall, A. (1988). Networks as personal communities. In B. Wellman & S. D. Berkowitz (Eds), *Social Structures: A Network Approach* (pp. 130–184). Cambridge: Cambridge University Press.

Wells, A. J. (1988). Variations in mothers' self-esteem in daily life. *Journal of Personality and Social Psychology,* **55**(4), 661–668.

Werner, C., Altman, I., Brown, B. & Ginat, J. (1993). Celebrations in personal relationships: A transactional/dialectical perspective. In S. W. Duck (Ed.) *Social contexts of relationships [Understanding Relationship Processes 3]* (pp. 109–138). Thousand Oaks, CA: Sage.

West, C. & Fenstermaker, S. (1993). Power, inequality, and the accomplishment of gender: An ethnomethodological view. In P. England (Ed.), *Theory on gender/ feminism on theory* (pp. 151–174). New York: deGruyter.

Weston, K. (1991). *Families we choose: Lesbians, gays, kinship.* New York: Columbia University Press.

Whitbeck, L. B., Hoyt, D. R. & Huck, S. M. (1994). Early family relationships, inter-generational solidarity, and support provided to parents by their adult children. *Journal of Gerontology: Social Sciences*, **49**, S85–94.

Whitbeck, L. B., Simons, R. L. & Conger, R. D. (1991). The effects of early family relationships on contemporary relationships and assistance patterns between adult children and their parents. *Journal of Gerontology: Social Sciences*, **46**, S330-S337.

White, K. M., Speisman, J. C. & Costos, D. (1983). Young adults and their parents: Individuation to mutuality. In H. D. Grotevant & C. R. Cooper (Eds), *Adolescent development in the family* (pp. 61–76). San Francisco: Jossey-Bass.

White, L. K. & Booth, A. V. (1985a). The quality and stability of remarriages: The role of stepchildren. *American Sociological Review*, **50**, 689–98.

White, L. K. & Booth, A. V. (1985b). The transition to parenthood and marital quality. *Journal of Family Issues*, **6**, 435–49.

White, L. & Rogers, S. (in press). Economic circumstances and family outcomes: A review of the 90s. *Journal of Marriage and the Family*.

Wilkie, J. R., Ferree, M. M. & Ratcliff, K. S. (1998). Gender and fairness: Marital satisfaction in two-earner couples. *Journal of Marriage and the Family*, **60**, 577–594.

Wilkie, J. R., Ratcliff, K. S. & Ferree, M. M. (1992, November). Family division of labor and marital satisfaction among two-earner married couples. Paper presented at the annual conference of the National Council on Family Relations, Orlando, FL.

Williams, N. (1990). *The Mexican–American family: Tradition and change*. Dix Hills, NJ.: General Hall.

Wilson, M. N., Tolson, T. F., Hinton, I. D. & Kiernan, M (1990). Flexibility and sharing of child care duties in Black families. *Sex Roles*, **22**, 409–25.

Wilson, S. M., Larson, J. H., McCulloch, B. J. & Stone, K. L. (1997). Dyadic2 adjustment: An ecosystemic examination. *American Journal of Family Therapy*, **25**, 291–306.

Wimberley, H. (1973). Conjugal-role organization and social networks in Japan and England. *Journal of Marriage and the Family*, **35**, 125–130.

Wood, J. T. (1993). Engendered relations: Interaction, caring, power, and responsibility in intimacy. In S. W. Duck (Ed.), *Social context and relationships* (pp. 26–54). Newbury Park, CA: Sage.

Wood, J. T. (1995). Feminist scholarship and the study of relationships. *Journal of Social and Personal Relationships*, **12**, 103–120.

Wood, J. T. & Cox, J. R. (1993). Rethinking critical voice: materiality and situated knowledge. *Western Journal of Communication*, **57**, 278–287.

Yi, E. K. (1986). Implications of conjugal role segregation for extrafamilial relationships: A network model. *Social Networks*, **8**, 119–147.

Youniss, J. (1983). Social construction of adolescence by adolescents and parents. In H. D. Grotevant & C. R. Cooper (Eds), *Adolescent development in the family* (pp. 93–109). San Francisco: Jossey-Bass.

Youniss, J. & Ketterlinus, R. D. (1987). Communication and connectedness in mother– and father–adolescent relationships. *Journal of Youth and Adolescence*, **16**, 265–280.

Youth of the Rural Organizing and Cultural Center (1991). *Minds stayed on freedom: The Civil Rights struggle in the rural south*. Boulder, CO: Westview Press.

Zarit, S. H. & Eggebeen, D. J. (1995). Parent–child relationships in adulthood and old age. In M.L. Bornstein (Ed.), *Handbook of parenting. Vol I: Children and parenting*. Mahwah, NJ.: Lawrence Erlbaum.

Zaslow, M., McGroder, S., Cave, G. & Mariner, C. (1999). Maternal employment and measures of children's health and development among families with some history of welfare receipt. In T.L. Parcel (Ed.), *Work and family: Research in the sociology of work* (Vol. 7, pp. 233–259). Stamford, CT: JAI Press.

Zvoncovic, A. M., Greaves, K. M., Schmiege, C.J. & Hall, L.D. (1996). The marital construction of gender through work and family decision making: A qualitative analysis. *Journal of Marriage and the Family*, **58**, 91–100.

AUTHOR INDEX

SUBJECT INDEX